Lecture Notes in Computer Science

Lecture Notes in Computer Science

Edited by G. Goos and J. Hartmanis

392

J.-C. Bermond   M. Raynal (Eds.)

Distributed Algorithms

3rd International Workshop
Nice, France, September 26–28, 1989
Proceedings

Springer-Verlag

Berlin Heidelberg New York London Paris Tokyo Hong Kong

Editors

Jean-Claude Bermond
Informatique, CNRS, 3, rue Albert Einstein, Sophia-Antipolis
F-06560 Valbonne Cedex, France

Michel Raynal
IRISA, Campus de Beaulieu
F-35042 Rennes Cedex, France

CR Subject Classification (1987): C.2.2, C.2.4, D.4.1, D.4.4, F.1.1, F.2.2

ISBN 3-540-51687-5 Springer-Verlag Berlin Heidelberg New York
ISBN 0-387-51687-5 Springer-Verlag New York Berlin Heidelberg

Printing and binding: Druckhaus Beltz, Hemsbach/Bergstr.
2145/3140-543210 – Printed on acid-free paper

PREFACE

The Third International Workshop on Distributed Algorithms was organized at La Colle-sur-Loup, near Nice, France, on September 26 to 28, 1989. It followed the first two successful International Workshops on Distributed Algorithms in Ottawa (1985) and Amsterdam (1987), the proceedings of which were published, respectively, by Carleton University Press in 1986 (eds. E. Gafni and N. Santoro) and by Springer-Verlag as LNCS 312 in 1988 (ed. J. van Leeuwen). This workshop was intended to provide a forum for researchers and other parties interested in distributed algorithms on communication networks, graphs, and decentralized systems. The aim was to present recent research results, explore directions for future research, and identify common fundamental techniques that serve as building blocks in many distributed algorithms.

Papers were solicited describing original results in all areas of distributed algorithms and their applications, including

- distributed combinatorial algorithms
- distributed graph algorithms
- distributed algorithms for control and communication
- distributed database techniques
- distributed algorithms for decentralized systems
- fail-safe and fault-tolerant distributed algorithms

- distributed optimization algorithms
- routing algorithms
- design of network protocols
- algorithms for transaction management
- composition of distributed algorithms
- analysis of distributed algorithms

The Program Committee consisted of

> J-C. Bermond (CNRS, LRI Orsay and Sophia-Antipolis, France)
> F. Mattern (University of Kaiserslautern, Fed. Rep. of Germany)
> M. Raynal (IRISA, Rennes, France)
> N. Santoro (Carleton University, Ottawa, Canada and Università di Bari, Italy)
> A. Segall (Technion, Haifa, Israel)
> S. Toueg (Cornell University, Ithaca, USA)
> P. Vitanyi (C.W.I. and University of Amsterdam, Amsterdam, Netherlands)

More than 80 papers were submitted, of which 73 arrived on time; 26 were selected for presentation at the Workshop and publication in these Proceedings.

We are grateful for the support from the CNRS and the French coordinated program C^3 (the three C's stand for Cooperation, Concurrency and Communication), the latter managed successively by J-P. Verjus and P. Quinton.

We also thank all those who made this Workshop possible, especially the members of the Program Committee, the referees (see list enclosed), not forgetting C. Lavault who was the main organizer, and C. Peyrat.

> Jean-Claude Bermond
> Michel Raynal
> Program Committee Chairmen
> July 1989

CONTENTS

CONTENTS

Random Leaders and Random Spanning Trees

Judit Bar-Ilan and Dror Zernik
Department of Computer Science
Hebrew University
Jerusalem, Israel

Abstract

The problem of distributively constructing a minimum spanning tree has been thoroughly studied. The root of this spanning tree is often elected as a leader, and then centralized algorithms are run in the distributed system. If, however, we have fault tolerance in mind, selecting a random spanning tree and a random leader are more desirable. If we manage to select a random tree, the probability that a bad channel will disconnect some nodes from the random tree is relatively small. Otherwise, a small number of predetermined edges will greatly effect the system's behavior.

In this paper we present an algorithm for choosing a *random leader* (RL), and *distributed random spanning tree* algorithms (RST), where *random* means, that each spanning tree in the underlying graph has the same probability of being selected. We give optimal algorithms for the complete graph and the ring. We also describe an RST algorithm for the general graph, and discuss the relation between RST and RL algorithms.

1 Introduction

When looking into distributed systems, and the current research on distributed problems, a central issue is the breaking of symmetry. This problem has many forms, and many aspects. One of the most elementary issues is how to choose a leader. Another elementary issue is how to perform broadcast. There are several hidden assumptions about distributed computations which cause these two problems to be the center of attention: The easiest way to establish a consistent behavior is to choose a leader and then run a centralized algorithm. A leader is a distinguished processor, and the identity of this processor is known to all the other processors. It is necessary to be able to select a leader, because the structure of a distributed system assumes that there is no *predefined leader*.

In order to select a leader and to facilitate the leader with a "quick", message efficient communication tool, a minimum spanning tree (MST) is usually computed. A side result of this computation is a distinguishable channel of communication between every pair of processors. However, choosing a leader as the root of the MST prevents some nodes from being elected as a leader, or gives them a very poor chance of becoming one. Usually, nobody cares about such a small injustice. However, when one considers one of the main problems in working with a distributed system - overcoming faulty nodes - it seems that the above injustice is rather harmful, because the probable leader can be a malicious one. Therefore, choosing a random leader is desirable.

By similar arguments, it is desirable to have a random spanning tree. By a *random spanning tree* (RST) we mean, that each spanning tree in the underlying graph has the same probability of being selected (uniform generation). If we manage to select a random tree, the probability that a bad channel will disconnect some nodes from the random tree is relatively small. If the algorithm for choosing a spanning tree was such, that a small set of trees was chosen with high probability, then malfunction in a small number of predetermined edges would greatly effect the system's behavior.

In addition to the importance of the problem for distributed computations, this problem is an interesting sequential problem ([B],[G]).

In a distributed system, creating a *random* spanning tree, seems more difficult then creating the *minimum* spanning tree. In most of the solutions for the MST problem, it was assumed, that all the weights on the edges are distinct. In this case, the MST is unique. It is easier for a distributed system to strive toward a unique goal (a unique tree), than to select one solution from a large set of possible solutions. This holds, even if the processors do not know in advance, what this unique solution is. The idea of defining a unique goal appears, for example, in [MVV]'s algorithm for finding a matching in a graph.

On the other hand, for the sequential case, generating a RST (with uniform distribution) seems to be easier, than creating an MST. For the complete graph on N edges, a minimum spanning tree algorithm has to examine all the edges, therefore must have complexity $\Omega(N^2)$. Broder's algorithm for uniform generation of a spanning tree by the use of Markov chains ([B]) works for the complete graph in expected time $O(N \log N)$.

The two problems (RST and MST), are related, but cannot be compared easily. The input for generating a RST is a graph, and the algorithm for solving the problem must use randomization. The input for constructing a minimum spanning tree is a graph with weights on the edges. In this problem, the output is almost predetermined by the input (if the weights are all distinct, only a single spanning tree exists), while for the random case, one spanning tree out of a huge number of possibilities is selected.

We can, however, say something about the complexity of the RST problem for regular graphs. For such graphs, the root of the tree is chosen uniformly (see section 4), and therefore can be chosen as a random leader. Hence, the complexity of selecting a RST for regular graphs has to be at least as much as the complexity for choosing a leader. We achieve these bounds for the ring (synchronous and asynchronous) and for the complete graph (for the asynchronous case, we achieve the bound on the message complexity only).

The paper is organized in the following way: in section 3, we describe a simple algorithm for selecting a random leader. In section 4, we implement a sequential algorithm (see [B]) for random generation of spanning trees, and also discuss the difference between choosing a random leader and creating a RST. In section 5, we give two algorithms for random generation of a spanning tree in a complete graph, the first is message optimal and works in deterministic time $O(\log N)$, the other works in constant time, but the size of the communication is $O(N^2)$ bits. In section 6, we describe two algorithms for picking a spanning tree in a ring.

2 Problem Definition

We work in an *asynchronous* model (unless otherwise stated), with N processors. Each processor has *polynomial computational power* (for local computation). Each processor has an ID, and each processor knows an upper bound, M, on the number of processors. Note that there are MST algorithms (see [A], [GHS]) work without knowing the size of the distributed system. There is an undirected *graph*, $G = (V, E)$, induced by the system: each node corresponds to a processor, and each edge to a communication link. A distributed algorithm is *correct* if it terminates, and each processor decides on the same value. An *RST algorithm* produces a *random spanning tree*, where each spanning tree in the underlying graph is equiprobable. A *correct RST algorithm* is an RST algorithm that is correct. Similarly, an *RL algorithm* chooses a single node, a *random leader*, where each node is chosen with the same probability.

Our algorithms have to be randomized, since we want random generation or a random leader. Some of the algorithms we present have deterministic termination. We also present Las-Vegas algorithms. In a Las-Vegas algorithm, at termination we have a spanning tree, however the exact time of termination is not known. For these algorithms, we give the *expected time complexity*. For all our algorithms, we give the *expected message complexity* - the expected total number of messages sent. A message is the name of a processor, or the weight of an edge, with some additional information , where the size of the name is dominant.

2.1 Background in Probability

Some of our algorithms are based on *random walks*. Here we describe in short the terms we use. For more details see [KS]. Let G be a connected, undirected graph on N vertices, and consider a particle that is on a node of the graph. At each step, it moves from the node it is on to one of the neighboring nodes. This node is chosen randomly and uniformly. The first time the particle visited all the nodes of the graph is the *cover time*. The random walk is a *Markov chain*, since the next move is dependent only on the present location of the particle. With the Markov chain, we associate a *transition probability matrix*, P, where p_{ij} is the transition probability from node i to node j in a single step. If we are currently at node i, the distribution on the particle's location at the next step is given by multiplying the vector of length N with all zeros, except for a 1 in the ith place, by the matrix P. The *stationary distribution* is defined as the vector π of length N, such that the sum of the entries is 1, such that $\pi P = \pi$. In our case, it is easy to see that the stationary distribution is unique. Intuitively, the stationary distribution is the distribution on the location of the particle after a "long" time, and is independent of the starting point of the random walk. The stationary distribution on a connected, undirected graph G, with N nodes, where the ith node has d_i edges (the *degree* of the node), is the vector: $\left(\frac{d_1}{\sum d_i}, \ldots, \frac{d_N}{\sum d_i} \right)$.

3 Random Leader

The following algorithm chooses a single node, where each node has equal probability of being chosen:

Each node independently picks a random number. If the random numbers are selected from a large enough range (e.g. $r \in \{1, 2, ..., N^3\}$), then with high probability all the numbers will be distinct. The weight on the edge between processors i and j will be $r_{\max\{i,j\}}$ concatenated with $r_{\min\{i,j\}}$. If the weights are all distincts, we can use the spanning tree algorithm given in [A], which has time complexity $O(N)$ and message complexity $O((E + N \log N))$. The algorithm in [GHS] works also for nondistinct weights, but has time complexity $O(N \log N)$. After a spanning tree is constructed, the node with the minimal random number can easily be found. This node will be chosen as the leader. Since every node has the same probability of picking the minimal number, the result of this algorithm is a random leader. In case the minimal number is not unique, the algorithm is rerun. This happens with probability $1 - \frac{\binom{N^3}{N}}{N^{3N}} \approx 1 - e^{\frac{1}{N}} \to 0$. The processors know an upper bound, M, on the number of processors, so they choose numbers from the range $\{1, ..., M^3\}$.

Can this algorithm serve us as an RST algorithm? Notice, that this algorithm is equivalent to defining a random permutation on the edges, and then constructing a spanning tree by considering the edges in the order defined by the permutation. It is easy to see that this algorithm generates all possible spanning trees, but are they generated uniformly? For a ring, the answer is positive, but even for the complete graph the generation is non-uniform (for a complete graph on four nodes, each star-shaped tree has probability $\frac{1}{15}$, and each of the other trees are generated with probability $\frac{11}{180}$). At the end of the next section, we formally show, that in a general graph, the two problems are not equivalent.

4 Random Generation through Markov Chains

Broder [B], in his sequential algorithm, uses Markov chains for uniform generation of spanning trees:

To each random walk in the graph corresponds a spanning tree. For each node, i, let e_i be the edge through which the node was visited the first time. After each node was visited at least once, there is an edge e_i for every node, except the node where the random walk started. This set of N-1 edges is a spanning tree. A spanning tree on N nodes is a set of N-1 edges without cycles. In "our" set there are no cycles, since each edge we add reaches a yet unvisited node. If the initial distribution of the random walk is the stationary distribution, then the spanning trees in the graph are generated uniformly. The sequential expected time is $O(N \log N)$ for most graphs, and $O(N^3)$ in the worst case. The expected time of the RST algorithm is the expected cover time. For bounds on cover time see [AK], [B]. The message complexity per step is constant.

Let us describe a simple implementation of this algorithm in a distributed system:

1. Choose a leader ($O(E+N \log N)$ bits and $O(N)$ time), (see section 3 or use any other algorithm for selecting a leader).

2. Count the number of nodes in the graph (after we have a spanning tree from the previous phase, this only takes $O(N)$ time and $O(N)$ messages using DFS).

3. Send the leader the number of edges connected to you (degree of each node), through the shortest path you know (time $O(N)$, and $O(N^2)$ messages).

4. The leader computes the stationary distribution of the canonical random walk on the graph (the stationary distribution is $\frac{d_i}{\sum d_j}$ for each vertex, i, where d_i is the degree of the node). He picks the starting node of the random walk according to this distribution, and sends a message to this node (time $O(N)$, $O(N)$ messages).

5. This node will be the root of the tree. It starts a random walk by choosing, with equal probability, one of its neighbors. Sends the chosen neighbor the number of nodes already visited by the random walk. This node continues similarly. Each node remembers the first edge through which it received a message in the random walk. This will be an edge of the random spanning tree. When the number of nodes already visited is N, stop. A spanning tree was created.

   This takes expected time $O(N^3)$ in the worst case, but only $O(N \log N)$ for most graphs. In each step of the Markov process, a single message is sent along a single edge.

6. Send a message of termination to the other nodes (time $O(N)$, number of messages $O(N)$).

The expected time complexity of this algorithm for most graphs is $O(N \log N)$, and the expected message complexity is $O(E + N^2 + N \log N)$.

Now, we can formally see why the root of a uniformly generated spanning tree cannot be a random leader. Vertex i is the root of the RST with probability $\frac{d_i}{\sum d_j}$, and if the graph is not regular, not all the roots are equiprobable.

Therefore, it is not clear how an RL algorithm give an RST. On the other hand, given an RST (a spanning tree), we can use the tree for election, and in $O(N)$ time and $O(N)$ messages a random leader can easily be chosen. This observation suggests that RST is "more difficult" than RL.

If the graph is regular, the output of the RL algorithm can be used as the starting point of the random walk (all roots are equiprobable). If it is known, that the graph is regular, we can skip phase 3 of the algorithm, and in phase 4 choose a starting node uniformly. If the graph is an expander, then the expected cover time of the random walk is $O(N \log N)$, and the message complexity for random generation becomes $O(E + N \log N)$. Since "most" regular graphs are expanders, we get quite a good result in terms of message complexity for expanders.

5 RST Algorithms on the Complete Graph

In this section, we give two algorithms for the complete graph, one is message and time optimal (when using an optimal number of messages), the other is not message optimal, but selects an RST in constant time.

5.1 A Message-Optimal Algorithm

1. Choose a leader ($\Theta(N \log N)$ messages, see [AG]).

2. This leader chooses one of the nodes of the graph as the root of the spanning tree (a single message).

3. This root chooses a random tree (local computation - will be described in section 5.2).

4. The root sends a message to each of the other nodes, telling them a single edge of the tree (like in the random walk) ($O(N)$ messages).

This algorithm takes $O(N \log N)$ messages, and $O(\log N)$ time, when the system is synchronous. This algorithm is both message and time optimal. The algorithm also works asynchronously, but the time is worse ($O(N)$, see [AG]).

5.2 Local Computation

Locally, the root can compute a RST, using the Markov chain approach (see [B]). We can, however, create a RST using $O(N)$ steps (deterministic, *not* expected). We count this as a single time unit in the distributed algorithm, since the processors have polynomial computational power. The root sends only a single message in a single time unit to all the other processors.

When we construct the tree using the random walk, all we care about is the first time a vertex is visited. In this algorithm we skip the walk through vertices that have already been visited. In each stage of the algorithm, we add a new edge and a new vertex to the tree:

Suppose the walk has visited m vertices already. Let these vertices be $W_m = \{i_1, i_2, ..., i_m\}$, and the random walk is at i_1 now. Then choose the vertex through which the random walk will leave the set W_m according to the distribution $(\frac{N-m+1}{N}, \frac{1}{N}, ..., \frac{1}{N})$.

Let the vertex chosen be i. Choose, with equal probabilities one of the $N - m$ neighbors of i not in W_m. Add this vertex, j, to the set of vertices already visited, and add the edge (i, j) to the tree. At this point, the set of vertices already visited has size $m + 1$, $W_{m+1} = W_m \cup \{j\}$, and the random walk is at j. Repeat this, until the set is of size N.

The above algorithm generates spanning trees exactly with the same distribution as the random walk algorithm (that is, the generation is uniform):

Let P_1 be the probability, that the random walk leaves W_m through the vertex at which the random walk is now. Let P_2 be the probability that the random walk leaves W_m through a vertex different from the vertex at which the walk is now. The only distinct node is the node at which the particle is located. Then, since the random walk leaves eventually:

$$P_1 + (m - 1)P_2 = 1$$

What is the probability, that the walk will leave through the vertex, i_1, the walk is at now? With probability $\frac{N-m}{N-1}$, it will leave the set straight away (in the coming step), and if it doesn't succeed on the first trial, it will visit another vertex, k, of W_m and will eventually leave through i_1, a vertex different from k:

$$P_1 = \frac{N - m}{N - 1} + \frac{m - 1}{N - 1}$$

The solution to these equations is:

$$P_1 = \frac{N - m + 1}{N} \qquad P_2 = \frac{1}{N}$$

Thus, the algorithm is correct.

5.3 A Constant Time Algorithm for the Complete Graph

If we do not mind large message size, we can create a random spanning tree in constant time. This algorithm doesn't involve choosing a leader first. All the processors pick a random vector in a distributive manner.

This algorithm is based on Cayley's theorem, that states, that there are N^{N-2} different labeled trees on N vertices. One of the proofs of this theorem (Prufer's proof, see [E]), shows a 1:1 correspondence between the spanning trees on N vertices, and the set of vectors of length $N - 2$, where each coordinate is a number in the set $\{1, 2, \ldots, N\}$. This correspondence can be easily computed with $O(N \log N)$ comparisons/additions, using an appropriate data structure (like 2-3 trees, see [AHU]).

The distributed algorithm:

1. Wake all the processors.

2. Send your ID and a random number in the range $\{1, \ldots, N\}$ to all the other processors.

3. (Local computation):
   Arrange the ID's in decreasing order, and create a vector of size N-2 from the random numbers the first N-2 processors sent. (Notice, that every processor has the same vector). Now use Prufer's correspondence to create a spanning tree from the vector.

The message complexity of this algorithm is $O(N^2)$, and the time complexity is $O(1)$, and the local computation required by each processor is $O(N \log N)$. Since each vector of length $N - 2$ is equiprobable, the spanning tree is generated uniformly.

6 The RST for the Ring

In this section, we give optimal algorithms for the ring, and another algorithm which is not optimal, but possibly, can be extended to the general graph.

6.1 An Optimal Algorithm on the Ring

On a ring, the problem of choosing a leader, and generating a RST are equivalent. The root of the spanning tree is a random leader. Given a random leader, it is easy to generate a random spanning tree: The random leader decides which one of his neighboring edges to delete from the tree (a tree on a ring is all the edges but one). This way, we do not get the correct distribution on the rooted trees, but now he passes on the leadership to a node randomly chosen by him. This only takes $O(N)$ time and $O(N)$ messages more, but there is a lower bound of $\Omega(N)$ messages and time on any synchronous algorithm for leader election (see [FL]), for algorithms that achieve this bound, see [V], [FL] or [Ga]. It is not necessary for the processors to know the size of the ring. For asynchronous algorithms, there is a lower bound of $\Omega(N \log N)$ (see [Bu]).

6.2 Random Spanning Tree on a Ring - RRST in O(N) Time

We describe here a synchronous algorithm that has worse message complexity, than the above mentioned algorithms, but we hope, that this algorithm can be extended to general graphs.

The algorithm described below assumes, that the nodes have distinct ID's or that they have knowledge of the ring size, and that they are arranged in a ring.

In general, edges have two stages before they are accepted as members of the spanning tree. The first stage - a candidate edge is selected with the proper probability by one of the edge's nodes. (1/2 in the case of the ring). The second stage - the edge is accepted iff its two nodes have selected it as candidate, otherwise it is rejected.

RRST algorithm

- Initially all nodes are part of the spanning forest, and each node
  is considered the leader of that tree.

- **While** there is more than a *single tree* do

- If you are the current leader of the tree then

  - Synchronize - according to the size of the maximal possible subtree at that stage. (In each stage each subtree makes one choice only, this ensures, that trees are created uniformly, that is each edge has equal probability to be left out of the tree.)

  - Choose randomly (with equal probability) one of the tree's *two* out going edges.

  - If you agree with your neighbor on the edge you chose then
    begin

    * Accept this edge.
    * Agree with your neighbor on the node that is going to be the leader of the joined tree.
    * Pass to all the nodes in the united tree the name of the leader (and possibly the size of the current tree).

    end-if

- **end-while**

Deciding if there is a single current tree can be done using the ID's (each node in the forest knows at each phase its root), or using the ring size.

Deciding randomly who is going to be the leader between the two former leaders, can be done using a single message. (If this fails, the edge is rejected). It is more efficient to choose the (temporary) leader as the central node, or one of the two central ones if there is an even number of nodes.

The expected number of edges that will be accepted is 1/4 of the number of trees at each stage. Therefore, the expected number of stages is $\log N$. In each stage, the synchronization is proportional to the length of the largest tree. The maximal length can grow at most twice during a stage, therefore the time complexity is:
$$c(1 + 2 + 4 + \ldots + N) = c(2^{\log N} - 1) = cN$$

Counting the expected number of messages is based on the assumption that each subtree has a unique leader which is located in the "center" of the tree. This leader has to send his decision in the correct direction, and wait for a reply from that direction. The messages that are sent include a single bit, yet the other side of the tree has to be informed about the new leader and length of the tree, thus a message of size $\log N$ is sent in this direction. This is done in every phase, for every subtree. Therefore, the expected message-complexity of the algorithm is $O(N \log N)$.

The algorithm is a Las-Vegas algorithm. When the algorithm stops it results in a tree. The tree, T, is selected uniformly among all possible trees. In every phase of the algorithm, each of the remaining edges has equal probability of being chosen.

The above algorithm relies on the assumption that the size of the ring is known and that each processor has a unique ID. It is easy to see, that the knowledge of the size of the ring is sufficient in order to generate unique ID's (with a small probability of error). If random binary strings of length $3 \log N$ are chosen, then with very high probability, all N strings will be distinct and can serve as ID's. Notice, that to have distinct ID's with high probability, it is enough to have an upper bound on the size of the ring.

If there are no ID's, but the size of the ring, N, can be computed exactly, the algorithm terminates, when there is a subtree of size N.

7   Conclusion

In this paper we discuss several algorithms for generating a random spanning tree. In a distributed system, a leader and a spanning tree have great importance, but because of possible faults, what is really needed, is a *random* leader and a *random* tree.

Our version of Broder's algorithm, doesn't use the whole power of the distributed resources. The core of the algorithm is the random walk, during which in each step only a single processor out of the N is active. In order to overcome the above shortcoming, we tried to form a distributed Markov process. This motivation lead us to the solution described in section 6 for a synchronous ring.

We hope to apply this method to a larger family of graphs, such as the highly symmetric graphs (for example the k dimensional cube) (see [H], [Bi]).

The main question that is yet to be answered is, to what extent the spanning forest technique can be useful in generating a random tree. This requires that each subtree is able to select an edge using only local knowledge or just the knowledge of the structure of the graph, but independently of the other subtrees.

Another approach for finding a spanning tree was studied in the parallel environment (see [QN]), where fast solutions relied on breaking cycles. The question is whether this approach can be applied to the distributed RST problem.

Finding lower bounds for the RST problem in the general graph are also of interest.

8 Acknowledgements

Our work has benefited from discussions with Ilan Newman and Eli Shamir. We express our thanks to Tal Rabin.

References

[AG] Afek, Y. and Gafni, E., *Time and Message Bounds for Election in Synchronous and Asynchronous Complete Networks,* PODC 1985, pp 199-207.

[AHU] Aho, V. A., Hopcroft, J.E. and Ullman, J.D., *The Design and Analysis of Computer Algorithms,* Addison-Wesley, 1974.

[A]   Awerbuch, B., *Linear Time Distributed Algorithms for Minimum Spanning Trees, leader election, counting and related problems,* 19th STOC, 1987, pp. 230-240.

[B]   Broder, A. Z., *Generating Random Spanning Trees,* To appear in 30th FOCS, 1989.

[Bi] Biggs, N., *Algebraic Graph Thory*

[BK] Broder, A. Z. and Karlyn, A. R., *Bounds on Cover Time* 29th FOCS, 1988.

[Bu] Burns, J. E., *A Formal Model for Message Passing Systems,* TR-91, Indiana University, 1980.

[E]   Even, S., *Graph Algorithms,* Maryland, Computer Science Press, 1979.

[FL] Fredrickson, G. N. and Lynch N. A., *The Impact of Synchronous Communication On the Problem of Electing a Leader in a Ring,* STOC84, pp. 493-503.

[Ga]   Gafni, E., *Improvements in the Time Complexity of Two Message-Optimal Election Algorithms*, PODC85, pp 175-184.

[GHS] Gallager, R. G., Humblet, P. A. and Spira, P. M., *A Distributed Algorithm for Minimum Weight Spanning Trees*, ACM Trans. Program. Lang. Syst., vol 5. pp. 66-77, January 1983.

[G]   Guenoche, A., *Random Spanning Trees*, J. Algorithm, vol 4, pp. 214-220, 1983.

[H]   Harary, F., *Graph Theory* Addison-Wesley, 1972.

[KS]   Kemeny, J.G and Snell, J.L., *Finite Markov Chains* Lect. Notes in Math, vol 69.

[MVV] Mulmuley, K., Vazirani, U. V. and Vazirani, V. J., *Matching is as Easy as Matrix Inversion*, 19th STOC, 1987, pp. 345-354.

[QN]   Quinn, M. J. and Narsingh Deo, *Parallel Graph Algorithms*, Computing Surveys, vol 16. No. 3, September 1984, pp 319-348.

[V]   Vitanyi, P., *Distributed Election in an Archimedian Ring of Processors*, STOC84, pp 542-547.

Fault-Tolerant Critical Section Management in Asynchronous Networks

Amotz Bar-Noy [*]   Danny Dolev [†]   Daphne Koller [‡]   David Peleg [§]

Abstract

The topic of the paper is managing a fault-tolerant critical section in a completely asynchronous distributed network. Assume that processors may fail while using the critical section and therefore the critical section must have at least $t + 1$ slots. (t is the maximum number of possible faulty processors).

There are several possibilities for defining a priority rule that achieves fairness among the processors. In [FLBB] processor p has a higher priority than processor q if p asked to access the critical section "before" q. In [ABDKPR] p has a higher priority than q if p used the critical section less than q. The drawback of the first rule (that motivated the second rule) is that a "fast" processor could use the critical section much more than a "slow processor". The drawback of the second rule is that processors should use the critical section infinitely often in order to prevent deadlock. In this paper we modify the second rule to circumvent this last drawback. Processor p has higher priority than processor q only if p used the critical section less times than q, p wants to access the critical section and q "knows" this fact.

We present two algorithms which require $t + 1$ and $2t + 1$ slots respectively. The second is a modification of the first which trades extra slots for simplicity and overcomes Byzantine faults as well.

[*]Computer Science Department, Stanford University, Stanford, CA 94305. Supported in part by a Weizmann fellowship, by contract ONR N00014-88-K-0166 and by a grant of Stanford's Center for Integrated Systems.

[†]IBM Almaden Research Center, 650 Harry Road, San Jose, CA 95120 and the Computer Science Department, Hebrew University, Jerusalem.

[‡]The Hebrew University of Jerusalem.

[§]Department of Applied Mathematics, The Weizmann Institute, Rehovot 76100, Israel. Part of this work was carried out while this author was visiting Stanford university. Supported in part by a Weizmann fellowship, by contract ONR N00014-88-K-0166 and by a grant of Stanford Center for Integrated Systems.

1 Introduction

An important issue in the theory of distributed systems is the extent to which processor cooperation and coordination can be achieved in the presence of faults. There are several parameters influencing this question. The first major parameter is the level of synchronism that exists in the system. A basic result [FLP] states that in a completely asynchronous system, a collection of $n \geq 3$ processors cannot deterministically achieve "nontrivial consensus" in a faulty environment, even if at most one processor may fail, and even when this can only be a benign fail-stop fault (i.e., a processor may either fail to start or stop functioning at some stage). This result and later stronger versions of it [DDS] characterize agreement as a "possibly too powerful" goal, and force us to limit ourselves to weaker forms of processor cooperation, hoping that these will be sufficient for executing various common tasks within such a system.

The topic of this paper is how to accomplish a basic task that requires a certain degree of processor cooperation — a controlled access to a shared resource. This task is generally referred to as critical section management. It is necessary there to achieve mutual exclusion for accessing the resource, i.e., at most one processor can be in the critical section at any time. This goal is obviously unachievable when processors may fail while being inside the critical section. We consider an extension of the problem in which there are several "copies" or slots of the resource, and the number M of such slots bounds the number of processors allowed to concurrently access the resource. This models a common situation in parallel operating systems [PS,Ru], and was introduced first in [FLBB].

Note that almost all previous studies of the critical section problem assumed a shared memory (cf. [R]) and that no processor fails in the critical section. Failure within a critical section was studied in [ABDKPR, DGS]. Other achievable goals in a faulty asynchronous message passing networks received some attention in [ABDKPR, BW, BMZ, DLPSW, K].

Three requirements characterize the critical section problem: exclusion, non-starvation and fairness. The concept of fairness can be interpreted in many ways by introducing different priority rules where each priority rule achieves a different goal. The novelty of this paper is by introducing a priority rule that is more "fair" when the processors access the critical section an equal number of times.

When considering possible access methodologies for a multi-slot resource, there are two viable alternatives for defining the exclusion requirement. One approach in designing the access algorithms asserts that a processor's responsibility is limited only to ensuring itself the right to enter the critical section, and it is not required to locate and secure itself a particular slot. This approach allows processors to view the critical section as a "black box", containing equal, externally indistinguishable slots. A more demanding approach requires the processor to be responsible to the entire assignment process, including finding itself a specific slot and making sure that this slot is not occupied by any other processor at the same time. The two approaches can be illustrated by considering the different procedures of buying a ticket for a bus ride or a flight. In the first case, the passenger needs only to make sure that there is room on the bus, but not to reserve a particular seat. In the second case, it is necessary to have a seat assignment before boarding the aircraft. In this paper we concentrate in implementing the first approach; an implementation of the second approach appears in [ABDKPR].

The identical-slot critical section problem (identical CS, for short) can be formalized by imposing the following three requirements:

1. **Exclusion:** At most M of the processors are in the CS at any given time.

2. **Non-Starvation:** Every non-faulty (or correct) processor that wants to enter the CS eventually succeeds.

3. **Fairness:** If a correct processor p enters the CS, then it is among the first M processors according to a given priority rule.

There are several possibilities for assigning the priorities among the processors. In [FLBB], processor p has higher priority than processor q if p asked to access the critical section "before" q. The drawback of this rule is that a "fast" processor could use the critical section much more than a "slow processor". To overcome this drawback, [ABDKPR] suggested the global priority rule where processor p has higher priority than processor q if p used the critical section less times than q.

An apparent limitation of the global priority rule is that it forces correct processors to use the critical section infinitely often; if M correct processors stop accessing the critical section at some stage, then some time later they will have the highest priority and deadlock the system.

Here, we modify the second rule to circumvent this limitation. The rule is based on $\#p$, the actual number of times that p has ever used slots of the CS.

- **The Transient priority rule:** processor p has higher priority than processor q only if $\langle \#p, p \rangle < \langle \#q, q \rangle$, p wants to enter the CS, and furthermore, q knows that fact.

Solving the critical section problems when all the processors are non-faulty is not difficult. Here, we solve it in the presence of faulty processors, where the fault model is assumed to be fail-stop. In this model, a faulty processor may suddenly stop functioning, regardless of the state it is in. In particular, a processor may fail while in the critical section, as well as in the process of sending messages. Our second algorithm can be run even in the presence of worse types of faults, such as Byzantine faults. In the Byzantine model, the faulty processors may be malicious and even collude to prevent a correct solution.

Note: Throughout, n denotes the number of processors in the system and t is a prescribed upper bound on the number of faulty processors. This number n is known and the processors are named $1, \ldots, n$. Also, whenever we compare two tuples $\langle a_1, \ldots, a_m \rangle$ and $\langle b_1, \ldots, b_m \rangle$, we assume a lexicographical ordering with the first component being the most significant.

Solutions to the CS problems should strive to minimize M. However, there may be as many as t faulty processors in the system, and each of them might stop functioning while inside the critical section. The asynchronous model implies that one cannot distinguish between a faulty processor and a slow one. Therefore, any algorithm needs at least $t + 1$ slots in order to prevent starvation. This proves:

Proposition 1.1 Any algorithm for the critical section problem requires $M \geq t + 1$ slots.
∎

Clearly, if $M \geq n$ we can dedicate a distinct slot to each processor and trivially meet all the requirements. Thus Proposition 1.1 is complemented by the following:

Proposition 1.2 There exists an algorithm for either of the critical section problems using $M = n$ slots. ∎

Another consideration besides the number of required slots is the amount of memory and communication used by the algorithm. The definition of the fairness necessitates the usage of an internal memory proportional to the number of times processors have accessed the critical section. Nevertheless, it does not impose the use of messages of that unbounded size.

For the global priority rule, [ABDKPR] present an algorithm that requires $M = t + 1$ slots, matching the above lower bound. This algorithm is very simple, the size of its messages is only one bit and it overcomes Byzantine faults as well. However, each processor is required to maintain information about the usage of the critical section by all the other processors.

Here, we present an algorithm for the transient priority rule. In this algorithm each processor p stores locally only $\#p$, the number of times it has accessed the critical section, and collects additional information only when it wants to access again the CS. This algorithm also requires $M = t + 1$ slots, but the size of its messages is proportional to the number of times processors have accessed the critical section. Another algorithm for the transient identical CS problem which requires $M = 2t + 1$ slots is described. This algorithm overcomes Byzantine faults as well.

The system model is the standard asynchronous model [FLP,DDS]. Each processor has a message buffer modeled as an unordered set; sending a message to processor p is represented as appending the message to p's buffer. In each step the processor either receives or sends messages, but not both (i.e., we assume non-atomic receive/send). When receiving, it reads some arbitrary (possibly empty) subset of the messages in its buffer; when sending, it can only transmit a message to a single processor. There are no restrictions or assumptions on the order in which messages are received, nor are there any restrictions on the order in which processors take steps, except that each non-faulty processor takes an infinite number of steps during any infinite run. In addition, every message sent from a non-faulty processor to another non-faulty processor will eventually be received.

2 The Transient Identical CS Problem

2.1 The $M = t + 1$ Algorithm

In algorithm **TCS** (transient critical section) described below, processors that do not want to access the CS are asked only to reply by sending some **acknowledge** message, and do not need to maintain any information about other processors. The algorithm requires $t + 1$ slots. Whenever a processor intends to use the CS, it registers itself by sending an appropriate message to every processor. Only processors that at present want to use the CS need to keep track of how many times each processor has visited the CS. Every other processor stores only the number of times it has previously visited the CS.

In the algorithm for the global priority rule described in [ABDKPR], whenever a processor finds itself ranked $t + 1$ or less in the global ordering $\langle \#q, q \rangle$, it may safely enter the critical section. The transient rule for fairness does not allow us to use such a simple criterion. A processor needs to inform others that it intends to access the CS. Similarly, before entering the CS, it has to make sure that no processor of higher priority has changed its state. Thus, the process of entering the CS is composed of two rounds of acknowledgment collection. This process is best described by identifying special states through which the processor has to go. Each processor is initially in PASSIVE state. A processor p that wishes to enter the CS first changes its state into REGISTERING and sends announcements informing all other processors of its wish. It then has to await acknowledgments for its announcement. These acknowledgments enable p to collect information regarding other processors' states. It switches into the state TRYING when it finds itself ranked $t+1$ or less among the processors that want to enter the CS. Upon entering state TRYING, p has to start a second round of sending announcements and awaiting acknowledgments. If, while collecting these acknowledgments, p learns of any higher priority processor that changed its state, it has to return to state REGISTERING and go through the entire process once again. The delicate part of the algorithm is to guarantee the Exclusion Property.

Let us now give a slightly more formal definition of the various states and messages used in the algorithm. Every processor can be in one of four states:

- PASSIVE (not interested at the moment) – encoded by 3.
- REGISTERING (to enter the CS) – encoded by 2.
- TRYING (to enter the CS) – encoded by 1.
- ACCESSING (at present in the CS) – encoded by 0.

There are two types of messages sent by processors. Announcement messages of the form "$\langle S, c \rangle$", where S is the current state of the sender and c is its counter, or acknowledgment messages of the form "$\langle S, c, S', c' \rangle$" as a reply to an announcement message "$\langle S', c' \rangle$", where S and c are defined as above.

During any run of the algorithm processors may send the same announcement message more than once. Therefore, they need to be able to associate each acknowledgment with the appropriate announcement in order to recognize when an acknowledgment to the current announcement is received. This can be achieved by either adding a counter to messages, or assuming FIFO on the lines and counting the acknowledgments received. It can also be solved by transmitting an announcement only after the acknowledgment to the previous announcement is received. Applying the last method to the algorithm does not require storing all outstanding announcements; it is sufficient to remember the last one. Throughout the algorithm we assume that one of these methods is applied. Hence, a processor eventually receives an acknowledgment to its last announcement from any non-faulty processor.

While a processor p attempts to enter the CS, it maintains three vectors, K_p, S_p and C_p, each of length n, containing information about the other processors. The vector C_p is as in the previous section. The q'th entry in the vector S_p indicates q's state. In the vector K_p, the q'th entry indicates whether q has acknowledged knowing that p is in a REGISTERING or TRYING state (encoded by $K_p(q) = 1$), or such an acknowledgment has not arrived p yet (encoded by $K_p(q) = 0$). Throughout the run of the algorithm, each processor maintains information about itself (even when it is in state PASSIVE). The initial values are: $K_p(p) = 1, S_p(p) = 3, C_p(p) = 0$. Thus, every processor starts in a PASSIVE state with a zero counter.

Denote by DB_p the **database** that processor p holds, i.e., the above three vectors. In every database DB_p the processors q are ordered dynamically by the quadruples

$$\langle K_p(q), S_p(q), C_p(q), q \rangle$$

which are ordered lexicographically. The rank of a processor q in a database DB_p (in this ordering) is denoted by $R_p(q)$.

Each processor is instructed by the algorithm to respond to certain messages arriving while it is in certain states, but is allowed to ignore these messages while being in other states. Consequently, the description of the algorithm prefixes each instruction by the states in which that instruction is applicable.

Algorithm TCS /* For a processor p */

1. /* Initialization */
   Create vectors K_p, S_p and C_p of length n. $K_p(p) \leftarrow 1$; $S_p(p) \leftarrow 3$; $C_p(p) \leftarrow 0$.

2. In every state:
   /* acknowledgments and book-keeping */
   if you receive "$\langle s, c \rangle$", from q then

   (a) Send "$\langle s, c, S_p(p), C_p(p) \rangle$" to q.
   (b) If not in state PASSIVE then $C_p(q) \leftarrow c$; $S_p(q) \leftarrow s$.

3. In state PASSIVE:
   if you want to enter the CS then

   (a) Change your state to REGISTERING ($S_p(p) \leftarrow 2$).
   (b) Send "$\langle S_p(p), C_p(p) \rangle$" to every processor.
   (c) For every processor q initialize the vectors:
       $K_p(q) \leftarrow 0$; $S_p(q) \leftarrow 0$; $C_p(q) \leftarrow -1$.

4. In state REGISTERING:

   (a) If you receive "$\langle s, c, s', c' \rangle$" from q such that $s = S_p(p)$ and $c = C_p(p)$,
       then $K_p(q) \leftarrow 1$; $C_p(q) \leftarrow c'$; $S_p(q) \leftarrow s'$.
   (b) If $R_p(p) \leq t + 1$ then

    i. Change your state to TRYING ($S_p(p) \leftarrow 1$).

    ii. For every q, $K_p(q) \leftarrow 0$.

    iii. Send "$\langle S_p(p), C_p(p) \rangle$" to every processor.

5. In state TRYING:

    (a) If you receive "$\langle s, c, s', c' \rangle$" from q such that $s = S_p(p)$ and $c = C_p(p)$, then $K_p(q) \leftarrow 1$; $C_p(q) \leftarrow c'$; $S_p(q) \leftarrow s'$.

    (b) If an announcement message was received from some q such that $\langle C_p(q), q \rangle < \langle C_p(p), p \rangle$, then

        i. Change your state to REGISTERING ($S_p(p) \leftarrow 2$).

        ii. For every q, $K_p(q) \leftarrow 0$.

        iii. Send "$\langle S_p(p), C_p(p) \rangle$" to every processor.

    (c) If $R_p(p) \leq t + 1$ then

        i. Change your state to ACCESSING ($S_p(p) \leftarrow 0$).

        ii. enter the CS.

6. In state ACCESSING:
upon leaving the CS:

    (a) Change your state to PASSIVE ($S_p(p) \leftarrow 3$).

    (b) $C_p(p) \leftarrow C_p(p) + 1$.

    (c) Send $\langle S_p(p), C_p(p) \rangle$ to every processor.

Lemma 2.1 (Exclusion) In every run of algorithm **TCS** at most $t+1$ correct processors are in the critical section at any given time.

Proof: Assume to the contrary that there is a set Z of $t + 2$ processors in the critical section at a certain time in some run. Let x be the last processor from this set that changed its state from REGISTERING to TRYING before accessing the critical section. Since x accessed the critical section, there must be a processor y in the set Z such that according to the data in x's vectors just before switching from TRYING to ACCESSING

$$\langle K_x, S_x, C_x, x \rangle < \langle K_y, S_y, C_y, y \rangle.$$

As $K_x = 1$ we conclude that $K_y = 1$ and $S_y \geq S_x = 1$. On the other hand, S_y was extracted by x from an acknowledgment sent by y. This acknowledgment was sent in response to an announcement sent by x after switching into state TRYING (in Step 4(b)). Since x was the last to change its state into TRYING, it follows that y was already TRYING or ACCESSING, i.e., $S_y \leq 1$. Thus, necessarily $S_y = S_x = 1$. Hence it should be the case that $\langle C_x, x \rangle < \langle C_y, y \rangle$. But then if y has received x's announcement while being in state TRYING, the algorithm instructs y (in Step 5(b)) to change its state back to REGISTERING and retry. Thus if y is in the CS now, it must have switched back into TRYING after x has done so, contradicting the assumption that x was the last to switch from REGISTERING to TRYING. ∎

Lemma 2.2 (Non-Starvation) In every run of algorithm TCS every non-faulty processor that wants to enter the critical section eventually succeeds.

Proof: Assume to the contrary that starvation has occurred in some run of the algorithm. Let p be the correct processor with the smallest pair $\langle C_p, p \rangle$ among the starved processors. Consider the time at which all faulty processors stopped functioning. Every non-faulty processor q will either be in the state PASSIVE forever or eventually have a pair $\langle C_q, q \rangle$ greater than p's pair in p's database. When this happens to all the correct processors, p will no longer return from state TRYING to state REGISTERING, and therefore will access the CS after all the correct processors acknowledge its registering announcement; a contradiction. ∎

Lemma 2.3 (Fairness) In every run of algorithm TCS, if a correct processor p enters the CS, then at the time p enters the critical section, there is a slot available for every processor with higher priority that wants to use the critical section.

Proof: If $\langle \#q, q \rangle < \langle \#p, p \rangle$ and q wants to enter the CS and p knows that, then by definition q has higher priority than p. If q did not yet enter the CS, q occurs before p in p's database. Hence p takes q into account (and leaves it a slot) when it decides to enter the CS. ∎

Theorem 2.1 follows from Lemmas 2.1, 2.2 and 2.3.

Theorem 2.1 Algorithm TCS solves the transient identical CS problem with $t + 1$ slots. ∎

2.2 The $M = 2t + 1$ Algorithm

In algorithm TCS, state TRYING is necessary because the CS has only $t + 1$ slots. In the case where $M = 2t + 1$, one can implement the transient rule for fairness without state TRYING, i.e., with only one round of announcements and acknowledgements. The necessary modifications involve canceling Step 5 of the algorithm; in Step 4(b)i, instead of entering state TRYING, the processor directly switches into state ACCESSING. We refer to this modified algorithm as algorithm TCS-1.

In order to prove that algorithm TCS-1 is correct, it suffices to prove the exclusion property. The proofs for the non-starvation and fairness properties remain as for algorithm **TCS**.

Lemma 2.4 (Exclusion) In every run of algorithm TCS-1 at most $2t + 1$ processors are in the critical section at the same time.

Proof: Assume to the contrary that there are $2t + 2$ processors in the critical section at a certain time in some run. Construct the following directed graph over the set of the processors that are at the critical section. The directed arc $\langle p, q \rangle$ is in the graph if the quadruple associated with p is larger than that of q in p's database. It is impossible that in this graph the arcs $\langle p, q \rangle$ and $\langle q, p \rangle$ occur together (but it might be that there is no arc between p and q).

Each processor draws at least $t + 1$ outgoing arcs from itself, otherwise it cannot enter the CS. Therefore, there exists at least one processor with indegree at least $t + 1$ which should prevent it from entering the CS; a contradiction. ∎

Theorem 2.2 follows from Lemmas 2.4, 2.2 and 2.3.

Theorem 2.2 Algorithm TCS-1 solves the identical CS problem with $2t + 1$ slots. ∎

Algorithm **TCS-1** is correct even when faulty processors are malicious, as long as a correct processor can identify the immediate sender of any message it receives. The worst a faulty processor can do is to occupy a slot forever, which may happen to a fail-stop processor as well. Algorithm **TCS** cannot overcome Byzantine faults, because a faulty processor can force a correct processor to continually retry entering the CS without success (i.e., switching between the states TRYING and REGISTERING).

References

[ABDKPR] H. Attiya, A. Bar-Noy, D. Dolev D. Koller, D. Peleg, and R. Reischuk, Achievable Cases in an Asynchronous Environment, *Proc. 28th Symp. on Foundations of Comp. Science*, pp. 196-203, 1987.

[BMZ] O. Biran, S. Moran, and S. Zaks, A Combinatorial Characterization of the Distributed Tasks which are Solvable in the Presence of One Faulty Processor, *Proc. 7rd ACM Symp. of Principles of Dist. Computing*, pp. 263-273, 1988.

[BW] M. F. Bridgland, and R. J. Watro, Fault-Tolerant Decision Making in Totally Asynchronous Distributed Systems, *Proc. 6rd ACM Symp. of Principles of Dist. Computing*, pp. 52-63, 1987.

[DDS] D. Dolev, C. Dwork and L. Stockmeyer, On the Minimal Synchronism Needed for Distributed Consensus, *Journal of the ACM*, **34** pp. 77-97, 1987.

[DGS] D. Dolev, E. Gafni, and N. Shavit, Toward a Non-Atomic Era: L-Exclusion as a Test Case, *Proc. 19th ACM SIGACT Symposium on Theory of Computing*, pp. 78-92, 1988.

[DLPSW] D. Dolev, N. A. Lynch, S. Pinter, E. Stark, and W. E. Weihl, Reaching Approximate Agreement in the Presence of Faults, *Journal of the ACM*, **33** pp. 499-516, 1986.

[FLBB] M.J. Fischer, N.A. Lynch, J. E. Burns, and A. Borodin, Resource Allocation with Immunity to Limited Process Failure, *Proc. 20th Symp. on Foundations of Comp. Science*, pp. 234-254, 1979.

[FLP] M.J. Fischer, N.A. Lynch, M.S. Paterson, Impossibility of Distributed Consensus with one Faulty Processor, *Journal of the ACM*, Vol. 32, No. 2, April 1985, pp. 374-382.

[K] D. Koller, Token Survival: Resilient Token Algorithms, *M.Sc. Thesis, Hebrew University*, 1986.

[PS] J. L. Peterson, and A. Silberschatz, *Operating Systems Concepts*, 2nd Edition, Addison-Wesley Publishing Co., 1985, Ch. 8,9,13.

[R] M. Raynal, *Algorithms for Mutual Exclusion*, North Oxford Academic Publishers Ltd, 1986.

[Ru] L. S. Rudolph, Software Structures for Ultra Parallel Computing, *Ph.D. Dissertation, Courant Institute, New York University*, 1981.

Efficient Emulation of
Single-Hop Radio Network with Collision Detection
on Multi-Hop Radio Network with no Collision Detection

Reuven Bar-Yehuda*   Oded Goldreich[†]   Alon Itai

Department of Computer Science
Technion - Israel Institute of Technology
Haifa 32000, ISRAEL

ABSTRACT

This paper presents an efficient randomized emulation of *single-hop* radio network *with* collision detection on *multi-hop* radio network *without* collision detection. Each step of the single-hop network is emulated by $O((D+\log\frac{n}{\varepsilon})\log\Delta)$ rounds of the multi-hop network and succeeds with probability $\geq 1-\varepsilon$. (n is the number of processors, D the diameter and Δ the maximum degree). It is shown how to emulate any polynomial algorithm such the probability of failure remains $\leq\varepsilon$.

A consequence of the emulation is an efficient randomized algorithm for choosing a leader in a multi-hop network.

1. INTRODUCTION

The purpose of this paper is to present a close relation between several different models of radio communication. In particular, the most restricted model is emulated by the most general one.

The easiest model to work with (i.e., for developing protocols) is that of the Ethernet. In this model all processors share a single "broadcast channel", through which they communicate in synchronous rounds. In each round, each processor may place a message on the channel. In case a single processor placed a message on the channel, all processors receive it at the end of the round. If no processor placed a message, all processor receive nothing. In case two or more processors placed messages on the channel, all processors, including the transmitters, receive noise at the end of the round. This last feature is called *Collision Detection*, and is

---

* Partially supported by Technion V.P.R. Fund - Albert Einstein Research Fund.
[†] Partially supported by grant No. 86-00301 from the United States - Israel Bi-national Science Foundation (BSF), Jerusalem, Israel.

hereafter abbreviated by CD.

The Ethernet is a good model for local networks, but is somewhat unrealistic for describing radio communication between distant stations. A better model for distant radio communication postulates that the underlying graph of the network is an arbitrary connected graph, rather than a complete graph (as in the Ethernet model). Such a network is called *multi-hop* (contrasted with the Ethernet model which is *single-hop*).

As before, communication in this network proceeds in (synchronous) rounds in which each processors can act either as a transmitter or as a receiver. A processor acting as a receiver receives a message only when some of its neighbors transmit. When one neighbor transmits then the message is indeed received. When more than one neighbor transmits the receiver may either receive one of the messages transmitted, receive noise or not receive anything. In particular, a receiver cannot necessarily distinguish the case of no transmission from the case of multi-transmission; namely, there is no Collision Detection (CD). The absence of CD characterizes noisy networks since the noise does not allow a processor to distinguish no transmission from multi-transmission. Note that the presence of CD does not invalidate our results, it has not been postulated because the proposed protocols do not make use of it. For the same reason we do not require the processors to have (unique) identities.

Due to the practical importance of multi-hop radio networks, the development of protocols for the second model is of interest. However, developing such protocols is a complicated task. The difficulties emerge both from the unknown topology of the network and from the absence of CD mechanism. A useful methodology is to first design protocols for the Ethernet and then emulate them to get protocols for the multi-hop radio network without CD. This methodology becomes more attractive if this compilation can be done automatically without losing too much efficiency.

In this paper, we present an efficient emulation of the Ethernet on arbitrary (multi-hop) radio networks without CD. In section 2 we show how to emulate a single Ethernet step, then in section 3 we show how to implement any Ethernet protocol.

Throughout the paper n denotes the number of processors, Δ and D the maximum degree and diameter of the multi-hop network, respectively. All logarithms are to base 2.

1.1 Previous Work. Chlamtac and Kutten [CK85] showed that, given a network and a designated source, finding an optimal broadcast schedule (i.e., broadcasting schedule which uses the minimum number of rounds) is NP-Hard. Chlamtac and Weinstein [CW87] presented a polynomial-time (centralized) algorithm for constructing a broadcast schedule which uses $O(D\log^2 n)$ time-slots. This centralized algorithm can be implemented in a distributed system assuming the availability of special control channels, but the number of control messages sent may be quadratic in the number of nodes of the network [We87].

Bar-Yehuda et al. [BGI87] described a randomized single-source broadcast protocol. To ensure that with probability $1-\varepsilon$ all nodes receive the message the protocol requires an average of $O((D + \log\frac{n}{\varepsilon})\log\Delta)$ time slots. For $D=O(1)$, they have also shown a $\Omega(n)$ lower bound for deterministic protocols. Thus, for this problem there exist randomized protocols that are much more efficient than any deterministic one.

Alon et al. [ABLP89] presented networks with diameter $D=2$ in which every broadcast schedule has length $\Omega(\log^2 n)$. The randomized protocol of [BGI87] is thus optimal for these networks. They also showed how to emulate a point-to-point *message-passing* model on a radio network. The main difference between the message-passing model and a (multi-hop) radio network with CD is that in the first model a processor must receive all messages sent to it by its neighbours in the current round, while in radio network receipt of messages is only required in case of no conflict. Thus the emulators described in [ABLP89] address a completely different model and are not applicable for our setting.

In [BII89], Bar-Yehuda et al. discuss several other radio communication tasks; namely, they study multiple broadcast and point-to-point communication. Efficient probabilistic protocols of the Las Vegas type (i.e., no error in case an acknowledgement is received) are presented. In particular, k point-to-point requests are handled in $O((k+D)\log\Delta)$ rounds (on the average), and k broadcast requests are handled in $O((k+D)\log\Delta\log n)$ rounds.

1.2 Our Results. Our main result is a probabilistic emulation of a single round of a single-hop radio network with CD on an arbitrary multi-hop radio network with no CD mechanism. The emulation of one round requires $O(B_\varepsilon)$ time slots, where $B_\varepsilon = O((D+\log\frac{n}{\varepsilon})\log\Delta)$ is the time required to implement broadcast with error probability bounded by ε on the underlying multi-hop network.

A simpler and more efficient for implementing a CD mechanism on an arbitrary multi-hop network is also presented. The emulation of one round with CD mechanism, on a network with the same topology but without CD, requires $O(\log\varepsilon^{-1} \log\Delta)$ (where ε is the error probability).

1.3 Subprotocols Used. Our emulations uses two protocols *Decay* and *Broadcast*, first discussed in [BGI87].

Decay is a protocol that enables a processor to receive, with probability $> \frac{1}{2}$, a message sent by one of its neighbours regardless of the number of neighbours wishing to send him a message.

procedure *Decay* (*m*);
    repeat at most 2logΔ times
        transmit *m* to all neighbors;
        flip *coin* $\in_R$ {0,1}
    until *coin* = 0;
    wait until round 2logΔ.

Decay is a probabilistic protocol, with the following properties:

(1) It lasts 2logΔ rounds.

(2) If several neighbors of a node *v* use *Decay* to send messages then with probability greater than ½ the node *v* receives one of the messages.

(3) *Decay* is oblivious of the contents of the messages sent.

    The second protocol is *Broadcast*. It makes use of *Decay* and has the following property: if several nodes initiate Broadcast at round 0 then at round $B_\varepsilon = O\left((D + \log\frac{n}{\varepsilon})\log\Delta\right)$ with probability > 1−ε all nodes have received a message of one of the initiators. (In particular, if there is only one initiator then all the nodes received the same message.) *Broadcast* is also oblivious to the contents of the message.

2. THE EMULATION OF A SINGLE ROUND.

Consider the following two models of radio networks.

Model 1: Complete graph with conflict detection.

Model 2: Arbitrary connected graph, in case of a conflict at vertex *v* any of the the following may occur:

(1) The conflict is detected, or

(2) *v* receives one of the messages, or

(3) *v* does not receive any message and is not aware that any message has been sent.

Aim: Show how one round in model 1 can be emulated by several rounds in model 2.

2.1 The emulation procedure.

Let *l* denote the number of processors (hereafter called *initiators*) which wish to transmit in the current round (of model 1). Let ε be the desired bound on the failure probability.

Variables: Let $k=2.5\log 3/\varepsilon$. For each processor v we use the following variables

msg_v A message v wishes to transmit in the current round (of model 1). $msg_v=\lambda$ if v does not wish to transmit.

$conflict_v$, m_v Output variables holding the result of the current round: $conflict_v$ is a Boolean variable while m_v is assigned messages.

tag_v, t_v k-bit variables used in the program.

The emulation consists of three phases: *propagation*, *detection* and *notification*.

Propagation: Initially, $conflict_v=0$ for all v. Each processor v with $msg_v \neq \lambda$ (wishing to transmit) selects tag_v at random in $\{0,1\}^k$ and initiates Broadcast of the pair (msg_v,tag_v). If $msg_v \neq \lambda$ and processor v receives a message other than (msg_v,tag_v) then v sets $conflict_v \leftarrow 1$. Every processor sets (m_v,t_v) to be the first message received during this phase (for v having $msg_v \neq \lambda$ we take the natural convention of setting (m_v,t_v) to (msg_v,tag_v)).

Detection: The purpose of this phase is to detect if there was more than one initiator (i.e., a processor v with $msg_v \neq \lambda$). To this end, each processor v having $m_v \neq \lambda$ (i.e., either an initiator or a receiver of a message during the propagation phase) proceeds as follows:

> **for** $i := 1$ **to** k **do**
>   **if** the i-th bit of t_v is 1
>   **then** $Decay\,(t_v)$
>   **else if** v receives a message during the next $2\log\Delta$ rounds
>   **then** it sets $conflict_v \leftarrow 1$.

(A processor v with $m_v=\lambda$ remains idle throughout the entire detection phase.)

Notification: Each processor, v, having $conflict_v = 1$ initiates a broadcast of a standard message (e.g., "conflict"). A processor, u, receiving this ("conflict") message sets $conflict_u \leftarrow 1$. (In case no such message was received, $conflict_u$ remains unchanged.)

2.2 Analysis.

Lemma 1: Suppose there is at least one initiator and that the propagation phase succeeded (every vertex received at least one message).

(i)   If there is a single initiator, denoted u, then at the end of the detection phase for all vertices v, $conflict_v = 0$ and $m_v = msg_u$.

(ii)   If there is more than one initiator then with probability $\geq 1-\varepsilon/3$ at the end of the detection phase there exists a vertex v for which $conflict_v = 1$.

Proof:

(i)   If there is a single initiator (u) all vertices v have the same value of t_v (which equals tag_u). Thus in every iteration of the detection phase, either all the vertices participate in *Decay* or all of them listen. Therefore, whenever a vertex listens no vertex transmits and the value of $conflict_v$ remains 0. Clearly, in this case $m_v = msg_u$.

(ii)   Assume that there was more than one initiator. If any vertex v received a message from more than one initiator then $conflict_v = 1$. Furthermore, by the properties of Broadcast and the connectivity of the network, there (must) exist two adjacent processors u and v which have received messages initiated by two different processors r and s (u may be equal to r – this is the case iff u is an initiator itself). It follows that $t_u = tag_r$ and $t_v = tag_s$. Since Broadcast is oblivious to the contents of the messages, the distribution of tag_u and tag_v is independent of the fact these messages have reached u and v respectively. Thus, for every i, with probability $\frac{1}{2}$, the strings t_u and t_v differ in the i-th bit. In this case, in the i-th iteration of the detection phase, one of them, say u, transmits and the other, v, listens, and there is probability $\geq \frac{1}{2}$ that the listening vertex, v, received a message, whereupon it sets $conflict_v$ to 1. Thus with probability $\geq \frac{1}{4}$ during some iteration, some $conflict_w$ variable is set to 1. The probability that this did not occur during any iteration is

$$\leq (1-\tfrac{1}{4})^k = \tfrac{3}{4}^{2.5\log\varepsilon^{-1}} < \varepsilon. \qquad \square$$

Lemma 2: The entire protocol requires $(2+o(1))B_\varepsilon$ rounds, where $B_\varepsilon = O(D\log\Delta + \log\Delta\log(n/\varepsilon))$.

Proof: The propagation and notification phases consist of executing broadcast, which by [BGI 87] can be implemented in B_ε rounds. The detection phase consists of $k = 2.5\log 3\varepsilon^{-1}$ iterations of *Decay* each of which requires $2\log\Delta$ rounds. Thus, the time is dominated by the number of rounds required for broadcast. $\qquad \square$

Theorem 1: Let the vertices of model 2 follow the above protocol. If there is a single initiator then with probability $\geq 1-\varepsilon/3$ all the vertices receive its message, and if there are more initiators then with probability $\geq 1-\varepsilon$ all vertices sense a conflict in model 1. The above protocol requires $O(D\log\Delta + \log\Delta\log(n/\varepsilon))$ time.

Proof: In case there is one or more initiators, *Broadcast* executed in the propagation phase fails with probability $\leq\varepsilon/3$. In case there are several initiators, conflict detection (in the second phase) fails with probability $\leq\varepsilon/3$. The failure probability in the (possible) broadcast of the notification phase is again bounded above by $\varepsilon/3$. The theorem follows. $\qquad \square$

2.3 Implementing a CD mechanism in arbitrary multi-hop networks.

In this subsection, we take a small detour, presenting a method for implementing a CD mechanism in arbitrary multi-hop radio networks. Namely, we show how to probabilistically emulate the following model 1' on model 2:

Model 1': A multi-hop network where conflicts are detected with probability $1-\varepsilon$.

Model 2: A network with the same underlying graph but no guarantee whatsoever concerning conflict detection.

Let $k = 2\log\dfrac{3}{\varepsilon}$. The emulation of a single round of model 1' proceeds as follows. Processor v wishing to transmit a message msg_v in the current round (of model 1') selects uniformly $tag_v \in \{0,1\}^k$ and repeats $Decay(msg_v, tag_v)$ k times. Processor u acting as receiver in the current round (of model 1') listens during the $2k\log\Delta$ rounds (i.e., the duration of k executions of $Decay$) and sets $conflict_u \leftarrow 1$ if it heard two messages with different tags (otherwise $conflict_u$ remains 0). Processor u sets m_u to be the message field in the first message it has received during the above rounds.

The reader may easily verify that the above procedure guarantees collision detection (at a single processor in one round) with probability $>1-\varepsilon$.

3. EMULATING AN ENTIRE ALGORITHM

In the previous section we presented a probabilistic protocol to emulate a single round of a single-hop network with CD (i.e., model 1) by a multi-hop radio network with no CD (i.e., model 2). The simulation is probabilistic and the probability of failure is bounded by a parameter ε. For a given ε the number of rounds is $S_\varepsilon = O((D+\log\dfrac{n}{\varepsilon})\log\Delta)$.

In general, the emulation of an algorithm (designed for model 1) on model 2, requires several such rounds. If the probability of error for a single round is ε', then the probability that the entire t rounds of the algorithm are error free is $(1-\varepsilon')^t > 1-t\varepsilon'$. To make sure that the algorithm succeeds with probability ε, we must choose $\varepsilon' = \varepsilon/t$. Thus a single round requires

$$O((D+\log\dfrac{n}{\varepsilon'})\log\Delta) = O((D+\log\dfrac{n}{\varepsilon/t})\log\Delta) = O((\log t + D + \log\dfrac{n}{\varepsilon})\log\Delta) = O(S_\varepsilon + \log t\log\Delta),$$

and the entire algorithm requires $O(t(\log t\log\Delta + S_\varepsilon))$.

In order to proceeds in such a simulation, one needs to precompute the value of ε', using an upper bound on the running time of the algorithm. In some cases, such a bound may not be known a-priori. An adaptive approach, which does not require a-priori knowledge of the running time, is to gradually decrease the ε' used in the single-round emulation. This yields also a slightly better simulation (in terms of number of rounds).

Let $\varepsilon_i = \dfrac{6\varepsilon}{\pi^2 i^2}$. In the emulation of the i-th round of the algorithm, we use ε_i instead of ε'.

Thus the i-th round requires $S_{\varepsilon_i} = O((D + \log\dfrac{n}{\varepsilon_i})\log\Delta) = O((D + \log\dfrac{n}{\varepsilon/i^2})\log\Delta) = O((2\log i + D + \log\dfrac{n}{\varepsilon})\log\Delta)$. Consequently, the emulation of a t-round algorithm requires

$O(t(\log t + D + \log\dfrac{n}{\varepsilon})\log\Delta) = O(t(\log t\log\Delta + S_\varepsilon))$.

The probability that the i-th round failed is ε_i. Thus the probability that no round failed is

$$\prod_{i=1}^{t}(1 - \varepsilon_i) > 1 - \sum_{i=1}^{t}\varepsilon_i = 1 - \sum_{i=1}^{t}\frac{6\varepsilon}{\pi^2 i^2} > 1 - \sum_{i=1}^{\infty}\frac{6\varepsilon}{\pi^2 i^2} = 1 - \varepsilon.$$

Theorem 2: For every ε, any Ethernet algorithm can be probabilistically emulated on a multi-hop network with no CD, such that

(1) The emulation fails with probability $\le \varepsilon$;

(2) The emulation takes $O(t(\log t \log\Delta + B_\varepsilon))$, where t is the round complexity of the Ethernet algorithm and $B_\varepsilon = O((D + \log\dfrac{n}{\varepsilon})\log\Delta)$ is the round complexity of broadcast (in model 2).

Note that an Ethernet algorithm with round complexity polynomial in the network size or in the inverse of the error probability (i.e., $t = poly(n/\varepsilon)$) can be emulated at an average cost of $O(B_\varepsilon)$ rounds per each round of the algorithm. In general, this seems the best result possible.

4. APPLICATIONS AND CONCLUSIONS

We now show how the emulation of section 3 can be used to choose a leader in a multi-hop radio network. Willard [W86] proposed an algorithm for leader election in the Ethernet model. The algorithm uses conflict detection and requires $O(\log\log n)$ rounds. Applying our emulation yields a probabilistic algorithm of $O(B_\varepsilon \log\log n)$ rounds for leader election in a multi-hop radio networks with no CD.

Our emulation results are general and apply to all Ethernet algorithms. In many cases (e.g. for polynomial-time algorithms) the overhead of the emulation is merely a multiplicative factor of the time required to complete broadcast on the underlying (multi-hop) network. As a general result this seems the best possible, but it may be improved in special cases. In particular, can one improve the $O((D + \log\dfrac{n}{\varepsilon})\log\Delta \log\log n)$ rounds algorithm for leader election in arbitrary radio networks?

REFERENCES

[ABLP89] Alon N., Bar-Noy A., Linial N. and Peleg D., "On the complexity of radio communication", *21st STOC*, pp. 274-285, 1989.

[BGI87] Bar-Yehuda R., Goldreich O. and Itai A., "On the time complexity of broadcast in
radio networks: an exponential gap between determinism and randomization", 6th
Symposium on Principles of Distributed Systems, (Aug. 1987).

[BII87] Bar-Yehuda R., Israeli A. and Itai A., Multiple Communication in Multi-Hop Radio
Networks, 8th Symposium on Principles of Distributed Systems, (Aug. 1989).

[CK85] Chlamtac, I. and Kutten, S., "On Broadcasting in Radio Networks- Problem Analysis
and Protocol Design", December (1985), Vol COM-33, No. 12.

[CW87] Chlamtac, I. and Weinstein O., "The wave expansion approach to broadcasting in
multihop radio networks", *INFOCOM* (April 1987).

[DIX80] Digital-Intel-Xerox, "The Ethernet data link layer and physical layer specification
1.0" (Sept. 1980).

[Ga85] Gallager, R., "A perspective on multiaccess channels", *IEEE Trans. on Inf. Theory*,
Vol. IT-31 (1985), 124-142.

[We87] Weinstein O., "The wave expansion approach to broadcasting in multihop radio networks", M.Sc. Thesis, Computer Science Dept., Technion, Haifa, Israel, (1987).

[Wi86] Willard D.E., "Log-logarithmic selection resolution protocols in a multiple access
channel", SIAM J. on Comput. 15(2), 468-477, (1986).

Applying a Path–Compression Technique to Obtain an Efficient Distributed Mutual Exclusion Algorithm*

José M. Bernabéu-Aubán

Departamento de Sistemas Informáticos y Computación
Universidad Politécnica de Valencia
Apartado 22012, 46020 VALENCIA (Spain)

Mustaque Ahamad

School of Information and Computer Science
Georgia Institute of Technology
ATLANTA, GA 30332–0280 (USA)

Abstract

In this paper we present a distributed algorithm for mutual exclusion. The algorithm maintains a dynamic forest structure in which the paths between nodes are compressed as a result of requesting the Critical Section. We develop a formal model of the algorithm's execution, which enables us to prove its correctnes. The formal model is also used to show that an execution history of the algorithm when concurrent requests are made (the ususal case) is equivalent to a history in which the requests are made serially. Based on this fact we are able to prove a logarithmic upper bound on the average number of messages needed per critical section grant.

1 Introduction

Distributed systems offer many advantages including sharing of resources by processes executing at different nodes. In many applications, a process needs to obtain mutual exclusion before it can use a resource. We address the problem of designing an efficient distributed algorithm that can be used to achieve mutual exclusion in a distributed system.

A number of distributed mutual exclusion algorithms have been proposed [1]. The operation of many of the algorithms can be characterized by an information structure [2] that defines a set of processes that must be informed before acquiring the Critical Section (CS), and another set must be informed when the process releases the CS. Examples of these algorithms include [3,4,5,6,7,8]. The communication cost of all the algorithms except [5] is $O(N)$ where N is the number of nodes that share access to a resource. The algorithm described in [5] reduces the communication cost to $O(\sqrt{N})$ by imposing a logical structure on the processes.

Recently tree-based algorithms have been proposed for achieving mutual exclusion that require smaller number of messages [9,10,11]. However, in these algorithms some nodes need to

---

*This work was supported in part by NSF grants CCR-8806358 and CCR-8619886.

process more messages than others even when the requests by all the nodes are uniform. For instance, in [10], internal nodes in the tree receive and send a higher number of messages compared to the leaf nodes. Furthermore, in [10] it is argued that in many networks the average number of messages exchanged is $O(\log N)$ but only informal arguments are presented to show how the cost is derived. Also, in [12] a general framework is presented, based on which several of the above mentioned algorithms can be modeled. In all the above algorithms, the number of messages a node has to process on behalf of other nodes between two consecutive critical section requests is potentially unbounded. We present a fully distributed algorithm whose average cost is bounded by $\log N$. This algorithm will process a maximum of N messages on behalf of other nodes between to consecutive critical section requests. We also use a formal model to argue about the correctness and cost (number of messages sent) of the proposed algorithm.

Our algorithm is similar to the *forwarding address* scheme that has been used for finding the location of moving resources in distributed systems. It was used in Demos [13] to find migrating processes and Fowler [14] studied the performance of a number of resource finding algorithms based on forwarding addresses. The main idea of such an algorithm is that each node stores the address of the node where the resource moved after it left the node. The current location of the resource is found by following these pointers. In distributed mutual exclusion, the CS privilege (also used in [7,10,9]) is the virtual resource, and to acquire the CS, the node where the privilege currently resides must be located. A dynamic structure that changes as requests are made is used by our algorithm to locate the CS privilege. Since the set of nodes that process a request message is not known to the node where the request originates, these algorithms use a dynamic information structure which is distributed.

In the algorithm presented in this paper, a node never stores more than one request of some other node and hence it only requires $O(\log N)$ bits to store the variables used by the algorithm. This is not true of the other tree-based algorithms because a node may have to queue upto $N - 1$ requests. Another desirable property is that message size is also $O(\log N)$ bits. Some of the other distributed mutual exclussion algorithms require variable size messages which can be up to $O(N \log N)$ bits (e.g., [7]). Since the algorithm does not use a static tree to find the CS privilege, which is the scheme presented in [10,9], our algorithm is fully distributed.

We present the details of the algorithm in section 2. In section 3 we describe a model of a system using the algorithm. The correctness of the algorithm is proven in section 4. In section 5 we prove a serialization property of the algorithm which permits us to establish an upper bound of $K(2 + 3 \log N)$ for K CS grants. Finally, in section 6 we present some concluding remarks.

2 Basic Algorithm

We assume that our system consists of a set V of N nodes numbered from 1 to N. The basic idea on which the algorithm is based is to maintain a rooted directed tree of the network nodes, where the root is the node containing the privilege. The edges of the tree are maintained by having one node pointer variable, t_addr_i, at each node i, where $t\_addr_i = j \neq 0$ indicates that the parent of i is j. $t\_addr_i = 0$ would imply that i is the root of the tree. We first consider the simple case in which a request for the CS is made by a single node at a time and the CS is available when the request is made. In such a situation, when a node, i, wants to enter the CS and it does not have the privilege, it sends a *request* message to its parent, t_addr_i, and changes t_addr_i to 0. A node j, on receiving a request message, forwards it to its parent, t_addr_j, and changes t_addr_j to i. When the request message arrives at the node, k, with $t\_addr_k = 0$, which under the current assumptions will be the root node at the time the request was initiated, k will send a *privilege* message to i, also changing t_addr_k to i. When i receives the privilege message it becomes the privilege owner and can enter its CS. Since all nodes that processed i's request now point to it, when i receives the privilege the path from the requesting node to the root has been compresed, and the requesting node becomes the new root of the tree, having the privilege. The path compression makes the tree structure dynamic.

It is clear that when requests are not made concurrently, the above scheme is valid. But if such were the case we would not need a mutual exclusion algorithm anyway. To make the basic algorithm work when requests are made concurrently we extend it by adding a second pointer variable, p_addr_i, which is stored at node i. Initially p_addr_i will be 0, and in general, $p\_addr_i = j$, will mean that node i will send the privilege to node j when node i exits its critical section. If $p\_addr_i = i$, the privilege will simply stay at i even after i exits its CS. When concurrent requests are allowed, we will have a forest instead of a single tree. Thus, when a request message for node i arrives to node j, with $t\_addr_j = 0$, there is no guarantee that node j will have the privilege, or that j is not in its CS. However, if $t\_addr_j = 0$ but j cannot pass the privilege, j is also requesting the CS (see section 4. In this case, p_addr_j will be set to i, so that j will send the privilege message to i when it exits its CS. The t_addr_j pointer is updated in this case also so it points to i.

The algorithm executed at node i as well as the handling of the request and privilege messages is shown in figure 1. The system is considered to start from a star configuration, with node 1 at the center (root) of the star. No node is assumed to be requesting the critical section and all p_addr pointers are 0. Variable req_i is **true** whenever the node is in the process of requesting the CS (or has got it already). Finally, variable $priv_i$ is **true** only if node i has the privilege. Thus, initially req_i is **false** for all i and variable $priv_i$ is only **true** for $i = 1$.

We take the view that there are two processes at each node, one of them requests the CS while the other is in charge of message handling. In general there would be more than one process at each node trying to access the CS. We will assume that each node sequences requests made by processes at the node, so that a node starts a request for the CS only if the node is not already requesting CS. A process wanting to enter the critical section at node i will execute procedure $requestCS(i)$. When a process at node i exits its critical section it will execute procedure $exitCS(i)$. The Message Handler at node i executes procedure $M\_handler(i)$. It is assumed that $requestCS(i)$, $exitCS(i)$, as well as the processing of each received message at node i is executed atomically within node i.This can be easily implemented using semaphores or other similar mechanisms.

3   Model of Execution

In the model, we will assume the existence of a logical communications link between every pair of nodes. The only assumption we will make about message transmission is that all sent messages are eventually delivered. From now on we will denote nodes with lowercase greek letters.

In the previous section we presented the operations used by the algorithm to synchronize access to the CS. Each one of the procedures presented above is executed atomically. We will now show a formal model of the system which we will use to prove its correctnes. The model will

```
t_addr_i    : node_id; (* parent pointer in tree *)      t_addr_i   := 1; (* for i not 1 *)
p_addr_i    : node_id; (* privilege list pointer *)      t_addr_1   := 0;
priv_i      : boolean; (* is the privilege at i? *)      p_addr_i   := 0;
req_i       : boolean;                                    priv_i     := false (* for i different from 1 *)
                                                          priv_1     := true
                                                          req_i      := 0;
```

```
procedure requestCS(i)                                   procedure exitCS(i)
    req_i := true;                                            j := p_addr_i;
    p_addr_i := i;                                            req_i := false;
    if (t_addr_i ≠ 0) then                                   p_addr_i := 0;
        send Request(i) message to t_addr_i                  if (j ≠ i) then
        t_addr_i := 0                                            send Privilege message to node j
        wait until priv_i = true.                            priv_i := false;
    endif                                                    endif
    (* Critical Section can be entered now. *)           endproc exitCS
    (* exitCS(i), to be executed afterwards *)
endproc requestCS
```

```
            procedure M_handler(i)
                while (true) do
                    wait for message m
                    case m of
                    Request(j):
                        k := t_addr_i
                        if (k ≠ 0) then
                            send Request(j) message to k
                        elsif ((req_i = false) ∧ (priv_i = true))
                        then
                            send Privilege message to j;
                            priv_i := false;
                        else
                            p_addr_i := j;
                        endif
                        t_addr_i := j;
                    Privilege:
                        priv_i := true;
                    endcase
                done
            endproc M_handler
```

Figure 1: Mututal Exclusion Algorithm

also help us in determining an upper bound on the cost of using the algorithm. The approach taken is very similar to that of I/O Automata models [15]. We will view the system as an automata with a set of states denoted by S, a set of operations denoted by $\mathcal{O}$, and a set of transitions denoted by T. The set of states is defined by the set of values that the variables in figure 2 can take. The set of possible messages and operators is also shown in figure 2.

The meaning of t_addr_α, p_addr_α, $priv_\alpha$, and req_α has already been explained above. I_α is a boolean variable which, when true, indicates that node α is executing its CS. J_α contains the number of the last request made by node α. On the other hand, C_α is the number of the last execution of the CS completed by node α (note: we consider that a node has finished executing its critical section only after it has finished executing the code in $exitCS$). The variable $L_{\alpha,\beta}$ is a set containing the messages in transit from node α to node β. $\mathcal{R}(\alpha, i)$ is the request message which will circulate on behalf of node α's i^{th} request and $\mathcal{P}$ is the privilege message.

Let $s \in S$, we will represent the variable X of the system in state s by $X(s)$. Sometimes the dependency of the variables on the state is not shown explicitly when the context in which it appears is unambiguous. We will denote the set of initial states in which the system may start by S_0. A state s will be in the set of initial states if it satisfies the following conditions

(a) The graph $D(s)$ where the set of edges $DE(s)$ is given by

$$DE(s) = \{< \alpha, t\_addr_\alpha(s) > | t\_addr_\alpha(s) \neq 0\}$$

forms a directed tree.

(b) Let ρ be the root of tree D, then $priv_\rho = \text{true}$, and $priv_\alpha = \text{false}$, for all other nodes α.

(c) $p\_addr_\alpha = 0$ for all α.

(d) $req_\alpha = \text{false}$ and $I_\alpha = \text{false}$ for all α.

(e) $J_\alpha = C_\alpha \geq 0$ for all α.

(f) $L_{\alpha,\beta} = \phi$ for all pairs of nodes.

The set of operators, $\mathcal{O}$, is given in figure (2). $(R_{\alpha,i}, \beta)$ represents the receipt and processing by node β of a request message for the ith request made by node α. (P, α) represents the receipt of the privilege by node α. (r_i, α) represents node α starting its ith request. (CS, α) represents node α entering the critical section. (ES, α) represents node α finishing the execution of the procedure $exitCS$.

The set of transitions, T, will consist of triples of the form (s, Γ, s'). We will specify T by associating two predicates with each operator Γ: the precondition $\textbf{Precond}(\Gamma)$, and the postcondition, $\textbf{Postcond}(\Gamma)$. These predicates have to be evaluated in the context of a possible transition (s, Γ, s'). Then $\textbf{Precond}(\Gamma)$ can depend only on s whereas $\textbf{Postcond}(\Gamma)$ can depend on s and s'. To make this dependence explicit we will write $\textbf{Precond}(\Gamma)[s]$ and $\textbf{Postcond}(\Gamma)[s, s']$. Thus the set of transitions allowed is defined by

$$T = \{(s, \Gamma, s') | \Gamma \in \mathcal{O} \wedge \textbf{Precond}(\Gamma)[s] \wedge \textbf{Postcond}(\Gamma)[s, s']\}$$

The set of preconditions and postconditions for our operators is shown in figure (2). When variable X is not mentioned in the postcondition, it is assumed that $X(s') = X(s)$. Based on

$$\begin{aligned}
t\_addr_\alpha &\quad: \text{node\_id;} \\
p\_addr_\alpha &\quad: \text{node\_id;} \\
priv_\alpha &\quad: \text{boolean;} \\
req_\alpha &\quad: \text{boolean;} \\
l_\alpha &\quad: \text{boolean;} \\
L_{\alpha,\beta} &\quad: \text{Set of Message; for } \alpha \neq \beta
\end{aligned}$$

$$\textbf{Message} = \{\mathcal{R}(\alpha,i) | 1 \leq \alpha \leq N \wedge i > 0\} \cup \{\mathcal{P}\}$$

$$\mathcal{O} = \{(R_{\alpha,i},\beta), (r_i,\alpha), (P,\alpha), (CS,\alpha), (ES,\alpha)\}$$

Operator	Precondition	Postcondition

$(R_{\alpha,i},\beta)$	$\exists \gamma : \mathcal{R}(\alpha,i) \in L_{\gamma,\beta}(s)$	let $\mathcal{R}(\alpha,i) \in L_{\gamma,\beta}(s)$, then
		$L_{\gamma,\beta}(s') = L_{\gamma,\beta}(s) - \{\mathcal{R}(\alpha,i)\}$
		if $(t\_addr_\beta(s) \neq 0)$ then
		$\quad$ let $\delta = t\_addr_\beta(s)$
		$\quad L_{\beta,\delta}(s') = L_{\beta,\delta}(s) \cup \{\mathcal{R}(\alpha,i)\}$
		elsif $(\neg req_\beta(s) \wedge priv_\beta(s))$ then
		$\quad L_{\beta,\alpha}(s') = L_{\beta,\alpha}(s)) \cup \{\mathcal{P}\}$
		$\quad \neg priv_\beta(s')$
		else
		$\quad p\_addr_\beta(s') = \alpha$
		endif
		$t\_addr_\beta(s') = \alpha$

(P,α)	$\exists \delta : \mathcal{P} \in L_{\delta,\alpha}(s)$	$priv_\alpha(s')$ $L_{\delta,\alpha}(s') = L_{\delta,\alpha}(s) - \{\mathcal{P}\}$

(r_i,α)	$\neg req_\alpha(s)$
	$J_\alpha(s) = i - 1$
		$t\_addr_\alpha(s') = 0$
		$req_\alpha(s')$
		$J_\alpha(s') = J_\alpha(s) + 1 = i$
		$p\_addr_\alpha(s') = \alpha$
		if $(t\_addr_\alpha(s) \neq 0)$ then
		$\quad$ let $\gamma = t\_addr_\alpha(s)$
		$\quad L_{\alpha,\gamma}(s') = L_{\alpha,\gamma}(s) \cup \{\mathcal{R}(\alpha,i)\}$
		endif

(CS,α)	$priv_\alpha(s) \wedge req_\alpha(s) \wedge \neg l_\alpha(s)$	$l_\alpha(s')$

(ES,α)	$l_\alpha(s)$	$\neg l_\alpha(s') \wedge \neg req_\alpha(s')$
		$p\_addr_\alpha(s') = 0$
		if $(p\_addr_\alpha(s) \neq \alpha)$ then
		$\quad \neg priv_\alpha(s')$
		$\quad$ let $\gamma = p\_addr_\alpha(s)$
		$\quad L_{\alpha,\gamma}(s') = L_{\alpha,\gamma}(s) \cup \{\mathcal{P}\}$
		endif

Figure 2: Variables and operators with their pre and postconditions

the above definition of transitions we will now define the set of possible histories of the system, $\mathcal{H}$, as the set of all possible infinite sequences, Π, of the form

$$\Pi = s_0 e_1 s_1 e_2 s_2 e_3 \ldots e_n s_n \ldots$$

where $s_0 \in S_o$ and for all $i \geq 0$, $(s_i, e_{i+1}, s_{i+1}) \in T$. That is, the system starts in one of the initial states and an operator can act on state s only if it is enabled (by its precondition) in s, resulting in another state satisfying the operator's postconditions. Finally, there are a set of assumptions we make about the system:

Assumptions

(a) $\mathcal{R}(\alpha, i) \in L_{\delta, \beta}(s_n) \Longrightarrow (\exists m > n : e_m = (R_{\alpha, i}, \beta))$.

(b) $\mathcal{P} \in L_{\alpha, \beta}(s_n) \Longrightarrow (\exists m > n : e_m = (P, \beta))$.

(c) $(req_\alpha(s_n) \wedge priv_\alpha(s_n) \wedge \neg l_\alpha(s_n)) \Longrightarrow (\exists m > n : l_\alpha(s_m))$.

(d) $l_\alpha(s_n) \Longrightarrow (\exists m > n : \neg l_\alpha(s_m))$.

(a) and (b) guarantee that all messages sent are eventually delivered (although no assumption is made about the order in which they will be delivered). (c) guarantees that if a node requested the C.S. and got the privilege it eventually enters its C.S. Finally (d) guarantees that a node executing its critical section will eventually release it.

4   Correctness

We will now show how the formal model presented above can be used to prove the correctness of the proposed algorithm. The proof of correctness has two different aspects: firstly, we have to prove that at any moment in time, at most one node is executing its critical section (the safety property), Also, we have to prove that if a node requests the critical section it will eventually obtain it (the liveness property). Both these properties are expressed in the following two theorems

Theorem 1 $l_\alpha(s_n) \Longrightarrow (\forall \beta \neq \alpha : \neg l_\beta(s_n))$

Theorem 2 $req_\alpha(s_n) \Longrightarrow (\exists m > n : l_\alpha(s_m))$

We will not give a full proof of the above theorems, instead we will give a sketch of the process followed to prove them. For the complete set of proofs the reader is referred to [16].

Lemma 1 *The following properties hold*

(a) $l_\alpha(s_n) \Longrightarrow req_\alpha(s_n) \wedge priv_\alpha(s_n)$.

(b) *Let* **toks**(s_n) *be defined as*

$$\mathbf{toks}(s_n) = \sum_{\alpha \neq \beta} \mathbf{1}(\mathcal{P} \in L_{\alpha, \beta}(s_n)) + \sum_{\alpha} \mathbf{1}(priv_\alpha(s_n))$$

Then **toks**$(s_n) = 1$.

Proof: Both properties can be shown by a simple induction proof. We will only show (b). (b) holds for any initial state. Assume it holds for s_i when $i < n$.

| case 1 | $\mathcal{P} \in L_{\alpha,\beta}(s_{n-1})$

By I.H. we know that $\textbf{toks}(s_{n-1}) = 1$, thus $priv_\gamma(s_{n-1}) = \textbf{false}$ for all γ. From the preconditions of the operators, the only operator which could change the values of $\textbf{1}(\mathcal{P} \in L_{\alpha,\beta})$ or $\textbf{1}(priv_\gamma)$ is $e_n = (P, \beta)$, and $\textbf{Postcond}((P, \beta))$ indicates that $\mathcal{P}$ will not be in any link in s_n and that $priv_\beta$ will be the only one with a **true** value.

| case 2 | $priv_\alpha(s_{n-1})$ holds

Then, by I.H., $\mathcal{P}$ is not on any link at s_{n-1} and all other $priv_\beta(s_{n-1})$ are **false**. By the preconditions of the operators, $priv_\beta(s_n) = \textbf{false}$ for $\beta \neq \alpha$ and any operators setting $priv_\alpha$ to false also send $\mathcal{P}$ on some link (and viceversa). Thus the property still holds.

■

Theorem 1 follows immediately from Lemma 1, which proves the safety property of our algorithm. To prove the livenes property we have to follow a more laborious path. It is easy to show that req_α holds if and only if $p\_addr_\alpha \neq 0$. Then the equivalence relation $\equiv_n$ defined as the transitive and reflexive closure of $=_n$, where $=_n$ is given by,

$$\alpha =_n \beta \qquad \text{if } p\_addr_\alpha(s_n) = \beta \;\; \vee \;\; p\_addr_\beta(s_n) = \alpha$$

will be defined on the set of requesting nodes in state s_n. Let us denote by $\mathcal{W}(s_n)$ the set of equivalence classes defined by $\equiv_n$

$$\mathcal{W}(s_n) = \{W_1, \ldots, W_{k_n}\}$$

It can be seen that a request message never visits the same node twice, and it never goes back to the originating node. It can also be shown that if $p\_addr_\alpha = \beta \neq \alpha$ then for all other $\gamma \notin \{\beta, \alpha\}$ $p\_addr_\gamma \neq \beta$, and this is so because once a node β sets its p_addr_β pointer to α, the request message for α is not retransmitted. Also, no other request message for α will appear in the links until α requests the CS again, which can only happen after β sends α the privilege message (consequently zeroing p_addr_β). Based on this, it can also be shown that class W_i with the set of edges $E_i = \{< \alpha, p\_addr_\alpha(s_n) > | \alpha \in W_i \; \wedge \; p\_addr_\alpha(s_n) \neq \alpha\}$ forms a path digraph. Moreover, denoting by ν_i the head node of the path W_i, the following can also be shown:

Lemma 2 *Let $\mathcal{W}(s_n) = \{W_1, \ldots, W_{k_n}\}$, then we have that $\exists! \, i\{priv_{\nu_i}(s_n) \cup \mathcal{P} \in L_{\alpha,\nu_i}\}$, and the nodes in W_i will enter their CS before any other node. For all other $j \neq i$ we will have that $\exists! \, (m_j, \alpha_j, \beta_j)\{\mathcal{R}(\nu_j, m_j) \in L_{\alpha_j, \beta_j}(s_n)\}$ and $\beta_j \notin W_j$, and the above are the only request messages present in the system in state s_n.*

Proof of Theorem 2: Assume that $req_\alpha(s_n)$ holds, but the theorem is violated, that is, for all $m \geq n$, $\neg I_\alpha$ holds. Let's denote by $W_\alpha(s_n)$ the class to which α belongs in s_n. If α never gets the privilege, then, by the previous lemma none of the nodes in $W_\alpha(s_n)$ ever will either. This means that $W_\alpha(s_m) \subseteq W_\alpha(s_{m+1})$ for all $m \geq n$. On the other hand the request messages eventually disappear from the links, and when a message for node γ disappears after arriving to node δ in event e_n then either, node δ sends a privilege message to γ or $p\_addr_\delta(s_m) = \gamma$. From our assumption, there will never be a $\mathcal{P}$ message heading for ν_α, thus if the request message for $\nu_\alpha(s_n)$ disappears in s_{n+1}, there will be a node $\beta \notin W_\alpha(s_n)$ such that $p\_addr_\beta(s_{n+1}) = \alpha$, and thus $|W_\alpha(s_{n+1})| > |W_\alpha(s_n)|$. Repeating the same argument we can see that there must exist an infinite sequence of m_i such that $|W_\alpha(s_{m_i})| < |W_\alpha(s_{m_{i+1}})|$, which is not possible, because there are only a finite number of nodes in the system. Thus our assumption has to be false and eventually α enters its critical section. ∎

5 An Upper Bound on the Number of Messages

We first define what we understand as the *cost* incurred by a history.

Definition 1 *We define the number of completions of a history at s_n by* $\#(\Pi, n) = \sum_\alpha C_\alpha(s_n) - \sum_\alpha C_\alpha(s_0)$. *We also define the cost of an event e_m with respect to s_n by*

$$\mathcal{L}_n(\Pi, e_m) = \begin{cases} 1 & \text{for } m \le n \quad \wedge \quad e_m = (R_{\alpha,i}, \beta) \quad \wedge \quad i \le C_\alpha(s_n) \\ 1 & \text{for } m \le n \quad \wedge \quad e_m = (P, \alpha) \quad \wedge \quad J_\alpha(s_m) \le C_\alpha(s_n) \\ 0 & \text{otherwise} \end{cases}$$

Based on this we also can define the cost of history Π with respect to s_n as $\mathcal{L}_n(\Pi) = \sum_{j=1}^n \mathcal{L}(\Pi, e_j)$. Finally we define the cost incurred by history Π in granting K critical sections by $C(\Pi, K) = \mathcal{L}_n(\Pi)$ for some n such that $\#(\Pi, n) = K$.

Thus, a message sent between two nodes will have cost one. Notice that thanks to theorem 2, for any K there will always be some n such that $\#(\Pi, n) = K$. In this section we will prove the following:

Theorem 3 $C(\Pi, K) \le K(2 + 3log(N))$ *for* $K \ge N - 1$

From the results in the previous section it can be seen that if $(s, \Gamma, s') \in T$ then that is the only transition starting at state s and having Γ as an operator. Thus the histories can actually be represented by the sequence of operators alone. We will take this view in the present section. We say that two histories $\Pi = e_1 \ldots e_n \ldots$ and $\Pi' = e_1' \ldots e_n' \ldots$, are equivalent if there is a bijection f in the set of natural numbers such that:

(a) $e'_{f(k)} = e_k$

(b) If $e_m = (ES, \alpha)$ with $J_\alpha(s_m) = i$ and $e_n = (ES, \beta)$ with $J_\beta(s_n) = j$ and $m < n$ then $f(m) < f(n)$ and $J_\alpha(s'_{f(m)}) = i$ and $J_\beta(s'_{f(n)}) = j$.

In other words, the same events occur in both histories and the critical sections are granted in the same order. A direct consequence of the above definition is that if Π and Π' are equivalent then $C(\Pi, K) = C(\Pi', K)$ for all K.

We can show that if e_n and e_m, with $m - n > 1$, and $J_\alpha(s_n) = J_\alpha(s_m)$, fulfill one of the following properties, then the history Π' defined by the bijection $f(i) = i$ for $i \notin \{m, m-1\}$ and $f(m) = m - 1, f(m-1) = m$, is equivalent to Π and $s_m = s'_m$.

e_n	e_m	additional condition
(CS, α)	(ES, α)	
(P, α)	(CS, α)	
(r_i, α)	(CS, α)	$priv_\alpha(s_n)$
(ES, β)	(P, α)	$p\_addr_\beta(s_n) = \alpha \ne \beta$
$(R_{\alpha,i}, \beta)$	(P, α)	$priv_\beta(s_{n-1}) \wedge req_\beta(s_{n-1})$

It is also possible to show that when e_n and e_{n+1} fulfill one of the following properties, the history Π' obtained from Π by the bijection $f(i) = i$ for $i \notin \{n, n+1\}$ and $f(n) = n+1, f(n+1) = n$, is equivalent to Π and $s_{n-1} = s'_{n-1}$ and $s_{n+1} = s'_{n+1}$.

e_n	e_{n+1}	additional condition
$(R_{\alpha,i}, \gamma)$	$(R_{\beta,j}, \lambda)$	$\alpha \neq \beta \wedge \gamma \neq \lambda$
(r_i, α)	(r_j, β)	
$(R_{\alpha,i}, \gamma)$	(r_j, β)	$\gamma \neq \beta$

On the other hand let $n(\alpha, i)$ stand for the event number in which the ith request for the critical section of node α is satisfied. Then if $e_n = (R_{\alpha,i}, \gamma)$ and $e_m = (R_{\beta,j}, \gamma)$ and $n < m$ then $n(\alpha, i) < n(\beta, j)$. Also if $e_n = (R_{\alpha,i}, \beta)$ and $J_\beta(s_n) < j$ then we would also have that $n(\alpha, i) < n(\beta, j)$. Based on these properties we can prove the following lemma:

Lemma 3 *Let $\Pi = e_1, \ldots, e_n, \ldots$, then there is a $\Pi' = e'_1, \ldots, e'_\ell, \ldots, e'_n, \ldots$ equivalent to Π where the bijection f is such that $f(m) = m$ for $m > n$ and $s'_n = s_n$ and $\#(\Pi, n) = \#(\Pi', n) = \#(\Pi', \ell)$ and $e'_\ell = (ES, \beta)$ for some β. Also for any $m < \ell$, if $e'_m = (r_i, \alpha)$ then there is a $t \leq \ell$ such that $e'_t = (ES, \alpha)$ and $C_\alpha(s'_t) = i$ and for all $m < x < t$ we have that e'_x is one of the following: $(R_{\alpha,i}, \beta_x)$, or (CS, α), or (P, α).*

In other words, the above lemma says that we can reorder the events in a history so that all events relating to the ith CS request of a node α (from the request proper until the release) appear consecutively, obtaining an equivalent history. Thus to talk about the costs of histories we can assume that our histories are serialized. In that case it is easy to see that if $e_\ell = (ES, \alpha)$ then s_ℓ will be a possible initial state with α at the root of the directed tree. When only serialized histories are considered we only have to record the "request events" $(e_n = (r_i, \alpha))$ to obtain a complete description of the history, and we can assume that all states s_n are valid initial states. The algorithm, when considering only serialized histories, behaves very much like a path–compression algorithm. Thus we can follow an approach very similar to that used by Yao [17] in finding an upper bound for the message cost of granting K critical section entrances.

We start by stating a variation on a lemma due to Paterson [18,17]. Let $w_n(\alpha)$ be the number of descendants of node α in the tree of state s_n. Then we define the entropy of state s_n as $H_n = \sum_\alpha \log w_n(\alpha)$. It is evident that $H_n \leq N \log N$, for any state s_n.

Lemma 4 *Let $e_n = (r_i, \alpha)$, with α being at distance $t+2$ from the root of the tree in s_{n-1}. Assume that nodes $\alpha_0, \ldots, \alpha_t, \alpha_{t+1}$ (with $\alpha = \alpha_0$) are the only nodes in the path from α to the root (α_{t+1}) of the s_{n-1} tree. Then there exists M, $1 < M \leq (w_{n-1}(\alpha_t))^{1/t}$ such that*

$$H_{n-1} - H_n \geq t \log \frac{M}{M-1} - \log N$$

Proof: We can see that $H_{n-1} - H_n$ can be expressed as,

$$H_{n-1} - H_n = \sum_{1 \leq j \leq t} (\log w_{n-1}(\alpha_j) - \log(w_{n-1}(\alpha_j) - w_{n-1}(\alpha_{j-1})))$$

$$+ \log N - \log(N - w_{n-1}(\alpha_t)) + \log w_{n-1}(\alpha) - \log N$$

The sum of the last four terms is always greater than $-\log N$ and it can be shown that the summation, under the constraint $1 \leq w_{n-1}(\alpha_{j-1}) < w_{n-1}(\alpha_j)$, for $1 \leq j \leq t$, is minimized when

$\{w_{n-1}(\alpha_j)\}$ form a geometric progression $\{AM^j\}$ with $A \geq 1$ and $AM^t = w_{n-1}(\alpha_t)$. The lemma then follows by explicitly evaluating the summation. ∎

Proof of Theorem 3: Let's consider K critical section grants of a history. Let's assume that of those K, C are performed by nodes which are at a distance less than or equal to $\log N + 2$ from the root of the tree. Thus each of those requests will cost at most $2 + \log N$. The rest of the requests $(K - C)$ will be at a distance $t + 2 > \log N + 2$. Let's denote by $t_i + 2$, for $1 \leq i \leq K - C$, the costs of each of the expensive requests. It can be seen that for the expensive requests, the constant M of lemma 4 satisfies $M \leq 2$, and thus $\log \frac{M}{M-1} \geq 1$, which implies that the decrease of entropy for those operations is greater than $t_i - \log N$. Also, the minimum entropy decrease caused by a cheap operation is $-\log N$. On the other hand, the entropy of a state can never be lower than $\log N$, thus the entropy of the initial state minus the sum of all entropy decreses has to be larger than the minimum entropy

$$\log N \leq H_0 - \Delta H \leq H_0 - \left[-C \log N + \sum_{i=1}^{K-C} (t_i - \log N) \right]$$

from where, considering $H_0 \leq N \log N$, we can get

$$\mathcal{C}(\Pi, K) \leq C(2 + \log N) + 2(K - C) + (K + N - 1) \log N$$

which for $K \geq N - 1$ leads to

$$\mathcal{C}(\Pi, K) \leq K(2 + 3 \log N)$$

thus finishing the proof. ∎

6 Concluding Remarks

In this paper we have shown a novel mutual exclusion algorithm for distributed systems with an upper bound of $K(2+3 \log N)$ messages for granting K critical section entrances. The algorithm makes use of a dynamic forest structure which gets modified every time a node makes a request for the CS. The modification of the forest which is achieved by doing path compression has the desirable property that only those nodes need to handle request messages which are competing for the CS.

To prove the correctness of the algorithm, we have developed a formal model of its execution. Using the formal model we were also able to prove that the execution histories produced by the algorithm can be serialized resulting in an equivalent history with the same cost properties. This allowed us to use available techniques to show the logarithmic upper bound on the number of messages needed to grant the CS.

References

[1] M. Raynal, *Algorithms for Mutual Exclusion. Series in Computer Systems*, Cambridge, Massachussets: MIT Press, 1st ed., 1986. Translated by D. Beeson.

[2] B. A. Sanders, "The information structure of distributed mutual exclusion algorithms," *ACM Trans. Computer Systems*, vol. 5, pp. 284–299, August 1987.

44

[3] L. Lamport, "Time, clocks and the ordering of events in a distributed system," *Communications ACM*, vol. 21, pp. 558–565, July 1978.

[4] G. Ricart and A. K. Agrawala, "An optimal algorithm for mutual exclusion in computer networks," *Communications ACM*, vol. 24, pp. 9–17, January 1981.

[5] M. Maekawa, "A $\sqrt{N}$ algorithm for mutual exclusion in decentralized systems," *ACM Trans. Computer Systems*, vol. 3, pp. 145–159, May 1985.

[6] M. Singhal, "A dynamic information–structure mutual exclusion algorithm for distributed systems," Tech. Rep., Department of Computer and Information Science. The Ohio State University, 1988.

[7] I. Suzuki and T. Kasami, "A distributed mutual exclusion algorithm," *ACM Trans. Computer Systems*, vol. 3, pp. 344–349, November 1985.

[8] O. Carvalho and G. Roucairol, "On mutual exclusion in computer networks," *Communications ACM*, vol. 26, pp. 146–147, February 1983.

[9] D. Agrawal and A. El Abbadi, "An efficient solution to the distributed mutual exclusion problem," Tech. Rep., Department of Computer Science. University of California at Santa Barbara, 1988.

[10] K. Raymond, "A tree–based algorithm for distributed mutual exclusion," *ACM Trans. Computer Systems*, vol. 7, pp. 61–77, February 1989.

[11] J. L. van de Snepscheut, "Fair mutual exclusion on a graph of processes," *Distributed Computing*, vol. 2, pp. 113–115, 1987.

[12] S. J. Mullender and P. M. Vitány, "Distributed match-making," *Algorithmica*, no. 3, pp. 367–391, 1988.

[13] M. Powell and B. Miller, "Process migration in DEMOS/MP," in *Proceedings Of the 9th Symposium on Operating System Principles. (Breton Woods, N.H.)*, pp. 110–119, ACM, October 10–13 1983.

[14] R. Fowler, "Decentralized object finding using forwarding addresses," PhD Thesis 85-12-1, University of Washington, December 1985.

[15] N. A. Lynch and M. R. Tuttle, "Hierarchical correctness proofs for distributed algorithms," in *Proceedings of the 6th Annual ACM Symposium on Principles of Distributed Computing*, pp. 137–151, ACM SIGACT and ACM SIGOPS, ACM Press, August 1987.

[16] J. M. Bernabéu–Aubán and M. Ahamad, "Modeling an efficient mutual exclussion algorithm for distributed systems," Tech. Rep. GIT-ICS-89/18, School of Information and Computer Science, Georgia Institute of Technology, ATLANTA, GA 30332, April 1989.

[17] A. C. Yao, "On the expected performance of path compression algorithms," *SIAM Journal on Computing*, vol. 14, pp. 129–133, February 1985.

[18] M. Paterson, " ," 1972. MIT class notes for course 6.851J, by A.R. Meyer and M.J. Fischer, 1973.

Combinatorics and Geometry of Consistent Cuts : Application to Concurrency Theory

Bernadette Charron-Bost

I.N.T., 9 rue C. Fourier, 91011 Evry

L.I.E.N.S., 45 rue d'Ulm, 75230 Paris Cedex 05

France.

Abstract: We define a concurrency measure of a distributed computation which is based on the number μ of its consistent cuts. We prove that counting consistent cuts takes into account the non-transitivity of the concurrency relation. Besides this combinatorial study, we give a geometric interpretation of μ using the clock designed by Fidge and Mattern for characterizing concurrency between two events. This geometric approach shows how much this clock is also a powerful tool for assessing the global concurrency. Moreover it provides a geometric picture of the concurrency phenomena in a distributed computation.

1 Introduction

There exists a great number of distributed algorithms which have the same function but there are few criterions to analyse and to compare them. The existing criterions stem from the sequential complexity measures and usually rely on message countings. Simple examples (*cf.* [4]) show that such measures are not significant since they disregard the specificity of the distributed algorithms. A basic notion that distinguishes sequential processing from multiprocessing is *concurrency*. In this paper, our aim is to define a measure which assesses concurrency of the distributed computations. The vector clock introduced by Fidge in [8] and Mattern in [10] for characterizing concurrency will be a fundamental tool for our purpose.

In Section 4, we discuss three principles inducing concurrency measures. The first two are thrown out because the measure cannot be computed or is not well-behaved for specific examples. Finally, we propose the following principle : the less the stop of one of the processes blocks the other processes, the more concurrent is the computation. That leads us to count the *consistent cuts* of a distributed computation (see 2.3 for the definition) for assessing its concurrency. These consistent cuts have been already considered for a different purpose, the detection of global states (*cf.* [7] and [10]).

Our main result (Theorem 1) asserts that the number μ of consistent cuts is equal to the number of *antichains*, *i.e.* of subsets of events in which any two events are concurrent. Thus for assessing concurrency we have to consider not only the pairs of concurrent events –which are the antichains of size 2– but the antichains of any size. In particular the number μ clearly takes into account the non-transitivity of the concurrency relation which is well-known to be a specific difficulty encountered in the study of distributed systems.

Besides its combinatorial expression in terms of antichains, the number μ has a simple geometric interpretation using a diagram in $\mathbf{R}^n$ built from the dates of the events assigned by the vector clock (here n is the number of processes). Indeed we show (see Theorem 4) that μ is the number of points in $\mathbf{N}^n$ located "between" n broken lines naturally associated to the n processes.

2 Description of the model

2.1 Model of a distributed system

A distributed system consists of a finite set of *processes* $\{P_1, \cdots, P_n\}$. A process P_i is characterized by a set of finite sequences C_i of *events*. This set is prefix closed. An event of C_i is either an internal event, the sending of a message to another process P_j or the receipt of a message which is sent to P_i. Notice that the processes are sequential since they are defined by sequences.

We assume that all the events and all the messages are different. Multiple occurences of the same message or of the same event could be distinguished by affixing subscripts to them. Every message sent by P_i to P_j contains the two names P_i and P_j. So a message cannot be sent (resp. received) by two different processes.

2.2 Computation of a distributed system

Let $\{P_1, \cdots, P_n\}$ be a distributed system and, for any i, let C_i be one of the sequences which define P_i. We define a relation $\prec$ on the set of events of $C_1 \cup \cdots \cup C_n$ as the smallest transitive relation satisfying the following conditions : (1) if a and b occur in the same process and if a comes before b then $a \prec b$; (2) if a is a sending of a message m and if b is the receipt of m, then $a \prec b$.

Definition 1 *A n-tuple $C = (C_1, \cdots, C_n)$ is a computation of $\{P_1, \cdots, P_n\}$ if it satisfies the following two properties : (1) $(C, \prec)$ contains no cycle; (2) for every receipt of the message m, there is a single sending of m.*

So, in this model, the communications are asynchronous and point to point. Moreover, the messages may be received in a different order than sent.

From (1), it follows that the events of C are partially ordered by the relation $\prec$ which is called the *causality* relation. We define the relation $\preceq$ by : $a \preceq b$ iff $a \prec b$ or $a = b$. We shall say that two events a and b of a distributed computation are *concurrent* (and we shall denote a co b) iff we have $\neg(a \preceq b)$ and $\neg(b \preceq a)$.

It is helpful to use the space-time diagrams introduced by Lamport in [6] to picture computations (see Figure 1). In these diagrams, the vertical lines denote processes; a send event and its corresponding receipt are joined together by a directed line. Such a diagram entirely defines a computation.

With respect to the causality relation, there are two opposite extremal classes of distributed computations : the *sequential* computations defined by the fact that the causality relation is a total order and the *entirely concurrent* computations which contain no receipt.

From now on, we consider a single distributed system. So, when we say that C is a computation, we mean that C is a computation of the distributed system considered here.

2.3 Cut of a distributed computation

Let $C = (C_1, \cdots, C_n)$ be a distributed computation and, for any index i, let a_i be an event of C_i. Consider the sets $\{x \in C_i, x \preceq a_i\}$ and their union denoted by $(\to a_1, \cdots, \to a_n)$. Such a set of events is called a *cut*. Since a cut may contain the receipt of a message but not its sending, a cut is not necessarily a computation.

Definition 2 *A consistent cut of a distributed computation C is a cut C' which is left closed by the causality relation.* [1]

Clearly a consistent cut is a computation. A basic example of a consistent cut is provided by the *past* of an event a denoted by $(\downarrow a)_C$, or $(\downarrow a)$ if no confusion can arise, and defined by $(\downarrow a) = \{x \in C, x \preceq a\}$. We shall denote $(\downarrow a)_i = (\downarrow a) \cap C_i = \{x \in C_i, x \preceq a\}$.

---

[1]That means that, for any events a and b of C, we have : $b \in C'$ and $a \preceq b \Longrightarrow a \in C'$. Observe that, for any subset C' of C, this condition implies that C' is a cut.

3 Clocks

In order to study concurrency in a distributed computation, we need a simple tool to decide whether two events are concurrent. We will use a characterization of concurrency which is based on the *dating* of events : we will assign a timestamp to every event and will establish that two events are concurrent by comparing their dates. Every procedure that allots a date to each event in a computation is called a *clock*.

3.1 Logical clocks

In this section, if a is an event of a distributed computation equipped with a clock, we shall denote $\chi(a)$ its date according to this clock. In [9] Lamport dates the events by integers and distinguishes the clocks that satisfy the following condition.

$$(*) \quad a \preceq b \Longrightarrow \chi(a) \leq \chi(b).$$

These clocks preserve the causality relation and are called *logical clocks*. In his paper Lamport explains how to construct such clocks by stamping the messages.

Let us observe that the implication converse of $(*)$ cannot hold because that would imply $\chi(a) < \chi(b) < \chi(a)$ if a and b are concurrent. Nevertheless if we want to assess concurrency in a distributed computation, it is crucial to have a simple way to detect whether two events are concurrent.

The previous remark on the converse implication of $(*)$ shows that $\mathbf{N}$ or $\mathbf{R}$ is not "large" enough to analyse concurrency. More precisely the information that we need about the structure of the computation cannot be coded by only one number.

Fidge and Mattern have independently constructed a clock that characterizes concurrency (see [8] and [10]); the dates which are assigned by this clock are not numbers but vectors. We now recall the construction and the properties of this clock that we shall use in this paper.

3.2 Vector clock

We shall use the following notations : if v is a vector in $\mathbf{R}^n$ then the i-th component of v will be denoted by $v[i]$. The set $\mathbf{R}^n$ is naturally ordered by the relation $\leq$ defined by : $a \leq b$ iff $a[i] \leq b[i]$ for any index i. If u and v are two vectors of $\mathbf{R}^n$ we shall denote $w = \sup(u, v)$ the vector of $\mathbf{R}^n$ the i-th component of which is $\max(u[i], v[i])$.

Here we describe the construction of a clock for the distributed computations with n processes. The dates assigned by this clock Θ will belong to $\mathbf{N}^n$.

Each process P_i is equipped with a clock Θ_i with values in $\mathbf{N}^n$. The initial value of Θ_i is $[0, \cdots, 0]$ and with each event on P_i the i-th component of Θ_i is incremented by 1 before any other event occurs on P_i. As in Lamport's scheme, every message m coming from P_i contains a timestamp that is equal to the value of Θ_i when m has been sent (timestamps are vectors). Upon receiving a message timestamped by t a process adapts its clock by $\Theta_i := \sup(\Theta_i, t)$. Finally to any event a we assign its vector date $\Theta(a) = \Theta_i(a)$ if a occurs in C_i. Figure 1 shows an example of the time propagation scheme.

3.3 Properties of the clock Θ

We now review and prove some properties [2] of the clock Θ. At first Θ satisfies the following property as a direct consequence of its definition.

---

[2]Theorem 1 and Proposition 2 have been stated by Mattern in [10].

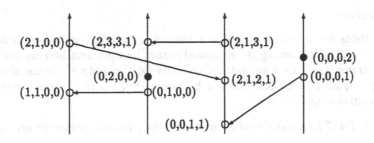

Figure 1

Proposition 1 *For any event a, $\Theta(a)[i]$ equals the number of the events of P_i that belong to the past of a : $\Theta(a)[i] =| C_i \cap (\downarrow a)| =| (\downarrow a)_i |$.*

This basic property allows to prove that Θ characterizes causality (or concurrency).

Theorem 1 *For any events a and b of a distributed computation, we have*

$$a \preceq b \Longleftrightarrow \Theta(a) \leq \Theta(b).$$

Proof First we check that Θ preserves the causality relation. As this relation is transitive, if $a \preceq b$ then for any index i $\{x \in C_i, x \preceq a\} \subseteq \{x \in C_i, x \preceq b\}$. So according to Proposition 1 we get $\Theta(a)[i] \leq \Theta(b)[i]$ for any index $i \in \{1, \cdots, n\}$, i.e. $\Theta(a) \leq \Theta(b)$.

Conversely assume that a and b are concurrent, $a \in C_k$ and $b \in C_l$. Let c be the greatest element of the totally ordered set $(\downarrow b)_k = \{x \in C_k, x \preceq b\}$. We have $c \prec a$ and $(\downarrow b)_k = (\downarrow c)_k \subset (\downarrow a)_k$. According to Proposition 1 we obtain $\Theta(b)[k] < \Theta(a)[k]$. By a symmetric argument we get $\Theta(a)[l] < \Theta(b)[l]$. So $\Theta(a)$ and $\Theta(b)$ are not comparable. $\square$

Thus using vectors of size n as dates it is possible to build a clock that characterizes concurrency. The use of of such vectors seems heavy from an implementation point of view; however it is worth noting that general theorems of combinatorics imply this size is necessary if we want to characterize concurrency (see [2]). In this sense the clock Θ is optimal.

The next statement makes easier the search of concurrent events when the clock Θ is built.

Proposition 2 *Let e and e' be two events of a computation that belong respectively to P_i and P_j. Then*

$$e \text{ co } e' \Longleftrightarrow \begin{cases} \Theta(e)[i] > \Theta(e')[i] \\ \quad\quad and \\ \Theta(e')[j] > \Theta(e)[j] \end{cases}$$

So concurrency between P_i and P_j can be checked by looking only at the i-th and the j-th components of Θ.

Proof It is sufficient to notice that if e and e' are concurrent then

$$(\downarrow e')_i \neq (\downarrow e)_i \text{ and } (\downarrow e')_i \subset (\downarrow e)_i . \quad \square$$

4 Concurrency measure

In this section our purpose is to rigorously define a "well-behaved" concurrency measure. Before we define a "good" measure, we discuss two attempts which will be thrown out for distinct reasons.

4.1 Preliminary

The usual methods for assessing equivalence relations (partitioning into equivalence classes, measure of the distribution among these classes) cannot be used here because the concurrency relation is not transitive. This is an essential difficulty for the study of the distributed systems. The following proposition, the proof of which is easy, shows that the non-transitivity of the concurrency relation is unavoidable.

Proposition 3 *Let C be a distributed computation; the following properties are equivalent :*

1. *the relation co is transitive;*

2. *co $= \emptyset$;*

3. *$(C, \prec)$ is a total order.*

Thus the concurrency relation cannot be reduced to a simple "equitemporality" relation that would be transitive (see [11]).

4.2 Counting pairs of concurrent events

A natural (but maybe too simple-minded) way for assessing concurrency would be counting the pairs of concurrent events[3] : the more a computation contains pairs of concurrent events, the more concurrent is this computation.

Such a basic principle seems to be correct for the extremal cases of sequential and entirely concurrent computations. More precisely, let $C = (C_1, \cdots, C_n)$ be a distributed computation such that C_i contains q_i events. The number of pairs of concurrent events cannot exceed $\sum_{1 \leq i < j \leq n} q_i q_j$. This value is reached if and only if C is entirely concurrent. On the other hand a computation is sequential if and only if it contains no pair of concurrent events.

So we could define a concurrency measure of the distributed computation C by the ratio

$$\omega(C) = \frac{|\{\{a,b\},\ a \text{ co } b\}|}{|\{\{a,b\},\ a \in C_i,\ b \in C_j \text{ and } i \neq j\}|}.$$

Clearly $\omega(C)$ belongs to $[0,1]$ and the bounds 0 and 1 respectively characterize the sequential and the entirely concurrent computations.

Let us consider the computations C and C' defined by Figure 2. We easily check that $\omega(C) = \omega(C') = 4/7$. Nevertheless C is intuitively "more concurrent" than C' : the three processes P_1, P_2 and P_3 can be simultaneously active in C whereas it is impossible in C'. Thus we need to define a more accurate measure than ω in order to distinguish computations such as C and C'.

4.3 Counting linear extensions

Let C denote a distributed computation. Using the terminology of combinatorics, a total order that extends the partial order $(C, \prec)$ will be called a linear extension of $(C, \prec)$. A fundamental theorem of Szpilrajn [12] asserts that the intersection of the linear extensions of a partial order equals this partial order. Thus a distributed computation is entirely defined by its linear extensions and we could think that the number of linear extensions of a distributed computation may be a good concurrency measure.

The study of the extremal cases is still in accordance to this intuition : if we consider the set Γ of the distributed computations $C = (C_1, \cdots, C_n)$ such that C_i contains q_i events, a

---

[3]Using the vector clock this counting is made easier by proposition 2.

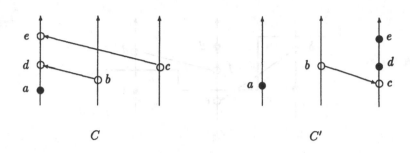

Figure 2

computation of Γ is sequential (resp. entirely concurrent) if and only if the number of its linear extensions is minimum (resp. maximum). More precisely, if $L(C)$ denotes the set of the linear extensions of a computation C we get the following equalities for the computations of Γ :

- if $(C, \prec)$ is sequential then $| L(C) |= 1$;

- if $(C, \prec)$ is entirely concurrent then $| L(C) |= \frac{(q_1 + \cdots + q_n)!}{q_1! \cdots q_n!}$.

Unfortunately there is no general formula expressing $| L(C) |$ in terms of some structural invariants of $(C, \prec)$ and the complexity of counting linear extensions of a partial order is unknown. So except for very simple classes of computations such a measure cannot be computed.

Moreover this point of view (counting linear extensions) is connected with the interleaving models. These models come from time sharing operating systems. For real distributed systems, interleaving independent events is not very natural for studying concurrency between these events. It is an additional argument for considering another concurrency measure.

4.4   The concurrency measure m

In this section we define a concurrency measure m based on the following principle[4] : the less the stopping of one of the processes blocks the other processes, the more concurrent is the computation. How to evaluate the tolerance of a distributed computation to the stopping of one process? The following example allows to guess an answer to this question.

Consider the computation C defined by Figure 3. If process P_2 stops after the event c, process P_1 can still proceed and even terminate whenever P_3 is blocked after the receipt of the message sent by P_1. If one cuts the computation C after c on C_2 one has to cut it after e on C_3 if one wants to get a well-defined computation. Thus the tolerance of a computation with respect to the stopping of one of its processes is closely related to its ability to be cut in a consistent way. That leads us to assess the concurrency of a distributed computation by counting its consistent cuts (cf. Definition 2).

Let us now compute the number of consistent cuts of a sequential and of an entirely concurrent computation in order to check the relevance of our basic principle for these computations. As before we introduce the set Γ of the distributed computations with n processes $C = (C_1, \cdots, C_n)$ such that C_i contains q_i events.

- If C is a sequential computation of Γ, the stopping of the working process stops the whole computation. Taking into account the empty cut the number of consistent cuts of C is equal to $\mu^s = 1 + q_1 + \cdots + q_n$.

---

[4]As T. Ehrhard pointed out to me, this principle is closely related to the definition of sequential algorithms given by Kahn and Plotkin in the framework of CDS (cf. [6] and [5]).

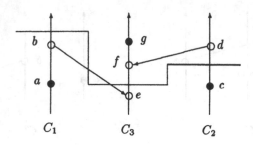

C_1 C_3 C_2

Figure 3

- If a computation is entirely concurrent, the stopping of a process does not interact with the other processes. Consequently one easily sees that the number of consistent cuts of an entirely concurrent computation in Γ equals $\mu^c = (1 + q_1) \cdots (1 + q_n)$.

We shall see in 5.3 that these two equalities characterize the sequential and the entirely concurrent computations.

According to 2.3, to any event a of a distributed computation we can assign the consistent cut $(\downarrow a)_C$. Clearly this mapping is one to one; thus the number μ of consistent cuts of a distributed computation in Γ is greater than μ^s. On the other hand μ is evidently less than μ^c. This motivates the following definition.

Definition 3 *The concurrency measure of a distributed computation $C = (C_1, \cdots, C_n)$ such that C_i contains q_i events is the ratio*

$$m(C) = \frac{\mu - \mu^s}{\mu^c - \mu^s}$$

where $\mu^s = 1 + q_1 + \cdots + q_n$, $\mu^c = (1 + q_1) \cdots (1 + q_n)$ and μ is the number of consistent cuts of C.

5   How to compute m

Contrary to linear extensions, counting consistent cuts is possible. In this section we describe two methods for counting consistent cuts. The first one comes from a property of the vector clock θ. The second one is based on a fundamental identity, which moreover allows to compare the measures ω and m.

5.1   Characterization of consistent cuts

Let $C = (C_1, \cdots, C_n)$ be a distributed computation. Recall (*cf.* 2.3) that any cut C' of C can be written $(\rightarrow a_1, \cdots, \rightarrow a_n)$ where a_i is the last event of C_i that belongs to C'. If Θ still denotes the vector clock described in 3.2 then we get the following proposition stated by Mattern in [10] (see [3] for a proof).

Proposition 4 *The cut $(\rightarrow a_1, \cdots, \rightarrow a_n)$ is a consistent cut if and only if*

$$\sup(\Theta(a_1), \cdots, \Theta(a_n)) = (\Theta(a_1)[1], \cdots, \Theta(a_n)[n]).$$

Thus the vector clock detects not only concurrency but also consistency in a simple way.

5.2 Consistent cuts and antichains

Recall that an *antichain* of a poset is a subset of this poset in which any two elements are incomparable. Thus the cardinality of an antichain in a distributed computation with n processes is not greater than n.

Let C be a distributed computation; let $\mathcal{A}$ denote the set of antichains of C and $\mathcal{C}$ the set of its consistent cuts.

Theorem 2 *The mapping $\Phi : \mathcal{A} \longrightarrow \mathcal{C}$ defined by*

$$\Phi(\{a_1, \cdots, a_p\}) = \bigcup_{i=1}^{p}(\downarrow a_i)$$

is bijective.

The proof will be divided into four steps.

Lemma 1 *For any events $a_1, \cdots, a_p$ of a computation C, $\bigcup_{i=1}^{p}(\downarrow a_i)$ is a consistent cut of C.*

We shall say that this consistent cut is *generated* by $a_1, \cdots a_p$.

Proof Let C' denote the union $C' = \bigcup_{i=1}^{p}(\downarrow a_i)$. Let x and y be two events of C such that $x \in C'$ and $y \prec x$. Then there exists an index i such that $x \in (\downarrow a_i)$. By transitivity of the causality relation we have $y \in (\downarrow a_i)$. Consequently y belongs to C'. Thus C' is a consistent cut of C. $\square$

This lemma proves that the images of Φ belongs to $\mathcal{C}$.

Lemma 2 *Every consistent cut is generated by a finite set of events located on distinct processes.*

Proof Let C' be a consistent cut of C. For any index i of $\{1, \cdots, n\}$, we consider the finite set $C' \cap C_i$. This set is totally ordered by the causality relation $\prec$. We denote $I = \{i \in \{1, \cdots, n\}, C_i \cap C' \neq \emptyset\}$. If $C' \cap C_i \neq \emptyset$ then it possesses a greatest element denoted by a_i. We claim that $C' = \bigcup_{i \in I}(\downarrow a_i)$.

Let x be an event of $\bigcup_{j \in I}(\downarrow a_j)$. There exists an index i of I such that $x \preceq a_i$. As a_i belongs to the consistent cut C' it follows that $x \in C'$.

Conversely let x be an event of C'; this event belongs to one sequence C_i. Thus $C' \cap C_i$ is not empty and from the definition of a_i we infer that $x \prec a_i$.

Thus $C' = \bigcup_{i \in I}(\downarrow a_i)$ and $\{a_i, i \in I\}$ generates the consistent cut C'. $\square$

Lemma 3 *Every consistent cut is generated by an antichain.*

Proof Let C' be a consistent cut. According to Lemma 2, C' is generated by some events $a_1, \cdots, a_p$. We shall prove that this set contains an antichain that generates C'.

By induction we construct an increasing sequence (for the relation $\subseteq$) of antichains denoted by (u_j) such that $(\downarrow a_1) \cup \cdots \cup (\downarrow a_j)$ is generated by u_j. The construction may be carried through as follows.

1. $u_1 = \{a_1\}$.

2. We suppose that u_j is built; let $u_j = \{b_1, \cdots, b_m\}$. We define u_{j+1} in the following way.

   (a) If there exists an index $l \in \{1, \cdots, m\}$ such that $a_{j+1} \preceq b_l$ then $u_{j+1} = u_j$.

   (b) If the set I of indices $l \in \{1, \cdots, m\}$ such that $b_l \prec a_{j+1}$ is not empty then $u_{j+1} = u_j \cup \{a_{j+1}\} \setminus \{b_l, l \in I\}$.

   (c) Else $u_{j+1} = u_j \cup \{a_{j+1}\}$.

It easily follows that u_{j+1} is an antichain and that u_{j+1} generates $(\downarrow a_1)\cup\cdots\cup(\downarrow a_{j+1})$. $\square$

According to lemma 2 and lemma 3, Φ is a surjective mapping. Next we prove that Φ is one to one.

Lemma 4 *A consistent cut is generated by a unique antichain.*

Proof Suppose that a consistent cut C' is generated by two antichains $\{a_1,\cdots,a_p\}$ and $\{b_1,\cdots,b_r\}$, i.e.

$$C' = (\downarrow a_1)\cup\cdots\cup(\downarrow a_p) = (\downarrow b_1)\cup\cdots\cup(\downarrow b_r).$$

Let a_k be an event of the first one. There exists an index i in $\{1,\cdots,r\}$ such that $a_k \preceq b_i$. Similary there exists j in $\{1,\cdots,p\}$ such that $b_i \preceq a_j$. By transitivity of the causality relation we get $a_k \preceq b_i \preceq a_j$. Since $\{a_1,\cdots,a_p\}$ is an antichain we obtain $a_k = b_i$. Finally

$$\{a_1,\cdots,a_p\} \subseteq \{b_1,\cdots,b_r\}.$$

By a symmetric argument we deduce that these two antichains are the same. $\square$

After proving this theorem we discovered a closely related result in [1] (page 400). However our proof is different and more direct. In this paper, we will only use the following consequence of Theorem 2.

Corollary 1 *The number of consistent cuts of a distributed computation is equal to the number of its antichains.*

5.3 Comparison of the measures ω and m.

It will be convenient to call k-*antichains* the antichains with k elements. Let C belongs to Γ; let μ still denote the number of its consistent cuts and let α_k denote the number its k-antichains. According to Corollary 1 we have

$$\mu = \alpha_0 + \alpha_1 + \cdots + \alpha_n.$$

The two first terms α_0 and α_1 do not depend on the causality relation : there is only one 0-antichain (the empty antichain) and the number of 1-antichains equals the number of events. So $\alpha_0 = 1$ and $\alpha_1 = q_1 + \cdots + q_n$. As a sequential computation has no k-antichain for $k \geq 2$, we find again that $\mu^s = \alpha_0 + \alpha_1$ in Γ. Thus for any computation $C \in \Gamma$ we obtain

$$\omega(C) = \frac{\alpha_2}{\alpha_2^c} \quad \text{and} \quad m(C) = \frac{\alpha_2 + \cdots + \alpha_n}{\alpha_2^c + \cdots + \alpha_n^c}$$

where α_k^c stands for the number of k-antichains of an entirely concurrent computation in Γ. [5] So if $n = 2$ the measures ω and m are equal. These identities show that all the antichains are taken into account in $m(C)$ contrary to $\omega(C)$ for which only 2-antichains are considered. In other words, when we count the consistent cuts we take into account the non-transitivity of the concurrency relation. In that, the measure m is better than ω.

Let us again consider the computations C and C' defined by Figure 2; C and C' have the same number of 2-antichains but C possesses a 3-antichain whereas C' has none. Consequently $\omega(C) = \omega(C') = 4/7$ and $m(C) = 1/2 > m(C') = 2/5$.

Contrary to what this example suggests, in literal meaning m is not more accurate than ω because there exist computations C and C' such that $\omega(C) < \omega(C')$ and $m(C) > m(C')$ (cf. [3]).

---

[5]Note that α_k^c is the kth symmetric polynomial in the numbers q_i, i.e. $\alpha_k^c = \sum_{1\leq i_1 < \cdots < i_k \leq n} q_{i_1} \cdots q_{i_k}$.

Observe that Proposition 4 and Corollary 1 give rise to two distinct algorithms for computing the measure m. For a complete description and a comparison of these two algorithms, the reader may refer to [3]. We only emphasize that the algorithm coming from Corollary 1 is efficient when the studied computation contains few 2-antichains.

Corollary 1 also provides a characterization of the sequential and entirely concurrent computations in term of m :

- if $m(C) = 0$ then C contains no pair of concurrent events. So C is sequential.

- if $m(C) = 1$ then $\alpha_2 + \cdots + \alpha_n = \alpha_2^c + \cdots + \alpha_n^c$. As $\alpha_i^c \geq \alpha_i$, we deduce $\alpha_2 = \alpha_2^c$. Any pair of two events that belong to distinct processes are concurrent. So C is entirely concurrent.

6 Geometric interpretation

Let $C = (C_1, \cdots, C_n)$ be a distributed computation such that for any index i, C_i contains q_i events. Let Θ still denote Fidge and Mattern's clock. To any event in C we associate the point in the space $\mathbf{R}^n$ which has its date as coordinates. For any i, $1 \leq i \leq n$, we get a broken line L_i contained in $[0, q_1] \times \cdots \times [0, q_n]$ by joining the points associated to the consecutive events of C_i by line segments in $\mathbf{R}^n$.

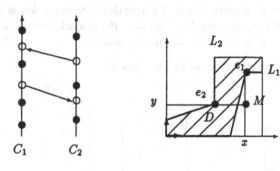

Figure 4

6.1 Distributed computations with two processes

First we assume that the number of processes is 2 (*cf.* Figure 4). One can prove the following proposition (see [3]).

Proposition 5 *The broken line L_2 is strictly above L_1.*

Let $\overline{D}$ denote the set of the points of $\mathbf{N}^2 \cap ([0, q_1] \times [0, q_2])$ located between the broken lines L_1 and L_2 or belonging to one of these lines (see Figure 4).

Theorem 3 *The number of consistent cuts of C is equal to the cardinality of $\overline{D}$.*

Proof (sketched). Let $M = (x, y)$ be a point of $\mathbf{N}^2$ such that $x \leq q_1$ and $y \leq q_2$. According to the definition of the clock Θ, there exists a unique event e_1 (resp. e_2) such that

$$e_1 \in C_1 \text{ and } x = \Theta(e_1)[1] \text{ (resp. } e_2 \in C_2 \text{ and } y = \Theta(e_2)[2]) .$$

Thus the points of $\overline{D}$ are characterized by

$$M = (x, y) \in \overline{D} \iff x \geq \Theta(e_2)[1] \text{ and } y \geq \Theta(e_1)[2] .$$

So if M belongs to $\overline{D}$ then $M = \sup(\Theta(e_1), \Theta(e_2))$ and Proposition 4 asserts that the cut $(\to e_1, \to e_2)$ is consistent. Conversely let us assume that $(\to e_1, \to e_2)$ is a consistent cut. Making again use of Proposition 4 it follows that $M = (\Theta(e_1)[1], \Theta(e_2)[2])$ belongs to $\overline{D}$. Thus the correspondence $M \in \overline{D} \longrightarrow (\to e_1, \to e_2) \in C$ is bijective. $\square$

The number μ has a geometric interpretation : it is essentially the "area" of the domain bounded by L_1 and L_2 in the rectangle $[0, q_1] \times [0, q_2]$. More generally, if we call area of a subset of $\mathbf{N}^2$ its cardinality, then the area of $D = \overline{D} \backslash (L_1 \cup L_2)$ equals the number of pairs of concurrent events and the concurrency measure $m(C) = \omega(C)$ equals the ratio of the area of D to the area of the reference rectangle $\mathbf{N}^2 \cap ([1, q_1] \times [1, q_2])$. Consequently the concurrency of a computation can be simply seen on the picture : the more the broken lines L_1 and L_2 diverge, the more concurrent is the computation.

6.2 General case

Suppose that the number of processes is arbitrary. Since the notion of domain located between n broken lines in $\mathbf{R}^n$ is meaningless for $n \geq 3$, we cannot directly generalize Theorem 3. Nevertheless this theorem suggests to consider the projections on the planes (O, x_i, x_j). Indeed, we get

Theorem 4 *The number of consistent cuts of a distributed computation is equal to the number of the points of $\mathbf{N}^n$ such that, for any $(i, j)_{1 \leq i < j \leq n}$, the projection of this point on the plane (O, x_i, x_j) lies between the projections of the lines L_i and L_j.*

The proof is a generalization of the proof of Theorem 3.

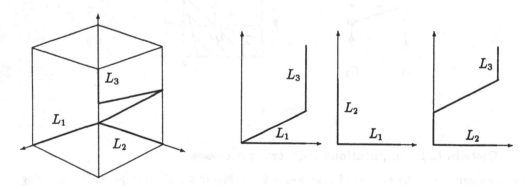

Figure 5: Diagrams of the computation defined in Figure 3

The projections of L_i and L_j on the plane (O, x_i, x_j) define a computation $C' = (C'_i, C'_j)$ that we can consider as the "projection" of C on the processes P_i and P_j. Let us notice that, contrary to [4], we know how to isolate the interactions between two processes thanks to the vector clock.

This geometric interpretation provides a picture of the concurrency phenomena among the events of a distributed computation. For instance it allows to locate the places where the broken lines converge, *i.e.* allows to detect the events which are the more responsible of the lack of concurrency.

7 Discussion

In this paper, we prove a close connection between the global evaluation of concurrency in distributed computations and the vector clock θ. This connection between two approaches of concurrency is obtained through a geometric construction (cf. section 6) which shed light on both of them.

For instance, the number μ of consistent cuts in a distributed computation, which is already a natural invariant of the concurrency relation from a combinatorial point of view, is the more natural as it can be defined in a simple way in terms of the associated diagram. Conversely, our result shows that the vector clock not only provides a simple characterization of concurrency between two events –what it was designed for– but also allows to assess the global concurrency in a distributed computation.

Acknowledgements: I would like to thank Friedemann Mattern, Joffroy Beauquier and Thomas Ehrhard for discussing this work with me and for suggesting improvements and extensions.

References

[1] M. Aigner. *Combinatorial Theory*. Springer-Verlag, 1979.

[2] B. Charron-Bost. *Au sujet de la taille des horloges*. Technical Report, LIENS, Paris, à paraître.

[3] B. Charron-Bost. *Concurrence dans les calculs répartis*. Technical Report, LIENS, Paris, à paraître.

[4] B. Charron-Bost. Measure of parallelism of distributed computations. In *STACS*, pages 434–445, AFCET, 1989.

[5] P.L. Curien. *Categorical Combinators, Sequential Algorithms and Functional Programming*. Pitman, 1986.

[6] G. Kahn et G. Plotkin. *Domaines concrets*. Technical Report 336, INRIA-LABORIA, 1978.

[7] K.M. Chandy et L. Lamport. Distributed snapshots : determining the global state of distributed systems. *ACM Trans. Comp. Systems*, 3(1):63–75, 1985.

[8] J. Fidge. Timestamps in message passing systems that preserve the partial ordering. In *Proc. 11th. Australian Computer Science Conference*, pages 55–66, 1988.

[9] L. Lamport. Time, clocks and the orderings of events in a distributed system. *Comm. of ACM*, 21,7:558–564, 1978.

[10] F. Mattern. Virtual time and global states of distributed systems. In *Parallel and Distributed Algorithms*, pages 215–226, North-Holland, 1988.

[11] C.A. Petri. Concurrency theory. In *Advances in Petri Nets*, pages 4–24, Springer-Verlag, 1986.

[12] E. Szpilrajn. Sur l'extension de l'ordre partiel. *Fund. Math.*, 16:386–389, 1930.

Distributed Fairness Algorithms for Local Area Networks

with Concurrent Transmissions

Israel Cidon and Yoram Ofek
IBM, T. J. Watson Research Center
P.O. Box 704, Yorktown Heights, NY 10598

Abstract

In this work, it is shown how multiple nodes can access a ring network concurrently with spatial reuse and in a fair manner. Traditionally, most ring and bus networks do not allow spatial reuse, e.g., FDDI, DQDB (IEEE 802.6). Concurrent access with spatial reuse enables the simultaneous transmissions over disjoint segments of a bidirectional ring, and therefore, can significantly increase the effective throughput, by a factor of four or more.

Spatial reuse can be easily implemented using a full-duplex buffer insertion or slotted techniques. However, these techniques may also cause starvation and thus have an inherent fairness problem. Two types of fairness algorithms are presented, global and local; both are shown to be stable and fault tolerant. The global fairness mechanism provides a complete fairness and is immune to control messages loss or duplication. This global algorithm views the whole ring as a single resource, while the local fairness algorithm views the ring as multiple disjoint resources. The local fairness mechanism is triggered only if potential starvation exists and is usually restricted only to segments of interfering nodes. If the segment of the interfering nodes covers the whole ring, we show that the local mechanism is equivalent to the global one.

The combination of a full-duplex buffer insertion ring, spatial reuse, reliable fairness mechanism and the exploitation of the recent advent in fiber-optic technology are the basis for the Metaring network architecture. This network is currently being prototyped at the IBM T.J. Watson Research Center.

1.0 Introduction

Local/metropolitan area networks (LANs/MANs) form an efficient and cost-effective solution for the in-site data communication problem. They are simple to control, manage and access, and make use of a low cost hardware that occupies small space. To reduce the complexity of the LAN, most designs focus on simple topology structures in the form of a bus or ring [1,2,5-12]. Traditionally, most ring networks allows only a single user to transmit concurrently (e.g., token ring). A user must wait for a token in order to insert its message into the ring. The existence of a single token in the ring must be then guaranteed. Token rings have an inherent fairness property since nodes are being served in a strict round-robin fashion.

In this work, we show how to increase the throughput of a ring based local area network far beyond its single link capacity and still to conserve its basic simplicity and fairness properties [3].

Spatial reuse and the ability to provide concurrent transmission over distinct segments of the ring can significantly increase the effective ring throughput. This potential throughput gain is further increased for the recent introduced bidirectional (or full-duplex) ring and bus structures [1,2,6,10,12]. By a simple observation one might realized that if the traffic pattern is homogeneous, a factor of 2 can be gained in a unidirectional ring structure by introducing spatial reuse. (The average distance of a path is half of the ring length.) When a bidirectional ring structure is used, with a shortest path routing rule, the average distance becomes only 1/4 of the ring circumference, and the average spatial reuse is of 4 nodes transmitting at the same time (on each direction).

Spatial reuse can be easily implemented using a buffer insertion technique. In this scheme, a node can transmit a packet at any time as long as its insertion buffer is empty, meaning, no transmission of up-stream users is detected. Spatial reuse is accomplished by the removal of packets at their destination. However, this technique may also cause starvation. This may happen if some node is constantly being 'covered' by an up-stream ring traffic and thus is not able to access the ring for a very long period of time.

This work introduces simple global and local fairness mechanisms that regulate the access to the buffer insertion ring, for solving the starvation problem with a minimum impact on the network throughput and delay. A global fairness mechanism views the whole ring as a single resource and gives all nodes equal transmission opportunity. We present a very simple and efficient global fairness solution which is based on a single control message. In the case of a full-duplex ring, the control message is rotating in the opposite direction to the data traffic that it regulates and has a preemptive resume priority over the regular data packets (i.e., data packets are kept intact). The global fairness mechanism is immune to message loss or duplication. This mechanism can also be extended to provide functions like asynchronous priority handling and the integration of synchronous and asynchronous traffic [4].

We also introduce the notion of local fairness where fairness is defined only among interfering nodes. Here the fairness mechanism is triggered locally, by an arbitrary condition, only if potential starvation exists. It attempts to regulate the transmissions of the interfering nodes without affecting others. We present a simple local fairness algorithm that is usually restricted only to segments of interfering nodes. The local fairness mechanism minimizes the performance hit caused by the additional constraints of the nodal transmission.

The combination of buffer insertion ring, spatial reuse, built in reliable fairness mechanism and exploitation of the recent advent in fiber-optic technology are the basis of the Metaring network [4]. This network is currently being prototyped at the IBM T.J. Watson research lab. The Metaring architecture also supports priorities and integration of synchronous and asynchronous traffic. It supports the transmission of variable size packets. The planned prototype will operate at 100-200Mbps link speeds with aggregate throughput of 1Gbps. The design is scalable to link bandwidth of 1Gbps or more, in fact, as the bandwidth increases the system's performance improves.

2.0 Principles of Operation

In this section, we describe the basic principles of the proposed solution, which is a full-duplex buffer insertion ring. An initial discussion on buffer insertion rings can be found in [7]. We than introduce the basic fairness problems and distinguish between two basic solutions, global and local fairness algorithms.

2.1 Buffer Insertion

Buffer insertion is a random and distributed access technique to a unidirectional ring network. On the receiving side of each link there is an insertion buffer (IB), which can contain one maximal size packet, as shown in Figure 1. A packet which is received by the node will be routed either into the node's input buffer or down-stream via the insertion buffer. Packets which arrives from the host to be transmitted over the ring are placed in the output buffer. A node can start a packet transmission from its output buffer as long as its insertion buffer is empty. If ring traffic arrives when the node is in the middle of a packet transmission, then the ring traffic will be stored in the insertion buffer (IB), until this packet transmission is completed. The node does not transmit anymore until the insertion buffer becomes idle again, i.e. a non-preemptive priority is given to the ring traffic. If the node is idle, the ring traffic will cut-through the insertion buffer. (This means that a packet does not have to be completely received before it is started to be forwarded).

Clearly, the buffer insertion access control may enable the concurrent access or spatial reuse of the ring by more than one node. Since the buffer insertion ring access control is distributed, i.e., each node uses only local information (buffer insertion full or empty) in order to determine its access to the ring, there is no degradation in its performance as the bandwidth or physical size increases. We consider a bidirectional or full-duplex ring where packets are sent via the shortest path. We also assume that nodes' identities are ordered according to the nodes' location on the ring. The ring has n nodes, which are numbered sequentially (clock wise) from 1 to n. This means that we distinguish between routing names that are actually used for access in the ring and global names that are known externally. Routing names are given to nodes in the

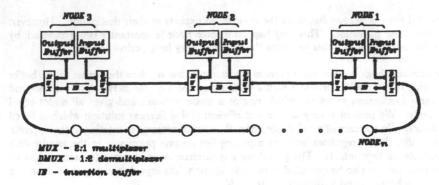

Figure 1. Buffer Insertion Ring

ring according to the ring topology and can be changed when the topology is changed. This naming organization can be manually programmed or be define at the time of the ring initialization through some simple naming algorithm.

The potential throughput is shown in Figure 2. It is assumed that the network has n nodes, numbered from 1 to n; routing is via the shortest path (which can be easily computed) and is under full load (i.e., at all times all nodes have something to send). Clearly, under uniform destination distribution the maximum distance is $n/2$, and the average distance is $n/4$. Therefore, the spatial reuse is of four nodes transmitting at the same time, in each direction on the average. As a result, the capacity of the full-duplex buffer insertion ring is eight times the single link transmission rate, which is 4 times more than a dual token-ring. If the destination distribution is inversely proportional, as shown in Figure 2, then the average distance is $n/6$ (spatial reuse factor is of 6 for each direction), which make possible to construct 1.2 Gigabit/sec ring by using 100 Mbps links!

2.2 Basic Problems with Buffer Insertion

The following are two problems or disadvantages which associate traditionally with buffer insertion rings:

- Large delay bounds - In a buffer insertion there is a possibility to accumulate a single packet store and forward queue at each hop. This could result in large ring delay bound when links speed is in the order of few Mbps. However, in the new environment of link speeds approaching Gbps, the problem disappears. For example with 200Mbps links and 1,000 bits packets the maximum nodal delay is only 5 μsec. It is only 1 μsec with 1Gbps link. So if 50 nodes are inserting packets in the same direction at the same time, then the worst case delay for traversing the ring will be 250 μsec or 50 μsec., for 200Mbps and 1Gbps rings, respectively. This worst case delay is smaller than the propagation delay around a metropolitan ring of 100km, which is 500 μsec.

- Starvation - the buffer insertion access control gives advantage to up-stream nodes, which can cause starvation. In Figure 3, for example, if node 2 will transmit continuously to node 10 and if node 9 will transmit continuously to node 12, then node 11 will not be able to transmit.

2.3 Hardware Control Messages or Control Signals

The hardware control messages are used for exchange of state information between neighboring nodes. These messages can be used for source fairness, back pressure and overflow prevention, and have the following characteristics:

- Very short - few characters (possibly one).

- Preemptive priority - can be sent in the middle of a data packet.

- Non-distractive - does not damage the data packets which they preempt.

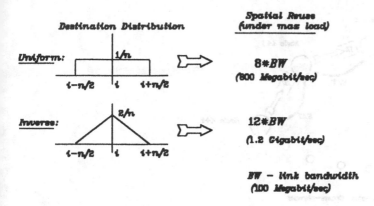

Figure 2.   Full-duplex Potential Ring Throughput

- Independent hardware - used for the ring control mechanism.

3.0 Global Fairness on a Full-duplex Ring

The access on each direction of the ring is regulated by a control message, SAT, which circulates in the opposite direction to the data traffic it is regulating. The hardware control message, SAT, is transferred up-stream from one node to its neighbor with preemptive priority, i.e., it can be sent in the middle of a data packet transmission. The SAT message is very short, one byte, and can be implemented by using the redundant codewords in the serial bit stream. Figure 4 describes the basic ring mechanism for one direction. Note that in principle, the SAT can be also transferred in the same direction as the data.

3.1 Informal Description of the Global Fairness

In principle, the node will forward the SAT message up-stream with no delay, unless it is not SATisfied or "starved." By "starved" we mean, that the node could not send the permitted number of messages from the last time it has forwarded the SAT message.

The node is SATisfied if between two SAT messages the node has sent at least l packets or if all packets in its output buffer, when the previous SAT was sent up-stream, were transmitted. When the node receives a SAT and it is SATisfied, it will forward the SAT up-stream. If the node is not SATisfied, it will hold the

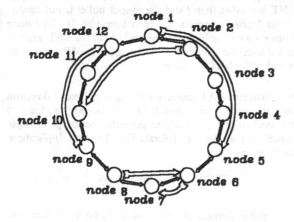

Figure 3.   Starvation on a Full-duplex Ring

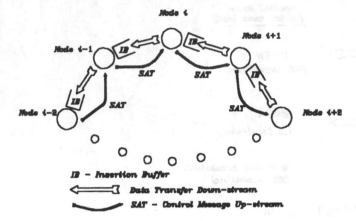

Figure 4. The Ring Basic Mechanism (one direction)

SAT until it is SATisfied and then forward SAT up-stream. After a node forwards a SAT it can send k more packets, $k \geq l$ (a simple case $k = l = 1$).

3.2 The Global SAT Algorithm

Figure 5 is a flow chart which describes the algorithm, and is divided into two parts, send packet and forward SAT.

Send Packet Algorithm

The node can transmit a packet from its output buffer when it is not empty, only if the following two conditions are true: (i) the variable COUNT is smaller than k, and (ii) the insertion buffer is empty. After the node transmits the packet, the COUNT is incremented by one.

Forward SAT Algorithm

This algorithm determines what the node does either after it receives the SAT message, or if the SAT message does not arrive after some maximum possible time has passed (time-out has been expired). The node will forward the SAT if the variable COUNT is greater than $l - 1$ or if the output buffer is empty. The node will hold the SAT if the variable COUNT is smaller than l and the output buffer is not empty. The node will hold the SAT until COUNT becomes l (after l packets has been transmitted). The node holds the SAT in order to prevent starvation. If during the time in which the node hold the SAT another SAT arrives, the second SAT will be discarded, and if time-out occurred it will be ignored. After the node forwards the SAT, it will set the COUNT to zero and will reload the timer.

Figure 6 illustrates the situation of having more than one SAT message rotating in the same direction in the ring. When two SAT messages meet at the same node, the second SAT is discarded, i.e., the two SAT messages are merged together. The time-out mechanism, the ability to generate and merge multiple SAT messages are enhancements to the fairness algorithms so they can tolerate SAT loss and duplication. This fault tolerant mechanism operates independently at any node.

3.3 Properties of the Global Fairness

The following summarizes the properties of the global fairness algorithm with its fault tolerance enhancement.

Send Packet

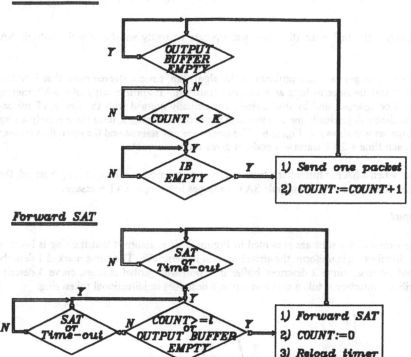

Forward SAT

Figure 5.   The Global Fairness Algorithm

Fairness Property - for a ring with a single SAT and $k = l$, after each round of the SAT message the subset of nodes with non-empty output buffer will transmit the same number of packets.

Proof - if at some round node i could not transmit k packets, then it will hold the following SAT message until up-stream becomes idle, and it is able to transmit its quota. Since the up-stream nodes are not allowed to transmit more than k packets before they see the SAT again, the up-stream of node i will eventually become idle.

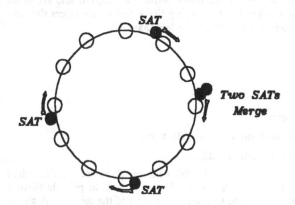

Figure 6.   Multiple SATs Merge

Liveness Property - the SAT can not be held indefinitely by a node, i.e., the global fairness algorithm is deadlock free.

Multiple SAT Property - the buffer insertion ring will operate correctly and fairly with multiple SAT messages.

Proof - multiple SAT messages cause no problem to the algorithm, since a starved node that is holding a SAT message will hold this message as long as it can not transmit. If another copy of a SAT message reaches this node, it will be ignored, and by that action, it is actually merged with the first SAT message being held. This mechanism will gradually merge more and more SAT messages, until there is only a single copy of the SAT message, as was shown in Figure 6. The nodes are not starved and the operation is clearly fair and correct, since each time a SAT traverse a node, it gives the same quota.

Lost SAT Property - when a SAT is lost, after a time-out, one or more SAT messages are generated, then SAT algorithm stabilizes itself, by merging multiple SAT messages to a single SAT message.

3.4 Delay-throughput

Initial discrete time simulation results are presented in Figure 7. It is assumed that the ring is homogeneous, the destination distribution is uniform, the arrival process is Bernoulli. The curve marked 1 describes buffer insertion without fairness, curve 2 describes buffer insertion with global fairness, curve 3 describes DQDB, curve 4 describes bidirectional token ring and curve 5 describes unidirectional token ring.

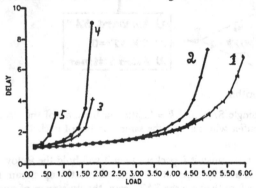

Figure 7.   Delay-Throughput for Global Fairness ($k = l = 1$)

The simulation result of buffer insertion with fairness shows a small performance degradation (20%) in compare to buffer insertion ring without fairness, and still three times better than DQDB and six times better than FDDI. Further simulation results [4] shows that by varying the k and l parameters the performance degradation of buffer insertion with fairness can be reduced to less than 10%.

4.0 The Local Fairness Algorithm

4.1 Motivation

The global fairness algorithms have two basic drawbacks:
1.   It is GLOBAL (have the same transmission constraints for all nodes), and
2.   it is CONTINUOUS (operates even if there is no starvation).

The first drawback, being global, is demonstrated in Figure 8. In this example there are 3 independent subsets of users that communicate only among themselves. A reasonable approach is to provide fairness within each subset while maintaining the maximal achievable throughput in each of the subsets. A global fairness algorithm will force all groups to maintain fairness (the same maximal throughput) among themselves, even if they do not interfere at all.

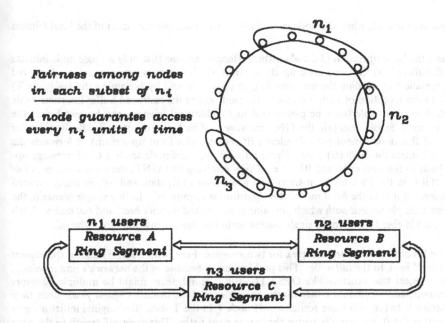

Fairness among nodes in each subset of n_i

A node guarantee access every n_i units of time

Figure 8.   Local Resources on a Ring

In this respect our global fairness algorithm can be made a local one by enabling different nodes to transmit different amount of data following the reception of the SAT message. However, it is not clear how these amounts can be defined dynamically and the problem is still open.

The second drawback, being continuous, means that the fairness algorithm is operational even if no node starves. This may result in some unnecessary performance degradation if the fairness parameters are not set properly. This problem is considerably less important.

These drawbacks motivate the development of an event-driven fairness algorithm, that is initiated only when starvation occurs. In addition, the algorithm should only involve segments of interfering nodes. In the above example of Figure 8, the local algorithm will be executed independently among the three nodes' subsets with no interference or message exchange. Under worst case load scenarios, the local fairness algorithm can "degenerate" to a global fairness.

4.2 Description of the Local Fairness Algorithm

The local fairness algorithm distinguishes between two basic nodal modes. Each mode is basically, a class of different algorithmic states.

- Non-restricted buffer insertion mode - Nodes can transmit at any time as long as the buffer insertion protocol permits it (priority to up-stream traffic). This mode is identified by the Buffer-Insertion (BI) state.

- Restricted buffer insertion mode - Nodes can transmit only a single packet before they transit back to the non-restricted mode (the exact states of this mode will be later described).

Nodes in the non-restricted mode are not involved in any control message exchange. However, they may asynchronously trigger the operation of the fairness algorithm upon starvation. The algorithm uses two types of control messages:

- REQ(REQ_ID) - This message initiates the restricted period of operation and is forwarded over the congested segment of the ring.

- GNT - This message is used, when the node is satisfied, to terminate the operation of the local fairness algorithm.

Figure 9 demonstrates the basic operation of the algorithm. Here we assume that only a single node initiates the algorithm and that there is at least one node up-stream to it which has no up-stream traffic. A starved node i triggers the operation by sending the message $REQ(i)$ up-stream and by becoming the *tail* (state T) of the segment. Upon the reception of such a message, the node enters the restricted buffer insertion mode of operation, in which only a single (may be generalized to k) additional message can be sent before the down-stream node indicates satisfaction (via the GNT message). If its buffer insertion is idle, it will enter the *head* (H) state. If this node cannot provide silence (it senses traffic from up-stream), it forwards the $REQ(i)$ up-stream, and enters the *body* (B) state. Upon satisfaction, a *tail* node sends a GNT message up-stream and transit back to the non-restricted BI state. Upon receiving this GNT, the node up-stream follows similar rules: If it is in the *body* mode, it transits to a *tail-body* (TB) state and will similarly forward GNT upon satisfaction. If it is in the *head* mode, the algorithm is terminated. In this simple scenario, the algorithm has created a simple *request path* which contains a unique and distinct *head* and *tail* nodes. Each node of the *request path* is able to transmit a single packet including the original initiator - the tail.

The picture might become much more complex for two reasons. First, with a single initiator the *request path* might be "stretched" back to the *tail* node. This problem exists because of the network's ring topology, and it is avoided on a linear bus structure like QPSX [2,6,10]. Second, there might be multiple initiators of the fairness algorithm, and we should either merge or sequence these distinct *request paths* once they overlap. We distinguish between two basic scenarios: If node i, in the T state (the original initiator), gets a REQ(j) message (where $j \neq i$), we basically merge the two request paths. This node will transit to the *body* mode and will forward the REQ(j) message only in the case that $j > i$ (or $j < i$ in the other direction). Since nodes are organized in an increasing order (clock wise), only the highest request ID will be ever forwarded. The forwarding is done in order to ensure that there are clearly defined end points for the merged *request path*. Basically, this task is a simple election algorithm in which, we assign a single *tail* to the *request path*. If $j = i$ it is clear that the merged *request path* is covering the whole ring. In such a case the *tail* node has received back its own request and it transits to the *tail-head* (HT) state. This node will function both as a *head* and as a *tail*.

The other scenario is that a node in the *tail-body* state receives a REQ(j) message. (This is not the original initiator of the algorithm). In this case, we do not merge the two *request path* but rather sequence them in time. The node will queue this request and transit to the TBH state. Only after it is satisfied and sent GNT for the previous round, it will forward the new outstanding request (unless it has already received a corresponding GNT). The reason for that is that the node has already heard a GNT message from down-stream and thus has provided its down-stream nodes with the opportunity to transmit in this current round of the algorithm. Merging the new *request path* with the old one, can cause starvation to the up-stream nodes. This message is therefore queued and treated as a new round of request.

4.3 Formal Description of the Local Fairness Algorithm

The formal description of the local fairness algorithm for node i is depicted in Figure 10, in terms of an event-driven finite-state-machine. The notes on the arcs of the finite-state-machine have the following form: *event/action*, i.e., the event that causes transition and the following action taken.

In the following we summarize the different states of the algorithm and their relationship to the *request path*.

- BI - the node is in the buffer insertion (BI) state and follows the non-restricted operation mode.
- T - node i is in the *tail* (T) state if it was "starved" did not receive REQ(j) (R_REQ(j)) from a node down-stream, and sent REQ(i) up-stream. It will stay in this state until it will send its packet and forward GNT (S_GNT) message up-stream. Additional REQ(j) message (R_REQ(j)) will cause it to transit to the B state.
- B - a node is in a *body* (B) state if it is in the middle of a *request path*. It will stay in this mode until it receives GNT (R_GNT) message from down-stream and then transit to the TB state.

- H - a node is in a *head* (H) state if it received REQ(*i*) from a node down-stream <u>but did not forward it up-stream.</u> It will stay in this state until it receives GNT (R_GNT) message from a node down-stream and transit back to the BI state or it will not be able to provide silent and then forward the request up-stream.

- HT - the node is both a *head*, and the original *tail*, which means that it's *request path* covers the whole ring.

- TB (*tail-body*) - last node in the chain of restricted nodes, but not the initiator. If an additional REQ message is received at this state the node will transit to the TBH state.

- TBH - as the TB state and in addition, the node queues an outstanding round of request.

4.4 Results of the Local Fairness Algorithm

The local fairness algorithm restricts the solution of local starvation problems to segments of the ring. It is triggered only by the event of starvation that is not likely to be too frequent in the case of high-speed links. If this is the case, there is a very small throughput and delay degradations compared to the basic buffer insertion ring, with the addition of starvation freedom. We use a simple and linear complexity symmetry breaking approach which is a by-product of the nodal identity ordering on the ring. We prevent nodes from abusing the fairness mechanism and causing the reverse starvation (by triggering too many requests). This is done by holding new requests until old ones are being satisfied. There are additional mechanisms that can be added in order to tolerate a-normal conditions.

- Message loss - after time-out return to the non-restricted mode.

- Fault tolerant - after any number of link or node failures, the local algorithm will operate correctly on any disconnected segment of the ring. Note that if the ring is open there is no need to include the requester's ID. The ID is used only for breaking the circular symmetry over the ring, and a linear chain of nodes has no circular symmetry.

In the following, we present some key definitions and properties of the local fairness algorithm.

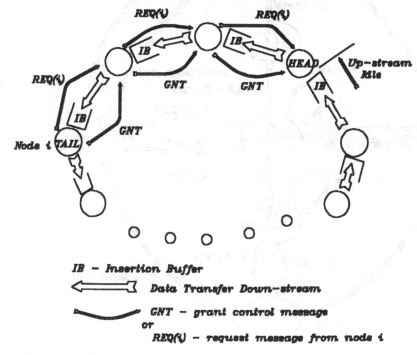

IB - *Insertion Buffer*

Data Transfer Down-stream

GNT - grant control message
or
REQ(*i*) - request message from node *i*

Figure 9.   Local Fairness Mechanism

Definition 1: A *valid request path* is a continuous segment of nodes that have one of the following structures:

1. It starts with a node in either T, TB or TBH states follows by some nodes in the B state and ends in a node in the H or TBH state.

2. It covers the whole ring where a single node is in the TH state and the rest in the B state.

3. As before, but the beginning and/or end of the *valid request path* is in transition, i.e., the control message are on their way from one node to its neighbor.

Theorem 1: At any given time t, the ring contains only *valid request paths* and nodes which are in the BI state. There is no message on the way which can violate this invariant upon its reception. If the last node of some *valid request path* is in the TBH state than this node is also the first node of a *valid request path* (might be the same one).

Proof: We will prove theorem 1 by an induction on the sequence of possible events. At the time of initialization, all nodes are in the BI state. Assume that some event takes place at time t and assume that the theorem holds until this time. We will show that it still holds after the event of time t. Since the number of possible events and state transition is quite large, we describe in details only some of them.

If the event causes no state transition or if the reception of these messages that are on their way as defined in line 3 of definition 1, then the induction still holds. Therefore, we consider only events that cause

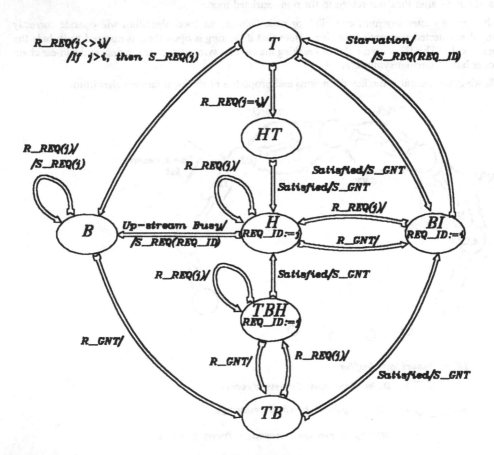

Figure 10.   Local Algorithm - State Diagram for Node *i*

a state transition at some node *i* which is part of a *valid request path* as defined by lines 1 and 2 of definition 1.

If the event is Satisfied it causes no transition in the B or H states. In the T state this causes transition to the BI state and the transmission of GNT messages up-stream. Since the node up-stream can be either in the B, H or TBH, the reception of the GNT will keep our invariant. The same holds for the TB, TBH and HT states.

If the event is Up-stream Busy, this affects only nodes in the H states. In that case, a REQ message is forwarded up-stream. If the node up-stream is in the BI state, this just replaces the head. If it is in the TB, it will transit to TBH. If it is in the T state, this will cause the transition to B only when the ID in the message is different from its own ID. In such a case, there must be a different node down-stream in either T, TB or TBH state. If the ID is the same as that of the up-stream node, it will transit to the TH state.

By a similar arguments it is easy to show that the induction holds for the events: R_REQ(j) and Starvation.

Corollary 1: a node that starts a *valid request path* is equivalent to a node in the global fairness algorithm which holds the SAT message.

Corollary 2: multiple *valid request paths* around the ring is equivalent to the global fairness algorithm with multiple SAT messages.

5.0 Discussion and Conclusions

The solutions presented in this paper are suitable for many applications and environments. In particular, it is the basis for the Metaring [4] architecture. The Metaring uses the combination of buffer insertion or slotted ring, global fairness algorithm and some additional extensions for fault tolerance, priority handling and real-time traffic support. It ranges from connecting a cluster of high speed machines, to large metropolitan area network.

The following list summarizes the essential properties of this architecture:

- Variable Size Packets - in the buffer insertion mode the transmission over the ring is asynchronous and with packet of variable sizes.

- Utilization vs. Bandwidth or Physical Size - as opposes to FDDI the utilization does not decrease as the bandwidth and physical increases.

- Fault Tolerant - the set of solutions presented in this work can be easily extended to operate independently and correctly on every connected arc (or segment) of the ring [4].

- Cost Effectiveness - the implementation of this architecture does not require new technology. The design complexity and technology are the same as FDDI, with performances which are much higher and more reliable. Thus, this solution has much better cost effectiveness characteristics (i.e., "you get much more for the same money").

The proposed architecture is a viable alternative for current FDDI and DQDB (IEEE 802.6) as a future network solution. The advantages of this architecture become more apparent as the bandwidth increases.

REFERENCES

1. W. E. Burr, "The FDDI Optical Data Link," *IEEE Communication Magazine*, Vol. 24, No. 5, May 1986, pp. 18-23.

2. Z. L. Budrikis et al., "QPSX: A Queue Packet and Synchronous Circuit Exchange," *ICCC'1986*, pp. 288-293.

3. I. Cidon and Y. Ofek, "Fairness Algorithm for Full-duplex Buffer Insertion Ring," U.S. Patent Pending.

4.   I. Cidon and Y. Ofek, "Metaring - A Ring with Fairness and Spatial Reuse," *IBM Research Report*, in preparation.

5.   A. Hopper and R. M. Needham, "The Cambridge Fast Ring Networking System," *IEEE Trans. on Comp.*, Vol. 37, No. 10, October 1988, pp. 1214-1223.

6.   J. L. Hullet and P. Evans, "New Proposal Extends the Reach of Metro Area Nets," *Data Communications*, February 1988, pp. 139-147.

7.   M. T. Liu and D. M. Rouse, "A Study of Ring Networks," *Proc. IFIP WG6.4/University of Kent Workshop on Ring Technology Based Local Area Networks*, September 1983, pp. 1-39.

8.   T. Minami et. al., "A 200 Mbit/s Synchronous TDM Loop Optical LAN Suitable for Multiservice Integration," *IEEE J. on Selected Areas in Comm.*, Vol. SAC-3, No. 6, November 1985, pp. 849-858.

9.   M. Misson, J-J. Mercier and A. El Oussoul, "A Fair Management of Communication Establishment for a Ring LAN," *1988 Local Computer Network Conference*, pp. 395-404.

10. R. M. Newman and J. L. Hullet, "Distributed Queueing: A Fast and Efficient Packet Access Protocol for QPSX," *ICCC'1986*, pp. 294-299.

11. A. Patir et al., "An Optical Fiber-Based Integrated LAN for MAGNET's Testbed Environment," *IEEE J. on Selected Areas in Comm.*, Vol. SAC-3, No. 6, November 1985, pp. 872-881.

12. F. E. Ross, "FDDI - a Tutorial," *IEEE Communication Magazine*, Vol. 24, No. 5, May 1986, pp. 10-17.

AN EFFICIENT RELIABLE RING PROTOCOL

Reuven Cohen & Adrian Segall
Dept. of Computer Science, Technion IIT
Haifa 32000, Israel

Abstract

In slotted- and token-rings, transmission errors and station failures may induce livelocks and deadlocks. In the present paper we address the problem of ring recovery from such faulty situations. We present a new protocol and prove that it recovers from any combination of transmission errors and station failures in at most 5 ring revolutions. The protocol requires no information about the current topology of the ring, like the number of stations or the ring revolution propagation time. It uses only two frame bits for access control and achieves minimum delay at the ring stations.

1. Introduction

One of the most popular approaches to local area networks is *slotted–rings* [1]-[5]. In such networks the stations are located on a ring, and a frame of fixed length travels around the ring. The frame is divided into a fixed number of fixed-size slots. Each slot contains a token that is responsible for the access control of the stations to this slot. Each slot operates independently of all other slots in the frame, so that in our description and analysis it will be convenient to assume that there is only one slot per frame, and use the term *frame* instead of *slot*.

The basic concept of a ring is that each station repeats the frame it receives, containing the token, to its downstream neighbor. A station that wishes to send data to another station waits for an *empty* token, changes it to *full*, and incorporates its own data in the frame. A station that recognizes a *full* token, or that has no data to send, passes the frame on unchanged to its downstream neighbor. If the destination address of a frame containing data matches the station address, then the contents of the frame is copied into a local buffer.

One of the basic requirements in the design of ring networks is minimum delay at each station. From this requirement follows that some of the frame fields, e.g. the token field, cannot be error protected by a CRC in the normal way. This is because such a protection would require each station to wait for the CRC before starting to transmit the frame to its downstream neighbor. Since the token field is unprotected, undetected errors may occur in this field, which may lead to faulty situations where no station can transmit data, or where data is not received by its destination. Such situations may also occur due to station failures.

There are many versions of the slotted-ring protocol. In this paper we assume that one of the ring stations functions as a *monitor*. The monitor is responsible for supervising the token operation and for invoking recovery actions in case of errors.

An efficient slotted-ring access control protocol must address the following issues:

1) Minimum delay at stations: since the station delays accumulate around the ring and contribute to the total transmission delay over the ring, the delay at each station must be minimized. The minimal bit delay is the time needed to copy a bit from the input channel to the output channel or to transmit a *constant* bit, namely one whose value has been determined independently of the current incoming bit value. This delay is called *one–bit–delay*. Some analytic results [7] demonstrate that there is a significant degradation in performance when the delay at stations is increased, especially in rings with a large number of active stations. On the other hand, the delay-throughput characteristic of the ring is fairly insensitive to the number of stations, if they work with a *one–bit–delay*.

2) The number of bits dedicated to the token must be as small as possible. The main reasons for this requirement are to minimize the probability of undetectable transmission errors and to reduce overhead.

3) The recovery time of the ring from failures must be as small as possible.

In the present paper we present a new access control protocol that addresses the above requirements. As in previous such protocols [1]-[4], [6]-[7], we dedicate only two bits to the token, and require a *one–bit–delay* at the ring stations and a maximum of three-bit-delay at the monitor. However, our protocol has the following improvements over previous ones:

(a) it enables recovery from any combination of transmission errors and station failures, whereas the protocols in [1]-[5] do not.

(b) recovery is completed in at most 5 ring revolutions whereas previous protocols [1], [2] require $N-1$ or $N/2$ ring revolutions, where N is the number of stations in the ring.

(c) it requires no knowledge of ring parameters like the number of stations or the ring revolution delay; the protocols of [1] and [2] require knowledge of the maximal number of stations in the ring, while those of [6] and [7] require the maximal ring revolution delay.

The organization of the rest of this paper is as follows: the next section introduces a well-known access-control protocol for slotted- rings called the *EM–protocol*; section 3 introduces our new protocol, called the *RE–protocol*; section 4 presents the proof of correctness for the *RE–protocol* and section 5 concludes the paper.

2. The EM-Protocol

Since our approach to the access-control protocol is partially based on the *EM–protocol* [1]-[4], we describe the latter in this section is some detail. The *EM–protocol* uses two bits for access control and recovery purpose (two *token* bits). The first bit, named E (empty), takes on values *empty* or *full*, while the second bit, named M (monitor), takes on values *new* or *old*. This protocol is destined for slotted-ring networks that use a monitor station. The format of the frame is depicted in Fig. 1.

The first field is the token field and afterwards come the destination field, the source field, the data field and the response field.

When any station wishes to send data, it waits for the token to arrive and examines the E bit. If E =empty, then the station changes it to full, sets the M bit to new, updates the destination field, writes its identity in the source field, writes its data in the data field and resets the response field. If E is already full, or if the station does not have data to send, it repeats the incoming frame, and copies the data field of this frame to a local buffer if it recognizes itself as the destination station. A station that has sent its data waits for the frame to circulate around the ring. When it receives the frame back, it sets the E bit, unconditionally, to empty, permitting other stations to send their data.

The M bit is used by the monitor for recovery purposes. A station sets this bit to new when it sends a new data-frame. When the monitor receives a frame with the values [full, new] in the token, it sets this pair to [full, old]. However, when it recognizes a [full, old] token, it sets it to [empty, *]. Such an action enables the ring to recover from transmission errors that change the E bit from empty to full and from a station failure that occurs after the data is sent and before it is received back.

In [1] and [2] it is shown how a single bit error from full to empty in the E bit may bring the ring into a livelock situation. Suppose such an error occurs after the station S_i sends its data. Consequently, other stations recognize an empty token, although the frame has not reached yet its destination. If another station, say S_j, wishes to send data, it changes the token to full and incorporates its own data in the frame. The data sent by S_i does not circulate around the ring, and possibly it is not received by its destination. Next time S_i receives the token it changes it to empty, since it does not know that the frame carries the data of S_j rather than its own. Now, another station may send its data, and the data sent by S_j does not complete a ring revolution. This situation will continue as long as stations will have data to send. A livelock situation may also occur due to a single bit error from new to old in the M bit. J. Pachl has shown how to detect livelock situations, and extensions to the basic EM −Protocol that allow the ring to recover from such a situation have been introduced in [1] and [2]. The main properties of the protocols of [1],

E	M	DEST	SRC	DATA	RESP

Fig. 1: Frame Format of the EM −protocol

[2] are:

- They do not require any change in the frame format and in the monitor protocol.
- The ring stations must know the maximum number of stations in the ring (N).
- The recovery time of these protocols is $N-1$ or $N/2$ ring revolutions.
- These protocols handle only errors in the token bits; they do not handle faulty situations caused by station failures, errors in the source field or combinations thereof.

A different approach of the *EM–Protocol* for livelock elimination was implemented in the Cambridge Ring [4]. Although it improves upon the protocols in [1], [2] in the sense that knowledge of N is not required, the recovery time of this protocol is still N ring revolutions.

The *IEEE* 802.5 standard for token-ring access method uses two token bits as well, with the same general purpose. The approach of this standard to prevent deadlocks and livelocks is based on timers held by both the monitor and the non-monitor stations. Such an approach has two deficiencies:

- It assumes that the stations have continuously updated information about the delay in the ring; alternatively the timer is set to the maximum possible delay, resulting in possibly very long recovery periods.
- This approach cannot be adapted efficiently to slotted-rings with multiple slots.

In the next section we introduce a new access control protocol, called the *RE–protocol*, that has the properties stated at the end of Sec. 1.

3. The RE-Protocol

The *RE–protocol* uses two token bits, as the EM and the *IEEE*–802.5 protocols, and hence requires no changes in the frame structure. As indicated in Sec. 2, the *EM–protocol* uses the M bit of the token for the purpose of recovery from an *empty→full* error in the E bit. Our *RE–protocol* does not dedicate a special bit for this purpose. Instead, the monitor records the source field of a *full* frame in a local variable called *last_source*, and if it recognizes either the same source field identity in two consecutive ring revolutions, or an unacceptable source field in a *full* frame, it waits for the next token arrival, and then resets the source field to *empty*. This requires an extra trip of the frame around the ring compared to the *EM–protocol*, but we shall show that still the *RE–protocol* is more efficient than the previous ones in terms of total recovery time.

In our protocol, the two token bits RE are used as follows:

- 00- denotes an *empty* frame; a station that recognizes such a token can change it to *full* and send its data.
- 01- denotes a *full* frame. A station that sees such a token cannot send its data; it has to transmit the frame unaltered to its downstream neighbor and to detect whether the frame is destined for itself. The station that sets the token to *full* (01) changes it back to *empty* (00) when the frame returns.
- 10- signals to the monitor that a reset ring revolution is required, due to a failure detection by a non-monitor station.

- 11- denotes a reset ring revolution trip that was initiated by the monitor.

One can observe that in this protocol the first bit, named R for *recovery*, indicates regular or irregular operation (values 0, 1 respectively). If $R=0$, then the second bit, named E, functions in the same way as the E bit of the *EM –protocol*. A similar approach was used in [1] for rings without a monitor. However, unlike the *RE –protocol*, livelocks may happen in that protocol for certain combinations of transmission errors (see [1]).

As mentioned before, the *RE –protocol* is designed for rings where one of the stations is distinguished from the others and functions as a monitor. In this paper we do not consider the election process, which is described in [6] and [7]. However, we assume that there is always a unique monitor station. In most applications, the monitor station operate as a non-monitor station in addition to its function as monitor. For clarity of exposition, we separate here the two functions and address this issue in the appendix.

The algorithm a for non-monitor station and for the monitor station are given in Fig. 2(a) and 2(b). If a non-monitor station receives a 00-token while its current mode is *LISTEN* and has data to send, then it changes the token to 01, sends its data, and makes a transition to the *ACTIVE* mode. In *ACTIVE* mode, a station has sent its data and is waiting for

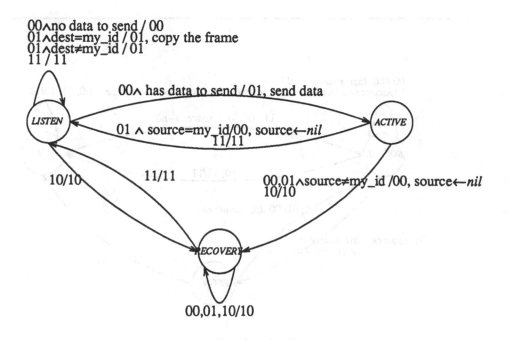

Fig. 2(a): Non-Monitor Algorithm

the data-frame to come back in order to remove it and to transmit a token-frame instead. Therefore the source field in the frame should normally indicate the identity of the station in *ACTIVE* mode. If this is the case, the station releases the token, changes the source field to *nil*, and returns to *LISTEN* mode.

Whenever a station detects abnormal operation of the ring, it enters the exception mode *RECOVERY*. The abnormal situation manifests itself by a station in *ACTIVE* mode receiving an *empty* token 00 or a *full* token 01 with source field different than its own, or as shown below, by a station in any mode receiving a 10 token. In the next round, the station in *RECOVERY* mode will change any token except 11 to a 10 token. The latter signals to the monitor and to any station before the monitor that abnormal operation has occurred. The *one–bit–delay* requirement bars transmission of the 10 token immediately when the station discovers the exception, hence the need for *RECOVERY* mode.

The monitor is in *NORMAL* mode as long as according to its information, the ring operates properly. The monitor has two exception modes. When it detects itself abnormal operation, it enters the *RESTORE* mode. This happens if two consecutive *full* frames contain the same source field or if a *full* frame contains source_field=*nil*. If the token received in the next round shows no further problems, i.e. if it is 00 or 01, then an *empty* token 00 is sent and the monitor returns to *NORMAL*. The second exception mode is *RESET*. This mode is entered when the monitor is informed with a 10 token by another station

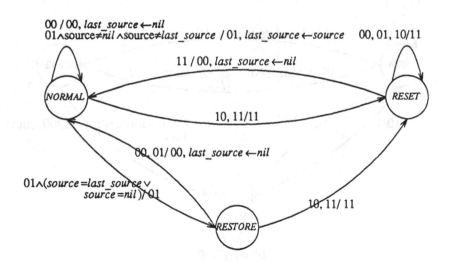

Fig. 2(b): Monitor algorithm

that the latter has detected an exception. In this case, the monitor releases a 11 token, that propagates around the ring and resets all stations to LISTEN mode. When the 11 token returns to the monitor, the latter returns to NORMAL and releases an *empty* token 00.

Theorem 1

In the *RE—protocol*, non-monitor stations work with *one—bit—delay*, while the monitor has a *one—bit—delay* in NORMAL or RESTORE modes, and a *three—bit—delay* in RESET mode.

Proof

A non-monitor station in LISTEN mode that receives a 00-token leaves it unaltered or changes it to 01. It leaves a 01, 10 or 11-token unchanged. Therefore, the algorithm of such a station is:

- *transmit the first bit as received.*

- *if the first bit was '0' and there is data to send, then transmit '1' as the second bit; use the frame to indeed send the data only if the received second bit was '0', otherwise transmit the received frame unaltered.*

- *if the first bit was '0' and there is no data to send, then transmit the second bit as received.*

- *if the first bit was '1', then transmit the second bit as received.*

The proof for all the other cases is similar and appears in [8]. □

Note that the three bit delay introduced by the monitor in RESET mode is not substantial, since there is only one monitor station and the monitor is in RESET only after an exception. In the *EM—protocol* the monitor operates always with a three-bit-delay.

4. Correctness Proof

The purpose of this section is to prove that the *RE—protocol* ensures recovery from *any combination* of transmission errors and station failures. We prove that the ring recovers in at most 5 ring revolutions from any faulty state, provided that no more errors or failures occur.

The following assumptions are made:

(1) Transmission errors may disrupt any bits in the frame, including the token bits and the source field bits, but the frame structure is not altered. Observe that in practice the source field bits are protected, but this protection is not used in our protocol.

(2) There is exactly one frame in the ring. We continue to consider, as indicated in Sec. 1, a one-slot frame, while recalling that the extension to multi-slot frames is trivial, since in this case each slot operates independently of the others.

(3) A non-monitor station can leave the ring at any time, due to a failure or any other reasons. Normally, it leaves when its mode is LISTEN. However, if because of a failure it leaves the ring in ACTIVE or RECOVERY mode, the ring will recover and continue to operate properly. As said before, we assume that the ring is always connected. Therefore, when a station either leaves the ring or fails, then its repeater enters a bypass-state, where it becomes a part of the link.

(4) A non-monitor station can join the ring at any time. Its initial mode is *LISTEN*.

(5) There is always *one* monitor station. However, a momentary monitor failure that disrupts its local variables is allowed.

State Definition- the state of the ring is defined by the following state variables:

(a) The location of the frame in the ring.

(b) The value of the token-field.

(c) The identity of the source-field in the frame.

(d) The modes of the stations.

(e) The value of the monitor variable *last_source*.

Although we allow stations to dynamically fail and/or join the ring, our discussion below addresses the recovery of the ring after topological changes and transmission errors cease. Consequently, we can consider a fixed ring topology. We denote by N the number of non-monitor stations in the ring. The monitor is station 0, the next station downstream is 1, and so forth around the ring. Station N is the last station before the monitor.

The variable T will be used to denote the frame location, the value of the token, and the source field of the token. We write $T=RE_l^i$ to show that the value of the first and second token bit is R and E respectively, the identity of the source field is i, and the location of the frame is between station l and station $(l+1) mod (N+1)$; namely, station l has already completed the execution of the protocol, and station $(l+1) mod (N+1)$ has not started it yet. When any state variable is irrelevant, it is not mentioned; for example $T=01_l$ denotes that the value of the token is 01, the last station to have executed the protocol is l, and the value of the source field is irrelevant; $T=11^{nil}$ denotes that the value of the token is 11, the value of the source field is *nil*, and the location of the frame is irrelevant. The variable $mode_i$ denotes the mode of station i. For clarity, we shall use $mode_M$ rather than $mode_0$ in order to denote the mode of the monitor. Another notation is required to define the set of non-monitor stations between any two given stations in the ring, i and j:

$$\{i \cdots j\} = \begin{cases} \{i, i+1, \cdots, j-1, j\} & \text{if } i \le j \\ \Phi & \text{otherwise} \end{cases}$$

The non-faulty states of the ring are:

$(S_1)\ mode_M=NORMAL \wedge \forall j \in \{1 \cdots N\}$ holds $mode_j=LISTEN \wedge T=00_l \wedge last\_source \notin \{l+1 \cdots$

$(S_2)\ mode_M=NORMAL \wedge \forall j \in \{1 \cdots N\}-\{i\}$ holds $mode_j=LISTEN \wedge mode_i=ACTIVE \wedge T=01_l^i \wedge$

$\quad ((l \ge i \wedge last\_source \ne i) \vee (l < i \wedge last\_source = i))$

State S_1 comprises all possible non-faulty situations with an *empty* token frame 00: the monitor is in *NORMAL* mode, all non-monitor stations are in *LISTEN* mode and the monitor variable *last_source* is either *nil* or in the range $\{1 \cdots l\}$, where l is the location of the token. Value *nil* denotes that the token was *empty* when it last traversed the monitor, value in $\{1...l\}$ indicates that it was *full* but was changed to *empty* by some station after it has traversed the monitor.

State S_2 includes all possible non-faulty situations with a *full* token frame 01: the monitor is in NORMAL mode; all non-monitor stations except one, i, are in LISTEN mode; station i is in ACTIVE mode after it has transmitted the data and before having received it back; the frame has the correct source field i and is located either after i and before the monitor while *last_source* (at the monitor) is not i yet, or after the monitor and *last_source* is i.

The next Theorem shows that if the ring is in a non-faulty state and operates properly, it stays in the non-faulty states forever. To be specific we shall denote by $S[t]$ the state just after a station processes the frame (i.e., the token and the source field) and by $S[t+1]$ the state just after the next station does so. A similar notation will be used to indicate the value of the various variables at the appropriate times.

Theorem 2

Suppose $S[t]$ is a non-faulty state, and until [t+1] there are no transmission errors and the ring topology does not change, namely stations neither leave nor join the ring. Then $S[t+1]$ is a non-faulty state.

Proof

With the notations above for S_1 and S_2, the next station to receive the token is $(l+1) mod (N+1)$.

- If $S[t]=S_1$ and $l=N$, namely, the next station to receive the token after t is the monitor, then the monitor remains in NORMAL mode and sets *last_source* $\leftarrow$ *nil*. Since *nil* $\notin \{0 \cdots N\}$, we have $S[t+1]=S_1$.

- If $S[t]=S_1$, $l \neq N$ and $l+1$ has data to send, then $l+1$ sets the receiving token to 01, copies its identity to the source field, and changes its mode to ACTIVE. Therefore, at time $[t+1]$ holds $T=01_{l+1}^{l+1}$. But *last_source* $[t] \neq l+1$, and since *last_source* does not change, holds *last_source* $[t+1] \neq l+1$. Therefore, $S[t+1]=S_2$.

- If $S[t]=S_1$, $l \neq N$ and $l+1$ has no data to send, the mode of $l+1$ and the value of the token remain unchanged. Since *last_source* $[t] \notin \{l+1 \cdots N\}$ and *last_source* does not change, holds *last_source* $[t+1] \notin \{l+2 \cdots N\}$. Therefore, $S[t+1]=S_1$.

- If $S[t]=S_2$ and $l=N$, then $l+1$ is the monitor. Since *last_source* $[t] \neq i$, the monitor remains in NORMAL mode, transmits the same token, and sets *last_source* $\leftarrow i$. Consequently, $S[t+1]=S_2$.

- If $S[t]=S_2$, $l \neq N$ and $l+1$ is in ACTIVE mode, then $l+1$ changes the token to 00, and its mode to LISTEN. Since *last_source* $[t]=l+1$ and *last_source* does not change, holds *last_source* $[t+1]=l+1$. Therefore, *last_source* $[t+1] \notin \{l+2 \cdots N\}$ and we have $S[t+1]=S_1$.

- If $S[t]=S_2$, $l \neq N$ and $l+1$ is in LISTEN mode, then $l+1$ remains in the same mode and transmits the same token. Since $i \neq l+1$, the following two cases are possible: (i) if $i < l+1$, then since *last_source* $[t] \neq i$ and *last_source* does not change, holds *last_source* $[t+1] \neq i$, and we have $S[t+1]=S_2$; (ii) if $i > l+1$, then since *last_source* $[t]=i$ and *last_source* does not change, holds *last_source* $[t+1]=i$, and we have $S[t+1]=S_2$. □

Our next step is to define, in Table 1, the faulty states (S_3–S_{18}). As shown in Lemma 1, states S_1–S_{18} cover all possible ring-states. For convenience, in Table 1 states S_1 and S_2

are repeated, so it covers all possible states of the ring.

(S_1) $mode_M{=}NORMAL \wedge \forall j \in \{1 \cdots N\}$ holds $mode_j{=}LISTEN \wedge T{=}00_l \wedge last\_source \notin \{l{+}1 \cdots N\}$

(S_2) $mode_M{=}NORMAL \wedge \forall j \in \{1 \cdots N\}{-}\{i\}$ holds $mode_j{=}LISTEN \wedge mode_i{=}ACTIVE \wedge T{=}01_l^i \wedge$
$\qquad ((l{\geq}i \wedge last\_source{\neq}i) \vee (l{<}i \wedge last\_source{=}i))$

(S_3) $mode_M{=}NORMAL \wedge \forall j \in \{1 \cdots N\}$ holds $mode_j{=}LISTEN \wedge T{=}00_l \wedge last\_source \in \{l{+}1 \cdots N\}$

(S_4) $mode_M{=}NORMAL \wedge \forall j \in \{1 \cdots N\}{-}\{i\}$ holds $mode_j{=}LISTEN \wedge mode_i{=}ACTIVE \wedge T{=}01_l^i \wedge (i{\leq}l \wedge last\_source{=}i)$

(S_5) $mode_M{=}NORMAL \wedge \forall j \in \{1 \cdots N\}{-}\{i\}$ holds $mode_j{=}LISTEN \wedge mode_i{=}ACTIVE \wedge T{=}01_l^i \wedge (l{<}i \wedge last\_source{\neq}i)$

(S_6) $mode_M{=}RESET \wedge T{=}11_l \wedge \forall j \in \{1 \cdots l\}$ holds $mode_j{=}LISTEN$

(S_7) $mode_M{=}RESET \wedge T{=}11_l \wedge \exists j \in \{1 \cdots l\}$ such that $mode_j{\neq}LISTEN$

(S_8) $mode_M{=}RESET \wedge (T{=}10 \vee T{=}01 \vee T{=}00)$

(S_9) $mode_M{\neq}RESET \wedge (T{=}10 \vee T{=}11 \vee \exists j \in \{l{+}1 \cdots N\}$ such that $mode_j{=}RECOVERY)$

(S_{10}) $mode_M{\neq}RESET \wedge (T{=}00_l \vee T{=}01_l) \wedge \not\exists j \in \{l{+}1 \cdots N\}$ such that $mode_j{=}RECOVERY \wedge \exists j \in \{1 \cdots l\}$
$\qquad$ such that $mode_j{=}RECOVERY$

(S_{11}) $mode_M{\neq}RESET \wedge T{=}00_l \wedge \not\exists j \in \{1 \cdots N\}$ such that $mode_j{=}RECOVERY \wedge \exists j \in \{l{+}1 \cdots N\}$ such that $mode_j{=}ACTIVE$

(S_{12}) $mode_M{\neq}RESET \wedge T{=}01_l^i \wedge \not\exists j \in \{1 \cdots N\}$ such that $mode_j{=}RECOVERY \wedge \exists j \in \{l{+}1 \cdots N\}$ such that
$\qquad (mode_j{=}ACTIVE \wedge j{\neq}i)$

(S_{13}) $mode_M{\neq}RESET \wedge T{=}00_l \wedge \not\exists j \in \{1 \cdots N\}$ such that $mode_j{=}RECOVERY \wedge \not\exists j \in \{l{+}1 \cdots N\}$ such that $mode_j{=}ACTIVE$
$\qquad \wedge \exists j \in \{1 \cdots l\}$ such that $mode_j{=}ACTIVE$

(S_{14}) $mode_M{\neq}RESET \wedge T{=}01_l^i \wedge \not\exists j \in \{1 \cdots N\}$ such that $mode_j{=}RECOVERY \wedge \not\exists j \in \{l{+}1 \cdots N\}$ such that
$\qquad (mode_j{=}ACTIVE \wedge j{\neq}i) \wedge \exists j \in \{1 \cdots l\}$ such that $(mode_j{=}ACTIVE \wedge j{\neq}i)$

(S_{15}) $mode_M{=}RESTORE \wedge T{=}01 \wedge \forall j \in \{1 \cdots N\}$ holds $mode_j{=}LISTEN$

(S_{16}) $mode_M{=}NORMAL \wedge T{=}01^i \wedge \forall j \in \{1 \cdots N\}$ holds $mode_j{=}LISTEN \wedge i{\neq}nil \wedge last\_source{\neq}i$

(S_{17}) $mode_M{=}NORMAL \wedge T{=}01^i \wedge \forall j \in \{1 \cdots N\}$ holds $mode_j{=}LISTEN \wedge (last\_source{=}i \vee i{=}nil)$

(S_{18}) $mode_M{=}RESTORE \wedge (T{=}01^i \wedge \forall j \in \{1 \cdots N\}{-}\{i\}$ holds $mode_j{=}LISTEN \wedge mode_i{=}ACTIVE) \vee$
$\qquad (T{=}00 \wedge \forall j \in \{1 \cdots N\}$ holds $mode_j{=}LISTEN)$

Table 1: All possible ring states

Lemma 1

S_1–S_{18} cover all the possible ring-states.

Proof

It is easy to check that all possible state are covered by S_1–S_{18}. The detailed proof appears in [8].

$\square$

Lemma 2

Suppose that the ring is in one of the faulty states S_i, $3 \le i \le 18$. Consider the situation just after the frame next traverses the monitor. At that time, the ring will be in one of the states indicated by arrows originating from S_i in Fig. 3.

Proof

For each faulty state, we examine the situation of the ring just after the token next traverses the monitor. Recall that we made the convention that the monitor is station 0, and, therefore, just after the token traverses the monitor holds $l=0$. Consequently, $\{1 \cdots l\}$ is the empty set, and $\{l+1 \cdots N\}$ is the set of all non-monitor stations. In this paper we prove the claim only for arrows originating from S_3 and S_4. The rest appears in [8].

S_3- Next time the token reaches the monitor, its value is either 00 or 01. If it is 00, then all non-monitor stations are in LISTEN mode and the monitor sets $last\_source \leftarrow nil$, causing the ring to enter state S_1. On the other hand, if the value of the token is 01, then all non-monitor stations are in LISTEN mode except one whose mode is ACTIVE and whose identity is the current value of the source field. In this case there are two possibilities: if the identity of the station in mode ACTIVE is the current value of $last\_source$, then the monitor enters mode RESTORE, causing the ring to enter S_{18}; otherwise, the monitor remains in LISTEN mode and copies the source field into the variable $last\_source$, causing the ring to enter S_2.

S_4- When the ring starts in this state, the token reaches the monitor before reaching the station in mode ACTIVE. Nothing changes until the time when the token reaches the monitor, namely, its value is still 01, all non-monitor stations are in LISTEN mode, except one that is in ACTIVE mode and the identity of the latter matches the current value of the frame source field. Since this value is identical to the value of $last\_source$, the monitor enters RESTORE mode. Thus, the ring enters state S_{18}.

$\square$

Theorem 3

If there are no further transmission errors or topological changes, the ring recovers from any faulty situation in at most 5 ring revolutions.

Proof

Suppose the ring is not in state S_1 or S_2, the non-faulty states, due to any previous combination of transmission errors and topological changes. Since no more transmission errors or topological changes occur subsequently, according to lemma 2, some transition of Fig.

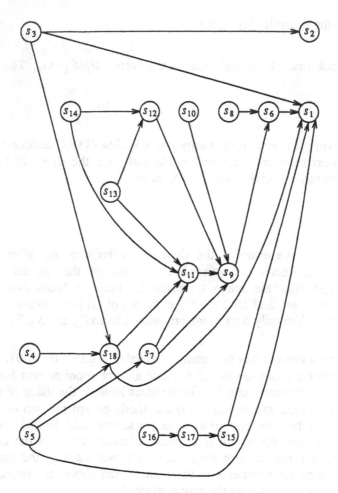

Fig. 3: State Transitions

3 must be performed every time the token traverses the monitor. It is easy to verify that the graph in Fig. 3 is an *acyclic directed graph* with sinks at S_1 and S_2 and longest directed path consists of 5 transitions. Therefore, the ring will reach the set $\{S_1, S_2\}$ in at most 5 ring revolutions, and according to Lemma 1, will stay there forever.

□

5. Conclusions

In this paper we have presented a new access control protocol for slotted-rings. This protocol requires only two bits of the frame format, so it can be applied instead of the *EM–protocol* with no need to alter the frame format. We have proved that the protocol can be performed with a minimum delay at the non-monitor stations. A minimum delay is achieved at the monitor as well, except in RESET mode, where the delay is three bits. We have defined the faulty and the non-faulty states of the ring and have proved that:

(1) if the ring is initialized at any time to a non-faulty state, it will stay in the non-faulty states as long as there are no transmission errors or station failures.

(2) the ring recovers from *any* combination of transmission errors and station failures.

(3) the recovery time is at most 5 ring revolutions.

References

[1] J. Pachl and L. Casey, "A robust ring transmission protocol". *Computer Networks and ISDN Systems* 13 (1987) 313-321.

[2] J. Pachl, "Livelocks in slotted ring networks". *Proceedings of IEEE INFOCOM 88* (March 29-31, 1988, New Orleans, Louisiana), pp. 174-179.

[3] D.T.W. Sze., "A metropolitan area network". *IEEE Journal on Selected Areas in Comm. SAC-3* (1985), 815-824.

[4] D. J. Wheeler, "The Livelock-Free Protocol of The Cambridge Ring", *The Computer Journal,* Vol. 32, No. 1, pp. 95, 1989.

[5] L.M. Casey, R.C. Dittburner and N.D. Gamage, "FXNET: a backbone ring for voice and data". *IEEE Communication Magazine 24,* 12 (December 1986), 23-28.

[6] IEEE Standards for Local Area Networks: Token ring access method and physical layer specification" ANSI/IEEE Std 802.5 (1985). Published by IEEE. Distributed in cooperation with Wiley-Interscience.

[7] W. Bux, F.H. Closs, K. Kuemmerle, H.J. Keller and H.R. Mueller, "Architecture and design of a reliable token-ring network". *IEEE Journal on Selected Areas in Comm.* Vol. SAC-1, No. 5, pp. 756-765, Nov. 1983.

[8] R. Cohen and A. Segall, "An Efficient Reliable Ring Protocol", submitted to *IEEE Transaction on Communication.*

AN EFFICIENT SOLUTION TO
THE DRINKING PHILOSOPHERS PROBLEM AND ITS EXTENSIONS

David Ginat, A. Udaya Shankar, A. K. Agrawala

Department of Computer Science
University of Maryland
College Park, Maryland 20742

ABSTRACT

We introduce a new solution to the drinking philosophers problem, using drinking session numbers. It is simple and easily adjusted to extensions of the problem. The number of messages per drinking session is between zero and twice the number of bottles needed for drinking, a considerable improvement over previous work.

1. INTRODUCTION

The drinking philosophers problem is a paradigm for sharing resources in distributed systems [1]. Contention between processes over "write locks" is abstracted in the problem into contention between philosophers over shared bottles. The problem was posed by Chandy and Misra [1] as a generalization of the dining philosophers problem [3]. Unlike the dining philosophers problem, in which a hungry philosopher needs *all* the forks he shares with his neighbors once he becomes hungry, in the drinking philosophers problem a philosopher may need only a *subset* of the bottles he shares with his neighbors upon becoming thirsty. Different subsets may be needed for different drinking sessions.

Chandy and Misra introduced a solution in which a thirsty philosopher can *concurrently* collect all the bottles he needs and all philosophers obey the same rule for resolving conflicts over shared bottles. Conflicts are resolved using an artificial dining layer below the drinking layer. However, due to the use of an artificial dining layer their solution is not simple and requires extra messages. We present a simple and efficient solution that eliminates this layer, by using drinking session numbers extended with ids. We provide an assertional proof of our solution. We then adjust our solution to extended versions of the problem. The number of messages per drinking session is between zero and twice the number of bottles needed for drinking, a considerable improvement over the result in [1]. The drawbacks of our solution are the lack of upper bound for drinking session numbers, and the use of ids for breaking ties between contending philosophers whose session numbers are equal.

In section 2, we present the problem as posed by Chandy and Misra. In section 3, we present our simple and efficient solution to the problem. In section 4 we provide its assertional correctness proof, and in section 5 we derive its message complexity and explain its improvement over Chandy and Misra's solution. In section 6, we adjust our solution to solve extensions of the original problem.

2. THE BASIC DRINKING PHILOSOPHERS PROBLEM

Philosophers are placed at the nodes of an undirected graph G, with one philosopher at each node. Neighboring philosophers communicate via messages subject to varying but finite transmission delays. Associated with each edge in G is a bottle shared between the two philosophers that are incident on the edge. A philosopher is either *tranquil*, *thirsty*, or *drinking*. A philosopher can be tranquil for an arbitrary period of time. A tranquil philosopher may become thirsty and need a *nonempty subset* of the bottles associated with his incident edges. He remains thirsty until he gets all the bottles he needs, at which point he starts drinking. He drinks for a finite time, after which he becomes tranquil and needs no bottles. A philosopher may need different subsets of bottles in different drinking sessions. Philosophers can drink concurrently from different bottles. The goal is to provide a solution which ensures that no two philosophers drink simultaneously from the same bottle, and that no philosopher remains thirsty forever.

3. ALGORITHM FOR THE BASIC PROBLEM

Philosopher u maintains two nondecreasing integer variables, s_num_u and max_rec_u. s_num_u, referred to as u's session number, identifies u's last drinking session if u is tranquil, u's upcoming drinking session if u is thirsty, and u's current drinking session if u is drinking. max_rec_u indicates the highest session number received by u from his neighbors so far.

(s_num_u, u) is referred to as u's extended session number. $(s\_num_u, u) < (s\_num_v, v)$ iff $s\_num_u < s\_num_v$ or $s\_num_u = s\_num_v$ and $u < v$ [5,8]. Each philosopher has an id which is different from the id's of his neighbors. (Ids of nonneighboring philosophers may be the same.) Thus, if u and v are neighbors, their extended session numbers are never equal.

Let u and v be two philosophers who share bottle b. Associated with bottle b is a request token req_b. Upon becoming thirsty, u sets s_num_u to a value higher than max_rec_u, and if u needs and does not hold the bottle b, u sends to v the request token for b, together with his extended session number, in the request message (req_b, s_num_u, u). u sends request messages *concurrently* to all his neighbors with whom he shares bottles he needs and does not hold. When the neighbor v receives a request (req_b , s , u), he obeys the following *conflict resolution rule*:

> if v does not need b or (v is thirsty and $(s , u) < (s\_num_v , v)$), then v immediately releases b.

If v does not release b immediately, then he needs b and will release it once he completes drinking from it. v will next use req_b only after he has released b. Thus, when req_b is in transit from v to u, b will either be in transit from v to u ahead of req_b, or will already be at u. s_num_u does not change while u is thirsty. Therefore, once b is released by v, it will not return to v before u drinks from it.

Initially, every philosopher u is tranquil and $s\_num_u = max\_rec_u = 0$. For every bottle b shared between two philosophers, one philosopher has b and the other has req_b.

Each philosopher u obeys the rules given in Table 1 below. Each rule execution is considered an atomic action. In addition to s_num_u and max_rec_u, each philosopher u has the boolean variables $need_u(b)$, $hold_u(b)$, $hold_u(req_b)$, indicating whether u needs b, holds b, and holds req_b, respectively. Below, Send(b) and Send(req_b , s_num_u , u) send the specified message to the philosopher with whom b is shared.

R1: becoming thirsty	when tranquil and "want to drink" do become thirsty; for each desired bottle b do $need_u(b) \leftarrow$ true; $s\_num_u \leftarrow max\_rec_u + 1$
R2: start drinking	when thirsty and holding all needed bottles do become drinking
R3: becoming tranquil, and honoring deferred requests	when drinking and "want to stop drinking" do become tranquil; for each consumed bottle b do $[need_u(b) \leftarrow$ false; if $hold_u(req_b)$ then [Send(b); $hold_u(b) \leftarrow$ false]]
R4: requesting a bottle	when $need_u(b)$, $\neg hold_u(b)$, $hold_u(req_b)$ do Send(req_b , s_num_u , u); $hold_u(req_b) \leftarrow$ false
R5: receiving a request, and resolving a conflict	upon reception of (req_b , s , v) do $hold_u(req_b) \leftarrow$ true; $max\_rec_u \leftarrow \max(max\_rec_u , s)$; if $\neg need_u(b)$ or (thirsty and $(s,v) < (s\_num_u , u)$) then [Send(b); $hold_u(b) \leftarrow$ false]
R6: receiving a bottle	upon reception of (b) do $hold_u(b) \leftarrow$ true

Table 1. Basic Algorithm: Rules for philosopher u

4. PROOF OF CORRECTNESS OF THE BASIC ALGORITHM

The assertions listed below should be viewed as an incremental description of the algorithm's basic properties. These assertions will be proved invariant, i.e., hold at any time during the distributed algorithm's execution.

Conventions. In an assertion, when we say *either A or B* we mean that exactly one of the conditions A or B holds. We assume that messages sent by one philosopher to another arrive in the order sent; a message m is *ahead of* (*behind*) a message n if m was sent before (after) n.

The following invariant properties derive from the problem definition:

A_0: For every bottle b shared between philosophers u and v:

　　　b is either held by u or held by v or in transit between u and v.

A_1: (a) u is not tranquil $\Leftrightarrow$ u needs at least one bottle.

　　(b) u is drinking $\Rightarrow$ u holds all the bottles he needs and drinks from them.

A_0 and A_1 imply that no two philosophers drink simultaneously from the same bottle.

Let u and v be two neighboring philosophers who share bottle b. The following invariant properties associate the locations of req_b and b:

B_0: req_b is either at u or at v or in transit between u and v.

B_1: req_b is in transit to u $\Rightarrow$ b is either held by u or is in transit to u ahead of

$$req_b.$$

B_2: req_b is held by u $\Rightarrow$ b is not in transit to u.

B_3: u does not need b $\Rightarrow$ (neither u nor v holds both b and req_b) and

　　　　　　　$((b$ is not in transit to $u)$ and $(req_b$ is not in transit to $v))$

Note that B_1 assures us that b is held by u when he receives req_b.

The following invariant properties relate extended session numbers, request tokens, and bottles:

C_0: b is in transit to u $\Rightarrow$ $(max\_rec_v \geq s\_num_u)$ and

　　　　　$(v$ does not need b or $(s\_num_u, u) < (s\_num_v, v))$

C_1: u holds both b and req_b $\Rightarrow$ $(u$ needs $b)$ and $(max\_rec_u \geq s\_num_v)$ and

　　　　　$(u$ is drinking from b or $(s\_num_u, u) < (s\_num_v, v))$

C_2: (req_b, s, v) is in transit to u $\Rightarrow$ $(s, v) = (s\_num_v, v)$.

C_3: $s\_num_u \leq max\_rec_u + 1$

The proof of invariance of the above assertions is as follows. All of them hold initially. A_0–A_1 are preserved by every rule. B_0–B_3 are preserved by every rule, assuming A_0 holds before the rule execution. C_0–C_3 are preserved by every rule, assuming A_0, B_0–B_3 hold before the rule execution.

C_3 ensures that R1 does not decrease s_num_u. This yields the next lemma.

Lemma 1.(a) s_num_u and max_rec_u never decrease.

(b) s_num_u does not change while u is thirsty.

Let u and v be two neighboring philosophers who share bottle b. We say that b is *dedicated* to u if u is thirsty and needs b and one of the following holds: (1) b is in transit to u; or (2) u holds b and $(s\_num_u, u) < (s\_num_v, v)$; or (3) u holds b, v does not need b, and $(max\_rec_v+1, v) > (s\_num_u, u)$.

Lemma 2. If b is dedicated to u, then b will not be released by u before he drinks from it.

Proof outline. Consider the period of time while u is thirsty and needs b. From Lemma 1 we know that s_num_u does not change during this period. Given that b is dedicated to u, it can be shown using B_1–B_3 and C_0–C_2 that a request (req_b, s, v) arriving at u during this period must have (s, v) higher than (s_num_u, u), and is therefore deferred. ∎

We now prove that every thirsty philosopher eventually drinks, by introducing a dynamic ordering of the philosophers according to their extended session numbers.

At any time, let the philosophers be grouped into classes, where each class consists of all philosophers with the same extended session number. Order the classes by increasing extended session numbers, and let $pos(u)$ be the position of philosopher u's class in this order. Thus, $pos(u) < pos(v)$ iff $(s\_num_u, u) < (s\_num_v, v)$. We prove progress by an inductive argument on the value of $pos(u)$.

Conventions. We use the temporal operator *leads–to* [2,9]. A *leads–to* B means that if the algorithm is in a state satisfying A, then within a finite number of rule executions it will be in a state satisfying B. We assume that drinking is finite, every message in transit is eventually received, and each of the rules R2 and R4 is fairly implemented, i.e., if it is continuously enabled, it is eventually executed.

Liveness Theorem. Philosopher u is thirsty *leads–to* philosopher u is drinking.

We prove the liveness theorem by proving the following assertion $D(i)$, for any i:

$D(i)$: $pos(u)=i$ and u is thirsty *leads–to* u is drinking.

We prove $D(i)$, for any i, by induction on i.

Proof of $D(1)$. The induction basis. We first prove the following assertion:

E_B: $pos(u)=1$ and u is thirsty and needs bottle b *leads–to* b is dedicated to u.

Let u be a thirsty philosopher who needs bottle b that he shares with philosopher v, and let $pos(u)=1$. $(s\_num_u, u) < (s\_num_v, v)$ since u is in the lowest class, and two neighboring philosophers cannot be in the same class. From Lemma 1, we know that $(s\_num_u, u) < (s\_num_v, v)$ holds continuously during the time that u is thirsty. If b is not already dedicated to u, then b must either be held by v or in transit to v. We show that b will eventually be dedicated to u by examining the possible locations of req_b.

(1)   Assume req_b is at v. b cannot be in transit to v, by B_2. Therefore, b is held by v, and from C_1 we can infer that v must be drinking from b. v will complete drinking in finite time, at which point rule R3 will be executed at v, resulting in b being sent to u and hence dedicated to u.

(2)   Assume (req_b, s, u) is in transit to v. It will arrive at v in finite time, when b is there (by B_1), and with $(s, u){=}(s\_num_u, u)$ (by C_2). Upon reception of req_b, v will either release b immediately and b will become dedicated to u, or v will defer u's request and we are back in (1).

(3)   Assume req_b is with u. R4 is continuously enabled at u. Thus, u will eventually send req_b to v and we are back in (2).

(4) req_b cannot be in transit to u, by B_1.

At this point, we can conclude $D(1)$. The number of bottles that u needs for drinking is finite. Each one of these bottles will be dedicated to u and held by him in finite time, after which it will not be released before u drinks, by Lemma 2. Therefore, once all of these bottles are held by u, R2 is continuously enabled at u, and u will eventually start drinking. ∎

Proof of $D(k+1)$ assuming $D(1), \cdots, D(k)$. The induction step. We first prove the following assertion:

E_S: $pos(u){=}k+1$ and u is thirsty and needs bottle b $leads{-}to$ b is dedicated to u or u is drinking.

Again, let u be a thirsty philosopher who needs bottle b that he shares with philosopher v, and let $pos(u){=}k+1$. $pos(v){\neq}k+1$ because u and v are neighbors. If $pos(v){\geq}k+2$, then E_S is proved using the same arguments given in E_B's proof. We prove E_S for the case where $pos(v){\leq}k$:

If b is not already dedicated to u, then b is not in transit to u. If b is held by u then it may be held by him until he starts drinking, or it may be released by u (upon receiving v's request) while he is still thirsty. The latter reduces to the case where b is not held by u.

If b is not held by u, then b is either held by v or in transit to v. We show that b will eventually be dedicated to u by examining the possible locations of req_b:

(1)   Assume req_b is at v. b must be held by v, by B_2, and v needs b, by C_1. If v is thirsty, then he will be drinking in finite time, since we assume $D(1), \cdots,$ $D(k)$. If v is drinking, he will complete drinking in finite time, and b will become dedicated to u.

(2)   Assume req_b is not at v. The arguments to show that b will eventually be dedicated to u are the same as those used in E_B's proof under cases (2), (3), (4).

At this point we can conclude $D(k+1)$. Either u will start drinking before all the bottles he needs are dedicated to him, or u will first have all the bottles he needs dedicated to him and then have R2 continuously enabled and start drinking. ∎

5. LOW MESSAGE COMPLEXITY

Let philosophers u and v share bottle b, and consider two consecutive drinking periods from b. If both periods are performed by the same philosopher, then no messages are sent for the second period. If the first period is performed by u and the second by v, then exactly *two* messages are sent for the second period: one transmission of req_b (by v) and one transmission of b (by u). Thus, a drinking session by a philosopher who needs k bottles requires between zero and $2k$ messages.

In Chandy and Misra's solution [1], there is a dining layer that runs concurrently with the drinking layer. Upon becoming thirsty, a philosopher also becomes hungry and needs *all* the forks associated with his incident edges. Thus, a drinking session by a philosophers who has d neighbors and needs k bottles $(k \leq d)$ may require up to $2d$ messages for obtaining the forks. Some of these messages may still be in transit even after drinking was completed. Our "single layer" solution does not require these messages. In addition, it does not have complications due to coordinating the drinking and dining layers [7].

We conjecture that the message complexity of our solution is optimal in a model where philosophers have no knowledge about the durations of tranquil periods and drinking sessions. In such a model, a thirsty philosopher who needs a bottle he does not hold must notify his neighbor about his need, and a bottle release should occur no later than one drinking session after a notification is received.

6. EXTENSIONS TO THE BASIC PROBLEM

The first extension to the drinking philosophers problem defined in section 2 is to associate with each edge in G multiple, identical instances of a bottle rather than one instance. A philosopher may need some (but not necessarily all) instances upon becoming thirsty. We call this extension *the multiple-instance extension*.

Consider two neighboring philosophers u and v who share $quantity(b)$ instances of bottle b. We provide each philosopher with his own request token for instances of b. req_{bu} is the request token used by philosopher u and req_{bv} is the request token used by philosopher v. Upon becoming thirsty, u sets s_num_u to a value higher than max_rec_u, and if u does not hold as many instances of bottle b as he needs, he sends the message $(req_{bu}, need_u(b), s\_num_u, u)$ to v, where $need_u(b)$ indicates the total number of instances of b needed by u. Note that $need_u(b)$ is not the additional number of instances that u needs, but the total number he needs. When v receives a request (req_{bu}, n, s, u), he obeys the following *conflict resolution rule*:

if $n \leq quantity(b) - need_v(b)$ or (v is thirsty and $(s, u) < (s\_num_v, v)$), then v immediately releases as many instances of b as the additional number of instances needed at u.

This conflict resolution rule is a generalization of the rule given for the basic algorithm (in section 3). Note that it is exactly the same rule when $quantity(b) = 1$.

We are interested in minimizing the number of messages per drinking session. Therefore, we require that v will release instances of b to u only once before u starts drinking. For this reason, v will release instances to u only at a time when he can give u all the additional instances needed at u. If v does not release instances of b immediately in response to u's request, then he will release them once he completes drinking. When releasing instances of b, v returns req_{bu} to u.

The key point is that when v decides to release instances of b to u, v knows exactly how many additional instances are needed at u and v holds at least that number of instances. The release can occur at one of the following times: (1) when u's request arrives at v and $quantity(b)$ is no less than the sum of the total needs of u and v; or (2) when u's request arrives at v and $quantity(b)$ is less than that sum, but u has priority and v is not drinking yet; or (3) when v completes drinking. At any of these times there are no instances of b in transit between the two philosophers. When no instances are in transit, v can determine the number of instances held by u (it equals $quantity(b)$ minus the number of instances held by v). Knowing the total number of instances needed by u, v can determine the additional number of instances needed by u.

When v receives u's request, there are no instances of b in transit from v to u. If u has priority over v, then there are also no instances in transit from u to v and v holds at least as many instances of b as the number of additional instances needed at u. If v has priority over u, then v either already holds as many instances as the additional need of u or v is thirsty, waiting for instances from u. In the latter case, v will eventually drink and upon drinking completion will have enough instances to release to u.

We now give the algorithm for the multiple-instance extension. The variables maintained by philosopher u are as follows: s_num_u and max_rec_u remain as in the basic algorithm (see section 3); $need_u(b)$ and $hold_u(b)$ are now integers indicating number of instances; $in\_hand_u(req_{bu})$ indicates whether u holds req_{bu}; $in\_hand_u(req_{bv})$ indicates whether u holds req_{bv}, where v is the neighbor with whom u shares instances of b; $hold\_neighbor_u(b)$ indicates the number of instances of b that u knows v to hold, and $need\_neighbor_u(b)$ indicates the total number of instances u knows v to need.

Initially, every philosopher u is tranquil and $s\_num_u = max\_rec_u = 0$. Given $quantity(b)$ instances of bottle b shared between two philosophers, some are with one philosopher and the rest are with the other. Each philosopher holds his own request token for instances of b.

Each philosopher u obeys the rules given in Table 2 below. As in section 3, each rule execution is considered an atomic action and messages regarding instances of a bottle are sent to the philosopher with whom they are shared.

R1': when tranquil and "want to drink" do
    become thirsty;
    $s\_num_u \leftarrow max\_rec_u + 1$;
    for each desired bottle b do
      $need_u(b) \leftarrow$ the number of instances of b needed

R2': when thirsty and holding enough instances of all needed bottles do
    become drinking

R3': when drinking and "want to stop drinking" do
    become tranquil;
    for each consumed bottle b do
    $[need_u(b) \leftarrow 0$;
     if $in\_hand_u(req_{bv})$ then
     $[hold\_neighbor_u(b) \leftarrow quantity(b) - hold_u(b)$;
     $release_u(b) \leftarrow need\_neighbor_u(b) - hold\_neighbor_u(b)$;
     Send ($release_u(b)$ instances of bottle b , req_{bv});
     $hold_u(b) \leftarrow hold_u(b) - release_u(b)$;
     $in\_hand_u(req_{bv}) \leftarrow$ false $]$ $]$

R4': when $need_u(b) > hold_u(b)$ and $in\_hand_u(req_{bu})$ do
    Send(req_{bu}, $need_u(b)$, s_num_u, u);
    $in\_hand_u(req_{bu}) \leftarrow$ false

R5': upon reception of (req_{bv}, n, s, v) do
    $in\_hand_u(req_{bv}) \leftarrow$ true;
    $max\_rec_u \leftarrow max(max\_rec_u, s)$;
    $need\_neighbor_u(b) \leftarrow n$;
    if $n \leq quantity(b) - need_u(b)$
     or (thirsty and $(s, v) < (s\_num_u, u)$) then
    $[hold\_neighbor_u(b) \leftarrow quantity(b) - hold_u(b)$;
    $release_u(b) \leftarrow need\_neighbor_u(b) - hold\_neighbor_u(b)$;
    Send ($release_u(b)$ instances of bottle b , req_{bv});
    $hold_u(b) \leftarrow hold_u(b) - release_u(b)$;
    $in\_hand_u(req_{bv}) \leftarrow$ false $]$

R6': upon reception of (i instances of bottle b , req_{bu}) do
    $hold_u(b) \leftarrow hold_u(b) + i$;
    $in\_hand_u(req_{bu}) \leftarrow$ true

Table 2. Multiple-Instance Algorithm: Rules for philosopher u

The liveness proof of the above algorithm is similar to the proof given in section 4 for the basic algorithm, since the use of extended session numbers for resolving conflict is identical in both algorithms. The additional component in the extension's proof involves correctness of the calculations performed by a philosopher determining the number of instances to be released (in rules R3' and R5'). This was intuitively justified earlier. The message complexity of the multiple-instance algorithm is identical to that of the basic algorithm. That is, at most two messages are transmitted per drinking from instances of a bottle.

Additional Extension. A second extension, referred to as *the multiple-type extension*, is to associate with each edge in G several types of bottles with multiple instances of each type. A philosopher may need instances from some of the types for a drinking session.

The solution to the multiple-type extension is based on the multiple-instance extension. When philosopher u needs additional instances of certain types of bottles he shares with his neighbor v, he notifies v of the total number of instances he (u) needs for each of these types. Philosopher v will obey a conflict resolution rule similar to the one provided for the multiple-instance extension. He will release all the additional instances needed at u in a single message, either immediately upon receiving u's request or upon drinking completion. In this extension too, the message complexity will remain as in the basic algorithm. A detailed discussion of both extensions appears in [4].

7. DISCUSSION

The drinking philosophers problem and its extensions model various paradigms of multiple mutual exclusion. We showed in this paper that resolving conflicts by using session numbers extended with ids provide simple, elegant and efficient solutions to these problems.

The emphasis in our paper is on simplicity, concurrency and minimization of message complexity. A recent work by Styer and Peterson [10] concentrated on minimization of chains of waiting processes. In their solution, as well as in Lynch's solution [6], collection of several "write locks" by a process may not be done concurrently. In addition, the message complexity of their solution is higher than ours. The tradeoffs between concurrent collection of locks, message complexity and the length of "waiting chains" is an interesting question for further research.

REFERENCES

[1] Chandy, M. and Misra, J., "The drinking philosophers problem," *ACM Trans. Prog. Lang. Syst.*, Vol. 6, 4, Oct. 1984, pp. 632-646.

[2] Chandy, M. and Misra, J., "An example of stepwise refinement of distributed programs: quiescence detection," *ACM Trans. Prog. Lang. Syst.*, Vol. 8, 3, July 1986, pp. 326-343.

[3] Dijkstra, E.W., "Two starvation free solutions to a general exclusion problem," EWD 625.

[4]   Ginat, D., "Decentralized ordering of contending processes in a distributed system," PhD Thesis, Computer Science Dept., Univ. of Maryland, in preparation.

[5]   Lamport, L., "Time, clocks, and the ordering of events in a distributed system," *Commun. ACM*, Vol. 21, 7, July 1978, pp. 558-564.

[6]   Lynch, N.A., "Fast allocation of nearby resources in a distributed system," *Proc. of the 12th ACM Symp. on Theory of Computing*, 1980, pp. 70-81.

[7]   Murphy, S.L. and Shankar, A.U., "A note on the drinking philosophers," *ACM Trans. on Prog. Lang. and Syst.*, Vol. 10, No. 1, pp. 178-188, January 1988.

[8]   Ricart, G., and Agrawala, A.K., "An optimal algorithm for mutual exclusion in computer networks," *Commun. ACM*, Vol. 24, 1, Jan. 1981, pp. 9-17.

[9]   Shankar, A.U., and Lam, S.S., "Time-dependent distributed systems: proving safety, liveness and real-time properties," *Distributed Computing*, Vol. 2, No. 2, Springer-Verlag, 1987.

[10] Styer, E. and Peterson G.L., "Improved algorithms for distributed resource allocation," *Proceedings of The Seventh Annual ACM Symposium on Principles of Distributed Computing*, August 1988, pp. 105-116.

Highly Concurrent Logically Synchronous Multicast

Kenneth J. Goldman*

M.I.T. Laboratory for Computer Science

Cambridge, MA 02139 USA

Abstract

We define the *logically synchronous multicast* problem, which imposes a natural and useful structure on message delivery order in an asynchronous system. In this problem, a computation proceeds by a sequence of *multicasts*, in which a process sends a message to some arbitrary subset of the processes, including itself. A logically synchronous multicast protocol must make it appear to every process as if each multicast occurs simultaneously at all participants of that multicast (sender plus receivers). Furthermore, if a process continually wishes to send a message, it must eventually be permitted to do so.

We present a highly concurrent solution in which each multicast requires at most $4|S|$ messages, where S is the set of participants in that multicast. The protocol's correctness is shown using a remarkably simple problem specification stated in the I/O automaton model. We also show that implementing a wait-free solution to the logically synchronous multicast problem is impossible.

The author is currently developing a simulation system for algorithms expressed as I/O automata. We conclude the paper by describing how the logically synchronous multicast protocol can be used to distribute this simulation system.

1 Introduction

We consider a set of n processes in an asynchronous system whose computation proceeds by a sequence of *multicasts* (or *partial broadcasts*). In each multicast, a process u sends a message m to an arbitrary subset S of the processes (including u). We say that a protocol solves the *logically synchronous multicast* problem if it guarantees the following conditions:

(1) Processes receive all messages in the same relative order. (Suppose messages m and m' are both sent to processes u_1 and u_2. If u_1 receives m before m', then u_2 does also, even if m and m' were sent by different processes.)

(2) If process u sends message m, it receives no messages between sending and receiving m.

(3) If process u continually wishes to send a message, then eventually u will send a message.

We may informally summarize the first two conditions by saying that it appears to all processes as if each multicast occurs simultaneously at all of its participants (sender plus receivers). Hence, the name *logically synchronous multicast*. Note that the hypothesis of the third condition does not require that u continually wish to send the *same* message, but only *some* message. This is a technical point that will be of importance later.

---

*This research was supported in part by the National Science Foundation under Greant CCR-86-11442, by the Office of Naval Research under Contract N00014-85-K-0168, by the Defense Advanced Research Projects Agency (DARPA) under Contract N00014-83-K-0125, and by an Office of Naval Research graduate fellowship.

The problem lends itself to a highly concurrent solution, since any number of multicasts with disjoint S sets should be able to proceed independently. Likewise, one would expect that the communication costs of an algorithm to solve this problem would be independent of n. We present a solution to this problem that takes advantage of the concurrency inherent in the problem and requires at most $4|S|$ messages per multicast. The strong properties of message delivery order imposed by the problem would make a fault-tolerant solution highly attractive for many applications. However, the properties of the message delivery order are strong enough to make a fault-tolerant solution impossible! By a reduction to distributed consensus, we show that there exists no wait-free solution to the logically synchronous multicast problem.

Various other approaches to ordering messages in asynchronous systems have been studied. Lamport [La] uses logical clocks to produce a total ordering on messages. Birman and Joseph [BJ] present several types of fault tolerant protocols. Their ABCAST (atomic broadcast) protocol guarantees that broadcast messages are delivered at all destinations in the same relative order, or not at all. Their CBCAST (causal broadcast) protocol provides a similar, but slightly weaker, ordering guarantee to achieve better performance. The CBCAST guarantees that if a process broadcast sends a message m based on some other message m' it had received earlier, then m will be delivered after m' at all destinations they share.

Like ours, the protocols of both [La] and [BJ] deliver messages to the destination processes according to some global ordering. However, these protocols do not solve the logically synchronous multicast problem because they allow messages to "cross" each other. That is, in their protocols a process u may send a message m and some time later receive a message ordered before m. Our problem requires that when a process u sends a message m, it must have "up to date" information, meaning that it has already received all messages destined for u that are ordered before m. (See Condition (2) above.)

Multiway handshaking protocols have been studied extensively for implementations of CSP [Ho] and ADA [DoD] (for example, see [Ba1] and [Ba2]). These protocols enforce a very strict ordering on system events, and therefore achieve less concurrency (than ours and the others mentioned above). This is necessary because the models of CSP and ADA permit processes to block inputs. Since a decision about whether or not to accept an input may depend (in general) on earlier events, each process can only schedule one event (input or output) at a time. Our problem permits processes to schedule multiple input events at a time.

One interesting feature of our problem is that it lies in between the two general approaches described above. It permits more concurrency than the multiway handshaking protocols, yet imposes a strong, useful structure on the message delivery order. Other related work includes papers by Awerbuch [Aw] and Misra [Mi], which study different problems in the area of simulating synchronous systems on asynchronous ones. In both cases, the computational models being simulated are very different from ours, but it is interesting to note that some of Misra's techniques, particularly those for breaking deadlock, can be applied to our problem.

The remainder of the paper is organized as follows. Section 2 provides a brief introduction to the I/O automaton model. In Section 3, we present the architecture of the problem and a statement of correctness in terms of the model. In Section 4, we formally present the algorithm using the I/O automaton model. In Sections 5 and 6, we sketch a formal correctness proof and present the message and time complexities. We prove in Section 7 that there exists no wait-free solution to the logically synchronous multicast problem.

The author is currently developing a simulation system for algorithms expressed as systems of I/O automata. The logically synchronous multicast problem was motivated by a desire to distribute the simulation system on multiple processors using asynchronous communication. We conclude the paper by describing how the logically synchronous multicast protocol can be used to achieve such a distributed simulation.

2 The Model

The logically synchronous multicast problem statement, protocol, and correctness proof are all formally stated using the I/O Automaton model [LT1, LT2]. We have chosen this model because it encourages precise statements of the problems to be solved by modules in concurrent systems, allows very careful algorithm descriptions, and can be used to construct rigorous correctness proofs. In addition, the model can be used for carrying out complexity analysis and for proving impossibility results. The following introduction to the model is adapted from [LT3], which explains the model in more detail, presents examples, and includes comparisons to other models.

2.1 I/O Automata

I/O automata are best suited for modeling systems in which the components operate asynchronously. Each system component is modeled as an I/O automaton, which is essentially a nondeterministic (possibly infinite state) automaton with an action labeling each transition. An automaton's actions are classified as either 'input', 'output', or 'internal'. An automaton can establish restrictions on when it will perform an output or internal action, but it is unable to block the performance of an input action. An automaton is said to be *closed* if it has no input actions; it models a closed system that does not interact with its environment.

Formally, an *action signature* S is a partition of a set $acts(S)$ of *actions* into three disjoint sets $in(S)$, $out(S)$, and $int(S)$ of *input actions*, *output actions*, and *internal actions*, respectively. We denote by $ext(S) = in(S) \cup out(S)$ the set of *external actions*. We denote by $local(S) = out(S) \cup int(S)$ the set of *locally-controlled actions*. An I/O automaton consists of an action signature $sig(A)$, a set $states(A)$ of *states*, a nonempty set $start(A) \subseteq states(A)$ of *start states*, a transition relation $steps(A) \subseteq states(A) \times acts(A) \times states(A)$ with the property that for every state s' and input action π there is a transition (s', π, s) in $steps(A)$, and an equivalence relation $part(A)$ partitioning the set $local(A)$ into at most a countable number of equivalence classes. The equivalence relation $part(A)$ will be used in the definition of fair computation. We refer to an element (s', π, s) of $steps(A)$ as a *step* of A. If (s', π, s) is a step of A, then π is said to be *enabled* in s'. Since every input action is enabled in every state, automata are said to be *input-enabled*. This means that the automaton is unable to block its input.

An *execution* of A is a finite sequence $s_0, \pi_1, s_1, \pi_2, \ldots, \pi_n, s_n$ or an infinite sequence $s_0, \pi_1, s_1, \pi_2, \ldots$ of alternating states and actions of A such that $(s_i, \pi_{i+1}, s_{i+1})$ is a step of A for every i and $s_0 \in start(A)$. The *schedule* of an execution α is the subsequence of α consisting of the actions appearing in α. The *behavior* of an execution or schedule α of A is the subsequence of α consisting of *external* actions. The same action may occur several times in an execution or a schedule; we refer to a particular occurrence of an action as an *event*.

2.2 Composition

We can construct an automaton modeling a complex system by composing automata modeling the simpler system components. When we compose a collection of automata, we identify an output action π of one automaton with the input action π of each automaton having π as an input action. Consequently, when one automaton having π as an output action performs π, all automata having π as an action perform π simultaneously (automata not having π as an action do nothing).

Since at most one system component controls the performance of any given action, we cannot allow A and B to be composed unless the locally controlled actions of A and B form disjoint sets. Also, we require that each action of a composition must be an action of only finitely many of the composition's components. If A is the composition of a set Q of automata, then $int(\mathcal{A}) =$

$\bigcup_{A' \in Q} int(A')$, $out(A) = \bigcup_{A' \in Q} out(A')$, and $in(A) = \bigcup_{A' \in Q} in(A') - \bigcup_{A' \in Q} out(A')$. Given an execution $\alpha = \vec{s_0} \pi_1 \vec{s_1} \ldots$ of A, let $\alpha | A_i$ be the sequence obtained by deleting $\pi_j \vec{s_j}$ when π_j is not an action of A_i and replacing the remaining $\vec{s_j}$ by $\vec{s_j}[i]$.

2.3 Fairness

We are primarily interested in 'fair' executions, those that permit each of the automaton's primitive components (i.e., its classes) to have infinitely many chances to perform output or internal actions. The definition of automaton composition says that an equivalence class of a component automaton becomes an equivalence class of a composition, and hence that composition retains the *essential* structure of the system's primitive components. In the model, therefore, being fair to each component means being fair to each equivalence class of locally-controlled actions. A *fair execution* of an automaton A is defined to be an execution α of A such that the following conditions hold for each class C of $part(A)$:

1. If α is finite, then no action of C is enabled in the final state of α.

2. If α is infinite, then either α contains infinitely many events from C, or α contains infinitely many occurrences of states in which no action of C is enabled.

We say that β is a *fair behavior* of A if β is the behavior of a fair execution of A, and we denote the set of fair behaviors of A by $fairbehs(A)$.

2.4 Problem Specification

A 'problem' to be solved by an I/O automaton is formalized essentially as an arbitrary set of (finite and infinite) sequences of external actions. An automaton is said to *solve* a problem P provided that its set of fair behaviors is a subset of P. Although the model does not allow an automaton to block its environment or eliminate undesirable inputs, we can formulate our problems (i.e., correctness conditions) to require that an automaton exhibits some behavior only when the environment observes certain restrictions on the production of inputs.

We want a problem specification to be an interface together with a set of behaviors. We therefore define a *schedule module* H to consist of two components, an action signature $sig(H)$, and a set $scheds(H)$ of *schedules*. Each schedule in $scheds(H)$ is a finite or infinite sequence of actions of H. Subject to the same restrictions as automata, schedule modules may be composed to form other schedule modules. The resulting signature is defined as for automata, and the schedules $scheds(H)$ is the set of sequences β of actions of H such that for every module H' in the composition, $\beta | H'$ is a schedule of H'.

It is often the case that an automaton behaves correctly only in the context of certain restrictions on its input. A useful notion for discussing such restrictions is that of a module 'preserving' a property of behaviors. A module *preserves* a property $\mathcal{P}$ iff the module is not the first to violate $\mathcal{P}$: as long as the environment only provides inputs such that the cumulative behavior satisfies $\mathcal{P}$, the module will only perform outputs such that the cumulative behavior satisfies $\mathcal{P}$. One can prove that a composition preserves a property by showing that each of the component automata preserves the property.

3 The Problem

In this section, we describe the architecture of the problem and then present a schedule module defining correctness for a multicast protocol.

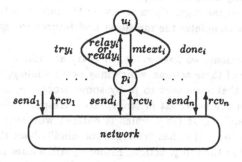

Figure 1: System Architecture. Arguments of actions are omitted.

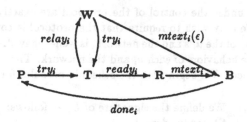

Figure 2: Region Changes for p_i. In region P, a $relay_i$ action does not cause a region change, and can be thought of as a self-loop.

3.1 The Architecture

Let $\mathcal{I} = \{1, \ldots, n\}$. Let $\mathcal{S}$ denote a universal set of text strings, and let $\mathcal{M}$ denote a universal set of messages, where both sets contain the empty sequence (ϵ). Let $u_i, i \in \mathcal{I}$, denote the n user processes engaged in the computation, and let $p_i, i \in \mathcal{I}$, denote n additional processes. Together, the p_i's are to solve the multicast problem, and each p_i is said to "work for" u_i. Each of the u_i's and p_i's is modelled as an automaton.

Each user u_i directly communicates by shared actions with the process p_i only. (One may think of u_i and p_i as running on the same processor.) The p_i's communicate with each other asynchronously via a network, also modelled as an automaton, that guarantees eventual one-time delivery of each message sent. Furthermore, we assume that all messages sent between each pair of processes are delivered in FIFO order. The boundary between u_i and p_i is defined by several actions. To summarize the relationship between u_i and p_i at each point in an execution, we say that p_i is in a certain *region*, according to which of these actions have occurred. We will formalize this later. Figure 1 illustrates the actions shared by u_i and p_i, and by p_i and the network. Figure 2 illustrates possible region changes for p_i, and the actions that cause them.

Initially, p_i is in its "passive" region (P). We say that p_i enters its "trying" region (T) when user u_i issues a $try_i(S \subseteq \mathcal{I})$[1] action, indicating that u_i would like to send a multicast message to processes named in the set S. When it is ready to perform a multicast on behalf of u_i, process p_i issues a $ready_i$ action and is said to enter its "ready" region (R). After receiving the $ready_i$

---

[1] That is, $try_i(S)$, where $S \subseteq \mathcal{I}$.

action as input, user u_i may issue a $mtext_i(m \in \mathcal{S})$ action, where the argument indicates the desired text of the multicast message. Upon receiving the $mtext_i$ action, p_i is said to enter its "bye" region (B), where it completes the multicast and returns to region P by issuing a $done_i$ action.

In addition to these actions, we have $relay_i(m \in \mathcal{S})$ actions, which are outputs of p_i and inputs to u_i. The purpose of these actions, which may occur while p_i is in P or T, is to forward multicast messages to u_i that were sent to p_i by some process p_j on behalf of user u_j. The argument m is the text of the multicast message. To correspond with this additional type of action, we have a "waiting" region (W), which is entered whenever p_i issues a $relay_i$ action while in T. In W, p_i waits to see if u_i has "changed its mind" about the multicast after hearing the information contained in the $relay_i$ action. Either u_i still wishes to perform some multicast and issues a $try_i(S')$ action, or u_i decides not to do a multicast after all and issues an $mtext_i(\epsilon)$ action.

3.2 Correctness

Note that the actions under the control of the protocol are exactly those actions that are the outputs of the p_i's. We only wish to require that the protocol is correct when its environment, namely the composition of the u_i's and the network, is well-behaved. We define schedule modules to specify the allowable behaviors of each u_i and the network. Then we define a schedule module for the multicast protocol. We begin with the schedule modules for the u_i's.

Schedule Module U_i: We define the signature of U_i as follows:
$$in(U_i) = \{relay_i(m \in \mathcal{S}), ready_i, done_i\}$$
$$out(U_i) = \{try_i(S \subseteq \mathcal{I}), mtext(m \in \mathcal{S})\}$$

Before defining the set of schedules of U_i, we define a "region sequence" to capture the series of region changes in a schedule, and then state a *well-formedness* condition which makes use of this definition. Let the alphabet $\Sigma = \{P, T, R, B, W\}$. If L is a language, we let *prefixes*(L) denote the set of all prefixes of strings in L. Let α be an arbitrary sequence of actions. We define the *region of i after* α, denoted $r(i, \alpha)$, to be an element of Σ defined recursively as follows. If $\alpha|U_i$ is empty (ϵ), then $r(i, \alpha) = P$. If $\alpha = \alpha'\pi$, then

$$r(i, \alpha) = \begin{cases} r(i, \alpha') & \text{if } \pi \notin U_i, \\ T & \text{if } \pi = try_i, \\ R & \text{if } \pi = ready_i, \\ B & \text{if } \pi = mtext_i, \\ W & \text{if } \pi = relay_i \wedge r(i, \alpha') \neq P, \\ P & \text{otherwise.} \end{cases}$$

Given an arbitrary action sequence α and an index $i \in \mathcal{I}$, let the *region sequence for i in* α, denoted *region-sequence*(i, α), be the string of characters over Σ constructed as follows. Let intermediate string σ be the concatenation of $r(i, \alpha')$ for each prefix of α in order, starting with $r(i, \epsilon)$ and ending with $r(i, \alpha)$. Then, to obtain *region-sequence*(i, α), remove from σ each character that is identical to its predecessor. Let α be an arbitrary sequence of actions. We say that α is *well-formed for i* iff

1. If $\alpha = \alpha'\pi$ with $\pi = mtext_i(m \neq \epsilon)$, then $r(i, \alpha') = R$, and

2. *region-sequence*$(i, \alpha) \in$ prefixes(L), where the language L over Σ is defined by the regular expression $P((TW)^*TRBP + (TW)^+BP)^*$.

The language L reflects the fact that u_i is allowed to "change its mind" about sending a multicast message whenever it is relayed a message. We can now define the set of schedules for U_i.

Let α be a sequence of actions in sig(U_i). Then $\alpha \in$ scheds(U_i) iff:

1. U_i preserves well-formedness for i in α, and

2. region-sequence(i, α) does not end in W or R.

The first condition will be used in the safety proof, and the second in the liveness proof.

Schedule Module N: We now define a schedule module specifying the allowable behaviors of the network. The signature is as follows:
$$\text{in}(N) = \{send(m \in \mathcal{M}, i, j \in \mathcal{I})\}$$
$$\text{out}(N) = \{rcv(m \in \mathcal{M}, i, j \in \mathcal{I})\}$$

Network well-formedness: Let α be an arbitrary sequence of actions. Then α is said to be *network well-formed* iff

1. For each $send(m, i, j)$ event in α, there exists at most one later $rcv(m, i, j)$ event in α. (We call this event the *rcv corresponding to* $send(m, i, j)$.)

2. For each $rcv(m, i, j)$ event in α, there exists an earlier $send(m, i, j)$ event in α (called the *corresponding send*).

3. If event $rcv(m, i, j)$ occurs in α before event $rcv(m', i, j)$, then their corresponding events $send(m, i, j)$ and $send(m', i, j)$ occur in the same order.

These conditions say that each message is delivered at most once, no spurious messages are delivered, and that messages between any pair of processes are delivered in the order sent. Given the network well-formedness definition, we can define the set of schedules of N. Let α be an sequence of actions of N. Then $\alpha \in$ scheds(N) iff

1. α is network well-formed, and

2. for each $send(m, i, j)$ event in α, there exists a $rcv(m, i, j)$ event later in α.

The second condition states that every message sent is eventually delivered.

Schedule Module M: We can now rephrase the correctness conditions informally stated in Section 1 in terms of the actions at the boundaries of the user processes. We do this with a schedule module M, which defines the multicast problem. Let sig(U) = $\cup_{i \in \mathcal{I}}$ sig(U_i).[2] We define the signature of M as follows:
$$\text{in}(M) = \text{out}(U) \cup \text{out}(N)$$
$$\text{out}(M) = \text{in}(U) \cup \text{in}(N)$$

Let α be a sequence of actions of sig(M). Then $\alpha \in$ scheds(M) iff:

1. $\forall i \in \mathcal{I}$, M preserves well-formedness for i in α.

2. If α is well-formed for every $i \in \mathcal{I}$ and α is network well-formed, then $\forall j \in \mathcal{I}$ and $\forall m, m' \in \mathcal{S}$,

---

[2]That is, component-wise union: $in(U) = \cup_{i \in \mathcal{I}} in(U_i)$, etc.

(a) If $relay_i(m)$, $relay_i(m')$, $relay_j(m)$, and $relay_j(m')$ occur in α, and if $relay_i(m)$ precedes $relay_i(m')$, then $relay_j(m)$ precedes $relay_j(m')$.

(b) If $mtext_i(m \neq \epsilon)$ occurs in α, then no $relay_i(m' \neq m)$ occurs between $mtext_i(m)$ and $relay_i(m)$.

3. If $\alpha|N \in$ scheds(N) and $\forall i \in \mathcal{I}$, $\alpha|U_i \in$ scheds(U_i), then the following hold:

(a) If a try_i occurs in α and each $relay_i$ thereafter is immediately followed by a try_i in $\alpha|U_i$, then a $ready_i$ occurs later in α.

(b) If an $mtext_i(m \neq \epsilon)$ occurs in α and $try_i(S)$ is the last preceding try_i action in α, then a $relay_j(m)$ occurs later in α for each $j \in S$.

Items (1) and (2) are the required *safety* properties, and item (3) is the required *liveness* property. A multicast protocol is *correct* iff it solves M.

4   The Algorithm

This section presents the multicast protocol. We present the algorithm by giving an explicit I/O automaton for each p_i, $i \in \mathcal{I}$. We show in Section 5 that the composition of the p_i's solves the schedule module M and is therefore a correct protocol.

The algorithm is based on logical time. We define a *logical time* to be an (integer, process-id) pair drawn from $\mathcal{T} = (\{1, 2, \ldots\} \cup \infty) \times \mathcal{I}$, and we let logical times be ordered lexicographically. Essentially, each process p_i maintains a logical time clock, and each multicast is assigned a unique logical time. The process p_i relays all multicast messages destined for u_i in logical time order.[3]

4.1   An Informal Overview

We begin with a discussion of the main ideas of the algorithm, which is followed by the formal automaton definition. Unless otherwise noted, the word "process" will refer to one of the processes p_i, $i \in \mathcal{I}$. Also, we use the words "time" and "logical time" interchangeably.

On receiving a $try_i(S)$ input, p_i remembers S as its *try-set*. In region T, p_i tries to set up a multicast for u_i to processes named in *try-set*, and it may request permission to do so from processes $p_j, j \in \mathcal{I}$ by sending "req-promise" messages. Permission is granted from a process p_j to p_i in the form of a "promise" message with an associated logical time t. The promise means that p_j will not perform any multicasts with a time greater than t until p_i either explicitly relinquishes the promise (by sending a "bye" message to p_j) or advances the promise (by sending an "adv-promise" message with the later time). One may think of this promise as a roadblock that p_i erects in u_j's computation at some future logical time. The process p_j doesn't allow u_j's computation to advance past that time until the roadblock is removed or moved forward by p_i. Processes are guaranteed of eventually getting a promise in response to every request.

Every multicast performed by p_i has an associated logical time (its *btime*), which is assigned by p_i to be at least as large as both p_i's *clock* and the maximum logical time among all promises held by p_i. Processes communicate their multicasts in "bye" messages, which have two arguments: the text of the multicast and its assigned logical time. (Upon receipt of a "bye" message, a process p_j keeps the (text, time) pair in a *pending* set until the message is relayed to u_j. It is safe to relay a message m when it is the message with the smallest time t in *pending* and

---

[3]We never assign a time of ∞ to a multicast message; it is used only as an upper bound.

all promises granted by p_j with times lower than t have either been relinquished or advanced past t.) After receiving a promise from each process p_j to whom a request was made, p_i is ready perform a multicast with $btime = t$ provided that (1) its *pending* set is empty, and (2) all promises p_i has granted with times lower than t have either been relinquished or advanced past t. The second condition is present to ensure that u_i receives no new messages with logical times less than t after p_i decides to send its multicast.

Finally, we explain those conditions under which p_i may advance promises. Suppose that p_i has received promises from all processes in its *try-set*, but has determined that it is not yet ready to perform a multicast to relinquish those promises. In order to not unnecessarily block the computation of those processes from which p_i has received promises, it may send "adv-promise" messages to those processes, informing them of the earliest possible time that p_i might actually use as its *btime*. Without these messages, it would be possible for the computation to deadlock.[4]

4.2 The Detailed Algorithm

We now present the formal algorithm description. The state of p_i has several components: A variable *region* $\in$ {P,T,W,R,B} is initially set to P. The variables *try-set*, *requested*, and *requests* are subsets of $\mathcal{I}$, initially empty. The variable *text* $\in \mathcal{S}$ is initially the empty string (ϵ). Two arrays of logical times indexed by $\mathcal{I}$ are kept: *promises-to* and *permission-from*. All entries of these arrays are initially greater than any possible logical time (∞, n). Two additional logical time variables, *clock* and *btime*, are initially $(0, i)$. Finally, the variable *pending* is an initially empty set of (text $\in \mathcal{S}$, time $\in \mathcal{T}$) pairs.

We let min(*promises-to*) denote the smallest time among the entries in that array. Similarly, we let max(*permission-from*) denote the largest time less than (∞, n) among the entries in that array; if all entries in that array are (∞, n), then max(*permission-from*) $= (\infty, n)$. Finally, we let min(*pending*) and max(*pending*) denote the pairs in the set having the least and greatest logical times, respectively; if *pending* is empty, then both values are $(\epsilon, (0, i))$.

In addition to the above variables, the algorithm description refers to a pseudo-variable, *try-time*, defined according to p_i's state components as follows: *try-time* is the smallest logical time having process-id i such that *try-time* $\geq$ max(*clock*, *btime*, max(*permission-from*)).

Automaton p_i has the following signature.

Input actions:		Output actions:	
	$try_i(S \subseteq \mathcal{I})$		$relay_i(m \in \mathcal{S})$
	$mtext_i(m \in \mathcal{S})$		$ready_i$
	$rcv(m \in \mathcal{M}, j \in \mathcal{I}, i)$		$done_i$
			$send(m \in \mathcal{M}, i, j \in \mathcal{I})$

The transition relation for p_i is shown in Figure 3. "P" and "E" denote precondition and effect, respectively. An action is enabled in exactly those states in which the precondition is satisfied. If an action has no precondition, it is always enabled. When an action occurs, p_i's state is modified according to the assignments in the effects clause. If a state component is not mentioned in the effect clause, it is left unchanged by the action.

The actions $relay_i$, $ready_i$, and $done_i$ are together in one equivalence class of $part(p_i)$. For each $j \in \mathcal{I}$, there exist four classes containing the sets of actions $send(\text{promise}(t \in \mathcal{T}), i, j)$, $send(\text{req-promise}, i, j)$, $send(\text{adv-promise}(t \in \mathcal{T}), i, j)$, and $send(\text{bye}(m \in \mathcal{S}, t \in \mathcal{T}), i, j)$.

---

[4] Consider a situation in which p_i and p_j are trying to send multicasts such that each is in the other's *try-set*. Suppose that all promises received by p_i are smaller than some promise received by p_j. If p_i has granted p_j a promise smaller than p_i's own *try-time*, neither can perform a multicast before the other.

Input Actions:

- $try_i(S)$
  E: $try\text{-}set = S \cup \{i\}$
        $region = \text{T}$

- $mtext_i(m)$
  E: $text = m$
        if $m = \epsilon$ then $try\text{-}set = \emptyset$
        $btime = try\text{-}time$
        $region = \text{B}$

- $rcv(\text{req-promise}, j \in \mathcal{I}, i)$
  E: $requests = requests \cup \{j\}$

- $rcv(\text{bye}(m \in \mathcal{S}, t \in \mathcal{T}), j \in \mathcal{I}, i)$
  E: $promises\text{-}to[j] = (\infty, n)$
        if $m \neq \epsilon$ then
            $pending = pending \cup \{(m, t)\}$

- $rcv(\text{adv-promise}(t \in \mathcal{T}), j \in \mathcal{I}, i)$
  E: $promises\text{-}to[j] = t$

- $rcv(\text{promise}(t \in \mathcal{T}), j \in \mathcal{I}, i)$
  E: $permission\text{-}from[j] = t$

Output Actions:

- $relay_i(m)$
  P: $region \in \{\text{P,T}\}$
        $(m, t) = \min(pending)$
        $t < \min(promises\text{-}to)$
  E: $pending = pending \setminus \{(m, t)\}$
        $clock = t$
        if $region = \text{T}$ then $region = \text{W}$

- $ready_i$
  P: $region = \text{T}$
        $pending = \emptyset$
        $\min(promises\text{-}to) \geq try\text{-}time$
        $\forall j \in requested,$
            $permission\text{-}from[j] < (\infty, n)$
  E: $region = \text{R}$

- $done_i$
  P: $region = \text{B}$
        $requested = \emptyset$
  E: $region = \text{P}$

- $send(\text{promise}(t \in \mathcal{T}), i, j \in \mathcal{I})$
  P: $j \in requests$
        $t > \max(try\text{-}time, \max(pending).time)$
  E: $requests = requests \setminus \{j\}$
        $promises\text{-}to[j] = t$

- $send(\text{req-promise}, i, j \in \mathcal{I})$
  P: $region \in \{\text{T,W}\}$
        $j \notin requested$
  E: $requested = requested \cup \{j\}$

- $send(\text{adv-promise}(t \in \mathcal{T}), i, j \in \mathcal{I})$
  P: $region \in \{\text{T,W}\}$
        $\forall k \in try\text{-}set,$
            $permission\text{-}from[k] < (\infty, n)$
        $permission\text{-}from[j] < try\text{-}time$
        $t = try\text{-}time$
  E: $permission\text{-}from[j] = try\text{-}time$

- $send(\text{bye}(m \in \mathcal{S}, t \in \mathcal{T}), i, j \in \mathcal{I})$
  P: $region = \text{B}$
        $permission\text{-}from[j] < (\infty, n)$
        $t = btime$
        if $(j \in try\text{-}set)$ then
            $m = text$
        else $m = \epsilon$
  E: $requested = requested \setminus \{j\}$
        $permission\text{-}from[j] = (\infty, n).$

Figure 3: Transition relation for p_i.

5 Proof of Correctness

Consider module P, the composition of all automata $p_i, i \in \mathcal{I}$. In this section, we show that module P solves schedule module M, which implies the correctness of the logically synchronous multicast protocol. The correctness proof follows the definition of schedule module M. Clearly, $\text{sig}(P) = \text{sig}(M)$. To show that P solves M, we need to show that all fair behaviors of P satisfy the safety conditions (1 and 2) and the liveness condition (3). To distinguish the state components of the different automata in P, we use subscripts. For example, $region_i$ is the $region$ variable in the local state of automaton p_i.

We only sketch the main ideas of the proof; the details may be found in [G].

5.1 Safety Proof

Condition (1), that P preserves well-formedness for all $i \in \mathcal{I}$, follows easily from the definition of language L and the preconditions on the actions of P:

Theorem 1: Module P preserves well-formedness for i, for all $i \in \mathcal{I}$.

Given this theorem, we need only consider executions in which well-formedness is preserved for all i. Let α be an execution of P. We say that α is *admissible* iff α is well-formed for every $i \in \mathcal{I}$ and α is network well-formed.

Next, we show that module P satisfies Condition (2a), that all multicast messages are delivered in the same relative order, and Condition (2b), that no message is relayed to u_i between an $mtext_i(m)$ event and its $relay_i(m)$ event. The following two lemmas are key to this part of the proof. Lemma 2 is usually applied to show the existence or nonexistence of certain events in a portion of an execution. Lemma 3 gives important invariants on the state of P.

Lemma 2: Let α be an admissible execution of P. Let α' be a subexecution of P between two successive $done_i$ actions (or between the beginning of α and the first $done_i$ action). Then if α' contains *any one* of the following five actions, then it contains *exactly one* of each of them such that they occur in the following order: $send(\text{req-promise},i,j)$, $rcv(\text{req-promise},i,j)$, $send(\text{promise}(t),j,i)$, $rcv(\text{promise}(t),j,i)$, and $send(\text{bye}(m,t''),i,j)$. Furthermore, if a $send(\text{adv-promise}(t'),i,j)$ occurs in α', then it occurs between the last two actions.

Lemma 3: Let α be an admissible execution of P. Then for all $i,j \in \mathcal{I}$, the following properties hold for all states s in α.

1. $i \in s.requests_j \Rightarrow s.promises\text{-}to_j[i] = (\infty, n)$
2. $s.promises\text{-}to_j[i] \leq s.permission\text{-}from_i[j]$
3. $s.clock_j < s.promises\text{-}to_j[i]$
4. $(s.region_i = \text{B} \wedge j \in s.try\text{-}set_i \cap s.requested_i) \Rightarrow s.permission\text{-}from_i[j] \leq s.btime_i$
5. $s.pending_j \neq \emptyset \Rightarrow s.clock_j < \min(s.pending_j).\text{time}$

The fifth invariant, which states that the minimum time in the pending set of a process p_i is always larger than the clock of that process, is a key piece of the safety proof. Informally, it tells us that no multicast message arrives "too late". Both of the above lemmas are proved by straightforward inductive arguments.

Given some simple lemmas (omitted here), showing that the state components *clock* and *btime* are nondecreasing, and that each multicast message is assigned a unique logical time, we can use the lemmas stated above to prove two theorems that correspond to Conditions (2a) and (2b). The fifth invariant of Lemma 3 is important in the proof of Theorem 4, while the second and fourth invariants are used to prove Theorem 5.

Theorem 4: Let α be an admissible execution of P. Then $\forall j \in \mathcal{I}$ and $\forall m, m' \in \mathcal{S}$, if $relay_i(m)$, $relay_i(m')$, $relay_j(m)$, and $relay_j(m')$ occur in α, and if $relay_i(m)$ precedes $relay_i(m')$, then $relay_j(m)$ precedes $relay_j(m')$.

Theorem 5: Let α be an admissible execution of P. Then $\forall j \in \mathcal{I}$ and $\forall m, m' \in \mathcal{S}$, if $mtext_i(m)$ occurs in α, then no $relay_i(m')$ occurs between $mtext_i(m)$ and $relay_i(m)$.

5.2   Liveness Proof

Let α be an fair execution of P. We say that α is *well-behaved* iff $\alpha|U_i \in \text{scheds}(U_i)$ for all $i \in \mathcal{I}$ and $\alpha|N \in \text{scheds}(N)$. The proof rests on two main lemmas, which are proved inductively. Informally, the first lemma states that if a promise is requested, then eventually it is granted. The second essentially states that, given certain simple conditions, processes cannot get stuck in their trying regions.

Lemma 6: Let α be a well-behaved execution of P. If event $\pi = send(\text{req-promise},i,j)$ occurs in α then a later $rcv(\text{promise}(t),j,i)$ occurs in α.

Lemma 7: Let α be a well-behaved execution of P, let s be some state in that execution, and fix $\mathcal{J} \subseteq \mathcal{I}$ such that $j \in \mathcal{J}$ iff $s.region_j \in \{T,W\}$ and for all states s' after s, $try\text{-}time_j$ does not increase beyond some time t. Then eventually an $mtext_j$ occurs after s for all $j \in \mathcal{J}$.

The following theorems correspond to Conditions (3a) and (3b), completing the liveness proof. In proof of Theorem 8, we assume that the $ready_j$ action does not occur and use Lemmas 6 and 7 to derive a contradiction. Theorem 9 follows easily from Theorem 8 and the simple liveness conditions placed on the u_i's.

Theorem 8: Let α be a well-behaved execution of P. If a try_i occurs in α and each $relay_i$ thereafter is followed immediately by a try_i in $\alpha|U_i$, then a $ready_j$ occurs later in α.

Theorem 9: Let α be an execution of P, where $\alpha|U_i \in \text{scheds}(U_i)$ for all $i \in \mathcal{I}$ and $\alpha|N \in \text{scheds}(N)$. If a $mtext_i(m \neq \epsilon)$ occurs in α and $try_i(S)$ is the last preceding try_i action in α, then a $relay_j(m)$ occurs later in α for each $j \in S$.

We conclude the correctness proof with the following theorem.

Theorem 10: Module P solves schedule module M.
   Proof: Immediate from Theorems 1, 4, 5, 8, and 9 and the definition of M.   ∎

6   Complexity Analysis

In this section, we present the message and time complexities of the multicast protocol. Let system A be the composition of modules $U_i, i \in \mathcal{I}$, module N, and modules $p_i, i \in \mathcal{I}$. Let α be an execution of system A. We say that α is an *undeviating execution for i* iff every pair of actions $try_i(S)$ and $try(S')$ either have a $done_i$ between them or $S = S'$. That is, in an undeviating execution for i, u_i does not "change its mind" about whether to issue a multicast message or which users to whom the the multicast should be sent.

If α is an execution of system A that is undeviating for all $i \in \mathcal{I}$, then for each $try_i(S)$ in α, the corresponding multicast requires at most $4|S|$ messages and a worst-case (real) time delay of at most $4nd + 2d$, where d is an upper bound on the (real) time between a *send* and the corresponding *rcv*. The proofs of the above facts are contained in [G], which also includes a worst-case analysis for executions that do not have the undeviating property and a discussion of possible optimizations of the protocol.

Note that the worst-case time complexity matches one's expectations about what must happen when all n processes attempt to send multicast messages to every process. A simple inductive argument shows that any pessimistic protocol requires an $O(dn)$ delay in this worst-case scenario: Since all processes send to all other processes, the conditions of the problem require that the protocol enforce a total order on the multicasts. Thus, the process u whose message is the kth message in the total order must wait at least $d(k-1)$ time before sending its message, or else it could not have received all $k - 1$ messages ordered before it. (This, of course, assumes that all messages take the maximum time d to arrive.)

7   Impossibility Result

Recall that our correctness proof depended upon certain liveness assumptions about the user processes. Namely, the user processes are not allowed to stop at certain points in their executions. It turns out that that these assumptions are, in fact, necessary in order to solve the logically synchronous multicast problem. In this section, we show that it is not possible to implement a solution to the logically synchronous multicast problem that tolerates even a single stopping fault of a user process. That is, we prove that there exists no wait-free implementation of a logically synchronous multicast protocol. The proof proceeds by a reduction, using techniques developed by Herlihy [He]. We first demonstrate that logically synchronous multicast can be used to solve distributed consensus. We then appeal to the known result that distributed consensus cannot be solved in a wait-free manner [FLP].

The consensus problem is defined as follows. Consider n user processes $u_1, \ldots, u_n$, where each u_i has an initial value $v_i \in \{0,1\}$ and output actions $decide(0)$ and $decide(1)$ to announce its decision. A consensus protocol is correct iff it satisfies the following properties.

1. Agreement: If any user outputs $decide(v)$, then that is the only decision value of any process.

2. Validity: If all processes start with v, then v is the only possible decision value.

3. Termination: All processes eventually output some decision.

We say that an implementation is *wait-free* if a process can complete an operation within finite time, regardless of the execution speeds of the other processes. Equivalently, an implementation is *wait-free* if a process can eventually complete an operation even if some number of the other processes halt at arbitrary times. For consensus, completing an operation means beginning the protocol and at some time later outputting a decision. For logically synchronous multicast, completing an operation means issuing a try_i output from region P and later receiving a $done_i$.

Lemma 11: If there exists a wait-free implementation of logically synchronous multicast, then there exists a wait-free implementation of distributed consensus.

Proof: Consider the following algorithm for reaching consensus among the n user processes $u_1, \ldots, u_n$ in system A, where each u_i has an initial value v_i in $\{0,1\}$. First, each process u_i

issues $try_i(\mathcal{I})$. Upon receiving a $ready_i$, process u_i issues $mtext_i(v_i)$. Upon receiving its first $relay_i(v)$, process u_i uses v as its decision value. (After receiving a $relay_i$, if u_i is in region W, it issues a $mtext_i(\epsilon)$.)

Agreement: Since all multicast messages are delivered in the same relative order to all user processes, they all decide on the same value. Validity: If all users start with 0, then the decision will be 0, since that is the only value sent in a multicast by any user. Similarly if all users start with 1, then the decision will be 1. Termination: By the liveness condition, some process p_i will eventually issue a $ready_i$, and eventually all processes u_i will receive a $relay_i(v)$ for some v. ∎

Theorem 12: There exists no wait-free implementation of logically synchronous multicast.

Proof: Suppose there were. Then by Lemma 11 there exists a wait-free implementation of distributed consensus. But it is known that there exists no wait-free implementation of distributed consensus [FLP]. ∎

8 Conclusion

We have defined the logically synchronous multicast problem and presented a highly concurrent solution. To conclude the paper, we illustrate an application of this protocol in the area of distributed simulation. Namely, we consider distributed simulation of I/O automata.

The I/O automaton model has proven useful for describing algorithms and proving their correctness (for examples, see [Bl, FLS, GL, LG, LM, LMF, LMWF, LT1, LW, WLL]). Therefore, we believe that a simulation system based on that model would be a useful tool to aid in the study and understanding of complicated algorithms. *Distributing* the simulation, besides being an interesting exercise in itself, can also reduce the simulation time.

Recall from the definition of the I/O automaton model that input actions of automata are always enabled, and that an action shared by a set S of automata is the output of only one automaton and occurs simultaneously at all automata in S. In general, the actions enabled in a given state of an automaton may depend upon all previous actions occurring at that automaton. Furthermore, the fairness condition requires that given an automaton $\mathcal{A}$ and an execution α of $\mathcal{A}$, if some class $C \in \text{part}(\mathcal{A})$ has an action enabled in a state s of α, then either no action in C is enabled in some state s' occurring in α after s', or an action from C occurs in α after state s.

We wish to construct a distributed system for simulating fair executions of a given automaton $\mathcal{A}$, where $\mathcal{A}$ has some finite number of components $\mathcal{A}_1, \mathcal{A}_2, \ldots, \mathcal{A}_n$. To simplify the discussion, we shall assume that each component $\mathcal{A}_i$ has exactly one class in its partition. (The generalization allowing each component to have a finite number of classes is straightforward.)

We simply "plug in" a particular transition relation for each u_i in system A such that all of its schedules are in $scheds(U_i)$: We assign process u_i to simulate component $\mathcal{A}_i$. When $\mathcal{A}_i$ has an action π enabled, u_i may issue a $try_i(S)$ action, where S is the set of automata having π as an action.[5] Then, upon receiving a $ready_i$ input, u_i issues an $mtext(\pi)$, where π is the action associated with the previous try_i. Furthermore, u_i can issue a $mtext(\epsilon)$ only if no actions are enabled in $\mathcal{A}_i$. The $relay_i(\pi')$ input actions are used to drive the simulation of $\mathcal{A}_i$. When a $relay_i(\pi')$ action occurs, process u_i updates its state based on action π' occurring in $\mathcal{A}_i$.

Given the schedule module M defined earlier, one can verify that the this distributed simulation satisfies the definitions of the model as described above. As far as each of the components of the simulation can tell, each action π occurring in the simulation happens simultaneously at every component having π in its signature. It is interesting to see how this construction and the liveness condition of the multicast problem work together to satisfy the fairness condition of the I/O automaton model.

---

[5] In a real implementation, one might have the system determine S based on π.

Although the problem described in this paper has an application to the simulation system just described, we have presented it here as a general problem in a modular framework. The problem statement, the algorithm and its correctness proof, and the impossibility result are therefore general results, independent of any particular system or application.

Acknowledgements

I would like to thank Hagit Attiya and Jennifer Welch for suggesting the impossibility result, and Nancy Lynch and Mark Tuttle for their helpful comments on earlier drafts.

References

[Aw]   Awerbuch, B. Complexity of Network Synchronization. JACM 32(4), October, 1985, pp. 804-823.

[Ba1] Bagrodia, R. A distributed algorithm to implement the generalized alternative command of CSP. *The 6th International Conference on Distributed Computing Systems*, May 1986, pp. 422-427.

[Ba2] Bagrodia, R. A distributed algorithm to implement N-party rendezvous. *The 7th Conference on Foundations of Software Technology and Computer Science*, Pune, India, December 1987. Lecture Notes in Computer Science 287, Springer Verlag, 1987.

[BJ]   Birman, K.P., and Joseph, T.A. Reliable Communication in the Presence of Failures. *ACM Transactions on Computer Systems*, 5(1):47–76, 1987.

[Bl]   Bloom, B. Constructing Two-Writer Atomic Registers. *6th ACM SIGACT-SIGOPS Symposium on Principles of Distributed Computing*, Vancouver, British Columbia, Canada, August, 1987, pp. 249-259. Also, to appear in Special Issue of IEEE Transactions on Computing, on Parallel and Distributed Algorithms.

[DoD] Department of Defense, Ada Programming Language, ANSI/MIL-STD-1815A-1983.

[FLS] Fekete, A., Lynch, N., and Shrira, L. A Modular Proof of Correctness for a Network Synchronizer. *2nd International Workshop on Distributed Algorithms*, Amsterdam, The Netherlands, July,1987.

[FLP] Fischer, M., Lynch, N., and Paterson, M. Impossibility of distributed consensus with one family faulty process. *Journal of the ACM*, 32(2):374–382, 1985.

[G]   Goldman, K.J., Highly Concurrent Logically Synchronous Multicast. M.I.T. Laboratory for Computer Science Technical Memo MIT/LCS/TM-401, July 1989.

[GL]   Goldman, K.J., and Lynch, N.A. Quorum Consensus in Nested Transaction Systems. *6th ACM SIGACT-SIGOPS Symposium on Principles of Distributed Computing*,Vancouver, British Columbia, Canada, August, 1987.

[He]   Herlihy, M. Impossibility and Universality Results for Wait-Free Synchronization. In *Proceedings of 7th ACM SIGACT-SIGOPS Symposium on Principles of Distributed Computing*. Toronto, Ontario, Canada, August, 1988, pp. 276-290.

[Ho]   Hoare, C. A. R. Communicating Sequential Processes. Prentice-Hall, 1985.

[La] Lamport, L. Time, clocks, and the ordering of events in a distributed system. *Communications of the ACM*, 27(7):558–565, 1978.

[LG] Lynch, N.A., and Goldman, K.J. Distributed Algorithms. MIT Research Seminar Series MIT/LCS/RSS-5, May 1989.

[LM] Lynch, N.A., and Merritt, M. Introduction to the Theory of Nested Transactions. *ICDT'86 International Conference on Database Theory.* Rome, Italy, September, 1986, pp. 278-305. Also, MIT/LCS/TR-367 July 1986. A revised version will appear in *Theoretical Computer Science.*

[LMF] Lynch, N., Mansour, Y., and Fekete, A. Data Link Layer: Two Impossibility Results. In *Proceedings of 7th ACM SIGACT-SIGOPS Symposium on Principles of Distributed Computing.* Toronto, Ontario, Canada, August, 1988, pp. 149-170.

[LMWF] Lynch, N., Merritt, M., Weihl, W., and Fekete, A. Atomic Transactions. In progress.

[LT1] Lynch, N.A., and Tuttle, M.R. Hierarchical Correctness Proofs for Distributed Algorithms. Master's Thesis, Massachusetts Institute of Technology, April, 1987. MIT/LCS/TR-387, April, 1987.

[LT2] Lynch, N.A., and Tuttle, M.R. Hierarchical Correctness Proofs for Distributed Algorithms. In *Proceedings of 6th ACM SIGACT-SIGOPS Symposium on Principles of Distributed Computing.* Vancouver, British Columbia, Canada, August, 1987, pp. 137-151.

[LT3] Lynch, N.A., and Tuttle, M.R. An Introduction to Input/Output Automata. *CWI Quarterly*, CWI Amsterdam, September 1989.

[LW] Lynch, N.A., and Welch, J.L. Synthesis of Efficient Drinking Philosophers Algorithms. In progress.

[Mi] Misra, J. Distributed Discrete-Event Simulation. *Computing Surveys*, 18(1):39–65, 1986.

[WLL] Welch, J., Lamport, L., and Lynch, N. A Lattice-Structured Proof of a Minimum Spanning Tree Algorithm. In *Proceedings of 7th ACM SIGACT-SIGOPS Symposium on Principles of Distributed Computing.* Toronto, Ontario, Canada, August, 1988, pp. 28-43.

Reliable Broadcast in Synchronous and Asynchronous Environments (Preliminary Version)

Ajei Gopal   Sam Toueg

Department of Computer Science
Upson Hall, Cornell University
Ithaca, New York 14853

Abstract

This paper studies the problem of reliable broadcast of a sequence of values in a system subject to processor failures. We consider three failure models – *crash*, in which a processor may stop executing at any time, *send omission*, in which processors may intermittently fail to send messages and *general omission*, in which processors may intermittently fail to send and receive messages – in both *synchronous* (the "round model") and *asynchronous* systems. In contrast to the Byzantine Generals formulation of reliable broadcast, the problem we consider can be solved for asynchronous systems. In synchronous systems, we first present an algorithm tolerant of crash failures, and use *translation* techniques to derive algorithms tolerant of send omission failures and general omission failures. For asynchronous systems, we present simple algorithms tolerant of all three failure models.

1 Introduction

This paper studies the problem of reliable broadcast in both synchronous and asynchronous distributed systems that are subject to processor failures. We consider three failure models – crash, in which processors may prematurely halt, send omission failures, in which a processor may intermittently fail to send a message, and general omission failures, in which a processor may intermittently fail to send and receive messages.

The reliable broadcast problem we consider is best understood as a modification of the Byzantine Generals Problem (BG) [LSP82] [Fis83]. In BG, processors may be *correct* or *faulty*. A distinguished processor (the transmitter), broadcasts a single value (the transmitter's value) to all processors, each of which must irrevocably *write* a value such that:

[**Validity**] If the transmitter is correct, then all correct processors eventually write the transmitter's value.

[**Agreement**] If any correct processor writes a value v then every correct processor must eventually write the value v.

[**Termination**] All correct processors eventually write a value.

We make two modifications to the statement of BG; the first concerns the Termination condition. A well known result [FLP85] implies that BG cannot be solved in an asynchronous[1] system, even if *at most* one processor may crash fail. This impossibility is

---

[1] In an asynchronous system there is no bound on the message passing delays.

a consequence of the following aspect of the Termination condition: all correct processors must write some value *even if* the transmitter is faulty. For example, even if the transmitter crashes *before* it is able to send any message to any other processor in the system (and thus the processors have no evidence of the transmitter's "willingness" to transmit a value), the correct processors are required to agree on a broadcast value. When there is no *a priori* knowledge of a processor's willingness to transmit a value, it is reasonable to drop this termination requirement, especially in an asynchronous environment. Hence, we weaken BG by requiring only the Validity and Agreement conditions: either all the correct processors write the transmitters value, or no correct processor writes any value. A similar idea was explored in [BT85].

Our second modification concerns the Agreement condition. When [LSP82] proposed the BG problem, they did so in the context of arbitrary (malicious) failures. However, when considering weaker failure models (upto general omissions), one can strengthen the agreement condition by requiring that faulty processors behave "consistently" with the correct processors. Thus we require:

[**Uniform Agreement (Uniformity)**] If *any* (faulty or correct) processor writes a value v, then every correct processor must eventually write v. Furthermore, v is either the transmitter's value or the symbol $\mathcal{F}$, but v can only be $\mathcal{F}$ if the transmitter is faulty.

Note that although the Agreement condition of the BG problem allows faulty processors to write a value different from that written by correct processors, the Uniformity condition forces *all* the values written to be the same.[2] Furthermore, since we are not considering arbitrary failures, we require that any value written to be the transmitter's value, or, in the event the transmitter is faulty, the symbol $\mathcal{F}$. [NT88] studied a weaker notion of the Uniformity.

1.1 Single-value Agreement (SA)

The Single-value agreement problem is a reliable broadcast by the transmitter such that the conditions of Validity and Uniformity are met. Unlike BG, there are algorithms that achieve SA in asynchronous systems (for the failure models we consider), due to the removal of the Termination condition. However, SA's Uniformity condition is strictly stronger than the Agreement condition used in BG, and hence SA and BG are *incomparable*.

1.2 Sequence Agreement (SeqA)

We generalize the SA problem by assuming that the transmitter wishes to transmit an infinite sequence of values, initially stored on a one-way read-once tape (called the *input tape*). Each processor (including the transmitter) must write on an initially blank one-way write-once output tape. SeqA requires:

[**Sequence Validity**] If the transmitter is correct, then $\forall k > 0$, each correct processor must eventually write the prefix of length k of the transmitter's input tape.

---

[2] The specification of the Database Commit Problem requires Uniformity rather than just Agreement on the commit/abort outcome of a transaction.

[Sequence Uniformity] If any processor writes v into the kth location of its output tape, every correct processor must eventually write v into the kth location of its output tape. Furthermore, v is either the kth value on the transmitter's input tape or the symbol $\mathcal{F}$ (only if the transmitter is faulty).

Thus, SeqA requires that the output tapes of all the processors be a prefix of the input tape, where the symbol $\mathcal{F}$ (used only in the event of a transmitter failure) can match any input tape symbol. The output tapes of all correct processors must be identical, and the output tape of a faulty processor must be a prefix of the output tape of a correct processor.

1.3 Model and Notation

We use a standard model, presented intuitively here; a formal description of the model is presented in [NT88]. Recall that we are considering a message passing distributed system with no shared memory. Processors may fail, but links are FIFO and reliable. If a processor halts prematurely it is said to *crash*; however, it behaves correctly (i.e. according to the protocol it is executing) until it crashes. A processor subject to *send-omission* failures may crash or may occasionally fail to send a message. A processor subject to *general-omission* failures may crash or may occasionally fail to send or receive a message. In an asynchronous system, there is no upper bound on message delivery. In synchronous systems, there is a known upper bound on message delivery and on processor's relative speeds, and thus computation can proceed in "rounds". In each round a processor sends messages according to its local state, then receives all the messages sent at the beginning of the round, then performs local computations and changes its state.

We will use the following notation: let n be the number of processors, t be the maximum number of faulty processors in the system, $\mathcal{I}$ denote the input tape, and $\mathcal{I}(k)$ denote the kth symbol on the input tape. Note that many proofs have been omitted from this paper due to space limitations.

2 Synchronous Systems

2.1 Single-valued Agreement

The solution of SA tolerant of crash failures is trivial and omitted in this paper. For send-omission failures we can derive a solution by adding an extra round to the $(t + 1)$-round protocol for BG given in [PT86], and then compressing rounds $t + 1$ and $t + 2$ into a single round, giving a round optimal solution described below. The send-omission algorithm is shown in Figure 1. The proof of the algorithm follows from the sequence of lemmas given below (proofs omitted).

Lemma 1 *For all processors, in all rounds, $tnt \in \{\mathcal{I}(1), \mathcal{F}\}$.*

Lemma 2 *At the end of round $t + 1$, if a correct processor p has $tnt = \mathcal{I}(1)$ then all non-crashed processors have $tnt = \mathcal{I}(1)$.*

Init:
    if p is the transmitter **then** $tnt := \mathcal{I}(1)$
        else $tnt := \mathcal{F}$
    for rounds r, $1 \leq r \leq t+1$
    do:
        if $tnt \neq \mathcal{F}$ and p never broadcast an (ECHO:m) message earlier **then**
            broadcast(ECHO:tnt)
        if received any (ECHO:m) in this round with $m \neq \mathcal{F}$ **then** $tnt := m$
    od
    in round $t+2$:
        broadcast(FINAL:tnt)
        if received any (FINAL:m) message with $m = \mathcal{F}$ **then**
            write $(\mathcal{F})$
        else /* p received (FINAL:m) with $m \neq \mathcal{F}$ from all correct processors */
            write(m)

Figure 1: $t + 2$ round synchronous algorithm that solves SA tolerant of $t < n$ send-omission failures – executed by p

Corollary 3 *At the end of round $t + 1$, if any non-crashed processor has $tnt = \mathcal{F}$ then all correct processors have $tnt = \mathcal{F}$.*

Lemma 4 *If any processor receives a (FINAL:$\mathcal{F}$) message in round $t + 2$, then every non-crashed processor must receive a (FINAL:$\mathcal{F}$) message in round $t + 2$.*

Theorem 5 *The $(t + 2)$-round algorithm shown in Figure 1 uses $n > t$ processors to solve the SA problem in a synchronous system, and is tolerant of up to t send-omission failures.*

Proof: Validity: Omitted. Uniformity: Consider round $t + 2$. There are two cases:
Case 1: Suppose a processor receives a (FINAL:$\mathcal{F}$) message. Then by Lemma 4 all non-crashed processors also receive such a message. Hence, by Figure 1, all non-crashed processors write $\mathcal{F}$.
Case 2: No non-crashed processor receives a (FINAL:$\mathcal{F}$) message. By Lemma 1 and since $n > t$, all non-crashed processors must receive at least one (FINAL:m) message with $m = \mathcal{I}(1) \neq \mathcal{F}$. Hence, by Figure 1, all non-crashed processors write m. □

We can compress the rounds $t + 1$ and $t + 2$ of the algorithm in Figure 1 into a single round, giving a $(t + 1)$-round algorithm. The resulting algorithm, shown in Figure 2 is based on the procedure *send-omission-consensus*; the proof is omitted. The algorithm for general-omission failures requires $n > 2t$ and uses a different consensus procedure, called *general-omission-consensus*[3]. Requiring a majority of correct processors can be shown to be necessary:

---

[3] We have a similar procedure *crash-consensus* for crash failures.

/* Procedure send-omission-consensus(TAG, tnt, t) is tolerant of t send-omissions */
/* It returns the consensus value in the the variable tnt */
/* TAG is used to distinguish different instances of this procedure */
Procedure *send-omission-consensus(TAG, tnt, t)*:
    for t **rounds**
    do:
        if $tnt \neq \mathcal{F}$ and p never broadcast a (ECHO:TAG:m) message earlier **then**
            broadcast(ECHO:TAG:tnt)
        if received any (ECHO:TAG:m) in this round with $m \neq \mathcal{F}$ **then** $tnt := m$
    od
    in round $t + 1$:
        if $tnt \neq \mathcal{F}$ and p never broadcast an (ECHO:TAG:m) message earlier **then**
            broadcast(ECHO:TAG:tnt)
        broadcast(FINAL:TAG:tnt)
        if received any (ECHO:TAG:m) in this round with $m \neq \mathcal{F}$ **then**
            $tnt := m$
        else if received any (FINAL:TAG:m) message with $m = \mathcal{F}$ **then**
            $tnt := \mathcal{F}$
        else /* received (FINAL:TAG:m) with $m \neq \mathcal{F}$ from all correct processors */
            $tnt := m$

---

    if p is the transmitter **then** $tnt := \mathcal{I}(1)$
        else $tnt := \mathcal{F}$
    call *send-omission-consensus*(TAG, tnt, t)
    write(tnt)

Figure 2: $t + 1$ round synchronous algorithm that solves SA tolerant of $t < n$ send-omission failures – executed by p

---

Theorem 6 *Any solution to SA tolerant of general-omission failures in synchronous systems requires $n > 2t$.*

2.2 The Consensus Protocols

This subsection gives an informal description of our consensus procedures, omitting a formal proof of correctness. Suppose a set S of processors invokes the procedure consensus(TAG, v_i, f), in the same round k, where $v_i \in \{\mathcal{F}, m\}$ and f is the maximum number of faulty processors in S.

● In *crash-consensus* and *send-omission-consensus*, if $|S| > f$ and any correct processor invokes the procedure with $v_i = m$, then in round $k + f$, all non-crashed processors $p_j \in S$ will terminate their executions of the protocol with $v_j = m$.

● In *general-omission-consensus*:

    ○ if $|S| > 2f$, and any correct processor invokes the procedure with $v_i = m$, then in round $k + f$, all non-crashed processors $p_j \in S$ will terminate their executions of the protocol with $v_j = m$.

o if $|S| \leq 2f$ then in round $k + f$, all non-crashed processors $p_j \in S$ will terminate their executions of the protocol with the same value of either m or $\mathcal{F}$.

2.3 Sequence Agreement

2.3.1 Tolerating Crash Failure

An obvious solution for SeqA would be to run a separate SA algorithm for each value on the input tape. However, this is too expensive in terms of messages and rounds.

Observation I: Assume processors may only fail by crashing. Suppose that the transmitter broadcasts a message m_r in each round r. If any processor receives m_r then all correct processors must have received m_{r-1} (in round $r-1$). If any processor that has not crashed by the end of round r fails to receive m_r (but received m_{r-1}), then the transmitter failed in round r or $r-1$.

Observation I leads to a communication efficient algorithm for SeqA tolerant of crash failures (Figure 3). If the transmitter remains correct, it broadcasts a new value in each round, and every correct processor writes each broadcast value exactly one round after it was broadcast by the transmitter. The overhead of a $t + 1$ round protocol is only incurred when the transmitter fails, and then only for the last two values the transmitter sent before it crashed.

The following shows the correctness of the algorithm in Figure 3. Lemma 7 is proved by induction using Observation I.

Lemma 7 *If the transmitter does not crash by the end of round $r > 1$, then every correct processor writes the sequence $\mathcal{I}(1) \ldots \mathcal{I}(r-1)$ at output tape locations $1 \ldots r-1$.*

Lemma 8 *If the transmitter fails in round $r \geq 1$, then:*
* *for $k = r - 1$ or r, and $k > 0$, if processor p writes $\mathcal{I}(k)$, then it writes it at location k on its output tape, and every correct processor writes $\mathcal{I}(k)$.*
* *no processor will write any value at output tape location $r + 1$.*

Proof Outline: Suppose the transmitter fails in round $r > 1$ (the case for $r = 1$ is similar). By the end of round r, all the non-crashed processors will have received the message $m_{r-1} = \mathcal{I}(r-1)$ (in round $r-1$); let R be the set of processors that received a message $m_r = \mathcal{I}(r)$ from the transmitter in round r, and let S be the remaining processors. The non-crashed processors in R write $m_{r-1} = \mathcal{I}(r-1)$ at the end of round r. However, the processors in S cannot distinguish the current scenario from one in which there are processors that failed to receive the transmitter's round $r-1$ message. Thus, in round $r + 1$ the non-crashed processors in S begin a $t - 1$ failure tolerant crash-consensus procedure for $\mathcal{I}(r-1)$ ($t - 1$ failures are the most that can occur, as the transmitter has already failed). This procedure terminates in round $r + t$ with $\mathcal{I}(r-1)$ chosen as the consensus value. By Figure 3 and Lemma 7, $\mathcal{I}(r-1)$ is then be written by the non-crashed processors in S in round $r + t$ at output tape location $r - 1$. Thus, by the end of round $r + t$, all processors will have written the sequence $\mathcal{I}(1) \ldots \mathcal{I}(r-1)$ in output

In round $r = 1$:
    if p is the transmitter **then** broadcast($\mathcal{I}(1)$)
    if received no message from the transmitter **then** go to recovery
For round $r \geq 2$
do:
    if p is the transmitter **then** broadcast($\mathcal{I}(r)$)
    if received any message m_r from the transmitter in round r **then**
        write(m_{r-1}) /* m_{r-1} is the message received in the previous round*/
    else /* the transmitter must have crashed in round r or $r-1$ */
        go to recovery
od
recovery: /* p detected the transmitter's failure at the end of round r */
    in round $r + 1$:
        if $(r - 1) > 0$ **then** call *crash-consensus*(TAG_{r-1}, m_{r-1}, $t - 1$)
    in round $r + 2$:
        $m_r = \mathcal{F}$
        call *crash-consensus*(TAG_r, m_r, $t - 1$)
    in round $r + t$: /* m_{r-1} is the result of crash-consensus called in round $r + 1$ */
        if $(r - 1) > 0$ **then** write(m_{r-1})
    in round $r + t + 1$: /* m_r is the result of crash-consensus called in round $r + 2$ */
        if $m_r \neq \mathcal{F}$ **then** write(m_r)

Figure 3: Synchronous algorithm that solves SeqA tolerant of $t < n$ crash failures – executed by p

tape locations $1 \ldots r - 1$.

The processors in R realize that there are processors that may not have received the round r message, and the processors in S realize that some processors may have received the round r message. Hence, in round $r + 2$, all non-crashed processors begin a consensus to determine the transmitter's round r broadcast. This terminates in round $r + t + 1$, the round *after* the consensus for $\mathcal{I}(r - 1)$ terminated. If this consensus value is $\mathcal{F}$, nothing is written; else it must be $\mathcal{I}(r)$, which is written by all the non-crashed processors at output tape location r.

The processors in R cannot distinguish the current scenario from one in which the transmitter failed in round $r + 1$ after sending its round $r + 1$ value to some processors. Thus, in round $r + 3$, the non-crashed processors in R also begin a consensus to determine the transmitter's round $r + 1$ broadcast (if any was sent). This terminates in round $r + t + 2$, with the value $\mathcal{F}$, and is not written by any processor.

The processors in S and R execute no further actions in after rounds $r + t + 1$ and $r + t + 2$ respectively. Thus no processor writes anything at output tape location $r + 1$. $\quad \square$

Theorem 9 *The algorithm shown in Figure 3 uses $n > t$ processors to solve the SeqA problem in a synchronous system, and is tolerant of up to t crash failures.*

Proof: Sequence Validity: Assume that the transmitter is correct, and hence every correct processor must receive $\mathcal{I}(r)$ in round r and write it in round $r + 1$. Sequence Uniformity: Follows from Lemmas 7 and 8. □

2.3.2 Tolerating Omission Failures

We derive algorithms for send and general-omission failures by applying translation techniques to the algorithm that tolerates only crash failures (see Figure 3). A *translation* from one (more benign) fault model to another (more severe) one is an automated procedure that converts algorithms that are tolerant of the first (benign) fault model into ones that are tolerant of the more severe fault model.

Recall the crash tolerant algorithm in Figure 3 consisted of two parts; the first was a sequence of consecutive broadcasts by the transmitter before it fails, and the second consisted of the non-crashed processors agreeing on the last two values sent by the transmitter before it crashed. We apply translation techniques only to the first part of this algorithm; the second part (recovery) is handled by a consensus protocol tolerating the appropriate type of failure. Hadzilacos's techniques [Had84] result in a protocol tolerant of send-omission failures (omitted in this paper), and Neiger and Toueg's techniques [NT88] result in a protocol tolerant of general-omission failures that is presented below.

A direct application of Neiger and Toueg's technique would limit the transmitter to broadcast at most one message every two rounds. We are able to modify this technique so that the transmitter can broadcast a message every round (as in the case of the crash tolerant algorithm) through the inclusion of fault masking [Coa87] [BNDDS87] and the special nature of the algorithm being translated. This modification is incorporated into the matching pair of procedures *broadcast-cg* and *accept-cg* shown in Figure 4; the former is invoked by the transmitter in round k and the latter is invoked by all processors in round $k + 1$. When executing in a system with general-omission failures, these procedures simulate the communication in a crash-only environment.

The proof of correctness of our general-omission algorithm for SeqA (Figure 5), consists of two parts. The first part consists of showing that the transmitter is able to perform a series of consecutive broadcasts until it fails, and these broadcasts are accepted by all non-crashed processors in the order in which they were sent. The second part consists of showing that when the transmitter fails, the non-crashed processors agree on the last two values the transmitter sent before it failed. The proof of the first part follows from the correct simulation of crash comunication by the broadcst-cg/accept-cg pair, and the correctness of the crash algorithm shown in Figure 3. (We assume that the procedures are invoked in a system with general-omission failures, and $n > 2t$.)

Lemma 10 *Suppose that the transmitter sends a message m_k in each round k by calling the procedure broadcast-cg(k, m_k), and every processor attempts to accept m_k by calling the procedure accept-cg(k, v) in round $k + 1$. Assume faulty-transmitter is initialized to*

/* Procedure broadcast-cg and accept-cg are executed in a general-omission failure */
/* model to simulate the communication in a crash failure environment */
/* *faulty-transmitter* is set to *true* when p detects the transmitter is faulty */
Procedure *broadcast-cg(k, v)*: /* to broadcast a message v in round k */
   in round k:
        broadcast(SEND-INIT: k, v)

Procedure *accept-cg(k, v)*: /* to *accept* v broadcast in round k by the transmitter */
   in round $k + 1$:
        if received (SEND-INIT: k, m) in round k **and** *faulty-transmitter* = *false* **then**
           broadcast(SEND-ECHO: k, m)
        else
           broadcast(SEND-ECHO: $k, \mathcal{F}$)
        if received fewer than $n - t$ (SEND-ECHO: $k, \ldots$) messages **then**
           halt   /* p detected its own failure to receive */
        if received fewer than $n - t$ (SEND-ECHO: k, m) messages, for $m \neq \mathcal{F}$, **then**
           faulty-transmitter := *true*   /* p detected the transmitter is faulty */
        if received any (SEND-ECHO: k, m) with $m \neq \mathcal{F}$ **then**
           $v := m$ /* set the *accepted* value */
        else
           $v := \mathcal{F}$

Figure 4: Procedures broadcast-cg and accept-cg – executed by p in rounds k and $k + 1$

false *by all processors. Then:*
Faulty-Recipient: *If the transmitter correctly executes broadcast-cg(r, m_r) in round r, and a processor p executes accept-cg(r, v) in round $r + 1$, but does not accept m_r, then p halts or crashes by the end of round $r + 1$. (p must be faulty.)*
Faulty-Transmitter: *If the transmitter executes broadcast-cg(r, m_r) in round r, and a processor p executes accept-cg(r, v) in round $r + 1$, but does not accept m_r, and neither halts or crashes by the end of round $r + 1$, then no processor will accept any message broadcast by the transmitter after round r. (The transmitter must be faulty.)*

Proof Outline: **Faulty-Recipient:** Since the transmitter correctly executed broadcast-cg, all correct processors must receive an (SEND-INIT: r, m_r) message in round r. Since *faulty-transmitter* is false at each processor at the start of round $r + 1$, all $n - t$ correct processors send a (SEND-ECHO: r, m_r) message in round $r+1$. Since each processor can send at most one (SEND-ECHO: $r, \ldots$) message in each round, at most t processors can send a (SEND-ECHO: $r, \mathcal{F}$) message. Suppose for contradiction, that p does not halt or crash by the end of round $r + 1$. Then p must have received at least $n - t$ (SEND-ECHO: $r, \ldots$) messages. Since at most t of these are (SEND-ECHO: $r, \mathcal{F}$) messages and since $n - t > t$, one of the received messages must be a (SEND-ECHO: r, m_r) message. Hence, by Figure 4 p must accept m_r; a contradiction.
Faulty-Transmitter: The proof is similar to the previous case.   □

in round $r = 1$:

    faulty-transmitter := false

    if p is the transmitter **then call** *broadcast-cg*$(1, \mathcal{I}(1))$

in round $r = 2$:

    if p is the transmitter **then call** *broadcast-cg*$(2, \mathcal{I}(2))$

    call *accept-cg*$(1, m_1)$ /* accept round 1 message */

    if $m_1 = \mathcal{F}$ **then** go to recovery

in round $r \geq 3$

do:

    if p is the transmitter **then call** *broadcast-cg*$(r, \mathcal{I}(r))$

    call *accept-cg*$(r - 1, m_{r-1})$ /* accept round $(r - 1)$ message */

    if $m_{r-1} \neq \mathcal{F}$ **then**

        write (m_{r-2}) /* write the round $(r - 2)$ message accepted in round $(r - 1)$ */

    else go to recovery

od

recovery: /* in round $r \geq 2$, p detected the transmitter's failure in sending m_{r-1} */

    in round $r + 1$:

        if $(r - 3) > 0$ **then call** *general-omission-consensus*$(\text{TAG}_{r-3}, m_{r-3}, t - 1)$

    in round $r + 2$:

        if $(r - 2) > 0$ **then call** *general-omission-consensus*$(\text{TAG}_{r-2}, m_{r-2}, t - 1)$

    in round $r + 3$:

        call *general-omission-consensus*$(\text{TAG}_{r-1}, m_{r-1}, t - 1)$

    in round $r + t + 1$: /* m_{r-2} is the result of crash-consensus called in round $r + 2$ */

        if $(r - 2) > 0$ **and** $m_{r-2} \neq \mathcal{F}$ **then** write(m_{r-2})

    in round $r + t + 2$: /* m_{r-1} is the result of crash-consensus called in round $r + 3$ */

        if $m_{r-1} \neq \mathcal{F}$ **then** write(m_{r-1})

Figure 5: Synchronous algorithm that solves SeqA tolerant of $2t < n$ general-omission failures – executed by p

We now have to show that when the transmitter fails, the non-crashed processors agree on the last two values the transmitter sent. This is achieved by the recovery section of the protocol. A processor p executes this section in round r, when it does not accept a message m_{r-1} from the (failed) transmitter. An informal description of the recovery section is given below. For simplicity, assume $r > 3$. By the end of round r, p must have accepted and written m_{r-3}, the round $r - 3$ message. However, it is possible that another processor may not have written that message; hence p participates in a consensus algorithm for the round $r - 3$ message, beginning in round $r + 1$. This general-omission tolerant consensus will terminate in round $r + t$, with the result being either m_{r-3} or $\mathcal{F}$ (in case fewer than $n - t$ correct processors participate in this consensus). In either case, p does not write the consensus value (p already wrote m_{r-3}).

By the end of round r, p must have accepted m_{r-2}, the round $r - 2$ message. However, it is possible that another processor may have written that message; hence p must participate in a consensus algorithm for the round $r - 2$ message, beginning in round $r + 2$. This consensus will terminate in round $r + t + 1$; if the result is $m \neq \mathcal{F}$ (i.e. if it is m_{r-2}), p writes m.

By the end of round r, p has not accepted the round $r - 1$ message. However, it is possible that another processor may have accepted that message; hence p must participate in a consensus protocol for the round $r - 1$ message, beginning in round $r - 3$. This consensus will terminate in round $r + t + 2$; if the result is $m \neq \mathcal{F}$, p writes m.

The remainder of the proof of correctness is similar to the crash tolerant protocol. Lemma 11 is proved by induction, using Lemma 10, and the proof of Lemma 12 is similar to that of Lemma 8, and follows from the correctness of the recovery section outlined above. The proof of Theorem 13 is based on Lemmas 11 and 12.

Lemma 11 *If every non-crashed processor accepts the transmitter's $r - 1$ round message by the end of round r, then every non-crashed processor writes the sequence $\mathcal{I}(1) \ldots \mathcal{I}(r - 2)$ at output tape locations $1 \ldots r - 2$.*

Lemma 12 *If some non-crashed processor fails to accept the transmitter's round $r - 1$ message in round $r \geq 2$, then:*
- *for $k = r - 2, r - 1$ and $k > 0$, if processor p writes $\mathcal{I}(k)$, $\mathcal{I}(k)$, then it writes it at location k on its output tape, and every correct processor writes $\mathcal{I}(k)$.*
- *no processor will write any value at output tape location r.*

Theorem 13 *The algorithm shown in Figure 5 uses $n > 2t$ processors to solve the SeqA problem in a synchronous system, and is tolerant of up to t general-omission failures.*

3 Asynchronous Systems

In Figure 6, we describe a simple solution to the SeqA problem tolerant of general-omission failures in an asynchronous system (the solution of the SA problem is a special case of this algorithm). Our algorithm works provided that a majority of the processors are correct ($n > 2t$). We can show that this is a necessary requirement; any solution to the SA problem in asynchronous systems requires $n > 2t$ even if *only* send-omission failures can occur (see Theorem 16). Following is the proof of our general-omission tolerant SeqA algorithm (Fig 6).

Lemma 14 *The algorithm in Figure 6 ensures that no processor writes $m \neq \mathcal{I}(k)$ in location k of its output tape. Furthermore, if any processor writes m at location k, then every correct processor also write m at location k.*

Proof Outline: We only show the second part of the lemma. Suppose processor p writes m in position k. By Figure 6 it must have received at least $n - t$ copies of the message (TAG_k, m). Since each processor broadcasts at most one (TAG_k, $\ldots$) message and $n - t > t$, at least one of the messages received by p was sent by a correct processor. Thus this message will also be received by all the correct processors, each of which will

```
    k := 1
    do /* for all values of k ≥ 1 */
        if p is the transmitter then
            broadcast (TAG_k, I(k))
        else
            wait to receive one copy of the message (TAG_k, m)
            broadcast (TAG_k, m)
        wait to receive at least n − t copies of the message (TAG_k, m)
        write(m)
        k := k + 1
    od
```

Figure 6: Asynchronous algorithm that solves SeqA tolerant of $2t < n$ general omission failures – executed by p

relay this message once. Hence every correct processor will eventually receive at least $n - t$ copies of (TAG_k, m) and write m. The proof that m is written in location k is by induction and is omitted. □

Theorem 15 *The algorithm shown in Figure 6 uses $n > 2t$ processors to solve the SA problem in an asynchronous system, and is tolerant of up to t send-omission or general-omission failures.*

Theorem 16 *Any solution to SA tolerant of send-omission failures in asynchronous systems requires $n > 2t$.*

Proof: Assume that Π is a solution to SA in an asynchronous system with $n = 2t$. Suppose that all processors run Π and the processors are partitioned into two sets, A and B, each of size t, with the transmitter in set A.

Scenario 1: Assume that all $p_a \in A$ are correct, all $p_b \in B$ are faulty and the transmitter's value is the symbol x. Let all communication be correct, except that when a processor $p_b \in B$ sends a message to $p_a \in A$, p_b performs a send-omission failure. By SA's Validity condition, all $p_a \in A$ must eventually write x on their output tapes. Let τ be the maximum amount of time it takes for all the processors in A to write that value.

Scenario 2: Assume all $p_b \in B$ are correct, all $p_a \in A$ are faulty and the transmitter's value is x. Let all communication be correct, except when $p_a \in A$ attempts to send a message to $p_b \in B$, it performs a send-omission failure. Additionally, when $p_b \in B$ sends a message to $p_a \in A$, the message arrives at p_a τ time units *after* the protocol has begun. Since scenarios 1 and 2 are indistinguishable to all $p_a \in A$ up to time τ after the protocol began, p_a must write x as in scenario 1. Since all $p_b \in B$ never receive any message from any $p_a \in A$ they are unable to determine the transmitter's value. However, to satisfy the Uniformity requirement, all $p_b \in B$ must eventually write the symbol x.

Scenario 3: This is exactly as in scenario 2, except the transmitter's value is the symbol

$y \neq x$. For all $p_b \in B$, the scenario is indistinguishable from scenario 2. Hence, all the processors in B eventually write the symbol x. This contradicts SA's Uniformity condition. □

3.1 Processors with Finite Memory

Consider an asynchronous system where processors have finite memory. The memory limitation implies that messages are restricted some maximum length; hence messages relating to different input values cannot be uniquely tagged as in the algorithm in Figure 6. Also, a processor can only store a finite number of messages. Hence even if a processor is waiting for the reception of a particular message, it cannot indefinitely delay the processing of all the messages that it receives while waiting. These two observations, in conjunction with the uncertainty of message delivery times in an asynchronous system can be used to show the following impossibility result.

Theorem 17 *In asynchronous systems where $n \geq 2$ processors have finite memory, there is no solution to the SeqA problem even if at most one crash failure may occur.*

4 Conclusions and Future Work

This paper studied the problem of reliable broadcast of a single value (SA) and of a sequence of values (SeqA) in synchronous and asynchronous systems subject to crash, send-omission and general-omission failures. Our formulation of reliable broadcast comes from a critical evaluation of the Byzantine Generals Problem (BG). In contrast to the BG problem, there are solutions to SA and SeqA for asynchronous systems. Hence the SA and SeqA problems can be used as powerful abstractions in the design of fault-tolerant asynchronous distributed algorithms. Furthermore, our formulation of reliable broadcast has a stronger agreement requirement than BG: it does not allow any faulty processor to write a value different from that written by the correct processors. This stronger agreement requirement is crucial to some important applications, such as the Database Commit Problem, where for example, a faulty processor cannot decide to abort when the correct processors decide to commit.

We presented both synchronous and asynchronous solutions to SA and SeqA tolerant of crash, send-omission and general-omission failures. The synchronous solution to SeqA is particularly efficient: it does not require an expensive $t + 1$ agreement protocol for each value broadcast. The overhead of a $t + 1$ round agreement protocol is only incurred when the transmitter fails, and then only to ensure consensus on the last two values the transmitter sent before it crashed.

We are continuing our study of finite memory asynchronous systems. Recall that SeqA has no solution in such systems. We are currently working on a problem closely related to SeqA; this problem is the Set Agreement problem (SetA), in which the transmitter seeks to broadcast a multi-set of values. SetA *has* an unusual solution if only one processor can crash; however, we conjecture that it has no solution if more than one processor can crash, or if at most one processor can commit send-omission failures.

References

[BNDDS87] Amotz Bar-Noy, Danny Dolev, Cynthia Dwork, and H. Raymond Strong. Shifting gears: Changing algorithms on the fly to expedite Byzantine agreement. In *Proceedings of the Sixth ACM Symposium on Principles of Distributed Computing*, pages 42–51, Vancouver, British Columbia, August 1987. ACM SIGOPS-SIGACT.

[BT85] Gabriel Bracha and Sam Toueg. Asynchronous consensus and broadcast protocols. *Journal of the ACM*, 32(4):824–840, October 1985.

[Coa87] Brian A. Coan. *Achieving Consensus in Fault-Tolerant Distributed Computer Systems: Protocols, Lower Bounds, and Simulations*. PhD thesis, Massachusetts Institute of Technology, June 1987.

[Fis83] Michael J. Fischer. The consensus problem in unreliable distributed systems (a brief survey). Technical Report DCS/RR-273, Department of Computer Science, Yale University, June 1983.

[FLP85] Michael J. Fischer, Nancy A. Lynch, and Michael S. Patterson. Impossibility of distributed consensus with one faulty process. *Journal of the ACM*, 32(2):374–382, April 1985.

[Had84] Vassos Hadzilacos. *Issues of Fault Tolerance in Concurrent Computations*. PhD thesis, Harvard University, June 1984. Department of Computer Science Technical Report 11-84.

[LSP82] Leslie Lamport, R. Shostak, and M. Pease. The Byzantine generals problem. *ACM Transactions on Programming Languages and Systems*, 4(3):382–401, July 1982.

[NT88] Gil Neiger and Sam Toueg. Automatically increasing the fault-tolerance of distributed systems. In *Proceedings of the Seventh ACM Symposium on Principles of Distributed Computing*, pages 248–262, Toronto, Ontario, August 1988. ACM SIGOPS-SIGACT.

[PT86] Kenneth J. Perry and Sam Toueg. Distributed agreement in the presence of processor and communication faults. *IEEE Transactions on Software Engineering*, 12(3):477–482, March 1986.

Observing global states of asynchronous distributed applications *

Jean-Michel HELARY

IRISA-IFSIC – Campus de Beaulieu– 35042 RENNES CEDEX

E.mail: helary@irisa.fr

Abstract

Observing global states of an asynchronous distributed application is a difficult task due to arbitrary messages transfer delays. Notion of global states and some of their properties – consistency, being transitless – are precisely stated, and the problem, in both FIFO and non FIFO communication models, is solved in a progressive way : local synchronization allows neighbour processes to record mutually consistent local states, then a sequence of consistent global states is obtained by composition with global wave synchronization; computing some functions over consistent global states becomes easier and an example is displayed (number of messages in transit). Solution generalizes and improves known results, both in FIFO (relaxation of synchronization constraints) and non FIFO (absence of message storing) situations.

1 Introduction

Computing global states of distributed systems or applications (also known as *computing snapshots*) is a difficult but major problem as previously pointed [CL85, CM88, FGL82, HPR89]. The difficulty is mainly from the lack of global clock and from non determinism inherent to arbitrary transfer delays of messages proper to asynchronism. The interest is yet multiple: on the one hand, it provides solution to a variety of control problems, e.g. detection of stable properties [CM86, Tel86, HJPR87], system recovery after failure [Mor85], etc.; on the other hand, its solution may give prominence to fundamental mechanisms for distributed application control. That's why several interesting results related to this problem have already been obtained. The first published snapshot algorithm was from Chandy and Lamport [CL85]; in this solution the communication channels need to be error-free, unidirectionnal and obey the first-in-first-out property. Synchronization rules use *markers* as control messages tranmitted on the main computation channels: reception of a *marker* on a channel is a synchronization event which, due to the FIFO assumption let processes record their local state consistently (we explain these terms in §2). Under the same communication hypotheses, Hélary et al. [HPR89] solved a stronger problem, namely repeated capture of consistent global states, allowing to detect

---

*This work was partly supported by the French Reserch Program C[3] on Parallelism and Distributed Computing

those without messages in transit; the derivation is based upon a principle of algorithm composition, more precisely a *phase synchronization* (using *markers*) is combined with a *sequential wave synchronization* (implemented with a *token* ring), and the obtained control algorithm is superimposed to the observed application. Among other proposed solutions, Lai and Yang [LY87] gave an interesting solution dropping out the FIFO assumption; markers aren't used and few synchronization is needed but storage of messages sent and received on every node makes a serious implementation problem. Also free from FIFO assumptions, Mattern [Mat89] gives a nice generalization of Chandy-Lamport's, based upon a generalized virtual time concept. In a related work, Taylor [Tay89] shows an fundamental impossibility result : in a non-FIFO asynchronous context, no consistent snapshot algorithm can be achieved without freezing, i.e. temporary inhibition of send or receive underlying events.

In this paper, we are interested in deriving snapshot computations based upon general, implementation free *wave synchronization* and improving previously known solutions in two directions : firstly under FIFO assumptions, *marker synchronization* constraints are weakened; secondly, we drop out the FIFO model, assuming only that channels are reliable, and unlike Lai and Yang's, only local counters storage, periodically reset to zero, is needed; in that sense, our result is similar to Mattern's one, but unlike the latter we achieve termination of a snapshot computation independantly of observed application behaviour, and our derivation and implementation are different.

In §2 we define precisely the notions of distributed application, its global state and some of their properties (consistency, no transit, etc.). In §3 we set synchronization rules allowing processes to record their local states consistently according to communication hypotheses; these rules define a distributed control algorithm superimposed to the underlying observed application, whereas §4 shows how a global synchronization technique – namely *wave sequence* – can be used to implement some computations on the set of recorded local states. An example of such a computation is given in §5 : number of intransit messages in a global state, allowing detection of global states without messages in transit, both in reliable FIFO and non-FIFO communication models.

2   Global state

2.1   Distributed application or system

Application (or system) to be observed consists of a set $X = \{P_1, P_2, \ldots, P_n\}$ of n computing processes, interacting through message exchange only; each process is located on a node, named a *computing node* in the following; messages circulate along a set $U \subseteq X \times X$ of communication channels[1]. We shall denote by c_{ij} the channel connecting P_i to P_j.

Several communication models can be defined, either synchronous : e.g. rendez-vous (instant communication), bounded delay (known maximum message transfer delay), or asynchronous : e.g. reliable FIFO (finite but impredictable message transfer delay : each channel acts like an unbounded FIFO buffer), bounded FIFO (like FIFO but with limited amount of storage : each channel acts like a bounded buffer and thus can lost messages

---

[1]Channels are assumed to be *logically* directed but *physically* bidirectionnal

or cause sender's blocking in case of full buffer), reliable non FIFO (messages can be desequenced but neither lost nor duplicated nor altered).

2.2 Global and local time

Whatever the model, some common features concerning time are to be noticed :

- There is no global clock, i.e. there is no concrete global time shared by the n processes,

- on the other hand, we will assume existence of an abstract global time (for purpose of reasonning only); this abstract time obeys to the *causality principle* : for any message m, emission precedes reception :

$$em(m) <_{agt} rec(m)$$

where $<_{agt}$ is the precedence relation in this abstract global time,

- each process is endowed with a local clock; local events (message sending or receiving and internal events) are sequential and totally ordered in the local time; this ordering is compatible with the abstract global time. In the following we shall use the term *time* for *local time*.

Several well-known implementations of such an abstract global time exist, e.g. [Lam78, Mat89]

2.3 Global and local states

For each process $P_i \in X$, the *local state* of P_i at a given time is defined by the local context of the distributed application (projection onto P_i of the global context). A *global state* is a set $GS = \{LS_1, LS_2, \ldots, LS_n\}$ containing processes local states. We shall denote by $\tau(LS_i)$ (τ_i in brief) the time when P_i has recorded its local state LS_i. For a message m_{ij}, sent from P_i to P_j (along channel c_{ij}) we shall say that :

- its emission belongs to LS_i iff $em(m_{ij}) < \tau(LS_i)$

- its reception belongs to LS_j iff $rec(m_{ij}) < \tau(LS_j)$

For a message m_{ij} and a pair of local states (LS_i, LS_j), we denote the four possible configurations in the following way:

(i) $em(m_{ij}) \in LS_i \land rec(m_{ij}) \in LS_j$ $\rightarrow$ consumed message
$m_{ij} \in consumed(LS_i, LS_j)$

(ii) $em(m_{ij}) \in LS_i \land rec(m_{ij}) \notin LS_j$ $\rightarrow$ intransit message
$m_{ij} \in transit(LS_i, LS_j)$

(iii) $em(m_{ij}) \notin LS_i \land rec(m_{ij}) \in LS_j$ $\rightarrow$ inconsistent message
$m_{ij} \in inconsistent(LS_i, LS_j)$

(iv) $em(m_{ij}) \notin LS_i \land rec(m_{ij}) \notin LS_j$ $\rightarrow$ inexistent message
$m_{ij} \in inexistent(LS_i, LS_j)$

Stress mut be laid on the fact that, in a distributed system, only processes local states are (locally) observable at a given time.

We now give the following definitions concerning global states :

Definition 1. Global state $GS = \{LS_1, LS_2, \ldots, LS_n\}$ is *consistent* if, and only if,

$$\forall i \; \forall j \; inconsistent(LS_i, LS_j) = \emptyset$$

Definition 2. Global state $GS = \{LS_1, LS_2, \ldots, LS_n\}$ is *transitless* if, and only if,

$$\forall i \; \forall j \; transit(LS_i, LS_j) = \emptyset$$

Definition 3. A global state is *strongly consistent* if, and only if, it is consistent and transitless [HPR89]

This last property means that, for any pair LS_i, LS_j, a message m_{ij} is received in LS_j if, and only if, it is sent in LS_i.

3 Synchronization rules for local mutual consistency

3.1 The problem

When a process P_i decides to record a local state LS_i it is necessary that it proceeds in co-operation with its neighbours, more precisely with processes P_j such that $(P_j, P_i) \in U$; in fact, inconsistent messages with respect to the pair (LS_j, LS_i) should be avoided, since they are messages having been received but not yet sent (in the global state $GS = \{\ldots, LS_j, \ldots, LS_i, \ldots\}$). The problem to be considered here can be stated more precisely : consider a pair of connected processes $(P_j, P_i) \in U$, each of them decides to record its local state respectively at times τ_j and τ_i. How to synchronise τ_j and τ_i in order to have $inconsitent(LS_j, LS_i) = \emptyset$? (Note that the problem investigated at this step is *not* symmetric : answers given below don't insure that $inconsistent(LS_i, LS_j) = \emptyset$ holds. The problem of global consistency for all pairs of connected processes will be addressed in section 4).

The answer depends on the communication model : we will not be concerned by synchronous models (rendez-vous, bounded delays) since problem here is obvious; we'll focus, in what follows, on two asynchronous models: FIFO (unbounded or not) and non FIFO. In order to implement a synchronization control which doesn't disturb the observed application, we will assume that on every computing node, there exists a control process CTL which performs the following tasks (let P be the application process associated to CTL on the same node):

i) monitor message sending and receiving on the account of P (this action must neither create nor modify nor desequence messages : it should be limited to observation and synchronisation),

ii) handle control messages, transparent to P,

iii) record local states on the account of P.

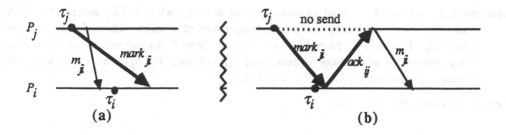

Figure 1: non-FIFO communication

3.2 FIFO communication model

This model is characterized by the following property : let m and m' two messages circulating over the same channel; then

$$em(m) < em(m') \Rightarrow (rec(m) < rec(m') \vee rec(m) = \infty)$$

(The second term handles with loss of messages in non reliable or bounded buffer models). The set of messages sent over a given channel has an ordered list structure which leads to use control messages acting like *end-of-(sub)file markers*.

Let two processes $(P_j, P_i) \in U$ having recorded local states LS_j, LS_i at respective times τ_j, τ_i. Let m_{ji} a message sent over channel c_{ji} and $\tau_j < em(m_{ji})$. To insure $inconsistent(LS_j, LS_i) = \emptyset$ it is sufficient that $\tau_i < rec(m_{ji})$. The following lemma is straightforward from FIFO assumption :

Lemma 3.1. Let $mark_{ji}$ a control message sent over c_{ji} when CTL_j records the local state LS_j of P_j. Then, for every local state LS_i of process P_i recorded by CTL_i not later than the reception of $mark_{ji}$, the property $inconsistent(LS_j, LS_i) = \emptyset$ holds.

3.3 non-FIFO communication model

In that case, the set of messages sent over a given channel is no more totally ordered and using markers is no more sufficient to insure the desired consistency property. Figure 1(a) shows that LS_i's recording occurs too late with respect to LS_j's recording, despite the marker's synchronization. A freezing technique is necessary in order to insure consistency : once P_j has recorded its local state LS_j, it cannot send any computation messages to P_i until it can be sure that P_i recorded LS_i; to this end, an *acknowledgement* technique can be used : when CTL_j decides to record P_j's local state LS_j, it sends a marker $mark_{ji}$ over channel c_{ji}; when CTL_i receives this marker, it sends back an acknowledgement message ack_{ij} to $CTLj$; when ack_{ij} comes back to CTL_j, the latter is sure that LS_i has been recorded. Thus it suffices that all underlying computation emissions are suspended on channel c_{ji} between times τ_j and $rec(ack_{ij})$. These considerations lead to the following result :

Lemma 3.2. Let $mark_{ji}$ a control message sent over c_{ji} when CTL_j records the local state LS_j of P_j, and ack_{ij} its acknowledgement of receipt. Then, for every local state LS_i of process P_i recorded by CTL_i not later than the reception of $mark_{ji}$, if no computation message is sent over c_{ji} between $\tau(LS_j)$ and $rec(ack_{ij})$, the property $inconsistent(LS_j, LS_i) = \emptyset$ holds.

Proof. Obvious from fig. 1(b).

4 Global synchronization for global state consistency

This section deals with the following problem : each process of the observed application has to record a sequence of local states

$$(LS_i^{(\mu)})_{\mu \in N} \text{ such that } \forall \mu \; \forall (P_i, P_j) \in U \; : inconsistent(LS_i^{(\mu)}, LS_j^{(\mu)}) = \emptyset$$

in other words : $\forall \mu \; GS(\mu) = \{LS_1^{(\mu)}, LS_2^{(\mu)}, \ldots, LS_n^{(\mu)}\}$ is a consistent global state. This problem will be treated here by composing two distributed algorithmic techniques :

1. Markers (resp. markers and acknowledgements) synchronization depending whether the communication model is FIFO or not, as seen in the preceeding section,

2. Wave sequence synchronization.

The first synchronization insures local mutual consistency for every pair (LS_i, LS_j) whereas the second one insures global state consistency and controls transition from a global state computation $GS(\mu)$ to the next one $GS(\mu + 1)$.

4.1 Wave sequences

A wave sequence is an abstract control scheme expressing the concept of global distributed iteration [HR89]. A wave [Sch85] is a control flow visiting every process in the system once, and only once, and allowing at least one process, predetermined or not, to know when this traversal is over. A wave defines the following events :

$\forall P_i \; visit(i) \equiv$ process P_i is visited by the wave
$\quad\quad return \equiv \forall P_i visit(i)$ happened

The set of visits is called a *traversal*.
As data flow, a wave has two functions : it broadcasts a datum $DIFF$ and collects a datum $COLL.P_i$ from each process P_i (these functions are performed on each process upon the visit); moreover, a computation $COLL = f(COLL.P_1, COLL.P_2, \ldots, COLL.P_n)$ can be performed over data collected. The logic associated to a wave is thus the following :

% $\forall i \; P_i$ knows $COLL.P_i \wedge$
$\quad \exists I \subseteq X, I \neq \emptyset \wedge (P \in I \Rightarrow P$ knows $DIFF)$ %
$$\left(\begin{array}{c} \|visit(i) \\ P_i \in X \end{array} \right);$$
$\quad\quad return$
% $\forall i \; P_i$ knows $DIFF \wedge$
$\quad \exists J \subseteq X, J \neq \emptyset \wedge (P \in J \Rightarrow P$ knows $COLL = f(COLL.P_1, \ldots, COLL.P_n))$ %

Moreover, following temporal relations hold (with straightforward notations) :

$$\forall \mu (\forall i \ visit(i, \mu)) <_{agt} return(\mu) <_{agt} (\forall i \ visit(i, \mu + 1))$$

A wave sequence ensures a strong global synchronization since the event $return(\mu)$ separates the two sets of events

$$\{visit(i, \mu) | P_i \in X\} \text{ and } \{visit(i, \mu + 1) | P_i \in X\}$$

In other words, a global state exists for which all the events of the first set and none of the second set occured [Tel86].

Wave sequences may be implemented by various traversal structures : directed or undirected spanning trees, rings, etc.. They lead to sequential or parallel structuration of wave events, centralized or distributed return control, and so on [HR88b, Tel86]

4.2 Synchronizations involved

Wave sequence will be useful to :

- Global synchronization of local states recordings; global state $GS(\mu)$ will be recorded along with wave μ,
- collection (resp diffusion) of informations related to global states recorded by the current wave (resp. previous wave).

Thus synchronization rules can be stated as follows :

R1) A controller CTL_i records local state $LS_i^{(\mu)}$ of process P_i upon the event $visit(i, \mu)$.

R2) When CTL_i records $LS_i^{(\mu)}$, it sends a marker $mark_{ij}(\mu)$ over each outgoing channel c_{ij}.

R3) (*reception* freezing rule) If CTL_i receives the marker $mark_{ji}(\mu)$ on the incoming channel c_{ji} before the occurence of event $visit(i, \mu)$, it prevents process P_i from receiving computations messages or markers on that channel until local state $LS_i^{(\mu)}$ is recorded.

We now state and proof rules to insure consistency of global state $GS(\mu)$, according to the communication model

4.2.1 Case of FIFO model

We state the main result of this subsection :

Theorem 4.1. If communications obey FIFO hypotheses and don't loose control messages (markers and wave implementation messages), rules R1) to R3) imply

$$\forall \mu \ GS(\mu) \text{ is consistent}$$

Proof is straightforward from lemma 3.1.

Absence of freezing. When waves are implemented by a diffusion of control messages (markers) issued from an initiator, we obtain Chandy-Lamport's algorithm [CL85] (also described in [Tay89]) : $visit(i, \mu)$ is triggered by the first reception of a marker belonging to wave μ, so that no freezing occurs.

4.2.2 Case of non FIFO communication model

Rules R1) to R3) remain the same. We add the following rules, related to *ack's* and *send freezing* :

R4) When CTL_i receives a marker $mark_{ji}(\mu)$ on c_{ji} it sends back an acknowledgement $ack_{ij}(\mu)$ on c_{ij}.

R5) (*emission* freezing rule) CTL_i prevents P_i from sending computation messages over outgoing channel c_{ij} during the interval $[\tau_i(\mu), \sigma_i(\mu)]$, where

$$\sigma_i(\mu) = \min(rec(ack_{ji}(\mu)), rec(mark_{ji}(\mu)), visit(i, \mu+1))$$

In fact, occurence of one of these three events indicates to CTL_i that $visit(j, \mu)$ (or, equivalently, $LS_j(\mu)$'s recording) has been done (due to lemma 3.2 for the first, rule R2 for the second, wave separation property for the third)

Thus we have the main result of this subsection :

Theorem 4.2. If communications are non FIFO and don't loose control messages (markers, acknowledgements and wave implementation messages), rules R1) to R5) imply

$$\forall \mu \; GS(\mu) \text{ is consistent}$$

4.2.3 Remarks

Absence of deadlock. Evident since record of local state depends only of wave visit. Moreover, any marker $mark_{ji}(\nu)$ arriving on incoming channel c_{ji} before time $\tau_i(\mu)$ has a number ν less or equal to μ (in the case $\nu = \mu$, and only in that case, receptions on channel c_{ji} are frozen until time $\tau_i(\mu)$); this remark is noteworthy as far as implementation is concerned : markers and wave numbers needn't to be explicit, each controller CTL_i handles a local counter array C_i, indexed by incoming channels, such that : $\forall j \; C_i[j] =$ difference between last wave number and last marker number.

Similar technique can be used for handling *ack's* in the non-FIFO case, in particular obsolete ones.

5 Computations over consistent global states

This section adresses the problem of computing functions defined over consistent global states recorded through a wave. The following example will be considered : compute the number $card(intransit(GS(\mu)))$ of intransit messages in the global state $GS(\mu)$ (for any μ). One of the applications of this computation is, for instance : is the recorded global state strongly consistent? The two communication models : reliable unbounded FIFO and reliable unbounded non FIFO will be considered.

5.1 FIFO communication

5.1.1 Abstract global definitions

With every wave number μ consider the global abstract counter vector $MT(\mu)$ defined by

$$MT(\mu)[i] = \sum_{j \neq i} card(\{m_{ji}|em(m_{ji}) < \tau_j(\mu)\}) - \sum_{j \neq i} card(\{m_{ji}|rec(m_{ji}) < \tau_i(\mu)\})$$

The following results are easy to show :

Proposition 5.1. If $GS(\mu)$ is consistent, then $\forall i\ MT(\mu)[i] = \#$ messages intransit towards P_i in $GS(\mu)$ (where $\#\cdots$ denotes "the number of $\cdots$").

This follows from

$$\bigcup_{j \neq i}\{m_{ji}|rec(m_{ji}) < \tau_i(\mu)\} \subseteq \bigcup_{j \neq i}\{m_{ji}|em(m_{ji}) < \tau_j(\mu)\} \text{ (consistency), whence}$$

$$\bigcup_{j \neq i}\{m_{ji}|rec(m_{ji}) < \tau_i(\mu)\} \text{ and the set of intransit messages towards } P_i \text{ in } GS(\mu)$$

form a partition of $\bigcup_{j \neq i}\{m_{ji}|em(m_{ji}) < \tau_j(\mu)\}$

Proposition 5.2.

$$
\begin{aligned}
\forall \mu\ \forall i\ MT(\mu)[i] = \ & MT(\mu - 1)[i] && \text{(a)} \\
& + \sum_{j \neq i} card\{m_{ji}|\tau_j(\mu - 1) < em(m_{ji}) < \tau_j(\mu)\} && \text{(b)} \\
& - \sum_{j \neq i} card\{m_{ji}|\tau_i(\mu - 1) < rec(m_{ji}) < \tau_i(\mu)\} && \text{(c)}
\end{aligned}
$$

5.1.2 Distributed implementation

The distributed computation of counters $MT(\mu)$ will be implemented using the wave sequence through which $GS(\mu)$ is recorded : informations $DIFF$ and $\forall i\ COLL.P_i$ have to be carried over by waves in order to maintain the following invariant :

Wave invariant. (When wave μ returns : $COLL(\mu) = MT(\mu)) \wedge DIFF(\mu + 1) = COLL(\mu)$

Progression. From proposition 5.2, line (a) is nothing else, from the invariant, than $DIFF(\mu)[i]$. Each of lines (b) and (c) can be computed from local counters : each controller CTL_i is endowed with two counters vectors s_i and r_i such that :

$\forall j \neq i\ : s_i[j] = \#\ m_{ij}$ sent over c_{ij} since last visit,
$\forall j \neq i\ : r_i[j] = \#m_{ji}$ received on c_{ji} since last visit.

$\rightarrow$ **Initially** (wave μ)
$\qquad COLL(\mu) \leftarrow COLL(\mu - 1)$

$\rightarrow$ **Upon** $visit(i, \mu)$
$\qquad \forall j \neq i\ COLL(\mu)[j] \leftarrow COLL(\mu)[j] + s_i(\mu)[j]$
$\qquad\quad COLL(\mu)[i] \leftarrow COLL(\mu)[i] - \sum_{j \neq i} r_i(\mu)[j]\ ;$

record $LS_i^{(\mu)}$;
reset to 0 counters s_i, r_i

$\rightarrow$ Upon $return(\mu)$
    % $\forall i \; COLL(\mu)[i]$ contains the number of intransit messages towards P_i in $GS(\mu)$ %

The result $"GS(\mu)$ is transitless" could be diffused by wave $\mu + 1$ (through a boolean $TL \equiv COLL(\mu) = 0$).

5.2 non FIFO communication

5.2.1 Abstract global definitions

In the following, we say that a message m_{ji} is sent (resp. received) in $GS(\mu)$ if, and only if : $\tau_j(\mu - 1) < em(m_{ji}) < \tau_j(\mu)$ (resp. $\tau_i(\mu - 1) < rec(m_{ji}) < \tau_i(\mu)$), (in other words, its emission – resp. reception – belongs to $GS(\mu)$ but not to $GS(\mu - 1)$) and we consider the following global abstract quantities :

$$S(\mu) = \#(\text{ messages sent in } GS(\mu)) \text{ (resp. } R(\mu), \text{ received in)}$$
$$NT(\mu) = \sum_{\nu \leq \mu} S(\nu) - \sum_{\nu \leq \mu} R(\nu) = \#(\text{intransit messages in } GS(\mu)$$
$$N(\mu) = \sum_{\nu \leq \mu} S(\nu) - \sum_{\nu \leq \mu-1} R(\nu)$$

Obviously, $N(\mu) = NT(\mu - 1) + S(\mu)$ and $NT(\mu) = N(\mu) - R(\mu)$

5.2.2 Distributed implementation

Each controller CTL_i is endowed with two counters :

s_i = total number of messages sent since the last time local state has been recorded
r_i = total number of messages received since the last time local state has been recorded.
    Moreover, upon each local state recording, CTL_i resets s_i, r_i to 0. Values obtained at time $\tau_i(\mu)$ will be denoted $s_i(\mu), r_i(\mu)$.
    Wave μ performs the following tasks :

- saves $NT(\mu - 1)$ as $NTBACK$(computed by wave $\mu - 1$),

- computes sums $S(\mu) = \sum_i s_i(\mu), R(\mu) = \sum_i r_i(\mu)$.

Upon return, the following computations can be performed :

$$
\begin{aligned}
N(\mu) &\leftarrow NTBACK + S(\mu) \\
NT(\mu) &\leftarrow N(\mu) - R(\mu) \\
NTBACK &\leftarrow NT(\mu)
\end{aligned}
$$

Boolean information $"GS(\mu)$ is transitless" is equal to $NT(\mu) = 0$ and can be diffused by wave $\mu + 1$.

6 Conclusion

Observing consistent global states is a fundamental problem in distributed systems, and a difficult one in asynchronous models. We gave a clear definition of global states, bringing out distinction between observable (processes) and not observable (channels) local states, and some of their properties (consistency, being transitless). The problem was tackled by steps : at first level, it was shown how a process can record its own local state consistently with its neighbours; the technique of markers, similar in the FIFO case to the one developped in [CL85, CM86], is generalized, through acknowledgements, to the non FIFO communication model. At second level, global synchronization requiring the wave sequence abstract control scheme solves the problem stated; from a methodological point of view, it displays yet another situation where this abstract network traversal scheme can be seen as a syntaxic scanner on which semantic actions are grafted : this approach has been previously enhanced in [HR88a]. Finally, at third level, a computation model is presented through an example : computing the number of intransit messages; clearly, other functions fit this model, e.g. set of intransit messages, or – in a bounded FIFO comunication context – number of lost messages due to full buffer (assuming that control messages have a specific storage buffer preventing them from loss), etc..

As conclusion, we lay stress on the fact that techniques developped lead to a whole family of algorithms devoted to observation of asynchronous distributed applications or systems.

Acknowledgements. Thanks to the anonymous referees for their useful comments on the preliminary version, which helped to obtain significant improvements.

References

[CL85]   K. M. Chandy and L. Lamport. Distributed snapshots: determining global states of distributed systems. *ACM TOCS*, 63–75, February 1985.

[CM86]   K. M. Chandy and J. Misra. An example of stepwise refinement of distributed programs: quiescence detection. *ACM TOPLAS*, 8(3), July 1986.

[CM88]   K. M. Chandy and J. Misra. *Parallel program design : a foundation*. Addison-Wesley, 1988.

[FGL82] M. J. Fischer, N. D. Griffeth, and N. Lynch. Global states of a distributed system. *IEEE trans. on soft. eng.*, SE-8:3:198–202, may 1982.

[HJPR87] J.-M. Hélary, C. Jard, N. Plouzeau, and M. Raynal. Detection of stable properties in distributed applications. *6th ACM SIGACT-SIGOPS, Symp. Principles of Distributed Computing, Vancouver, Canada*, 125–136, August 1987.

[HPR89] J.M. Hélary, N. Plouzeau, and M. Raynal. A characterization of a particular class of distributed snapshots. In *Submitted to International Conference on Computing and Information (ICCI'89), Toronto*, may 23–27 1989.

[HR88a] J.M. Hélary and M. Raynal. Les parcours distribués de réseaux: un outil pour la conception de protocoles. In R. Castanet et O. Rafiq, editor, *CFIP'88 Ingénierie des protocoles*, pages 159–170, Eyrolles, 1988.

[HR88b] J.-M. Hélary and M. Raynal. *Synchronisation et contrôle des systèmes et des programmes répartis.* Eyrolles, Septembre 1988. English translation to appear, Wiley, 1990.

[HR89] J.-M. Hélary and M. Raynal. An abstract distributed iteration scheme: application to the computation of weighted shortest paths. *Technology and Science of Informatics, Vol. 7, No 3*, May 1989. (In French).

[Lam78] L. Lamport. Time, clocks and the ordering of events in a distributed system. *Communications. of the ACM*, 21(7):558–565, July 1978.

[LY87] T.H. Lai and T.H Yang. On distributed snapshots. *Inf. Proc. Letters*, 25:153–158, 1987.

[Mat89] F. Mattern. Virtual time and global states of distributed systems. In Cosnard, Quinton, Raynal, and Robert, editors, *Proc. Int. Workshop on Parallel and Distributed Algorithms, Bonas, France, oct. 1988*, North Holland, 1989.

[Mor85] C. Morgan. Global and logical time in distributed algorithms. *Inf. Proc. Letters*, 20:290–294, 1985.

[Sch85] F. B. Schneider. Paradigms for distributed programs. In *Distributed Systems*, pages 431–480, Springer Verlag, 1985. LNCS 190.

[Tay89] K. Taylor. The role of inhibition in asynchronous consistent-cut protocols. *these proceedings.*

[Tel86] G. Tel. *Distributed Infimum Approximation*. Tech. report RUU-CS-86-12, University of Utrecht, 1986.

Building a Global Time on Parallel Machines *

Jean-Marc JEZEQUEL

I.R.I.S.A. Campus de Beaulieu
F-35042 RENNES CEDEX, FRANCE

Abstract

This paper presents a pragmatic algorithm to build a global time on any distributed system, which is optimal for homogeneous parallel machines. After some discution on time, clocks and distributed systems, we survey and criticize the classical approaches based on clock synchronisation techniques. Satisfying better our purposes, a statistical method is chosen as a building block to derive an original algorithm valid for any topology. This algorithm is particularly well suited for distributed algorithm experimentation purposes because, after an acquisition phasis, it induces neither CPU nor message overhead. We provide in the conclusion some data about its behavior and performances on some parallel machines.

1 Introduction

Whereas ordering two events occuring at the same place is straightforward, there is a problem if the events occur at different places, or if we want to compare various durations, because usually there is no common time reference among them.

In a distributed system, a common time reference (*i.e.* a global time) is very useful for two kinds of reasons. First, a global time availability allows to design simpler distributed algorithms to deal with synchronized behaviors, real-time constraints (like timeout for protocols) or actual ordering of events (Distributed Database Systems, version management...). Then, if we want to observe the behavior of a distributed algorithm on a distributed system (for test or debug or other purposes), a global time allows us to measure its performances, to observe the order of events, and to verify easily some properties (mutual exclusion...).

This paper discusses the way such a global time may be actually constructed on parallel machines. We define in section 2 some vocabulary and precise what kind of systems we are interested in. Section 3 is an overview of the software clock synchronization principles, methods and limits. To get rid of those limits (too constrainfull for our purposes), we present in section 4 a new hypothesis to justify an approach based on statistical estimations upon mutual dependencies of local clocks. Section 5 shows how this approach can be used as a building block to construct a global time in any distributed system, and that for some of them (the subclass of homogeneous parallel machines) this global time has the real time accuracy. We conclude with some practical results for this global time for some parallel machine, and on the interests and limits of this new service.

---

*This work has been partially supported by the French program on parallelism of the CNRS/C^3, and within the ADP research team of the IRISA laboratory.

2 General Framework

2.1 About Time

Agreeing with [10] we can define an *event* as a *point* on the time line, and a *duration* as the interval between two events. The real number $t(e)$ is associated to event e by the fonction *time*. We call *clock* any abstract device which is able to measure durations. A *physical clock* is a device which can count the occurrence of quasi-periodic events. Such events are generally the observable oscillations of some physical system where the variations of a state variable of the system (position, volume, electrical tension...) are related to time through a periodic physical law. The *granularity* of a physical clock is the duration g between two incrementations of the clock. The *local time* lt_i is the continuous time generated by a physical clock C_i, taking as time basis its average granularity g_i. We can say that $lt_i = g_i(C_i + e_i)$, where e_i is the "reading error" of the discrete clock C_i.

2.2 Distributed systems

In the following we consider that a distributed system is a set of processors (or sites, machines, nodes) communicating only by messages transmission through a point to point communication network. We call *parallel machine* any homogeneous distributed system built on a local network. The transmission delays of messages are *not* negligible in front of internal action durations on a processor. Massively parallel machines like hypercubes or local networks of workstations are good examples of distributed systems. In order to compare different synchronization algorithms on those machines, let us present some typical data about some parallel machines: a network of Sun workstations (located on various buildings), linked with *ethernet* (and optical couplers between buildings); an Intel hypercube iPSC/2, with 64 processors (80386) linked by special hardware; and a FPS hypercube T-40, with 32 processors (Transputers). Measures have been performed with the ECHIDNA system, which provides an homogeneous interface for an high level programming language (Estelle) on parallel machines (see [9] for a presentation).

Machines	Sun	iPSC/2	FPS-T40
minimum transmission delay of a message T_{min} (ms)	10	1	3
maximum transmission delay of messages T_{max} (ms)	> 100	> 10	> 20
granularity of the available physical clock g (ms)	20	1	0.064
physical clock medium drift d (s/day)	0	≈ 1	≈ 0.5

2.3 Physical clock for common processors

Let us look into the usual way physical clock are built on common computers. There are two basic methods, the simpler (used in our Sun network) uses the 110 or 220V power line to cause an interrupt on every voltage cycle (at 50 or 60 Hz). The other one needs a local oscillator, which is commonly a (cheap) quartz crystal. The cut of the crystal determines its resonant frequency, within 50.10^{-6} of its nominal frequency for common commercial purposes (1.10^{-6} for military applications). This actual resonant frequency depends on the temperature and on few others factors of lesser importance. When such a crystal is mounted under tension, it generates a periodic signal which is fed into a counter to make it count down to zero. There, it causes a CPU interrupt (called *clock tick*): the CPU increments an internal register (its local "physical clock") and loads again the counter with the accurate predefined value.

According to [5] and to various experiments made on our parallel machines, if the temperature is quite constant at each node then the trajectory of a local time generated by such a physical clock may be modeled with a constant frequency offset: as the frequency change rate is less than $10^{-7}/day$, the resulting bias error on the time offset will be less than 30 ns for 10 min. So, we can model the trajectory of a local time generated by such a physical clock with: $lt(t) = \alpha + \beta t + \delta(t)$, where α is the time offset at $t = 0$, β is the drift of the logical clock, $\beta = 1 + \kappa$, $\kappa = \frac{\Delta F}{F}$ (frequency offset) and $\delta(t)$ modelizes random perturbations and granularity.

2.4 Global time and logical clock

On each site of a distributed system there is such a physical clock showing a different time. Our goal is to build on each site a *logical clock* such that all logical clocks show the same hour at the same time.

We call *global logical clock (LC)* an application from $\Re$ to $\Re^n$, such that:

$LC_i(t)$ is the value of the ith component of LC at time t

Increasing $\forall i \in [1..n], \forall t \in \Re, \forall d > 0 \quad LC_i(t + d) - LC_i(t) \geq 0$

Agreement $\exists \epsilon \in \Re^+, \quad \forall i, j \in [1..n], \forall t \in \Re \quad | LC_i(t) - LC_j(t) | < \epsilon$

We call *global time* the time T generated on each site by the component LC_i. The imprecision of the global time is ϵ, and $G = 2\epsilon$ is its granularity.

As the major interest of a clock is to measure durations and to allow ordering of events, we are interested in the following properties for our logical clocks:

Accuracy $\exists \rho \in \Re, \forall t_1, t_2 \in \Re \times \Re, \forall i \in [1..n]$
$$(t_2 - t_1)(1 - \rho) < LC_i(t_2) - LC_i(t_1) < (t_2 - t_1)(1 + \rho)$$

i.e. the logical clock is within a linear envelope of real time. If LC_i is derivable, this property is equivalent to $| \frac{dLC_i(t)}{dt} - 1 | < \rho$.

Internal causality

$\forall e_i, e_j$ internal events of a distributed system $e_i \rightarrow e_j \Rightarrow LC_i(t(e_i)) < LC_j(t(e_j))$
There exist known hardware solutions to build systems having such a global time, using phaselock loops or satellite synchronization. Besides the fact that such machines are no longer distributed systems, those solutions are quite expensive and not currently available for common parallel machines. So we have to check for software solutions, which have aroused a profuse bibliography.

3 Software Clock Synchronization

3.1 Principles and Problems

The usual way to synchronize two clocks C_i and C_j consists in choosing one of them (say C_i) as a reference (*i.e.* $\forall t$, $LC_i(t) = C_i(t)$), and then to measure the offset Δ_{ij} between lt_i and lt_j in order to set $LC_j(t) = C_j(t) - \Delta_{ij}$.

But, as clocks have a granularity, we can only measure $\Delta_{ij} = C_j - C_i$ in place of $lt_j - lt_i$, and as a frequency offset may exist between clocks, lt_i and lt_j can drift, thus Δ_{ij} is time dependent. Furthermore, in distributed systems the evaluation of Δ_{ij} is not trivial, because any information interchange can only be done through messages: site P_i

has to send to site P_j the value at time t of its clock, $C_i(t)$. As the transmission time tm_{ij} of a message from P_i to P_j can't be known *a priori*, the error on the evaluation of Δ_{ij} can be as large as the maximum transmission time of a message.

It appears clearly that this method can be used only if transmission delays, granularities and frequency offsets are small enough with respect to the wanted agreement on the global time. Otherwise, we have to look for more sophisticated algorithms.

3.2 Lamport's logical clocks

Assuming the following hypothesis,

LH1 For every processor P_i having available a physical clock C_i, $\mid \frac{dC_i(t)}{dt} - 1 \mid < \kappa$

LH2 there exists a bound on the transmission delays of messages: $t_{del} = \mu + \xi$, where μ is the minimum delay of a message, and ξ the known bound on the unpredictable delay of messages.

LH3 every τ seconds a message is sent over every edge of the network

LH4 physical clock granularity is thin enough to timestamp two events of the same site with different values

Lamport presents in [13] an algorithm to build synchronous logical clocks, which can be adapted to synchronize physical clocks: as long as P_i doesn't receive any message, let $\frac{dLC_i(t)}{dt} \equiv \frac{dC_i(t)}{dt}$. But, upon sending a message, P_j timestamps it with the value $T_j = LC_j(t)$; and when P_i receives a message, it sets $LC_i(t) = max(LC_i(t), T_j + \mu)$

The properties of those logical clocks are:

LP1 $\forall i, j \, \forall t \mid LC_i(t) - LC_j(t) \mid < \epsilon \approx 2\kappa\tau + \xi$ which is for our examples: $\epsilon_{Sun} > 50ms, \epsilon_{iPSC} > 10ms, \epsilon_{FPS} > 20ms$

LP2 $\mid \frac{dLC_i(t)}{dt} - 1 \mid < \kappa$ between resets, but undefined during resets.

But we can remark that the resulting global time doesn't stay within a linear envelope of real time, because clocks are always reset forward, each τ in the bad case. On the other hand, if τ is large then ϵ is large, and thus the agreement poor.

Anyway, if the application doesn't send enough messages to complete LH3, additional messages are needed, and thus the application can be perturbed. Furthermore, granularity is not really taken into account, meanwhile in our systems LH4 is not valid (excepted for the FPS).

3.3 Improvements and limits

Numerous researchers improve the Lamport's idea: among them, Lamport himself in [14] (where clocks are no longer always reset forward, and can tolerate some faults), and Marzullo who formalizes the problem and its solution in [16]. Various algorithms are presented to deal with byzantine behaviors in [15, 8] and in [19](optimal solution with respect to the Accuracy property: its global time accuracy is as good as the harware one (quartz)); see [17] and [18] for an overview and a detailed comparison.

But, as it is highlighted in [11, 12], those algorithms are quite complex, and thus difficult to implement correctly and maintain, and exhibit high CPU and messages overheads as the number of tolerated faults increases. Furthermore, it is observed in [2] that the overall increase in reliability provided by those byzantine algorithms is not always significant, compared to other sources of system failure. Thus, restricting the class of faults to be resisted, [2] presents a simpler algorithm, which improves the precision of

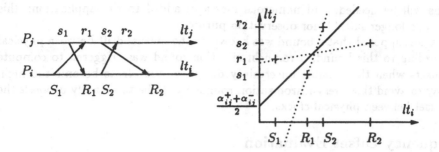

Figure 1: Statistical estimation of time and frequency offset

the global time (the trick is to lower $t_{del} = \mu + \xi$ (and thus ϵ), and to consider that a message whose transfer delay is greater than t_{del} is faulty).

So, apart for the accuracy and the fault tolerance problems, the primary solution of [13] has not been drastically improved. When extra messages are exchanged to control the mutual drift of physical clocks, the observational purpose of a global time is clearly unusable: those extra messages perturb the application that we want to observe. Furthermore, the precision of the global time is still not very good, because it depends closely on the variability of the transmission delays of messages, which is always the main factor of uncertainty. But, according to hypothesis LH1, LH2, LH3, [3] shows that much better results are impossible. So, if we want to go further, we have to study new hypothesis, reformulate the problem and present new methods.

4 Statistical Estimation of Clock Offsets

4.1 Elimination of the transmission delay uncertainty

In a first step, we are not interested in fault tolerance (in parallel machines, almost all faults are software bugs or fail stops). Furthermore, we think that clock synchronization is not an intrinsic problem of fault tolerance. As it is explicitly stated in [2], the major contribution brought by thoses techniques is to get rid of the transmission delay uncertainty (and eventually to deal with crash and join problems).

But transmission delays can be modelized by a random variable whose distribution is unknown, because they depend on the software overhead to access the network on the sending machine, on the network transmission time (depending on the size of the messages) and on the software overhead to deliver the incoming messages to the right tasks on the receiving machine, etc...

Reference [6] proposes a statistical method to eliminate this uncertainty when drift between clocks may be assumed negligible for short periods. Instead of performing only one message exchange when a resynchronization is needed, the algorithm performs numerous exchanges and selects the one with the best transmission delay to compute the time offset between two sites (and the precision of this evaluation).

The major advantage of this algorithm is its precision obtained on the global time, which is only limitated by the granularity of the physical clocks and the anisotropy of the network (*i.e.* difference between minimum transmission delays).

However, if the mutual drift between physical clocks is not negligible, frequent resynchronizations will be needed, and numerous messages added to the application: this global time is no longer suitable for observation purposes.

Until now we supposed that a bound was known on the mutual drift between physical clocks. According to this bound, a resynchronization round was triggered to compute new time offsets when the possible uncertainty due to mutual drifts became too high. The only way to avoid those resynchronization rounds would be to actually *compute* the frequency offset between physical clocks.

4.2 Frequency Offset Evaluation

The idea of [4] is also to use multiple message exchanges between P_i and P_j to estimate with a statistical method the time *and* the frequency offset between two sites. As for each site P_i we have $lt_i(t) = \alpha_i + \beta_i t + \delta_i$ (see 2.3), there exist α_{ij} and β_{ij} such that $lt_j(t) = \alpha_{ij} + \beta_{ij} lt_i(t) + \beta_{ij}\delta_{ij}$, where δ_{ij} is a random variable whose density function is the convolution between δ_j and δ_i density functions ($\beta_{ij} = \beta_j/\beta_i$ $\alpha_{ij} = \alpha_j - \beta_{ij}\alpha_i$ and $\delta_{ij} = \delta_j - \beta_{ij}\delta_i$). The actual purpose of [4] is thus to compute bounds for α_{ij} and β_{ij}.

Let S_i^k be the event of site P_i sending a message to P_j, R_j^k the corresponding reception on P_j, and τ_{ij} the positive random variable (whose distribution is unknown) modelizing the transmission delay of messages. Thus, we can write for messages received by P_j (see figure 1):

$$lt_j(t(R_j^k)) = lt_j(t(S_i^k) + \tau_{ij}) = lt_j(t(S_i^k)) + \beta_j \tau_{ij} = \alpha_{ij} + \beta_{ij} lt_i(t(S_i^k)) + \beta_j \tau_{ij} + \delta_{ij}$$

and symetricaly for messages sent by P_j:

$$lt_j(t(S_j^k)) = lt_j(t(R_i^k) - \tau_{ji}) = lt_j(t(R_i^k)) - \beta_j \tau_{ji} = \alpha_{ij} + \beta_{ij} lt_i(t(R_i^k)) - \beta_j \tau_{ji} + \delta_{ij}$$

If δ_{ij} (mainly the granularity) is small in comparison with transmission delays ($\delta_{ij} \ll \tau_{ij}$ so $\beta_j \tau_{ij} + \delta_{ij} > 0$ and $-\beta_j \tau_{ji} + \delta_{ij} < 0$), then the wanted line ($lt_j = \alpha_{ij} + \beta_{ij} lt_i$) geometrically lies between the two separate sets of points UP=(S_i^k, R_j^k) and LOW=(R_i^k, S_j^k); see figure 1. Thus, we can compute higher and lower bounds $\alpha_{ij}^+, \alpha_{ij}^-$ and $\beta_{ij}^+, \beta_{ij}^-$ for α_{ij} and β_{ij} using a geometrical algorithm[1]. Furthermore, as the duration and the number of points of the estimation increase, $\beta_{ij}^+ - \beta_{ij}^-$ decreases to 0, and $\alpha_{ij}^+ - \alpha_{ij}^-$ to the difference between minimum transmission delays in the two directions. Practically, this convergence is very fast for distributed systems built on local networks, because the transmission delay distribution has an important mass near the minimum (see [7] for details and proof).

Hence, the problem of transmission delay variability is solved, and as the mutual frequency offset is computed instead of being bounded, resynchronization is no longer needed. This last property is very interesting because, after an acquisition phasis, this algorithm induces neither CPU nor message overhead. The application is thus no longer perturbed by the global time construction.

In the following, we will select this statistical method as a building block to derive an original algorithm valid for any topology.

---

[1] The first idea was to use a linear regression to estimate α_{ij} and β_{ij}, but [4] shows that this method can't give 100% confidence intervals.

4.3 Optimisations and limits for parallel machines

First, let us see how we can optimize this method for parallel machines.

Let μ be a constant less than the minimum transmission delay (more precisely, μ is such that $\forall i, j \ 0 < \mu < \beta_j \tau_{ij}$), and δ such that $\forall i, j \ | \delta_{ij} | < \delta$. $\delta \approx g$ (the granularity) because $| \delta_{ij} | = | \delta_i \otimes \delta_j | < 2 \max(| \delta_i |)$, and $| \delta_i | \approx g/2$ is mainly the precision of the physical clock ($\otimes$ is the convolution product).

A problem arises when the granularity is not small with respect to transmission delays ($\delta > \mu$, see the Sun network example): the two sets of points (S_i^k, R_j^k) and (R_i^k, S_j^k) may overlap, because $\beta_j \tau_{ij} + \delta_{ij}$ is no longer always greater than $-\beta_j \tau_{ji} + \delta_{ji}$.

The solution to this problem consists in artificially increasing the minimum transmission delay so that $\mu' > \delta$. Geometrically, this leads to move away the two sets of points eachother. The required minimum value of this adjustment is thus $\nu = \delta - \mu$, so that $\nu + \beta_j \tau_{ij} + \delta_{ij} > -\nu - \beta_j \tau_{ji} + \delta_{ji}$.

We can use the same method to decrease the value of the minimum transmission delay downto $| \mu_{ij} - \mu_{ji} |$ (i.e. the difference between minimum transmission delays in both directions) as long as the two sets of points (S_i^k, R_j^k) and (R_i^k, S_j^k) remain separated each other, i.e. the adjustment ν is such that $\nu > \delta - \mu$ (if $\nu > 0$ the sets are moved away and else they are bring together).

This can be used to gain precision on the evaluation of β_{ij} and α_{ij} with the same acquisition period ΔT, as precision on α_{ij} depends on the precision on β_{ij} (and is limited by $| \mu_{ij} - \mu_{ji} |$), and the lower bound for $\Delta \beta_{ij} = \frac{1}{2}(\beta_{ij}^+ - \beta_{ij}^-)$ is $\frac{2\mu}{\Delta T}$.

If the network is highly symmetrical and homogeneous (as it is in our three examples), minimum transmission delays in both directions can be considered equal (isotropic networks), and thus lower bound for $\Delta \beta_{ij}$ is $\frac{2(\mu+\nu)}{\Delta T} = \frac{2\delta}{\Delta T}$.

5 Building a global time over any connected network

5.1 Theoretical solution

At this point, a site is able to evaluate its local linear dependencies with its neighbours. From those local dependencies, we want to derive some global dependencies in order to build on each processor a global time function $TG_i(lt_i(t))$ having the required properties.

We assume in this part that each processor P_i of the network N has computed (in parallel) its linear dependencies with all of its neighbours with the algorithm described in the previous part (let us call it A1). So, the following system (S) of inequations holds:

$$\forall P_i \in N, \ \forall P_j \in V_i, \ \alpha_{ij}^- < \alpha_{ij} < \alpha_{ij}^+, \ \beta_{ij}^- < \beta_{ij} < \beta_{ij}^+ \ and \ lt_j(t) = \alpha_{ij} + \beta_{ij} lt_i(t) + \delta_{ij}$$

where V_i denotes the set of P_i's neighbours. As $| \delta_{ij} | \approx g$, we have:

$$\forall P_i \in N, \ \forall P_j \in V_i, \ \alpha_{ij}^- - g + \beta_{ij}^- lt_i(t) < lt_j(t) < \alpha_{ij}^+ + g + \beta_{ij}^+ lt_i(t)$$

As $lt_i(t) = \alpha_i + \beta_i t + \delta_i$, and $| \delta_i | \approx g/2$, (S) is equivalent to

$$\forall P_i \in N, \forall P_j \in V_i, \alpha_{ij}^- - g + \beta_{ij}^-(\alpha_i - g/2) + \beta_{ij}^- \beta_i t < \alpha_j + \beta_j t < \alpha_{ij}^+ + g + \beta_{ij}^+(\alpha_i + g/2) + \beta_{ij}^+ \beta_i t$$

This is valid for each t, so:

$$\forall P_i \in N, \forall P_j \in V_i, \beta_{ij}^- \beta_i < \beta_j < \beta_{ij}^+ \beta_i \ ; \ \alpha_{ij}^- - g + \beta_{ij}^-(\alpha_i - g/2) < \alpha_j < \alpha_{ij}^+ + g + \beta_{ij}^+(\alpha_i + g/2)$$

As the method used in A1 is highly symetric, $\beta_{ij}^+ = 1/\beta_{ji}^-$ and $\alpha_{ij}^+ = -\alpha_{ji}^-/\beta_{ij}^-$, so half of the inequations are redondant. We want to solve this system, *i.e.* to find intervals $[\alpha_i^-, \alpha_i^+]$ and $[\beta_i^-, \beta_i^+]$ for all P_i that verify the system. There exists at least a solution: if every site has a linear dependency with all of its neighbours and if the graph is connected, every site has a linear dependency with every other by composition of the dependencies along any path. There exists even an infinity of solutions, each one being homothetic of the others (in terms of β).

The principle of the solution is to choose a reference site P_r (either statically or by regular dynamical election), where we state $\beta_r^- = \beta_r^+ = 1$ and $\alpha_r^- = \alpha_r^+ = 0$; and then to eliminate *all* the inequations of (S) by substitution.

Let $d(i,j)$ be the topological distance from P_i to P_j on N. Let $D_r(p) = \{j \in N \mid d(r,j) = p\}$ be the set of sites which are at distance p from P_r. We suppose that there exists a minimal spawning tree T over N (*i.e.* where distance from P_r to P_j along T is $d(r,j)$), whose root is P_r and diameter d, and that every process P_i knows its depth and its neighbour's one on this tree[2].

The system will be solved from near to near along T, *i.e.* for the neighbours of P_r, then for the neighbours of the neighbours etc...

We say that a site P_j is *synchronized* if and only if all the inequations of (S) with terms in α_{ij} or β_{ij} such that $d(r,i) \le d(r,j)$ have been eliminated (so we have found the wanted intervals $[\alpha_j^-, \alpha_j^+]$ and $[\beta_j^-, \beta_j^+]$). Let be S^p the system where $\forall P_j \in \bigcup_{k\in[0,p]} D_r(k)$, P_j is synchronized.

Theorem *If P_r is the root of a minimal spawning tree T and if P_r is synchronized, then it is possible to eliminate all the inequations of (S) in order to synchronize all the sites of T in d steps, where d is the depth of T.*

Demonstration (by induction on the depth of the graph):

Initially, only site P_r is synchronized, and $S^0 =$(S). Suppose that: $\forall P_j \in \bigcup_{k\in[0,p-1]} D_r(k)$, P_j is synchronized. The graph is synchronized until depth $p-1$, and remaining inequations form the system S^{p-1}. Let us see how to synchronize it at depth p.

Let be $P_j \in D_r(p)$ and $P_i \in V_j$. As $d(i,j) = 1$, $V_j \subset D_r(p-1) \cup D_r(p) \cup D_r(p+1)$. So we have to eliminate all the inequations of S^{p-1} having terms in α_{ij} or β_{ij} such that $P_i \in D_r(p-1) \cup D_r(p)$.

1. If $P_i \in D_r(p-1)$, then P_i is synchronized (by hypothesis), so there exist solutions such that $\alpha_i^- < \alpha_i < \alpha_i^+$ and $\beta_i^- < \beta_i < \beta_i^+$. In S^{p-1} we can extract the two following inequations (the symetric one, in terms of α_{ji} and β_{ji} being equivalent to those one):

$$\beta_{ij}^- \beta_i < \beta_j < \beta_{ij}^+ \beta_i \text{ and } \alpha_{ij}^- - g + \beta_{ij}^-(\alpha_i - g/2) < \alpha_j < \alpha_{ij}^+ + g + \beta_{ij}^+(\alpha_i + g/2)$$

This is valid for all $P_i \in V_j \cap D_r(p-1)$, so the conjonction of those inequations gives:

$$[\beta_j^-, \beta_j^+] = \bigcap_{P_i \in V_j \cap D_r(p-1)} [\beta_i^- \beta_{ij}^-, \beta_i^+ \beta_{ij}^+]$$

---

[2] If every site can know statically the topology of R, then T can be statically defined. Otherwise T has to be built, using for example the algorithm (say A2) provided in [1], after whom each site broadcasts its depth in T to its neighbours.

and

$$[\alpha_j^-, \alpha_j^+] = \bigcap_{P_i \in V_j \cap D_r(p-1)} [\alpha_i^- - g + \beta_{ij}^-(\alpha_i^- - g/2), \alpha_i^+ + g + \beta_{ij}^+(\alpha_i^+ + g/2)]$$

2. If $P_i \in D_r(p)$, let us notice that $D_r(p)$ forms a sub-network N_p, partitioned in a set of connected sub-networks $N_p^1..N_p^n$.

- If $N_p^j = \{P_j\}$, *i.e.* if $V_j \cap D_r(p) = \emptyset$, then there is no more inequations over P_j, so P_j is synchronized.

- Otherwise, for each of those connected sub-networks N_p^k we choose again (either statically or dynamicaly) a new reference site, root of a new minimal covering tree over N_p^k, and we synchronize those sub-networks with the same method as for the main network.

  As the number of sites in N_p^k is strictly less than the number of sites in N (the reference site of N can't be in N_p^k), this leads to build decreasing sequences (with the inclusion meaning) of unsynchronized sub-networks whose minimal size is one site. Upon synchronization of thoses last sites (a single site network is synchronized by definition), N_p^k becomes synchronized, thus $P_j \in N_p^j$ is synchronized.□

5.2 Algorithm derivation

From the mathematical resolution of (S), we can derive directly a distributed algorithm A3 to make the problem be solved by the considered distributed system.

$A3(N, P_r) :=$ -- Algorithm to synchronize network N, with P_r as reference[3].

for each process P_j do begin
  $p:=distance(P_j, P_r);$
  -- **STEP 1**, get the values from the already synchronized neighbours
  if $p > 0$ then begin
    $\forall P_i \in V_j \cap D_r(p-1) \quad P_i \; ? \; ([\alpha_i^-, \alpha_i^+], [\beta_i^-, \beta_i^+]);$
    $[\beta_j^-, \beta_j^+] := \bigcap_{P_i \in V_j \cap D_r(p-1)} [\beta_i^- \beta_{ij}^-, \beta_i^+ \beta_{ij}^+];$
    $[\alpha_j^-, \alpha_j^+] := \bigcap_{P_i \in V_j \cap D_r(p-1)} [\alpha_i^- + \beta_{ij}^- \alpha_{ij}^-, \alpha_i^+ + \beta_{ij}^+ \alpha_{ij}^+];$
  end;
  -- **STEP 2**
  if $V_j \cap D_r(p) \neq \emptyset$ then begin
    Perform $A2(N_p^j, P_s);$ -- to build a minimal covering tree (whose root is P_s)
                    -- over the subnetwork N_p^k (possible static knowledge)
    Perform $A3(N_p^j, P_s);$ -- recursive call
  end;
  -- **STEP 3**, as P_j is synchronized, it broadcasts its values deeper on the tree
  $\forall P_i \in V_j \cap D_r(p+1) \quad P_i \; ! \; ([\alpha_j^-, \alpha_j^+], [\beta_j^-, \beta_j^+]);$
end;

---

[3]Hereafter, "P_i ? " denotes the asynchronous reception of a message from P_i, and "P_i !" the emission to P_i.

So, the full algorithm is:

Perform A1;
All sites exchange their relatives values $\alpha_{ij}^+, \alpha_{ij}^-, \beta_{ij}^+, \beta_{ij}^-$ with neighbours
Perform A2(N, P_r);
Perform A3(N, P_r);

$$LC_i(C_i(t)) ::= (C_i(t) - \frac{\alpha_i^+ + \alpha_i^-}{2}) / (\frac{\beta_i^+ + \beta_i^-}{2});$$

5.3 Application to some classical topologies

Our algorithm doesn't need to know statically the actual topology of the network. But if it is known, we can derive from it simpler algorithms to suit the particularities of the network, because the second step of the general algorithm (which could be quite costly) will be streched.

Fully connected network In such a network, the depth of the covering tree is always 1. So, all sites are chosen one after the other to be the next reference site for the remaining subnetwork. During the STEP 1 of A3, the only message expected is from the reference site of the current subnetwork, and the STEP 3 is performed only by the site which is reference of its subnetwork. Supposing that A2 is not actually performed (static order is known to choose next reference site), the time complexity of A3 is the complexity on the last site chosen: $O(n)$. We can notice that we get there a distributed version of the algorithm first presented in [4].

Ring topology Let be R_n a network of n processors connected with a ring topology. We must study two cases, depending on the parity of n. If n is even, $\forall P_j \in R_n$, $V_j \cap D_r(p) = \emptyset$. So, the second step of A3 becomes useless, and its time complexity is $O(n/2)$.

But if n is odd, the two sites located at distance $\frac{n-1}{2}$ of P_r are neighbours. So, the second step of A3 is usefull only for those two sites, and time complexity is also $O(\frac{n}{2})$.

Star topology If we choose the center of the network as the reference site, the minimal covering tree depth is only one, and thus A3 complexity becomes $O(1)$.

Hypercube topology Let be P_r a site of an hypercube H, whose dimension (and thus diameter) is d. Hypercube topologies have numerous interesting particularities. Among them, if $P_s \in D_r(p)$, then $V_s \cap D_r(p) = \emptyset$: a site which is at distance p from P_r has no neighbour at the same distance p from P_r.

So, in the same way that for an even ring, the second step of A3 becomes useless, and time complexity is $O(d)$.

5.4 Global time and real time

As we have chosen the physical clock on one site to synchronize all the others, the resulting global time can't be better (in terms of accuracy) than the local time generated by the quartz of the reference site. This is generally not a problem when we are only interested in internal events observation. However, if we have to deal with external events references, a synchronization with a better external clock might be required. If such a clock is connected to the network, it is possible to select its site as the primary reference for our algorithm, so the accuracy of the global time is its accuracy.

However in almost all parallel machines, such a good clock is not available. But on homogeneous networks (such as hypercube machines), the available quartz have a resonant frequency that can be modelized on the set of all the quartz of the network by a random variable whose mean value is the nominal frequency of the quartz. So, $\frac{1}{N}\sum_{i=1}^{N}\beta_i = 1 \pm \varepsilon$, $\varepsilon \approx 10^{-10}$.

Thus it is possible to append to our algorithm a last phase where it adjusts all the computed frequency offset with their mean value. We can then have an accuracy very close to real time, without any reference to a better than quartz external clock (*e.g.* *atomic*).

6 Conclusion

The algorithm described above has been simplified for the hypercube topology and specified with the Estelle programming language in order to be compiled with ECHIDNA and experimented on Sun network, on iPSC/2 and on FPS-T40.

An initial acquisition period of 300 s yields to the following results:

Machines	Sun	iPSC/2	FPS-T40
Physical clock granularity g (ms)	20	1	0.064
Measured bound on $\Delta F/F$	0	2.10^{-5}	5.10^{-6}
Best precision with classical methods (ms)	80	10	20
Precision on β_i	6.10^{-5}	4.10^{-6}	5.10^{-7}
Initial precision of $LC_i(t)$ (ms)	50	2	0.2
Precision after one hour (ms)	200	15	2

The hypothesis of linearity between physical clocks (*i.e.* that frequency offset rate is actually negligible) has been verified for rather large periods ($\approx 12h$) through various experiments. However, the imprecision of our global time increases linearly with time: $G \approx 2g + 2\Delta\beta t \approx 2g + \frac{4\delta}{\Delta T}t$. So, if this algorithm is to be used continuously, resynchronization rounds should take place dynamically when the precision becomes too bad for the current purpose, or application messages can be used to enforce the precision on frequency mutual offsets during the application execution.

The granularity of our global time doesn't always allow us to check for internal causality, *i.e.* that messages are always sent before they are received (at least for the Sun and the iPSC). But, as shown by the FPS example, this is mostly an hardware problem, and there is no software possibility to get rid of physical clock granularity. However various experiments showed that our global time can be used to order (with high probability) communication events, even on the iPSC. But, if we would use this new service in the property verification field, it would be interesting to study the idea of a probabilistic order of events, in place of classical partial orders.

For the distributed algorithm experimentation purpose, this global time algorithm has been integrated in the ECHIDNA system (along with the Lamport's algorithm to ensure internal causality), so it is now possible to observe a distributed algorithm behavior on a parallel machine without perturbing it.

Acknowledgements.

Special acknowledgment is due to Y. Haddad for the original idea of frequency offset estimation, to C. Jard for his constant support and advices, and to all the members of the ADP team for their reviewing.

References

[1] A. T. Cheung. Graph traversal techniques and the maximum flow problem in distributed computing. *IEEE Trans. on SE*, SE-9(4):504–512, 1983.

[2] F. Cristian, H. Aghili, and R. Strong. Clock synchronization in the presence of omission and performance faults, and processors joins. In *Proc. of 16th IEEE Symposium on Fault-Tolerant Computing Systems, Vienna*, pages 218–223, July 1986.

[3] D. Dolev, J.Y. Halpern, and R. Strong. On the possibility and impossibility of achieving clock synchronization. In *Proc. of 16th ACM Symposium on Theory of Computing*, pages 504–511, April 1984.

[4] A. Duda, G. Harrus, Y. Haddad, and G. Bernard. Estimating global time in distributed system. In *Proc. 7th Int. Conf. on Distributed Computing Systems, Berlin*, 1987.

[5] C.E Ellingson and R.J. Kulpinski. Dissemination of system time. *IEEE Transactions on Communications*, COM-21(5):605–623, May 1973.

[6] R. Gusella and S. Zatti. A network time controler for a distributed berkeley UNIX system. *IEEE Distr. Proc. Tech. Comm. Newsletter*, SI-2(6):7–15, June 1984.

[7] Y. Haddad. Performance dans les systèmes répartis: des outils pour les mesures. Thèse de Doctorat, Univ. Paris-Sud, Centre Orsay, PARIS, Septembre 1988.

[8] J.Y. Halpern, B. Simons, R. Strong, and D. Dolev. Fault-tolerant clock synchronization. In *Proc. of the Third ACM Symposium on Principles of Distributed Computing, Vancouver, Canada*, pages 89–102, August 1984.

[9] C. Jard and J.-M. Jézéquel. A multi-processor Estelle to C compiler to experiment distributed algorithms on parallel machines. In *Proc. of the 9th IFIP International Workshop on Protocol Specification, Testing, and Verification, University of Twente, The Netherlands*, North Holland, 1989.

[10] H. Kopetz. Accuracy of time measurement in distributed real time systems. In *5th Symposium on Reliability in Distributed Software and Database Systems*, pages 35–41, IEEE Comp. Society, 1986.

[11] H. Kopetz and W. Ochsenreiter. Clock synchronization in distributed real time systems. In *IEEE Transaction on Computers, Special issue on Real Time Systems*, pages 933–940, August 1987.

[12] C.M. Krishna and K.G. Shin. Synchronization and fault-masking in redundant real time systems. In *Proc. of the FTCS 14, IEEE Press*, pages 151–157, 1984.

[13] L. Lamport. Time, clocks and the ordering of events in a distributed system. *Communications. of the ACM*, 21(7):558–565, July 1978.

[14] L. Lamport and P.M. Melliar-Smith. Synchronizing clocks in the presence of faults. *Journal of the ACM*, 32(1):52–78, Juanary 1985.

[15] J. Lundelius and N. Lynch. A new fault-tolerant algorithm for clock synchronization. In *Proc. of the Third ACM Symposium on Principles of Distributed Computing, Vancouver, Canada*, pages 75–88, August 1984.

[16] K. Marzullo and S. Owiki. Maintaining time in a distributed system. In *ACM Operating Systems Rev.*, pages 44–54, 1983.

[17] F.B. Schneider. A paradigm for reliable clock synchronization. In *Proc. Advanced Seminar Real Time Local Area Network*, pages 85–104, April 1986.

[18] B. Simons, J. Lundelius, and N. Lynch. *An Overview of Clock Synchronization*. Technical Report, IBM Research Division, October 1988.

[19] T.K. Srikanth and S. Toueg. Optimal clock synchronization. In *4th Annual ACM Symposium on Principles of Distributed Computing*, pages 71–86, August 1985.

FUNCTIONAL DEPENDENCIES OF VARIABLES
IN WAIT-FREE PROGRAMS
(Extended Abstract)

Evangelos Kranakis

Centre for Mathematics and Computer Science
P.O. Box 4079, 1009 AB Amsterdam, The Netherlands
(eva@cwi.nl)

ABSTRACT

Suppose that we are given a wait-free protocol for the asynchronous, concurrent processes $P_1, P_2, ..., P_r, Q_1, Q_2, ..., Q_s$, with $r \geq 2$, $s \geq 0$. For any run (or interleaving) ρ of the protocol and any initialization *init* of all the protocol variables let $X[\rho, init]$ be the value of the variable X at the end of the run ρ. The variables $X_1, X_2, ..., X_r$ "belonging" to the processors $P_1, P_2, ..., P_r$, respectively, are called functionally dependent for the initialization *init*, if for any runs ρ, σ of the protocol,

$$(\forall i, j)(X_i[\rho, init] = X_i[\sigma, init] \Leftrightarrow X_j[\rho, init] = X_j[\sigma, init]).$$

For any run ρ and any initialization *init* of the protocol define the evaluation mapping $eval_{X_1, X_2, ..., X_r}(\rho, init) = (X_1[\rho, init], X_2[\rho, init], ..., X_r[\rho, init])$. We show that for any protocol as above, the variables $X_1, X_2, ..., X_r$ are functionally dependent for the initialization *init* if and only if the quantity $eval_{X_1, X_2, ..., X_r}(\rho, init)$ is independent of ρ.

1. Introduction

There has been a lot of interest in the current literature on Distributed Computing for a more thorough examination of the computational possibilities offered by wait-free protocols. In particular, this has led to a re-examination of the necessity of using control primitives in the design of Concurrent Reader, Concurrent Writer protocols. The results obtained so far have been particularly interesting. Several researchers have been able to implement: (i) atomic, 1-reader, 1-writer registers from safe, 1-reader, 1-writer registers ([L], [K], [T]), and (ii) atomic, multireader, multiwriter registers from atomic, 1-reader, 1-writer registers, by using only wait-free protocols ([A2], [B], [K], [L1], [L2], [N], [P], [V]). Wait-free protocols are of particular interest not only because they are free from the usual control primitives (like, Mutual Exclusion, Test and Set, etc.), but also because they make possible a rather quantitative appraisal of the complexity of various algorithms, e.g. determining the wait-free protocol with the best running time ([P], [L2]).

There are certain instances of programming methodology which have "inherent" waiting requirements (e.g. whenever it is necessary to allocate a critical resource among many users). In such instances, the mechanism of waiting has been extensively used ever since its introduction by Dijkstra [D]. As it seems natural these considerations have led [H] to implement a hierarchy of objects such that objects at a certain level of the hierarchy are "stronger" (with respect to waiting mechanisms) than objects lying below this object in this same hierarchy. The purpose of the present paper is twofold: (1) to reappraise the computational aspects and limitations of wait-free programs, and (2) to "draw the line" between what is possible (e.g. solving the Concurrent Readers/Writers problem) and what is impossible (e.g. Mutual Exclusion problem) by using only wait-free programs. Before giving an outline of the main results it will be necessary to introduce some useful concepts.

1.1. Preliminaries

In order to motivate our results and facilitate the discussion we will first consider wait-free protocols consisting of processors each executing a sequence of assignment statements. In section 5 we will indicate all the modifications necessary to cover the most general wait-free protocols (such protocols in addition to assignment statements will include: **if** ... **then** ... **else** ... **fi**; and **for** $i = 1...n$ **do** ... **od** statements). Let Σ be a language consisting of the assignment symbol :=, the function symbols F, G,... (with subscripts and/or superscripts) each associated with a specified arity ≥ 0, (if the arity of F is 0 then F is also called a constant) and the variables $v_0, v_1,...,v_n,....$

An assignment statement of Σ is a formula of the form $x := F(x_1,...,x_n)$, where $x, x_1,...,x_n$ are variables and $F \in \Sigma$ is an n-ary function symbol. Suppose that P and Q are asynchronous, concurrent processors each executing a finite sequence $p_1,...,p_m$ and $q_1,...,q_n$, respectively, of assignment statements. These assignment statements form a program or protocol $P \parallel Q$. Call the variables occurring in all these assignment statements of $P \parallel Q$, protocol variables. If $x := F(x_1,...,x_r)$, is an assignment statement of P (respectively, Q) then the variable x is said to belong to P (respectively, Q). The protocol variables are supposed to satisfy certain atomicity conditions (see section 3, for formal definitions). The program $P \parallel Q$ can have numerous possible executions. We illustrate this in the example below.

Suppose that processor P (respectively Q) intends to execute the assignment statement p : "$x := F(x')$" (respectively q : "$y := G(y', y'')$"). In general, a possible execution might be given by the following sequence of statements: Q reads y''; P reads x'; Q reads y'; P writes $x = F(x')$; Q writes $y = G(y', y'')$. However, for the purposes of the investigations of the present paper such "lower level" interleavings will never be considered. In other words, although interleavings among the $p_1,...,p_m$, $q_1,...,q_n$ are possible, the actions p_i and q_j will be considered atomic, i.e. either all subactions of p_i precede all subactions of q_j or else all subactions of q_j precede all subactions of p_i. For this reason we will also call such assignment statements atomic.

Let $x_1,...,x_k$ be a list of all the protocol variables. An interpretation or model of the protocol $P \parallel Q$ is a structure $m = (M, F^m, G^m,...)$ together with a k-tuple $init \in M^k$, where

- if $F \in \Sigma$ is an n-ary function symbol then $F^m : M^n \to M$, and
- $init = (c_1,...,c_k)$ are the initial interpretations of the protocol variables $x_1,...,x_k$, respectively, where $c_1,...,c_k \in M$; the k-tuple $init$ is also called initialization of the protocol variables.

For any sequence $\sigma = (r_1,...,r_m)$ of atomic assignment statements $r_1,...,r_m$ of the protocol $P \parallel Q$, and any protocol variable X define the value $X[\sigma, init]$ of the variable X in the model $m = (M, F^m, G^m,...)$ with respect to the sequence σ by induction on the length of σ.(†) Suppose that X is the variable x_j in the list $x_1,...,x_k$ of all the protocol variables. If $\sigma = \varnothing$, i.e. σ is the empty sequence, then $X[\sigma, init] = c_j$. Let σ be the sequence $(r_1,...,r_{s+1})$ and let ρ be the sequence $(r_1,...,r_s)$. Suppose that r_{s+1} is the assignment statement $y := F(y_1,...,y_n)$. Then define $X[\sigma, init] = F^m(y_1[\rho, init],...,y_n[\rho, init])$ if $X = y$, and $X[\sigma, init] = X[\rho, init]$ if $X \neq y$.

We are interested in program executions (interleavings or runs) $\rho = (\alpha, <_\rho)$, of the

---

(†) The value of the variable X in a model m for the protocol $P \parallel Q$ at the end of the execution of the run ρ depends on $P \parallel Q, m, init, \rho$, where $init$ is a given initialization in m. Therefore a more correct notation is $X^m[P \parallel Q, \rho, init]$. Instead we use $X[\rho, init]$ by abuse of notation, because the model m and protocol $P \parallel Q$ will always be easily understood. Moreover, we will normally be referring to an initialization $init$ of the protocol variables without explicitly mentioning the model m.

assignment statements $p_1,...,p_m, q_1,...,q_n$, with $\alpha = \{r_1,...,r_{m+n}\} = \{p_1,...,p_m\} \cup \{q_1,...,q_n\}$. The order of actions in a run ρ is determined by the relation $<_\rho$, i.e. $p <_\rho p'$ if and only if p immediately precedes p' in the run ρ, where $p, p' \in \alpha$. We assume that the transitive closure $\to_\rho$ of $<_\rho$ is a partial ordering on the set α such that the natural ordering of the execution of the program $P \parallel Q$ is preserved, i.e. for any run ρ of the program $P \parallel Q$ the following order among the atomic assignment statements in α must be preserved:

$$p_1 \to_\rho p_2 \to_\rho \cdots \to_\rho p_m, \quad q_1 \to_\rho q_2 \to_\rho \cdots \to_\rho q_n.$$

In general, actions p_i, q_j may be concurrent in a run ρ; in our framework this can be expressed by simply stating that p_i, q_j are $\to_\rho$-incomparable. However, as explained before, here we are only interested in a specific type of runs (or "higher level" interleavings) for which $\to_\rho$ is a linear order. Let $RUN(P \parallel Q)$, or simply RUN, be the set of all these runs, where $P \parallel Q$ is a certain program as above.

Let m be a given model of the protocol and suppose that X, Y are variables belonging to P, Q, respectively. The evaluation mapping of the protocol $P \parallel Q$ (with respect to the model m) is a function $eval_{X,Y} : RUN(P \parallel Q) \times M^k \to M^2$, defined by the formula

$$eval_{X,Y}(\rho, init) = (X[\rho, init], Y[\rho, init]).(*)$$

1.2. Results of the Paper

In [A1], Anderson and Gouda proved that it is impossible to construct protocols of the form $P \parallel Q$ defined above, which also satisfy the following conditions for any initialization $init$:

the variables X, Y can only assume the values $0, 1$,

$eval_{X,Y}(\rho, init) \in \{(0,1), (1,0)\}$, for all runs ρ,

$eval_{X,Y}(p_1,...,p_m, q_1,...,q_n, init) = (0,1)$,

$eval_{X,Y}(q_1,...,q_m, p_1,...,p_m, init) = (1,0)$

(they call such protocols, binary disagreement protocols).

The present paper investigates even further the limitations of wait-free protocols, by analyzing and studying one of their main structural deficiencies, namely "their inability to make a processor wait". As a first step it was observed that the result mentioned above could be generalized to show that there exist no protocol $P \parallel Q$ such that the following conditions are met for any initialization $init$:

the variables X, Y can only assume the values $0, 1$,

$eval_{X,Y}(\rho, init) \in \{(0,1), (1,0)\}$, for all runs ρ,

$(\exists \rho, \sigma \in RUN)[eval_{X,Y}(\rho, init) \neq eval_{X,Y}(\sigma, init)]$.

Motivated from this, we define a new notion of functional dependency among protocol variables. Namely, we call the variables X, Y "belonging" to processors P, Q, respectively, functionally dependent for the initialization $init$, if for any runs ρ, σ of the protocol $P \parallel Q$,

$$X[\rho, init] = X[\sigma, init] \Leftrightarrow Y[\rho, init] = Y[\sigma, init]).$$

Using this notion it is possible to provide characterizations of those programs for which the variables X, Y are functionally dependent in terms of the evaluation function $eval_{X,Y}$ of the program (see section 3). In fact we show that for any model m of the given protocol and any possible

---

(*) The same remark as in the previous footnote applies to the notation used for the evaluation function $eval$.

initialization *init* of the protocol variables the following statements are equivalent:

● the variables X, Y are functionally dependent for the initialization *init*,

● the quantity $eval_{X,Y}(\rho, init)$ is independent of the run $\rho \in RUN$.

Intuitively, if both the binary relation $\{(X[\rho, init], Y[\rho, init]) : \rho \in RUN\}$ and its inverse are functions then the relation must be a singleton. This makes it possible to give very natural and elegant generalizations of the result of [A1] not only to multivalued variables (as opposed to boolean valued variables considered before), but also to multiprocessor protocols (see section 4). As in [A1] this implies the impossibility of constructing wait-free protocols for Mutual Exclusion. The main combinatorial lemma needed for our analysis is presented in section 2. Extensions to more general protocols are given in section 5.

2. A Combinatorial Principle

At the heart of the proof of the result on functional dependencies in wait-free programs lies a rather simple combinatorial principle. Before stating and proving this principle some definitions will be necessary. Let $A = \{a_1, a_2, ..., a_m\}$, $B = \{b_1, b_2, ..., b_n\}$ be two disjoint sets such that $|A| = m \geq 1$, $|B| = n \geq 1$. Let $[A,B]$ be the set of sequences $x = (x_1, ..., x_{m+n})$ of elements of $A \cup B$ such that

$$\{x_1, ..., x_{m+n}\} = A \cup B,$$

and if $a_i = x_{k(i)}$, $b_j = x_{l(j)}$, then both sequences $<k(i) : i = 1,...,m>$, $<l(j) : j = 1,...,n>$ are monotone increasing. For each i, j let $a^i = a_{i+1}, ..., a_m$ be the "final" segment of the sequence $(a_1,...,a_m)$ starting from a_{i+1}, and similarly $b^j = b_{j+1}, ..., b_n$. For $i, j \geq 1$, call a sequence $x \in [A,B]$, $\{a_i, b_j\}$-separated if x is of one of the following four forms

$$(s, a_i, b_j, a^i, b^j), (s, a_i, b_j, b^j, a^i), (s, b_j, a_i, a^i, b^j), (s, b_j, a_i, b^j, a^i),$$

where s is an arbitrary finite sequence of elements of $A \cup B$ of the appropriate length $(= i+j-2)$. For any $\{a_i, b_j\}$-separated sequence x let $x(a_i, b_j)$ (respectively, $x(a^i, b^j)$) be the sequence obtained from x by interchanging the position of a_i, b_j (respectively, a^i, b^j) in x. An elementary interchange of the type $x \to x(a_i, b_j)$ is called one-step interchange. Let $F : [A,B] \to S$ be a function defined on all the sequences in $[A,B]$ and with range the nonempty set S. Then we can prove the following theorem.

Theorem 1. (Combinatorial Theorem)

Assume that for some $i, j \geq 1$ there is an $\{a_i, b_j\}$-separated sequence $x \in [A, B]$ such that $F(x) \neq F(x(a_i, b_j))$. If $x \in [A,B]$ is an $\{a_i, b_j\}$-separated sequence such that $i + j$ is maximal with $F(x) \neq F(x(a_i, b_j))$ then we have that $F(x(a^i, b^j)) \neq F(x(a^i, b^j)(a_i, b_j))$.

Proof. Let $x \in [A,B]$ be an $\{a_i, b_j\}$-separated sequence such that $i + j$ is maximal with $F(x) \neq F(x(a_i, b_j))$. Clearly, in order to prove the theorem it is enough to show that both equations below

$$F(x) = F(x(a^i, b^j)), \tag{1}$$

and

$$F(x(a_i, b_j)) = F(x(a^i, b^j)(a_i, b_j)) \tag{2}$$

are true. We prove only (1). The proof of (2) is similar. Without loss of generality assume that $x = (s, a_i, b_j, a^i, b^j)$. The idea of the proof is to transform the given sequence x into the sequence $x(a^i, b^j)$ in stages via sufficiently many one-step interchanges.

Stage 1. Interchange the position of a_m and each b_s $(s = j+1,...,n)$ one at a time and let

$$x_{m,j} = x, x_{m,j+1} = x(a_m, b_{j+1}), x_{m,j+2} = x_{m,j+1}(a_m, b_{j+2}),...,x_{m,n} = x_{m,n-1}(a_m, b_n),$$

be the resulting sequences.

Stage 2. Start from the sequence $x_{m,n}$, interchange the position of a_{m-1} and each b_s ($s = j+1,...,n$) one at a time, and let

$$x_{m-1,j+1} = x_{m,n}(a_{m-1}, b_{j+1}), x_{m-1,j+2} = x_{m-1,j+1}(a_{m-1}, b_{j+2}),...,x_{m-1,n} = x_{m-1,n-1}(a_{m-1}, b_n),$$

be the resulting sequences. Continue in this manner.

Final Stage. Start from the sequence $x_{i+2,n}$, interchange the position of a_{j+1} and each b_s ($s = j+1,...,n$) one at a time, and let

$$x_{i+1,j+1} = x_{i+2,n}(a_{i+1}, b_{j+1}), x_{i+1,j+2} = x_{i+1,j+1}(a_{i+1}, b_{j+2}),...,x_{i+1,n} = x_{i+1,n-1}(a_{i+1}, b_n),$$

be the resulting sequences. Clearly, $x = x_{m,j}, x_{i+1,n} = x(a^i, b^j)$. It follows from the maximality of $i + j$ that the function F assumes the same value on all the above sequences, i.e.

$$F(x_{m,j}) = F(x_{m,j+1}) = \cdots = F(x_{m,n}) =$$

$$F(x_{m-1,j+1}) = F(x_{m-1,j+2}) = \cdots = F(x_{m-1,n}) =$$

$$\cdots$$

$$F(x_{i+1,j+1}) = F(x_{i+1,j+2}) = \cdots = F(x_{i+1,n}).$$

This shows that $F(x) = F(x(a^i, b^j))$ and completes the proof of part (1) of the theorem. The proof of part (2) is similar. •

The combinatorial theorem, as well as its proof will be used frequently in the sequel.

3. Two Processor Programs

In this section we prove the main result on functional dependencies for 2-processor protocols. Suppose that we are given two processes P, Q which are executing concurrently and asynchronously the atomic assignment statements $p_1, p_2,...,p_m$ and $q_1, q_2,...,q_n$. We assume that each of the p_i, q_j is an atomic assignment statement of the type $x_i := F_i(w_i)$, $y_j := G_j(z_j)$, respectively, where the variables satisfy the following atomicity conditions ([A1]):

Variable Atomicity Conditions:

- The sets $\{x_1, x_2,..., x_m\}$, $\{y_1, y_2,..., y_m\}$ of program variables are mutually disjoint.
- The atomic statements p_i satisfy the following conditions:

    either x_i is a local variable of P, and $F_i \in \Sigma$ is a function symbol and the variables $w_i = w_{i,1},...,w_{i,k_i}$ are either local or read variables of the process P,

    or x_i is a write variable of P, and $F_i \in \Sigma$ is a function symbol and the variables $w_i = w_{i,1},...,w_{i,k_i}$ are local variables of the process P.

- The atomic statements q_j satisfy the following conditions:

    either y_i is a local variable of Q, and $G_j \in \Sigma$ is a function symbol and the variables $z_j = z_{j,1},...,z_{j,l_j}$ are either local or read variables of the process Q,

    or y_j is a write variable of Q, and $G_j \in \Sigma$ is a function symbol and the variables $z_j = z_{j,1},...,z_{j,l_j}$ are local variables of the process Q.

Such a program will be denoted by $P \parallel Q$. The next theorem ties the notion of functional dependencies of variables with the evaluation mapping $eval_{X,Y}$ of the program $P \parallel Q$. This generalizes the main result of [A1] to the case of multivalued variables.

Theorem 2. (Two Processor Functional Dependencies)

Let $P \parallel Q$ be any wait-free program with X, Y variables of P, Q respectively. Let RUN be the set of all possible runs of $P \parallel Q$. Then for any initialization $init$ of the protocol variables (in a given model m) the following statements are equivalent:

(1)   The variables X, Y are functionally dependent for the initialization $init$.

(2)   The quantity $eval_{X,Y}(\rho, init)$ is independent of the run $\rho \in RUN$.

Proof. The implication $(2) \Rightarrow (1)$ is trivial. So we will only concentrate on the proof of $(1) \Rightarrow (2)$. As in theorem 1 we use the notation: $p^i = p_{i+1},...,p_m$, $q^j = q_{j+1},...,q_n$. Fix any initialization $init$ of all the protocol variables. First of all we prove the following claim.

Claim 1. For all i, j and all $\{p_i, q_j\}$-separated sequences ρ,

$$eval_{X,Y}(\rho, init) = eval_{X,Y}(\rho(p_i, q_j), init).$$

Proof of Claim 1. Assume on the contrary that there exist i, j and a $\{p_i, q_j\}$-separated sequence ρ such that $eval_{X,Y}(\rho, init) \neq eval_{X,Y}(\rho(p_i, q_j), init)$. For the given initialization $init$ let the function F be defined on the set RUN of runs of the protocol by $F(\rho) = eval_{X,Y}(\rho, init)$. Clearly, for any initialization of the variables the set RUN can be identified with the set $[\{p_1, ..., p_m\}, \{q_1, ..., q_n\}]$ considered in the previous section. Let ρ be $\{p_i, q_j\}$-separated, with $i + j$ maximal such that $F(\rho) \neq F(\rho(p_i, q_j))$. Without loss of generality assume that

$$\rho = \cdots \; p_i \; q_j \; q_{j+1} \; \cdots \; q_n \; p_{i+1} \; \cdots \; p_m,$$
$$\rho(p_i, q_j) = \cdots \; q_j \; p_i \; q_{j+1} \; \cdots \; q_n \; p_{i+1} \; \cdots \; p_m,$$
$$\rho(p^i, q^j) = \cdots \; p_i \; q_j \; p_{i+1} \; \cdots \; p_m \; q_{j+1} \; \cdots \; q_n,$$
$$\rho(p_i, q_j)(p^i, q^j) = \cdots \; q_j \; p_i \; p_{i+1} \; \cdots \; p_m \; q_{j+1} \; \cdots \; q_n.$$

The variable dependencies that will be proved below are summarized in table 1. Recall that due to the assumption of the functional dependence of the variables X, Y, if ρ and σ are runs such that either $X[\rho, init] = X[\sigma, init]$ or else $Y[\rho, init] = Y[\sigma, init]$ then it is true that $eval_{X,Y}(\rho, init) = eval_{X,Y}(\sigma, init)$. This simple observation will be used frequently in the sequel.

x_i	y_j	Variable Equalities
local	local	$X[\rho] = X[\rho(p_i, q_j)]$, $Y[\rho] = Y[\rho(p_i, q_j)]$
write	write	$X[\rho] = X[\rho(p_i, q_j)]$, $Y[\rho] = Y[\rho(p_i, q_j)]$
local	write	$Y[\rho] = Y[\rho(p_i, q_j)]$
write	local	$X[\rho(p^i, q^j)] = X[\rho(p^i, q^j)(p_i, q_j)]$

Table 1: Variable Equalities in $P \parallel Q$.

If x_i were a local variable of P and y_j were a write variable of Q then $x_i := F_i(w_i)$, where the w_i are local or read variables of P and $y_j := G_j(z_j)$, where the z_j are local variables of Q. But then in the runs ρ, $\rho(p_i, q_j)$, the actions $q_{j+1}, ..., q_n$ do not see the value assigned to x_i by p_i. Moreover, since y_j is a write variable of Q its value does not depend on p_i. Hence, $Y[\rho] = Y[\rho(p_i, q_j)]$.

If either both x_i, y_j are local variables of P, Q respectively or else both x_i, y_j are write variables of P, Q respectively then $X[\rho] = X[\rho(p_i, q_j)]$, $Y[\rho] = Y[\rho(p_i, q_j)]$.

Hence, the only case left is if y_j is a local variable of Q and x_i is a write variable of P. In view of theorem 1, $F(\rho(p^i, q^j)) \neq F(\rho(p^i, q^j)(p_i, q_j))$. However, since y_j is local to Q, we must have $X[\rho(p^i, q^j)] = X[\rho(p^i, q^j)(p_i, q_j)]$.

This gives contradictions in all four cases considered and completes the proof of claim 1.

Therefore for all i, j and all $\{p_i, q_j\}$-separated sequences ρ,

$$eval_{X,V}(\rho, init) = eval_{X,Y}(\rho(p_i, q_j), init).\tag{3}$$

But then it is not hard to show that (3) implies the conclusion of the theorem, i.e. there is a constant c such that for all runs ρ $eval_{X,Y}(\rho, init) = c$. More formally, the following claim is needed.

Claim 2. If the run ρ is $\{p_i, q_j\}$-separated with $i + j > 2$ then there exists a $\{p_{i'}, q_{j'}\}$-separated run ρ' such that $i' + j' < i + j$, $eval_{X,Y}(\rho, init) = eval_{X,Y}(\rho', init)$.

Proof of claim 2. Suppose that $\rho = (s, p_i, q_j, p^i, q^j)$, where s is a sequence of length $i + j - 2$. By repeatedly applying (3) it can be shown that

$$eval_{X,Y}(\rho, init) = eval_{X,Y}(\rho(p_i, q_j), init) = eval_{X,Y}(\rho(p^i, q^j), init).$$

On the one hand, if the last element of s is p_{i-1} then put $\rho' = \rho(p_i, q_j)$, which is a $\{p_{i-1}, q_j\}$-separated sequence. On the other hand, if the last element of s is q_{j-1} then put $\rho' = \rho(p^i, q^j)$, which is a $\{p_i, q_{j-1}\}$-separated sequence. This completes the proof of claim 2.

To finish the proof of the theorem start with an arbitrary run ρ and interchange the position of its atomic assignment statements one by one, by performing one-step interchanges, just like in the proof of theorem 1, until ρ is transformed into the run $(p_1, ..., p_m, q_1, ..., q_n)$. That this can be done is guaranteed from the result of claim 2. Hence,

$$eval_{X,Y}(\rho, init) = eval_{X,Y}(p_1, ..., p_m, q_1, ..., q_n, init). \bullet$$

4. Multiprocessor Programs

As a byproduct of our analysis on functional dependencies we can now generalize the previous results to multiprocessor, wait-free programs consisting only of assignment statements. Indeed, let

$$P_1 \| P_2 \| \cdots \| P_r \| Q_1 \| Q_2 \| \cdots \| Q_s,$$

be a wait-free program of $r+s$ processors: $P_1, P_2, ..., P_r$ are the active processors, and $Q_1, Q_2, ..., Q_s$ are the dummy processors, with $r \geq 2, s \geq 0$. The definitions and assumptions outlined in the previous sections are still assumed true for the case of multiprocessor protocols. In the sequel, we stress the most important of these aspects. We assume that each processor P_i (respectively, Q_j) executes a sequence of "atomic" assignment statements $p_1^i, p_2^i, ..., p_{m_i}^i$ (respectively, $q_1^j, q_2^j, ..., q_{k_j}^j$), where $i = 1, ..., r$ (respectively, $j = 1, ..., s$). The p_k^i, q_k^j are atomic assignment statements of the form $x := F(w)$, where $x, w = w_1, ..., w_t$ are variables of the corresponding process, and F is a function symbol in the language Σ. Let $W(P_i)$ be the set of variables x which are assigned a value by the process P_i, i.e. the set of variables x such that some assignment statement p_k^i of the process P_i is of the form $x := F(w)$.

Variable Atomicity Conditions:

- the sets $W(P_i)$ are pairwise mutually disjoint, for $i = 1, ..., r$, i.e. $W(P_i) \cap W(P_j) = \emptyset$, for $i \neq j$.

- Suppose that $x := F(w)$ is any assignment statement of processor P_i. Then the variables $x, w = w_1, ..., w_t$ are supposed to satisfy the following conditions:

  either x is a local variable of P_i, and F is a function symbol and the variables w are either local or read variables of the process P_i, or

  x is a write variable of P_i, and F is a function symbol and the variables w are local variables of the process P_i.

As before, we are interested in program executions (or runs) $\rho = (\alpha, <_\rho)$ of the above program, where α is the set of atomic assignment statements of the program. The order of actions in a run ρ is determined by the relation $<_\rho$, i.e. $p <_\rho p'$ if and only if p immediately precedes p' in the run ρ, where $p, p' \in \alpha$. We assume that the transitive closure $\rightarrow_\rho$ of $<_\rho$ is a partial ordering on the set A such that the "natural ordering" of execution among the actions— $\{p_k^i\}$ for P^i, and $\{q_k^j\}$ for Q_j— of the program is preserved,

$$p_1^i \rightarrow_\rho \cdots \rightarrow_\rho p_{m_i}^i, i = 1,...,r,$$

$$q_1^j \rightarrow_\rho \cdots \rightarrow_\rho q_{k_j}^j, j = 1,...,s.$$

For any run ρ of the protocol and any initialization *init* of the variables let $X[\rho, init]$ be the value of the variable X at the end of the run ρ, when all the variables are initialized by *init* (the formal definition of this which is given in introduction can be generalized easily). For each $i = 1,...,r$ let $X_i \in W(P_i)$ (in this case we say that the variable X_i belongs to the processor P_i). As before, for any run ρ and any initialization *init* of the program variables, define the evaluation mapping of the program by

$$eval_{X_1, X_2, ..., X_r}(\rho, init) = (X_1[\rho, init], X_2[\rho, init], ..., X_r[\rho, init]).$$

Call $X_1, X_2, ..., X_r$ functionally dependent if the following holds for any initialization *init*, where ρ, σ range over runs of the protocol $P_1 \| P_2 \| \cdots \| P_r \| Q_1 \| Q_2 \| \cdots \| Q_s$:

$$\forall \rho, \sigma \forall i, j (X_i[\rho, init] = X_i[\sigma, init] \Leftrightarrow X_j[\rho, init] = X_j[\sigma, init]).$$

In general, the values obtained by the evaluation function $eval_{X_1, X_2, ..., X_r}(\rho, init)$ depend on the initialization *init* of the protocol variables as well as on the protocol run ρ. However, as before we can prove a necessary and sufficient condition for the evaluation mapping to be independent of the given run ρ. This is done in the following theorem.

Theorem 3. (Multiprocessor Functional Dependencies)

Let $X_1, X_2, ..., X_r$ be variables belonging to the active processors $P_1, P_2, ..., P_r$, respectively, of the wait-free, multiprocessor program $P_1 \| P_2 \| \cdots \| P_r \| Q_1 \| Q_2 \| \cdots \| Q_s$, with $r \geq 2, s \geq 0$. Let *RUN* be the set of all its possible runs. Then for any possible initialization *init* of the protocol variables (in a given model m) the following statements are equivalent:

(1) The variables $X_1, X_2, ..., X_r$ are functionally dependent for the initialization *init*.

(2) The quantity $eval_{X_1, X_2, ..., X_r}(\rho, init)$ is independent of the run $\rho \in RUN$.

Proof. Clearly, theorem 2 proved in the previous section corresponds to the case $r = 2, s = 0$. The implication (2) $\Rightarrow$ (1) is trivial. Hence it only remains to prove the reverse implication. Assume that (1) is true. We want to show that (2) is true, as well. The proof of the present theorem is via two reductions. First we show that the special case $r = 2$ of the theorem implies the more general case $r \geq 2$. Next we show that theorem 2 implies the present theorem in the case $r = 2, s \geq 0$. Obviously, this is enough in order to give a complete proof of the theorem.

Claim. Without loss of generality we can assume $r = 2$.

Proof of the claim. Indeed, assume that the theorem is true for $r = 2$. It will be shown that the theorem is true for any arbitrary $r \geq 2$. Let $i < j \leq r$ be arbitrary, but fixed. Consider the program

$$P_i \| P_j \| (P_1 \| P_{i-1} \| P_{i+1} \| \cdots \| P_{j-1} \| P_{j+1} \| \cdots \| P_r \| Q_1 \| Q_2 \| \cdots \| Q_s) \quad (4)$$

with selected variables X_i, X_j and evaluation mapping $eval_{X_i, X_j}(\rho, init)$. By the assumption that the theorem is true for $r = 2$, if the variables X_i, X_j are functionally dependent in the program (4) then the quantity determined by its evaluation function $eval_{X_i, X_j}(\rho, init)$ is independent of the run ρ. But by assumption (1) of the theorem the variables $X_1, X_2,...,X_r$ are functionally dependent. Hence, for all i, j the quantity determined by the evaluation function $eval_{X_i, X_j}(\rho, init)$ is independent of the run ρ. But then it follows immediately that the quantity $eval_{X_1, X_2,...,X_r}(\rho, init)$ is also independent of the run ρ. This completes the proof of the claim.

In view of the claim just proved we can assume without loss of generality that we have the program $P \parallel Q \parallel Q_1 \parallel Q_2 \parallel \cdots \parallel Q_s$, with $Q_1 \parallel Q_2 \parallel \cdots \parallel Q_s$ the dummy processors, and two variables X, Y belonging to the active processors P, Q, respectively, which are functionally dependent, i.e. for any runs ρ, σ of the protocol $P \parallel Q \parallel Q_1 \parallel Q_2 \parallel \cdots \parallel Q_s$,

$$X[\rho, init] = X[\sigma, init] \Leftrightarrow Y[\rho, init] = Y[\sigma, init]). \tag{5}$$

Let R be the set of all possible runs of the program $P \parallel Q_1 \parallel Q_2 \parallel \cdots \parallel Q_s$. Any run $\rho \in R$ gives rise to a program $P_\rho \parallel Q$, where the processor P_ρ is executing the sequence of assignment statements determined by the run ρ, while Q is executing the sequence of assignment statements it was executing before in the program $P \parallel Q \parallel Q_1 \parallel Q_2 \parallel \cdots \parallel Q_s$. For each run $\rho \in R$ let $eval_{\rho, X, Y}$ be the evaluation mapping of the program $P_\rho \parallel Q$. It is clear that for all runs $\rho \in R$,

$$RUN(P_\rho \parallel Q) \subseteq RUN(P \parallel Q \parallel Q_1 \parallel \cdots \parallel Q_s).$$

In view of theorem 2, and equivalence (5) the quantity $eval_{\rho, X, Y}(\sigma, init)$ is independent of the run $\sigma \in RUN(P_\rho \parallel Q)$. Put $c_\rho(init) = eval_{\rho, X, Y}(\sigma, init)$. It remains to show that for all runs $\rho, \rho' \in R$, and all initializations $init$, $c_\rho(init) = c_{\rho'}(init)$. To this effect, let $\rho, \rho' \in R$ be two arbitrary but fixed runs, and consider the following two new runs of the program $P \parallel Q \parallel Q_1 \parallel \cdots \parallel Q_s$:

$$\sigma : q_1, q_2, ..., q_n, \rho \in RUN(P_\rho \parallel Q)$$

$$\sigma' : q_1, q_2, ..., q_n, \rho' \in RUN(P_{\rho'} \parallel Q),$$

i.e. σ (respectively, σ') is formed by executing the sequence of assignment statements $q_1, ..., q_n$ followed by the assignment statements occurring in ρ (respectively, in ρ'). Let $init$ be any initialization of the variables. Clearly,

$$eval_{X, Y}(\sigma, init) = eval_{\rho, X, Y}(\sigma, init) = c_\rho(init)$$

$$eval_{X, Y}(\sigma', init) = eval_{\rho', X, Y}(\sigma', init) = c_{\rho'}(init).$$

Moreover, since in the run σ (respectively σ') the subrun ρ (respectively ρ') cannot influence the value attained by the variable Y, it is immediate that $Y[\sigma, init] = Y[\sigma', init]$. Since by the assumption of the theorem the variables X, Y are functionally dependent it follows that also $X[\sigma, init] = X[\sigma', init]$. Hence,

$$c_\rho(init) = eval_{X, Y}(\sigma, init) = eval_{X, Y}(\sigma', init) = c_{\rho'}(init).$$

This completes the proof of the theorem. ●

4.1. Examples

Now a few illuminating examples are in order.

Example 1. The reader should pay special attention to the variable conditions mentioned at the beginning of this section; they are quite important for the validity of theorem 2. This is easily seen in the following example. Let P, Q be two processors executing the statements p : "$X := Y + 1$", and q : "$Y := X + 1$", respectively (where + denotes modulo 2 addition). Further, suppose that X is a write variable and Y is a read variable of P (respectively, Y is a write variable and X is a read variable of Q). Consider the runs $\rho = (p, q)$ and $\sigma = (q, p)$, and the initialization

$init = (0, 0)$ of the variables X, Y. It is then easy to see that at the end of the execution of the runs ρ, σ, $X[\rho, init] = 1$, $Y[\rho, init] = 2$, $X[\sigma, init] = 2$, $Y[\sigma, init] = 1$. Hence, the variables X, Y are functionally dependent for the initialization $init$, but the values assumed by the evaluation mapping $eval_{X,Y}(\cdot, init)$ are not independent of the run, since

$$eval_{X,Y}(\rho, init) = (1, 2) \neq (2, 1) = eval_{X,Y}(\sigma, init).$$

Example 2. If even one processor is allowed to execute a waiting loop then theorem 2 is false. For such an example the reader is referred to [A1].

Example 3. The following example illustrates theorem 2. Suppose that $P \parallel Q$ is a wait-free program, with distinguished variables X, Y belonging to the processes P, Q, respectively. Let $m = (M, F^m, G^m, ...)$ be a model of the protocol and suppose that $f : M \to M$ is a one-to-one function. An immediate consequence of the theorem is that the following claim can be proved. Let $init$ be any initialization of all the protocol variables. If for any run ρ of the protocol $P \parallel Q$, $f(X[\rho, init]) = Y[\rho, init]$ then $eval_{X,Y}(\rho, init) = (X[\rho, init], f(X[\rho, init]))$ is independent of the run ρ.

Example 4. Clearly, theorem 2 (and its extension given in the next section) implies that it is impossible to construct wait-free, binary disagreement protocols. Further, it is shown in [A1] that it is impossible to implement Mutual Exclusion without waiting. According to theorem 3 (and its extension given in section 5) this is also the case even if we assume that a finite number $Q_1,...,Q_s$ of "dummy" processors is present.

5. Extensions to More General Protocols

The previous two theorems on functional dependencies can easily be extended to programs, which—in addition to assignment statements—include the following additional types of statement constructions: if ... then ... else ... fi; for $i := 1,...,n$ do ... od. We extend the language Σ by adding relation symbols R, S, ..., (with subscripts and/or superscripts) each of a certain arity ≥ 1. Statements of the form $R(v_1,...,v_n)$ are called primitive statements. In addition, to assignment statements now we also have boolean statements, i.e. boolean combinations of primitive statements. The class of program statements is the smallest class of statements such that assignment statements are program statements, and is closed under

(a)   **if** α **then** p **else** p' **fi**, where α is a boolean statement,

(b)   **for** $i := 1,...,n$ **do** p **od**,

where p, p' are sequences of program statements. A processor P will now be executing a finite sequence of program statements each of which must satisfy one of the following conditions [A1]:

*   if it is an assignment statement then its variables satisfy the variable atomicity conditions for the processor P (see section 3),

*   if it is a program statement of the form (a) above then all the variables occurring in α must be local to P,

*   if it is a program statement of the form (b) above then both variables i, n must be local to P, and p has no assignments to either i or n.

An interpretation or model of the protocol is defined as before. For any run ρ and any initialization $init$ the definition of $X[\rho, init]$ as well as of the evaluation function $eval_{X,Y}$ is similar to the definition given in the introduction (however, the definition of $X[\rho, init]$ is given by induction on the length of ρ and the construction of the protocol formulas). In the sequel we outline a proof of the validity of theorems 2 and 3 in this more general context.

Proof of Theorems 2 and 3 (outline). Suppose we are given a program $P \parallel Q$ performed by processors P and Q, executing the program statements $\phi_1,...,\phi_m$ and $\psi_1,...,\psi_n$, respectively, and let X, Y be variables belonging to P, Q, respectively. We add extra local variables to the language according to the rules below in such a way that to each initialization *init* (in the old language) there corresponds an initialization $\overline{init}$ (in the new language), and vice versa. The main idea is to replace each program statement of type (b) or (c) with an appropriate sequence of assignment statements and form a new protocol $\overline{P} \parallel \overline{Q}$ such that:

- $\overline{P}$ (respectively, $\overline{Q}$)executes the sequence of assignment statements $\overline{\phi}_1,...,\overline{\phi}_{\overline{m}}$ (respectively, (respectively, $\overline{\psi}_1,...,\overline{\psi}_{\overline{n}}$),

- to every run $\rho \in RUN(P \parallel Q)$ there corresponds a run $\overline{\rho} \in RUN(\overline{P} \parallel \overline{Q})$ such that for any initialization *init*

$$X[P \parallel Q, \rho, init] = X[\overline{P} \parallel \overline{Q}, \overline{\rho}, \overline{init}], Y[P \parallel Q, \rho, init] = Y[\overline{P} \parallel \overline{Q}, \overline{\rho}, \overline{init}], \qquad (6)$$

and vice versa. The essential details of the construction are as follows (see [A1]). Take the first **for** statement occurring in P, say **for** $i := 1,...,n$ **do** p **od**, and consider the sequence s of statements preceding it in P. Let N be the maximal value of n over all concurrent executions of s and Q. Now replace the above statement with the following sequence of $2N$ statements: $i := 1$; **if** $i > j$ **then skip else** p **fi**;, ..., $i := N$; **if** $i > j$ **then skip else** p **fi**, where **skip** is an assignment statement of the form $x := x$, for some local variable x. We can thus eliminate one by one all **for** statements. Next we eliminate the **if** statements; since such statements can be nested they are eliminated one by one starting with the inner-most one. For every write variable x introduce a new local variable $\overline{x}$ and replace each assignment statement $x := F$ with the two assignment statements $x := F$; $\overline{x} := F$. Replace **if** α **then** p **else** p' **fi** by the sequence $a := \alpha$; $p[a]$; $p'[\neg a]$, where a is a new local variable and $p[a]$ is the same sequence as p except that each asignment statement $x := F$ in p with x a write variable is replaced in $p[a]$ by $x := F$, if a, and $x := x$ otherwise, and each asignment statement $x := F$ in p with x a local variable is replaced in $p[a]$ by $x := F$, if a, and $x := \overline{x}$ otherwise, and similarly for $p'[\neg a]$.

Now suppose that the variables X, Y are functionally dependent in the protocol $P \parallel Q$. Then we must show that the variables X, Y will be functionally dependent in the protocol $\overline{P} \parallel \overline{Q}$, as well. This follows from the fact that every run of $\overline{P} \parallel \overline{Q}$ is "essentially" of the type $\overline{\rho}$, for some run ρ of $P \parallel Q$. It follows from theorem 2 that the quantity $eval_{X,Y}(\overline{P} \parallel \overline{Q}, \overline{\rho}, \overline{init})$ is independent of the run $\overline{\rho}$. Hence, it follows from equality (6) that $eval_{X,Y}(P \parallel Q, \rho, init)$ is also independent of the run ρ, as desired. A similar proof will work for multiprocessor programs. •

Acknowledgements

Discussions with Paul Vitányi and John Tromp are gratefully acknowledged.

REFERENCES

[A1] J. H. Anderson and M. G. Gouda, *The Virtue of Patience: Concurrent Programming with and without Waiting (Draft)*, University of Texas, Department of Computer Science, 78712-1188, 1987.

[A2] Anderson, J. H., Gouda, M. G., and Singh, A. K., *The Elusive Atomic Register*, Proceedings of 6th ACM Symposium on Principles of Distributed Computing, Vancouver, Canada, 1987.

[B] Bloom, B., *Constructing Two-writer Atomic Registers*, Proceedings of 6th ACM Symposium on Principles of Distributed Computing, Vancouver, Canada, 1987.

[D] Dijkstra, E. W., *A Solution to a Problem in Concurrent Programming Control*, Comm. ACM, Vol. 8, No. 9, p. 569, 1965.

[H]   Herlihy, M. P., *Impossibility and Universality Results for Wait-Free Synchronization*, Proceedings of 7th ACM Symposium on Principles of Distributed Computing, 1988.

[K]   Kirousis, L. M., Kranakis, E., and Vitányi, P. M. B., *Atomic Multireader Register*, 2nd International Workshop on Distributed Algorithms, Amsterdam 1987, Springer Verlag Lecture Notes in Computer Science, 312 (1988), pp. 278-296.

[L1] Lamport, L., *On Interprocess Communication, Part I: Basic Formalism, Part II: Algorithms*, Distributed Computing, vol. 1, pp. 77-101, 1986.

[L2] Li, M. and P. Vitányi, *A Very Simple Construction for Atomic Multiwriter Register*, in proceedings of ICALP 1989.

[M]   Misra, J., *Axioms for Memory Access in Asynchronous Hardware Systems*, ACM Transactions on Programming Languages and Systems Vol. 8, No. 1, pp. 142-153, Jan. 1986.

[N]   Newman-Wolfe, R., *A Protocol for Wait-Free, Atomic, Multi-Reader Shared Variables*, Proceedings of 6th ACM Symposium on Principles of Distributed Computing, Vancouver, Canada, 1987.

[P]   Peterson, G.L. and J.E. Burns, *Concurrent Reading While Writing I*, Proceedings of 6th ACM Symposium on Principles of Distributed Computing, Vancouver, Canada, 1987.

[T]   Tromp, J., *How to Construct an Atomic Variable*, in present proceedings.

[V]   Vitányi, P. M. B., and Awerbuch, B., *Atomic Shared Register Access by Asynchronous Hardware*, 27th Annual Symposium on Foundations of Computer Science, Toronto, 1986.

Two Strategies for solving the Vertex Cover Problem on a Transputer Network *

R. Lüling, B. Monien

Department of Mathematics and Computer Science
University of Paderborn, West Germany
e-mail : rl@pbinfo.uucp, bm@pbinfo.uucp

Abstract

In this article, we present an implementation of a distributed branch and bound algorithm solving the Vertex Cover problem on a network of up to 63 Transputers.

We implemented two different strategies: The first parallelization of our branch and bound algorithm is fully distributed. Every processor performs the same algorithm but on a different part of the solution tree. In this case it is necessary to distribute subproblems among the processors to achieve a well balanced workload.

Our second strategy is based on a tree structured network, where all subproblems are stored at the root processor and the other processes work as slaves of this master process.

To show the performance of our strategies, we solved the Vertex Cover problem for graphs of up to 150 nodes and an average degree of 30. We were able to achieve a speedup of 57.35 for the first strategy on a 60 processor network and 62.11 for the second strategy on 63 processors, compared to a very efficient sequential algorithm.

1 Introduction

It is the objective of this paper to show, that also very efficient sequential branch and bound algorithms can be implemented on a parallel system with nearly linear speedup. Many problems from the areas of operations research and artificial intelligence can be defined as combinatorial optimization problems. Among these are the Travelling Salesperson Problem, the Vertex Coloring Problem, Scheduling Problems and also the Vertex Cover Problem. To solve such a problem, an integer solution vector has to be found which respects some finite set of constraints and minimizes/maximizes a given function f. There exists a finite solution space for such problems, because the range of the solution vector is known a priori.

A simple strategy for finding the optimal solution is the brute force method, which computes the optimal solution by examining all elements of the solution space. Since the solution space grows exponentially in the size of the input, this method leads to extreme computation times and although an efficient parallel execution of this strategy is extremely simple and achieves linear speedup, unaceptable computation times are achieved.

---

*This work was partly supported by the german research association (DFG)

Branch and bound is an universal algorithmic technique for solving problems of this type. This technique also performs a search through the solution space, but it uses heuristic knowledge about the solution to cut off parts of the search tree. Usually branch and bound techniques are combined with the use of dominance relations [14], leading to a further detraction of the search tree. Though these techniques lead to a dramatic reduction of the number of nodes in the search tree, the size of the search space is still growing exponentially with the size of the input. Therefore it is an intriguing research problem to study, whether parallelism can be fully exploited in solving problems of this type.

The name branch and bound describes a large class of search techniques. Among these are depth-first branch and bound and best-first branch and bound. Depth-first branch and bound performs a depth first search through the solution space and cuts off a branch whenever its bound is worse than the best solution found at that time. Best-first branch and bound always branches the subproblem with the best bound. Best-first branch and bound leads to a very good computational performance. It has to pay for this with large storage requirements.

In this paper we describe two parallel versions of best-first branch and bound. We implemented both versions using a network of up to 63 T800 Transputers.

Our first technique is fully distributed. It uses distributed memory. Every processor has its own local heap. In order to get a good speedup compared with sequential best-first branch and bound, it is essential, to avoid idle times.

The aim of our load balancing algorithm is to keep the heapweights (some function defined on the heapelements) of the whole system on an nearly equal level. For this purpose, each processor knows the heapweight of his neighbours in the network. He sends some subproblems to a neighbour if his own heapweight is large (relative to the heapweights of his neighbours) and sends his heapweight for work request, if it is small. This strategy will guarantee that a processor and his neighbours have nearly the same heapweight and will so lead to an equal heapweight level in the whole network. It will be shown that this strategy works on networks with small and with large diameters.

The speedup is influenced by the communication overhead (for exchanging informations between the processors) and the search overhead (usually the parallel version uses more nodes in the search space than the sequential one).

Our second technique simulates a parallel machine with shared memory in a rather straightforward way. One of the processors (we call it the "root processor") stores the heap. All the other processors perform just branching steps, i.e. they get a subproblem from the heap, compute the branching and the bounds of the new subproblems and send this information back to the root processor.

In this paper we describe a branch and bound algorithm for solving the vertex cover problem. This problem has applications in different areas, see [3]. For an undirected Graph G=(V, E) a subset U, U$\subseteq$V, of nodes is called a vertex cover, if every edge is covered by a node from U, i.e. {u, v} $\in$E implies u$\in$U or v$\in$U. The vertex cover problem consists of computing a vertex cover of minimal cardinality. This problem is known to be NP complete [6], an efficient backtracking algorithm has been described in [14].

Our algorithm uses the very efficient branching technique for solving the vertex cover problem described in [14] and also in [13]. We got a speedup of 57.35 for the distributed strategy on a 60 processor network and a speedup of 62.11 for the shared memory strategy on a 63 processor network. The instances we tested are random graphs with 150 nodes and an average degree of 30.

Other authors also studied parallel algorithms for solving the vertex cover problem and found rather good speedup values (29.36 on a 32 Transputer network in [17], 4.69 on a network of 7 conventional processors in [1]). However their sequential version is by far not as powerfull as ours (instances of 80 nodes in [17], no information about the instance size in [1]).

In general it is more difficult to achieve good speedups for efficient sequential algorithms. The speedup is determined by the search overhead and the ratio between the execution times for performing one branching step on a subproblem and the communication overhead necessary to obtain a good load balance. A sequential improvement which is gained mainly by performing one branching step faster, will make the same speedup difficult to obtain. If however the sequential algorithm is made more efficient by introducing a more sophisticated branching method, reducing this way the number of problems in the search space, then a good parallelization is still very likely. This is the case for our vertex cover algorithm and will hold also for other efficient branch and bound algorithms. On the other hand there are efficient sequential search algorithms (e. g. α-β-search for computing the value of a game tree) which find cut offs by using informations about other subproblems. For algorithms of this type it is still very hard to find good parallelizations (see[5]).

Our algorithms are implemented in OCCAM 2 and run on a network of up to 63 T800 Transputers [4]. The transputer, manufactured by INMOS, is a processor which has gained a lot of attention because of its efficient communication mechanism which is directly supported by the programming language OCCAM.

For analyzing the performance of distributed algorithms and to compare different algorithms the speedup factor is a common measurement criterian. Let C be a class of problem instances and let $T_k(P)$ be the execution time for problem P using k processors.

$S_k(P) := \frac{T_1(P)}{T_k(P)}$ speedup for problem P

$E_k(P) := \frac{S_k(P)}{k}$ efficiency for problem P

$S_k(C) := \frac{\sum_{P \in C} T_1(P)}{\sum_{P \in C} T_k(P)}$ average speedup for class C

$E_k(C) := \frac{S_k(C)}{k}$ average efficiency for class C

In section 2 we give a short description of our branch and bound procedure solving the vertex cover problem. In section 3 we present a parallelization of branch and bound which uses distributed heap management and dynamic load balancing , whereas in section 4 we describe the algorithm on a tree structured network.

2 Sequential Branch and Bound

In this section we give a short description of our branch and bound algorithm for the vertex cover problem. We assume familiarity with the general sequential branch and bound algorithm. For a introduction see [10]. All subproblems are coded as tupels (C, b) where C is a subcover, i.e. C is a set of nodes that covers some edges of the graph G, and b is a lower bound for the costs of all solutions containing C.

The branch and bound algorithm generates from a given subproblem (C, b) two new subproblems (C_1, b_1), (C_2, b_2). The generation of C_1 and C_2 by the branch procedure is done by searching for a node v with maximal degree in the restgraph (part of the original graph that has not yet been covered). $C_1 := C \cup \{v\}$, $C_2 = C \cup \{w \in V \mid \{v, w\} \in E\}$. The branch algorithm reduces the restgraph by applying the following rules:

- if there is an edge $\{v, v\}$ in the restgraph then v has to be added to the cover.

- if the restgraph contains an edge $\{v, w\}$ and v has degree 1, than w is added to the cover.

- if there are edges $\{v_1, v_2\}$, $\{v_2, v_3\}$ in the restgraph G=(V, E) and v_2 has degree 2, then a new graph G'=(V', E') is defined by:

  $V' := V \cup \{v'\} \setminus \{v_1, v_2, v_3\}$ where v' is a new node, and
  $E' := \{\{u, v\} \mid \{u, v\} \cap \{v_1, v_2, v_3\} = \emptyset\} \cup \{\{u, v'\} \mid \{u, x\} \in E, x \in \{v_1, v_3\}\}$.

  The vertex cover problem is solved for the graph G'. If v' in an element of the minimal vertex cover of G' then v_1 and v_3 are in the minimal cover of G, else v_2 is in the minimal cover of G.

Note that these rules can be applied as long as the restgraph has nodes of degree at most two. Therefore a branching step is performed only on graphs where every vertex has degree at least three. The cardinality of a maximal matching for a graph is a natural lower bound for the vertex cover. We obtained a better lower bound by first computing a maximal cover by triangles and then determing a maximal matching of the restgraph.

3 Distributed Algorithm

In this section we describe an algorithm which uses a distributed heap organization. Each processor has a local heap and performs the sequential branch and bound algorithm using this heap. Due to the fact that the workload must be efficiently distributed over the whole network to achieve a good utilization of each processor, a network topology with minimal diameter behaves extremely well in such a case [12]. So we have chosen a topology with 60 processors and diameter 5. There is a hamilton circuit in this topology, which is necessary for our termination detection algorithm. Additionally we run the same tests on a ring of 32 transputers.

Algorithm

Each processor performs the sequential branch and bound algorithm and a communication task which includes local heap management, distributed termination detection and the local balancing strategy. Our load balancing algorithm is based on the following ideas:

- if the heapweight of processor i increases more than "heap.up" percent, then processor i sends subproblems to his neighbours.

- if the heapweight of processor i decreases more than "heap.down" percent, then processor i sends the new heapweight to all his neighbours

- if processor i receives a heapweight h_j from one of his neighbours j, then i sends subproblems to processor j if $h_i > (1+$"threshold"$)*h_j$ and h_i is greater than a given constant.

- subproblems are only distributed by processor i, if $h_i >$ min.heap.weight.

The heapweight can be any function over the heapelements. In our case the heapweight is the number of subproblems in the local heap which may lead to a better solution. The communication process is given below (the distributed termination part is ommitted, see [2] for a description). Also the processes for simulating asynchronous communication are not presented.

```
procedure communicate(heap.up, heap.down, threshold, min.heap.weight)

c:=∞;
initialize each processor with one subproblem (for details see [17])
heapw.old:=heapw.new:=number of subproblems in local heap
∀ neighbours i : heapw(i):=0

loop
    if computing process is idle and heap contains subproblem x with bound(x)<c then
        send subproblem with minimal bound to computing process
        heapw.new:=heapw.new-1

    if computing process sends subproblem x then
        if bound(x)<c then insert x into the local heap
        heapw.new:=heapw.new+1

    if computing process has found a new solution x then
        if bound(x)<c then
            c:=bound(x)
            send c to all neighbours
            heapw.new:=number of problems x in the local heap with bound(x)<c
            send heapw.new to all neighbours

    if neighbour sends new bound c'<c then
        c:=c'
        send c to other neighbours
```

heapw.new:=number of problems x in the local heap with bound(x)<c.
send heapw.new to all neighbours

if heapw.new < heapw.old*(1-heap.down) then
send heapw.new to all neighbour processes
heapw.old:=heapw.new

if heapw.new > heapw.old*(1+heap.up) and heapw.new> min.heap.weight then
   while ∃ neighbour process j with heapw(j)*(1+threshold)<heapw.new and
   heapw.new>min.heap.weight
    send subproblem with minimal bound to j
    heapw(j):=heapw(j)+1
    heapw.new:=heapw.new-1
   send heapw.new to all neighbour processes
   heapw.old:=heapw.new

if some neighbour j sends his heapweight x then
   heapw(j):=x
   while heapw(j)*(1+threshold)<heapw.new and heapw.new>min.heap.weight
    send the best subproblem to j
    heapw.new:=heapw.new-1,
     heapw(j):=heapw(j)+1
   heapw.old:=heapw.new

Results

We have implemented this algorithm and made the experiments for 20 graphs each with 150 nodes and an average degree of 30. The parameters heapw.up=0.50, heapw.down=0.20, threshold=0.20 and min.heap.weight=5 were found experimentally.

The following results for 5 graphs show the typical behavior of our algorithm on a 60 processor topology.

Graph Id.	1 processor		60 processors			
	time	iterations	time	iterations	speedup	efficiency
0	11842.97	38100	205.79	38149	57.54	0.959
1	20998.21	66335	356.89	66343	58.84	0.981
2	20826.10	65951	354.27	65958	58.79	0.979
3	10796.53	33828	181.61	32513	59.44	0.991
4	10555.15	33003	209.53	37944	50.37	0.839
	75018.96	237217	1308.09	240907	57.35	0.956

Table 1: Results for 5 graphs (n=150, d=30) on a 60 processor topology, diameter 5

Table 2 shows our results on a network of 32 transputer connected as a ring. We have chosen the

Graph Id.	1 processor		32 processors			
	time	iterations	time	iterations	speedup	efficiency
0	11515.95	38100	369.09	37194	31.20	0.975
1	20414.90	66335	669.27	66766	30.50	0.953
2	20257.59	65951	666.81	66307	30.37	0.949
3	10500.24	33828	391.12	38360	26.84	0.839
4	10087.81	33003	344.52	34470	29.28	0.915
	72776.49	237217	2440.81	243097	29.81	0.932

Table 2: Results for 5 graphs (n=150, d=30) on a 32 processor ring

parameters heapw.up=20, heapw.down=10, threshold=10 and min.heap.weight=5 which were found experimentally. In general, load balancing on a ring with large diameter can not lead to the same good results as on a network with small diameter. Our load balancing algorithm ignores little differences in the workload of two neighbour processes. This can create great differences in the workload of processors which are not directly connected. So it was necessary to send subproblems to neighbour processes, even if the difference between this direct neighbours was not very great, to achieve a better workload balancing for the whole network.

4 Tree structured topology

In this section we describe a parallelization of our branch and bound method which is based on a ternary tree structure of the net topology. In this network topology, all subproblems are stored at the root processor, so that problems concerning the distributing of the global heap can be avoided. A common problem to such centralized algorithms is to avoid a bottleneck because each slave processor has exclusive access to the heap management capabilities of the root processor.

Algorithm

The algorithm works as follows:

- all subproblems are stored in the heap of the root processor

- an idle process sends a request for work to the root processor

- if a process receives a subproblem with bound b that is no vertex cover then it computes the two successor subproblems and their bounds b_1, b_2. If $b_1 \neq b \neq b_2$ then these new subproblems are sent to the root processor. If there is one new subproblem with bound b then this problem is held by the processor for the next branching step, the other is sent to the root processor.

- if the root processor receives a new solution it eventually updates the actual best solution and sends a new subproblem to the sending processor.

- if the root receives only one problem from a slave processor, this processor has locally stored the other generated subproblem. The received problem is inserted into the heap if its bound is less than the actual best solution.

- if the root processor receives two subproblems in one package from some processor i, then these subproblems are inserted into the heap, if their bounds are less the actual best solution. The subproblem with minimal bound is send to processor i.

- if a slave processor sends an explicit request for work at the beginning of the algorithm or an implicit request (sending two subproblems or a solution) and the global heap is empty or contains only subproblems with bound greater or equal to the actual best solution, then this process is marked idle. If all processes are idle, the algorithm terminates.

Configuration

This algorithm was implemented on a transputer network with a ternary tree topology (processors near to leave processors are of degree two). We used this tree topology, because every transputer has four communication links. Each non-leave slave processor performs a sequential branch and bound algorithm and a routing process in "parallel", because it is necessary to route subproblems very quickly through the network, to avoid long idle times of processors in a subtree. The leave processors perform only the sequential branch and bound algorithm. The root processor controls the heap, holds the actual best solution, detects termination, and performs the branch and bound algorithm in "parallel".

Results

To test the efficiency of our algorithm we solved the vertex cover problem on the described network for 20 random graphs, each having 150 nodes and an average degree of 30. Table 3 show the results for 5 graphs which are typically for the whole class of testgraphs.

Graph Id.	1 processor		63 processors			
	time	iterations	time	iterations	speedup	efficiency
0	5488.69	37953	88.64	38033	61.92	0.983
1	9499.36	66768	152.60	66815	62.25	0.988
2	9401.62	66017	150.88	66035	62.31	0.989
3	5015.47	34038	81.06	34188	61.87	0.982
4	4807.84	32949	77.70	33005	61.88	0.982
	34212.98	237725	550.88	238076	62.11	0.986

Table 3: Results for 5 graphs (n=150, d=30) on a 63 processor ternary tree

Table 4 shows idle times and iterations for graph 1. The small idle times for each processor

computation time	152.60
idle time root process	0.6350
min. idle time slaves	0.5496
max. idle time slaves	1.3743
avg. idle time slaves	1.1011
iterations root process	895
min. iterations slaves	1007
max. iterations slaves	1133
avg. iterations slaves	1063

Table 4: idle times, iterations of Graph 1

especially for the leave processors are very surprising and reflect the extremely efficient communication mechanism of OCCAM-programmed transputer networks. One can see that the root process which has to perform the whole heap organization is only little blocked by this additional work. We have done additional simulations of distributing workload over processors which are configured in a ternary tree structure. These results show, that for constant communication and storage management costs the speedup increases, if the computation time for a single subproblem on a slave processor is sufficiently high.

Since an efficient branch and bound algorithm must perform a great amount of computation for one branch and bound step, the tree structure might be a simple alternative to really distributed algorithms if the global memory management can be done efficiently by the root processor.

5 Conclusion

We have proposed two strategies for implementing distributed branch and bound algorithms on a distributed system.

The algorithm which is based on the tree structured network topology is a rather simple and straightforward method for parallelizing branch and bound algorithms. In our case, the relation between costs for communication and global heap management on one side and execution times for the branch and bound step on the other side, is extremely good. Thus a nearly linear speedup for 63 processors could be achieved. Shorter execution times of the sequential algorithm for one subproblem or longer communication and heap management times will lead to decreased speedup. Many efficient sequential branch and bound algorithms gain their efficiency by a sophisticated branching method which reduces the number of problems in the search space. We predict, that in these cases the tree based strategy will give good results.

Our distributed strategy, which is based on the proposed load balancing algorithm, is more independent from the execution times of one branch and bound iteration. This strategy may work for any other branch and bound algorithm.

A problem of this load balancing method is to find the optimal parameterset for a given network topology and sequential branch and bound algorithm. We will do further work on dynamically optimizing this parameters.

References

[1] E. Altmann, T. A. Marsland, T. Breitkreutz
    Accounting for Parallel Tree Search Overheads, Proceedings of the International Conference on Parallel Processing 1988, pp. 198 - 201

[2] C. Beilken, F. Mattern, M. Reinfrank
    Verteilte Terminierung ein wesentlicher Aspekt der Kontrolle in verteilten Systemen Sonderforschungsbereich 124 "VLSI Entwurfsmethoden und Parallelität", Bericht Nr. 41/85, Dezember 1985

[3] C. Berge
    The theory of graphs and its applications, Methuen, London 1962

[4] A. Burns
    Programming in OCCAM 2, Addison Wesely 1988.

[5] R. Feldmann, B. Monien, P. Mysliwietz, O. Vornberger
    Distributed Game Tree Search, to appear in: Kanal, Gopalakrishnan, Kumar, Parallel Algorithms for Machine Intelligence and Pattern Recognition, North Holland/ Elsevier Publ. Co.

[6] M. R. Garey, D.S. Johnson
    Computers and Intractability: A Guide to the Theory of NP-Completeness, 1979 Freeman, San Francisco, Calif.

[7] V. K. Janakiram, D. P. Agrawal, R. Mehrotra
    A randomized Parallel Branch and Bound Algorithm, Proceedings of the International Conference on Parallel Processing 1988, pp. 69 - 75

[8] R. M. Karp, Y. Zhang,
    A randomized Parallel Branch and Bound Procedure, Proceedings of the ACM Symposium on Theory of Computing 1988, pp. 290 - 300

[9] V. Kumar, V. Nageshwara Rao, K. Ramesh
    Parallel Depth First Search on the Ring Architecture International Conference on Parallel Processing, pp. 128 - 132

[10] E. L. Lawler, D. E. Wood
     Branch and Bound Methods: A survey, Operations Research 14, 1966, pp. 699-719

[11] F. C. H. Lin, R. M. Keller
     The Gradient Model Load Balancing Method, IEEE Transactions on Software Engineering, Vol. 13, No. 1 January 1987

[12] B. Monien and O. Vornberger
Parallel processing of combinatorial search trees, Processings International Workshop on Parallel Algorithms and Architectures, Math. Research Nr. 38, Akademie - Verlag Berlin, pp. 60-69, 1987

[13] B. Monien, E. Speckenmeyer, O. Vornberger
Upperbound for covering problems, Methods of operations research, 43, 1981, pp. 419-431

[14] R. E. Tarjan, A. E. Trojanowski
Finding a maximum independent set, SIAM J. Computing, Vol. 6, No. 3, September 1977, pp. 537-546

[15] O. Vornberger and B. Monien
Parallel alpha-beta versus parallel SSS*, Proceedings IFIP Conference on Distributed Processing, Distributed Processing, North Holland, pp. 613-625, 1987

[16] O. Vornberger
Implementing branch and bound in a ring of processors, Proceedings of CONPAR 86, Lecture Notes of Computer Science 237, Springer Verlag, pp. 157-164, 1986

[17] O. Vornberger
Load Balancing in a Network of Transputers, Distributed Algorithms 1987, Lecture Notes of Computer Science 312, Springer Verlag, pp. 116 - 126

Optimal Fault-Tolerant Distributed Algorithms for Election in Complete Networks with a Global Sense of Direction*

Toshimitsu MASUZAWA[1], Naoki NISHIKAWA[2], Ken'ichi HAGIHARA[1] and Nobuki TOKURA[2]

[1] Education Center for Information Processing, Osaka University
Machikaneyama, Toyonaka, Osaka, 560, JAPAN
[2] Faculty of Engineering Science, Osaka University
Machikaneyama, Toyonaka, Osaka, 560, JAPAN

Abstract

This paper considers the leader election problem (*LEP*) in asynchronous complete networks with undetectable fail-stop failures. Especially, it is discussed whether presence of a global sense of direction affects the message complexity of *LEP* in faulty networks. For a complete network of n processors where k processors start the algorithm spontaneously and at most f_p ($<n/2$) processors are faulty, this paper shows

(1) the message complexity of *LEP* is $\Theta(n + k\,f_p)$, if the complete network has a global sense of direction.

It is already known that *LEP* requires $\Omega(n \log k + k\,f_p)$ message exchanges, if the complete network has no global sense of direction. Therefore, our result implies that the message complexity of *LEP* can be greatly reduced by using a global sense of direction in faulty networks as well as in reliable networks. For a complete network with at most f_l ($<n-1$) faulty links (and no faulty processor), this paper also shows the similar result :

(2) the message complexity of *LEP* is $\Theta(n + k\,f_l + f_l \log f_l)$, if the complete network has a global sense of direction.

1. Introduction

Consider an asynchronous bidirectional network of n processors. The *leader election problem* (*LEP*) is the problem of choosing a unique processor as a leader. *LEP* is considered to be solved if (a) a unique leader is elected, (b) every processor knows that a leader has been elected, and (c) every processor knows the identity number of the leader. Since *LEP* is a central problem in the study of distributed algorithms, many distributed algorithms have been proposed for *LEP*. There are various models and cost measurements. In this paper, we consider *LEP* in a *complete network* (i.e. the network where every pair of processors is

* This work was supported in part by The Mazda Foundation's Research Grant and The Inamori Foundation's Research Grant.

directly connected by a link) and use the *message complexity* (i.e. the maximum total number of messages transmitted during any execution of the algorithm) to measure the efficiency of a distributed algorithm.

Korach *et al.* [4] and Afek *et al.* [1] showed that the message complexity of *LEP* in reliable *complete* networks is $\Theta(n \log k)$, where k is the number of the processors that start the algorithm spontaneously. Santoro [9] proposed "*a global sense of direction*" of a complete network as topological information, and Loui *et al.* [7] pointed out that *LEP* can be solved by using $O(n)$ messages *if the reliable complete network has a global sense of direction*. This fact means that presence of a global sense of direction can greatly affect (in a positive sense) the communication complexity of *LEP* in the case that there exists no failure.

Real systems, however, are subject to several types of failures. This paper proposes *fault-tolerant* distributed algorithms for *LEP* in *asynchronous* complete networks. This paper considers only *fail-stop* failure, that is, a failed processor stops sending messages, and a failed link stops transmitting messages. In asynchronous networks, the fail-stop failure is undetectable because any processor cannot distinguish between a slow processor (resp. a slow link) and a failed processor (resp. a failed link). Therefore, fail-stop failures further complicate *LEP*.

We first consider only processor failures under the assumption that there exists no faulty link. It is already known that *LEP* is *unsolvable* even if one processor may fail *during* execution of an algorithm [3]. Therefore, it is assumed throughout this paper that every failure occurs *prior to* execution of the algorithm. On the other hand, Kutten [6] pointed out that no algorithm can solve *LEP* in a complete network with $n/2$ faulty processors even if the failures occur before execution of the algorithm. Therefore, we assume that the number of faulty processors is less than $n/2$. Under the same assumptions several fault-tolerant distributed algorithms have been proposed [2,5]. It is obvious that no fault-tolerant leader election algorithm guarantees termination in *general* networks even with the assumption. Kutten *et al.* [5] proposed a leader election algorithm with the message complexity $O(n \log k + k f_p)$ for a *complete* network with at most f_p ($<n/2$) faulty processors, and they showed that the message complexity is optimal (within a constant factor). *Can the message complexity of LEP be reduced by using a global sense of direction in a faulty complete network as well as in a reliable complete network?*

This paper answers in the affirmative by showing

(1)   the message complexity of *LEP* is $\Theta(n + k f_p)$, if the complete network has a global sense of direction.

For a complete network where at most f_l ($<n-1$) *links* are faulty (and there exists no faulty processor), this paper also shows

(2)   the message complexity of *LEP* is $\Theta(n + k f_l + f_l \log f_l)$, if the complete network has a global sense of direction.

If no global sense of direction is available, the message complexity of *LEP* in a complete network with at most f_l ($<n-1$) faulty links is $\Theta(n \log k + n f_l)$. This result follows from the result Kutten *et al.* [5] showed. (Kutten *et al.* [5] considered the link failures as well as the processor failures, and showed the message complexity $\Theta(\min(n \log k + k f_l, n f_l))$. But this result contradicts the proven fact that the lower bound of the message complexity of *LEP* is $\Omega(n \log k)$ in a reliable complete network, because the result in [5] implies that a leader can be elected by using $O(n)$ messages in a reliable complete network.)

Table 1. Message complexity of *LEP* in complete networks

a complete network with	no failure	f_p faulty processors	f_l faulty links
no global sense of direction	$\Theta(n \log k)$ [1,4]	$\Theta(n \log k + k f_p)$ [5]	$\Theta(n \log k + n f_l)$
a global sense of direction	$\Theta(n)$ [7]	$\Theta(n + k f_p)$	$\Theta(n + k f_l + f_l \log f_l)$

results in this paper

Table 1 summarizes the existing results and our results for *LEP* in complete networks. A close look at Table 1 shows that our result is regarded as integration of the result for reliable complete networks with a global sense of direction and the result for faulty complete networks with no global sense of direction.

Kutten *et al.* [5] proposed the general method for making a *fault-intolerant* distributed algorithm *fault-tolerant*. Roughly speaking, in order to overcome the problem of tokens' loss, $f_p + 1$ tokens are used (in a faulty network) instead of one token (in a reliable network) in the method. Kutten *et al.* developed an *optimal fault-tolerant* leader election algorithm by applying the method to an *optimal fault-intolerant* algorithm (*AG-algorithm*) proposed by Afek and Gafni [1]. We also adopt the same method to design a fault-tolerant distributed algorithm for *LEP* in a complete network with a global sense of direction. However, even if we simply apply the method to an *optimal fault-intolerant* algorithm (*LMW-algorithm*) proposed by Loui *et al.* [7], an *optimal fault-tolerant* algorithm cannot be obtained. What makes it impossible to obtain an optimal fault-tolerant algorithm in this case? The reason why Kutten *et al.* succeeded in developing an optimal fault tolerant distributed algorithm is that AG-algorithm is *insensitive* to the order of links incident to a processor in which the links are used to transmit tokens. On the other hand, LMW-algorithm is *extremely sensitive* to the order.

To fill the gap, this paper introduces a method "*grouping*", that is, $f_p + 1$ processors are *grouped* together at first and all processors in the same group act for one processor in a reliable network. After *grouping*, we apply the method proposed by Kutten *et al.* to LMW-algorithm, and obtain an *optimal fault-tolerant* leader election algorithm in complete networks *with a global sense of direction.*

As the grouping method we use can be applied generally, we believe that the efficient fault-tolerant algorithms can be obtained by applying the method to efficient fault-intolerant algorithms for a complete network with a global sense of direction.

2. Model

Our model is standard one except that "a global sense of direction" and "fail-stop failures" are introduced, that is, (1) through (7) are assumptions of the standard model (before considering a global sense of direction and failures).

(1) The network is a *complete network* of *n* processors, that is, every pair of processors is directly connected by a bidirectional communication link.

(2) The processors communicate only by passing messages.

(3) The network is *asynchronous*, that is, the time to transmit a message along a link is finite but unpredictable.

(4) The processors are identical except that each processor *u* has a unique *identity number* (i.e. processor number) *ID*(*u*). Every identity number is represented in O(log *n*) bits. The processors all perform the same program.

(5) The program executed in each processor includes (a) its internal operations, (b) *send* operations to send messages via its ports, and (c) *receive* operations to receive messages from its ports. (Each processor can distinguish its ports each other.)

(6) The messages sent along the same link are delivered in the FIFO order.

(7) Any non-empty subset of processors may start the algorithm spontaneously, and each of other processors starts the algorithm when it receives a message. The processors which start the algorithm spontaneously are called *initiators*.

A global sense of direction

This paper considers the complete network with *a global sense of direction*. The complete network has a global sense of direction, if the ports of every processor are labelled as follows:

(a) a directed Hamilton cycle *H* is fixed; and

(b) each port of every processor *u* is labelled according to the distance in *H* from *u* to the adjacent processor via the port.

An example of the labelling is shown in Fig. 1.

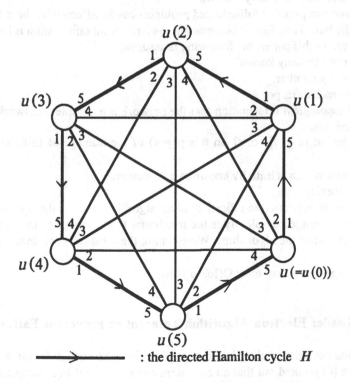

u(2)

u(3)

u(1)

u(4)

u(=u(0))

u(5)

———————⟶ ———— : the directed Hamilton cycle *H*

Fig. 1 A complete network with a global sense of direction

Throughout this paper, the following notations are used concerning a global sense of direction.

H: the directed Hamilton cycle that determines the labelling of the ports.

$u(p)$: the processor to which u connects via the port labelled p.

(For convenience, let $u(0)$ denote u itself.)

$u(p..q)$: the set of processors $\{u(i) \mid p \leq i \leq q\}$.

By making effective use of a global sense of direction, a processor u can directly send messages to a processor w, if u knows its port connected to v and v's port connected to w. For example, when $v = u(a)$ and $w = v(b)$ hold, then $w = u((a+b) \bmod n)$ holds in a complete network with a global sense of direction. This property is of great use to reduce the message complexity.

Fail-stop failures

This paper considers fail-stop failures.

(8) A faulty processor sends no message.

(9) A faulty link transmits no message.

In asynchronous networks, the fail-stop failure is undetectable because no processor can distinguish between a *slow* processor (resp. a *slow* link) and a *failed* processor (resp. a *failed* link).

It is known that *LEP* is unsolvable even if one processor may fail *during* execution of the algorithm [3]. Therefore, the following is assumed.

(10) No failure occurs *during* execution of the algorithm. Processors or links may recover during execution of the algorithm.

What each processor initially knows

The message complexity of distributed problems can be affected by the information each processor initially has. Therefore, it is important to clarify what information is initially available in each processor. In this paper, the following is assumed.

(11) Each processor initially knows

(a) its own identity number,

(b) the label on each of its ports,

(c) the global topological information that the network is a complete network with a global sense of direction, and,

(d) an upper bound (e.g. f_p or f_l in this paper) of the number of failures in the whole network.

No other information is initially known to a processor.

Message complexity

In this paper, to measure the efficiency of an algorithm, we use the *message complexity*. The (worst case) message complexity is the maximum total number of messages transmitted during any execution of the algorithm. We estimate the message complexity under the next assumption.

(12) Every message contains at most O($\log n$) bits.

3. Optimal Leader Election Algorithm Tolerant of Processor Failures

This section considers a distributed algorithm for *LEP* which is tolerant of processor failures. Kutten [6] pointed out that no algorithm can solve *LEP* in a complete network with $n/2$ faulty processors. This section shows a leader election algorithm tolerant of f_p ($<n/2$)

faulty processors, and shows that its message complexity is optimal within a constant factor. In this section, we assume that
(13) there exist at most f_p ($<n/2$) faulty processors and there exists no faulty link.

From the assumption (11), each processor initially knows the value f_p which is the upper bound of the number of faulty processors.

The fault-tolerant algorithm we propose is developed by modifying an already known algorithm (*LMW-algorithm*) which solves *LEP* in reliable complete networks with a global sense of direction. LMW-algorithm is the slightly modified version of the algorithm proposed in [7].

3.1 LMW-algorithm

Initially every initiator is a *king*, that is, a candidate for a *leader*. Each *king* u has its *kingdom* which consists of only u itself initially. Each *king* u tries to expand its *kingdom* along the directed Hamilton cycle H under the condition that
(a) there exists no *king* except for u in u's *kingdom*, and
(b) u's *kingdom* has the form of $u(0..a)$ for some non-negative integer a, that is, u's *kingdom* consists of consecutive processors in H beginning from u.

When the *kingdom* of a *king* covers more than $n/2$ processors, the *king* becomes a *leader*. Each *king* owns one token, and tries to annex other processors to its *kingdom* by sending the token. The token of a *king* u carries $ID(u)$, the message identity (ASK or ACCEPT) and the information about the *kingdom* of the annexed *king*.

Let u be any *king* and u's *kingdom* be $u(0..a)$. (Initially, $a=0$ holds.) The *king* u sends its token in the form of $<ASK, ID(u)>$ to v ($=u(a+1)$) in order to expand u's *kingdom*. When v receives the message, v acts as follows.

Case 1. v is an initiator (i.e. a *king* or a *loser*) and $ID(u)>ID(v)$ (this implies u is stronger than v): v returns u's token in the form of $<ACCEPT, b>$ to u, when v's *kingdom* is $v(0..b)$. This message informs u that all processors in v's *kingdom* are annexed to u's *kingdom*. Also, if v is a *king*, v becomes a *loser* and stops expanding v's *kingdom*.
Case 2. v is an initiator and $ID(u)<ID(v)$: The message $<ASK, ID(u)>$ is ignored. It indirectly makes u stop expanding its *kingdom*.
Case 3. v is not an initiator : v returns u's token in the form of $<ACCEPT, 0>$ to u. This message informs u that only v is annexed to u's *kingdom*.

When a *king* u receives the message $<ACCEPT, b>$ from $u(a+1)$, u's *kingdom* becomes $u(0..a+b+1)$. If the size of u's *kingdom* exceeds $n/2$ (i.e. $a+b+2>n/2$), u becomes a *leader* and terminates after broadcasting $ID(u)$ to all other processors. Otherwise (i.e. $a+b+2\leq n/2$), u sends $<ASK, ID(u)>$ to $u(a+b+2)$, i.e. the processor with the minimum distance in H among the processors outside u's *kingdom*. (u examines whether the processors outside u's *kingdom* are *kings* or not in the order in which the processors appear on H. We call the method for searching for the *nearest king* the *sequential search*.)

If the processor u which receives $<ACCEPT, b>$ is not a *king* (this case arises when u was defeated by another *king* before u receives the reply to $<ASK, ID(u)>$), then u ignores the message $<ACCEPT, b>$ it receives.

We can understand from LMW-algorithm that the following is the key to efficient distributed algorithms in complete networks with a global sense of direction.
[LMW-technique] Every *king* u tries to find the *nearest king* in H and to annex it to u's *kingdom*. Consider the case that a *king* u annexes the *nearest king* v. v informs u of v's ports connected to processors in v's *kingdom*. By utilizing a global sense of direction, u can

find u's ports connected to processors which *was* contained in v's *kingdom*. This prevents u from sending its token to them, that is, once a processor is annexed to the *kingdom* of any other *king*, it never receives a token for searching for the *nearest king*. Consequently, the total number of tokens for searching for the *nearest king* is $O(n)$. On the other hand, the information about any *kingdom* can be transferred by using *only log n bits*, that is, by using *only one message*. (Recall that any *kingdom* consists of consecutive processors in H beginning from its *king*). Consequently, the total number of messages for transferring the information about the *kingdoms* is $O(k)$. Therefore, the message complexity of LMW-algorithm is $O(n)$ (while $\Omega(n \log k)$ messages are required if no global sense of direction is available.) []

Difficulty on applying LMW-technique to faulty networks

As pointed out above, the key of LMW-technique is to find the *nearest king*. But unfortunately, the *nearest king* cannot be found in asynchronous faulty network if every initiator is initially a *king*, because a faulty processor cannot be detected in asynchronous network. For example, let u be a *king* and $u(0..a)$ be its *kingdom*. To find the *nearest king*, u has to decide whether $u(a+1)$ is a *king* or not. However, u cannot distinguish a faulty processor and a slow *king*. Therefore, LMW-technique cannot be simply utilized in faulty complete networks.

3.2 Making a Distributed Algorithm Fault-Tolerant

Kutten *et al.* [5] proposed the general method to make a *fault-intolerant* distributed algorithm *fault-tolerant*. They obtained an *optimal fault-tolerant* algorithm by applying the method to an *optimal fault-intolerant* algorithm (*AG-algorithm*) proposed by Afek and Gafni [1]. Similar to LMW-algorithm, every initiator is initially a *king* and owns one token in AG-algorithm. Every *king* uses a token to annex other processors to its *kingdom*. The algorithm may be deadlocked in presence of faulty processors, because tokens sent to faulty processors are lost. In order to overcome the problem of tokens' loss, Kutten *et al.* devised the following method.

[(f_p+1)-token method] Each *king* has f_p+1 tokens utilized for expanding its *kingdom*. []

3.3 (f_p+1)-token sequential search

In order to design a fault-tolerant algorithm for complete networks with a global sense of direction, we tried to combine the (f_p+1)-token method with LMW-technique. For example, we easily think of the following method of searching for another *king*. The method is regarded as the multi-token version of the sequential search.

[(f_p+1)-token sequential search] Consider the case that u's *kingdom* is $u(0..a)$ and u searches for another *king*. To overcome the problem of tokens' loss, the (f_p+1)-token method is adapted to the sequential search which is used to search for the nearest king in LMW-technique. Each king u owns f_p+1 tokens, and initially sends tokens to all processors in $u(a+1..a+f_p+1)$. As at least one processor in $u(a+1..a+f_p+1)$ is not faulty, at least one token returns eventually. When u receives a token, u sends a token to $u(a+f_p+2)$ if u does not find another *king* yet. (see Fig.2) u continues to search for another *king* in this way. []

Assume that u eventually finds a *king* $u(b)$ by the (f_p+1)-token sequential search. When u finds out the *king* $u(b)$, there are at most f_p processors in $u(a+1..b-1)$ which return no token. u cannot decide whether they contain a *king* or not. Therefore $u(b)$ is not necessarily the *nearest king*. As the *kingdom* of u is expanded *along H* (that is, the *kingdom* of u is expanded under the condition that it consists of consecutive processors in H beginning from

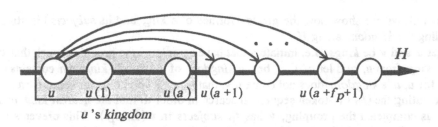

(a) Initially u sends f_p+1 tokens to all processors in $u(a+1..a+f_p+1)$.

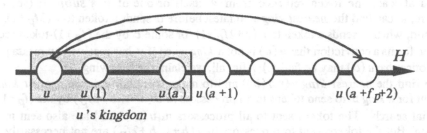

(b) When a token is returned to u, u sends it to $u(a+f_p+2)$.

Fig. 2 Execution of the (f_p+1)-token sequential search.

u), u cannot annex the *kingdom* of $u(b)$ until u forms a conviction that there exists no *king* in $u(a+1..b-1)$. Unfortunately as we pointed out in the section 3.1, u never forms the conviction because of the undetectable processor failures, if every initiator is initially a *king*.

Why did Kutten *et al.* succeeded in developing an optimal fault-tolerant distributed algorithm by using the (f_p+1)-token method? In (f_p+1)-token method, a *king* sends f_p+1 tokens via arbitrary f_p+1 unused ports simultaneously. We cannot predict which token is returned to the *king* first. But this indeterminacy poses no problem. Because the order of the ports in which the ports are used to send tokens is *insignificant* in AG-algorithm. In other words, in order to find another *king*, a *king* sends a token via an *arbitrary* unused port in AG-algorithm. On the other hand, the order of ports is very important in LMW-algorithm, because LMW-algorithm requires a *king* to find the *nearest king*. To fill up the gap, we introduce a technique "*grouping*" that makes it possible to *makes effective use of a global sense of direction in presence of failure.*

3.4 A key technique "grouping"

As we pointed out above, no *king* can find the *nearest king*, if every initiator is initially a *king*. To solve the difficult situation, we introduced a preprocessing phase called "*grouping phase*". At the beginning of our algorithm, every initiator is not a *king* but a *lord*. In the grouping phase, each *lord* u tries to capture f_p *subjects* in $u(1..2f_p)$, and becomes a *king* when it has captured f_p *subjects*. Every *king* tries to expand its *kingdom* along the directed Hamilton cycle H in the second phase of our algorithm as well as in LMW-algorithm. At the beginning of the second phase, the *kingdom* of u consists of u itself. Note that u's *subjects* are not contained in u's *kingdom*. They may be annexed to u's *kingdom* in the second phase.

In what follows, we show how the *group* (formed of a *king* and its *subjects*) is utilized for expanding the *kingdom* along *H.*

Let u and v be *kings* (i.e. initiators that have completed the grouping) such that v is the *nearest king* from u, and let $u(0..a)$ be the *kingdom* of u. As u's *kingdom* contains no *king* except for u, u's *kingdom* does not contain v, that is, $v=u(b)$ holds for some $b>a$. Assume u is executing the (f_p+1)-token sequential search in order to find the *nearest king*, that is, v. As v has completed the grouping, v has f_p *subjects* in $v(1..2f_p)$. This prevents u from sending a token to $v(2f_p+1)$ without receiving the token returned from v or one of v's *subjects* as follows. If u sends a token to $v(2f_p+1)$, then u has received tokens all processors in $v(0..2f_p)$ except for f_p processors. As v has f_p *subjects* in $v(1..2f_p)$, u has received at least one token returned from v itself or one of v's *subjects* (see Fig. 3). Therefore, u can find the *nearest king* v at latest before u sends a token to $v(2f_p+1)$. On the other hand, when u sends a token to $u(c+2f_p+1)$ for some c by the (f_p+1)-token sequential search, u forms a conviction that $u(c)$ is not a *king* even if u has received no message from $u(c)$. (Notice that $u(c)$ may be faulty.) After all, we claim the following.

To find the *nearest king* $v(=u(b))$ and to make sure that v is the *nearest king*, it is sufficient for a *king* u to send tokens to all processors in $u(a+1..b+2f_p)$ by the (f_p+1)-token sequential search. The tokens sent to all processors in $u(a+1..b)$ are also sent in LMW-algorithm. But the tokens sent to processors in $u(b+1..b+2f_p)$ are not necessarily sent in LMW-algorithm, if

(a) u is defeated by v, or
(b) some processors in $u(b+1..b+2f_p)$ are included in v's *kingdom*.
In these cases, the tokens sent to processors in $u(b+1..b+2f_p)$ are additional tokens to LMW-algorithm, which make the algorithm fault-tolerant.

3.5 Our Algorithm

This section shows an optimal algorithm which tolerates at most f_p $(<n/2)$ faulty processors in a complete network with a global sense of direction. For want of space, we describe only the outline of our algorithm and the outline of the estimate of the message complexity. The detailed algorithm, the detailed estimate of the message complexity and proof of correctness are reported in [8]. (We are now preparing a detailed report in English.)

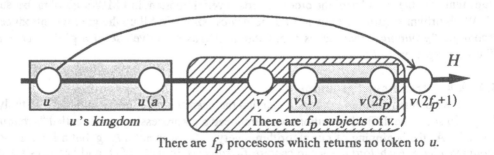

There are f_p processors which returns no token to u.

Fig.3 The situation when u sends a token to $v(2f_p+1)$.

3.5.1 Outline of the Algorithm

One of initiators is elected as a *leader* in our algorithm. Our algorithm consists of three phases.

First Phase (Grouping Phase)

Initially, every initiator is a *lord*. In this phase, every *lord* u tries to capture f_p *subjects* in $u(1..2f_p)$. When a *lord* has captured f_p *subjects*, it becomes a *king*. To capture *subjects*, u initially sends tokens (with $ID(u)$) to all processors in $u(1..2f_p)$. Since a *king* is a candidate for a *leader*, it is sufficient that at least one *lord* becomes a *king*. Therefore, a *lord* gives up his hope of becoming a *king* and releases its *subjects* when it finds either a *king* or a *lord* with a larger identity number. That is, when v receives the token from u, v acts as follows.

If (a) v is contained in the *kingdom* of some *king* (possibly v itself), or (b) v is a *subject* of a *king*, or (c) v is a *lord* s.t. $ID(v){>}ID(u)$ holds, or (d) v is a *subject* of a *lord* w s.t. $ID(w){>}ID(u)$, then v returns the token in the form of <REJECT> which makes u give up his hope of becoming a *king*. Otherwise, v returns the token in the form of <ACCEPT> to inform u that v becomes a *subject* of u.

Second Phase (Election Phase)

(A) In case of $f_p < n/4$

A *leader* is elected by utilizing LMW-technique. Every *king* tries to expand its *kingdom* along H, and becomes a *leader* when the size of its *kingdom* exceeds $n/2$. In order to find the *nearest king*, every *king* executes (f_p+1)-token sequential search in the way stated in the previous section. When a king u finds the nearest king v, u compares $ID(u)$ with $ID(v)$, and u annex v's *kingdom* to u's *kingdom* if $ID(u){>}ID(v)$ holds. As v's *kingdom* consists of consecutive processors in H, v can inform u of v's *kingdom* by using one message of $O(\log n)$ bits.

(B) In case of $f_p \geq n/4$

If we use the same method as that in the case of (A), a *king* u may send messages to all processors in $u(n/2..n/2+2f_p)$ in order to test whether $u(n/2)$ is a *king* or not. If $f_p \geq n/4$ holds, u is contained in $u(n/2..n/2+2f_p)$ and this may complicate the algorithm. Therefore, LMW-technique is not utilized in our algorithm, if $f_p \geq n/4$ holds.

In this case, every king u sends tokens with $ID(u)$ to all other processors when u becomes a *king*. If a processor v receives this token, v acts as follows.

(a) If v is a *king* s.t. $ID(v){>}ID(u)$ or if v is a *subject* of a *king* w s.t. $ID(w){>}ID(u)$, then v ignores the token sent from u.

(b) Otherwise, v returns u the token sent from u.

If a *king* u receives $n-1-f_p$ returned tokens, then u becomes a *leader*. As every *king* has f_p *subjects*, only the *king* with the largest identity number among all *kings* can become a *leader*.

Third Phase (Broadcast Phase)

In this phase, the *leader* elected in the second phase broadcasts its identity number to all other processors by sending the messages with $ID(u)$ from all of its ports.

3.5.2 Message complexity

[**Theorem 1**] For a complete network of n processors where k processors are initiators and at most f_p processors are faulty ($f_p < n/4$), the message complexity of *LEP* is $\Theta(n+kf_p)$, if a global sense of direction and the value of f_p are available at each processor.

(Sketch of Proof)

(1) *Upper bound* $O(n + kf_p)$: In the *first phase*, each *lord* sends $2f_p$ tokens. Each token causes at most 3 messages, that is, a message to inquire a *lord* whether the *lord* has become a *king* or not, a response to the inquiry, and the returned token. This implies that $O(kf_p)$ messages are used in the first phase. The message complexity of the *third phase* is clearly $O(n)$. In what follows, we estimate the number of messages used in the *second phase*.

(A) In case of $f_p < n/4$

A token sent by a *king* to search for the *nearest king* (in (f_p+1)-token sequential search) causes at most 3 messages in the second phase as well as in the first phase. Therefore we have only to estimate the number of tokens sent to search for the *nearest king*. Compared with LMW-algorithm, the following additional tokens are used in our algorithm.

(a) When a *king u* finds the *nearest king v*, u sends at most $2f_p$ additional tokens (as stated in the section 3.4).

(b) If u annexes a king v when v's *kingdom* is $v(0..a)$, v may have sent at most $2f_p+1$ additional tokens to processors outside v's *kingdom*.

It follows that at most $4f_p+1$ additional tokens are sent for every annexation of *kingdom*. As annexation of *kingdom* occurs $k-1$ times, $O(kf_p)$ additional messages are sent in the second phase. Therefore the total number of tokens to search for the nearest king is $O(n + kf_p)$.

(B) In case of $f_p \geq n/4$

Every *king* initially sends $n-1$ messages, and each message causes at most three messages. Therefore, the total number of messages used in the second phase is $O(kn)$, that is, $O(kf_p)$ in the case of $f_p \geq n/4$.

(2) *Lower bound* $\Omega(n + kf_p)$: It is trivial that $\Omega(n)$ messages are required. To overcome tokens' loss, each initiator must initially send at least f_p+1 messages. Therefore, $\Omega(kf_p)$ messages are required. (Kutten *et al.* [5] made the same argument to prove the same lower bound for LEP in complete networks with no global sense of direction.) []

4. Results about Leader Election Algorithm Tolerant of Link Failures

This section only shows the results of our research on leader election algorithms tolerant of *link* failures. If the number of faulty link is more than or equal to $n-1$, the network may be disconnected because of faulty links. Therefore, we assume that

(14) there exist at most f_l ($< n-1$) faulty links and there exists no faulty processor.

From the assumption (11), each processor initially knows the value f_l which is the upper bound of the number of faulty links.

Recall the optimal leader election algorithm we proposed in the previous section, which is tolerant of processor failures. The first phase and the second phase work correctly for the case of link failures as well as the case of processor failures, that is, the algorithm elects one leader for the case of link failures. (In case of $f_l \geq n/2$, we have to modify the algorithm a little so that at least one processor can capture f_l *subjects* in the first phase.) However, the third phase does not work well, if there exist faulty links. For example, if a link connecting to the leader is faulty, the leader cannot directly send the message with its identity number to the processor to which the leader is connected by the faulty link. Therefore, the only problem we have to consider is the *broadcast problem* (*BCP*) to disseminate a value (e.g. an identity number) to all processors. With regard to *BCP*, the following is shown. (Details are reported in [8].)

[Theorem 2] The message complexity of *BCP* in a complete network with at most f_l ($<n$-1) faulty links (and the value of f_l is known to every processor) is

(1) $\Theta(n + f_l \log f_l)$, if a global sense of direction is available, while

(2) $\Theta(n\, f_l)$, if no global sense of direction is available. **[]**

Notice that presence of a global sense of direction greatly affects the message complexity of *BCP*.

Since *LEP* includes *BCP* as a subproblem, it follows from Theorem 2 that the message complexity of *LEP* is $\Omega(nf_l)$ in a complete network with no global sense of direction. The lower bound $\Omega(n \log k)$ for a reliable network is also the lower bound for a faulty network. Therefore, the message complexity of *LEP* is $\Omega(n \log k + nf_l)$ in a complete network with no global sense of direction. By combining the broadcast algorithm we devised [8] with the fault tolerant leader election algorithm proposed by Kutten *et al.* [5], *LEP* can be solved by using $O(n \log k + nf_l)$ messages. Therefore, the message complexity of *LEP* is $\Theta(n \log k + nf_l)$, if no global sense of direction is available. On the other hand, for *LEP* in a complete network with a global sense of direction, the following theorem is proved from Theorem 2. Theorem 3 implies that presence of a global sense of direction greatly affects the message complexity of *LEP* in a complete network with faulty links.

[Theorem 3] For a complete network of n processors where k processors are initiators and at most f_l links are faulty ($f_l < n$-1), the message complexity of *LEP* is $\Theta(n + kf_l + f_l \log f_l)$, if a global sense of direction and the value of f_l are available at each processor. **[]**

References

[1] Y.Afek and E.Gafni, "Time and message bound for election in synchronous and asynchronous complete networks", Proc. 4th PODC, Minacki, Canada, pp.186-195 (Aug. 1985).

[2] R.Bar-Yehuda, S.Kutten, Y.Wolfstahl and S.Zaks, "Making distributed spanning tree algorithms fault-resilient", Proc. 4th Ann. Sympo. on Theoretical Aspects of Computer Science, LNCS 247, pp.432-444 (Feb. 1987).

[3] M.J.Fischer, N.A.Lynch and M.S.Paterson, "Impossibility of distributed consensus with one faulty process", JACM, Vol.32, No.2, pp.374-382 (Apr. 1985).

[4] E. Korach, S.Moran and S.Zaks, "Tight lower and upper bounds for some distributed algorithms for a complete network of processors", Proc. 3rd PODC, Vancouver, Canada, pp.199-207 (Aug. 1984).

[5] S.Kutten, Y.Wolfstahl and S.Zaks, "Optimal distributed t-resilient election in complete networks", Tech. Rep. #430, Computer Science Department, Technion, Israel (Aug. 1986).

[6] S.Kutten, "Optimal fault-tolerant distributed construction of a spanning tree", (the final version of [5]).

[7] M.C.Loui, T.A.Matsushita and D.B.West, "Election in complete networks with a sense of direction", Information Processing Letters, vol.22, No.4, pp.185-187 (Apr. 1986).

[8] T.Masuzawa, N.Nishikawa, K.Hagihara, N.Tokura and K.Fujita, "Leader election problem on faulty complete networks with global sense of direction" (in Japanese), Tech. Rep. IECEJ,COMP88-98 (Mar. 1989).

[9] N.Santoro, "Sense of direction, topological awareness and communication complexity", ACM SIGACT NEWS, vol.16, pp.50-56 (Summer 1984).

Simple and Efficient Election Algorithms for Anonymous Networks

Yossi Matias
Computer Science Dep.
Tel-Aviv University

Yehuda Afek
AT&T Bell Labs&
Computer Science Dep.
Tel-Aviv University

1 Introduction

We address the problem of electing a leader in an anonymous, asynchronous network of arbitrary topology. Our algorithms are considerably simpler than known algorithms and have equal or improved communication complexity.

In [Ang80] it was shown that from symmetry considerations, there is no deterministic algorithm to elect a leader (i.e., to break the symmetry) in a general anonymous network [ASW85]. Following [Ang80] many probabilistic algorithms for electing a leader, and/or breaking the symmetry were proposed [IR81, ASW85, AAHK86, CV86, FS86, SS89]. However, only Schieber and Snir have considered the general case of an arbitrary topology asynchronous network. The present paper was motivated by their work [SS89] and in particular by their list of open questions.

When discussing election algorithms for anonymous networks one has to consider *knowledge of the network size*, and *termination detection* [SS89, ASW85]. In [IR81] it was shown that a leader can be elected in a ring, with termination detection, and with fixed error probability $\epsilon < 1$, only if an upper bound is known on the network size. Furthermore, Itai and Rodeh continued to show that the problem can be solved with termination detection and without error only if the ring size is known up to a factor of two. In [SS89] Schieber and Snir extended all of these results to an arbitrary network, under a variety of assumptions on the processors *a priori* knowledge of the network. They presented efficient algorithms for constructing a spanning tree and electing a leader (see Figure 1 for summary of their results).

In this paper we present three types of algorithms. In Section 2 we give a simple elec-ion algorithm without termination detection for the case that nothing is known about the network size, n. In Section 3 we show that when a lower bound is given on the network size the algorithm of Section 1 can be made more efficient (still without termination detection). n Section 4 we turn to the design of election algorithms with termination detection when both lower and upper bounds are given (see Figure 1 for a summary of results). Finally, we how in Section 5 that for the problem of electing a leader, complete anonymous networks are more powerful than arbitrary networks. Specifically, we show that the complexity of probabilistically electing a leader in an anonymous complete network is the same as in an anonymous ring, the cost in both topologies being lower than in dense networks of arbitrary topology. (The same relationships hold in the case of deterministic election algorithms without anonymity.)

The results in this paper improve the bit complexity of [SS89]. Moreover, [SS89] suggest a way to reduce the message complexity by increasing the message size. Contrary to this approach the algorithms presented here have increased message complexity and reduced message size, which result in an overall decrease in bit complexity for sparse networks. Furthermore, the approach taken here leads to algorithms that require less state information at the nodes. The algorithms in Sections 2 and 3 require at most $O(\log \log n + \log 1/\epsilon)$ bits of state information per node (it is always equal to the message size), while in [SS89] the algorithms require $O(\log(n/\epsilon))$ bits of state information per link. In addition, algorithms here are considerably simpler. As in [SS89] all our algorithms construct a spanning tree which can then be used for many applications, such as counting the number of nodes, assigning unique id's to the nodes, constructing a minimum weight spanning tree, etc.

2   Networks with unknown size

In this section we present a simple probabilistic algorithm for leader election in an asynchronous network of processors. The processors are assumed to be anonymous and have no knowledge of the network size or topology. The only thing known to each processor is its collection of incoming and outgoing ports by which it receives and sends messages from and to its neighbors. The algorithm succeeds with probablity $1 - \epsilon$. Let $r = 1/\epsilon$.

The algorithm, denoted $ELECT$, proceeds in two steps. First, each node randomly selects an id, and second each node tries to broadcast its id over the network. Upon receiving an id a node forwards it only if it is larger than any id the node has seen so far. Thus, eventually the largest id captures the entire network. In addition, each node marks the link over which it received the largest id as its $parent$ link, thus constructing a spanning forest. If the largest id chosen is unique than the forest is a tree whose root is the leader.

The crux of the algorithm is the id selection procedure. It is designed such that two

Election	Know about n	Term. Detec.	Message Complexity	Message Size	Time
[SS-89]	nothing	w/o	$m \cdot \log n$ (worst case)	$\log n + \log r$	n (w.c.)
[SS-89]	nothing	w/o	$m \cdot \log \log n + n \log n$ ($m \cdot f(n) + n \log n$)	$\log n + \log r$ ($\log F(n) + \log r$)	$n \log \log n$
§2	nothing	w/o	$m \log n \cdot r \log r$	$\log \log n + \log r$	D
§3	$L \le n$	w/o	$m \cdot r \log r \log(rn/L)$	$\log \log(n/L) + \log r$	D
§3	$L < n \le kL$ $k \ge 1$	w/o	$m \cdot r \log(rk) \log r$ (worst case)	$\log r + \log \log(k)$	D (w.c.)
[SS-89]	$n \le U$	with	$n \cdot \log n + m$ (worst case)	$\log U + \log r$	n (w.c.)
[SS-89]	$L < n \le 2L$	with	$n \cdot \log n + m$ (no error)	$\log n$	n
§4	$L < n \le kL$ $k \ge 1$	with	$m \cdot r \log(rk) \log r$ (worst case)	$\log n$	D (w.c.)
§5	complete network	with	$n \cdot r \log^2 r$ (worst case)	$\log n$	$\log n$

Figure 1: Our Anonymous Election Algorithms versus Schieber Snir ones
($r = 1/\epsilon$; D is the network diameter; m is the total number of links; $F(n) = \max\{i : f(i) = f(n)\}$)

conditions are simultaneously satisfied with high probability: (a) a single node is distinguished from the rest; (b) the number of different id's is low. (The id selection procedure distributively estimates the size of the network without explicitly revealing this information to any single node. This idea was first introduced and applied in [GL83].)

More precisely, each processor P_i randomly selects two numbers t_i and s_i as follows: (1) it tosses a fair coin until it gets a $Head$ for the first time. Let t_i be the number of these tosses. (2) The second number, s_i, is randomly selected in the range $[1..d]$, where $d = O(r \log r)$. (The exact value of d will be given in the analysis.) Let id_i, the id of processor P_i, be the ordered pair $< t_i, s_i >$. A lexicographic order on the ids is naturally defined. Denote this procedure of choosing id_i as $Choose(id_i)$.

Algorithm $ELECT$

Procedure $Initialize(i)$ /* performed upon waking up or reception of first message - whichever comes first */

call $Choose(id_i)$;   /* P_i randomly selects $id_i = < t_i, s_i >$ */

$nax_i := id_i;$ $parent_i := 0;$
Send id_i to all neighbors.   /* P_i broadcasts its id */

Upon receiving id at node i over link l:

f id_i not defined then call $Initialize(i)$;
If $id \leq max_i$
then ignore   /* P_i purges this message */
else $max_i := id;$ $parent_i := l;$
    Send id to all neighbors.   /* P_i broadcasts the new max_i */

Analysis

Theorem 1 *Algorithm ELECT will eventually reach quiescence. Upon termination a unique leader is elected and a spanning tree is constructed with probability $1 - \epsilon$. The expected message complexity of ELECT is $O(mr \log n \log r)$, where each message is of expected size $O(\log \log n + \log r)$ bits. (Recall that $r = 1/\epsilon$ and m is the total number of links). The time complexity is $O(D)$, where D is the diameter of the network. All complexities are with probability $> 1 - \epsilon$.*

The following claim can be easily proved:

Claim 1 *Eventually, algorithm ELECT will reach quiescence at which time max_i is the same at all nodes.*

Let $M = \max\{id_i : i = 1, \ldots, n\}$. We have

Claim 2 *If there is a unique node with $id_i = M$ then algorithm ELECT produces a spanning tree of G, consisting of the pointers $parent_i$ (for all i).*

Claim 3 $\max\{t_i : i = 1, \ldots, n\} < \log(rn)$ *with probability* $\geq 1 - \epsilon$.

Proof: For a fixed i $Prob[t_i \geq \log(rn)] = (1/2)^{\log(rn)} = (1/rn)$. Therefore, $Prob[\exists i \in [1..n]$ s.t. $t_i \geq \log(rn)] \leq 1/r = \epsilon$. ∎

laim 4 *With probability $\geq 1-\epsilon$, the message complexity of algorithm ELECT is $O(mr \log n \log r$*

Claim 5 *The size of each message is $O(\log\log n + \log r)$ bits with probability $\geq 1 - \epsilon$.*

Corollary 6 *The bit complexity of algorithm ELECT is, with probability $\geq 1 - \epsilon$, $O(mr \log n \log r(\log\log n + \log r))$.*

Corollary 7 *Algorithm ELECT requires $O(\log\log n + \log r)$ bits of state information per node, with probability $\geq 1 - \epsilon$.*

The main idea in algorithm *ELECT* is based on the assumption that there is one node whose *id* is larger than all the other *ids*. The following lemma proves the existence, with high probability, of such a node.

Lemma 8 *There is a unique node P_i with $id_i = M$, with probability $\geq (1 - \epsilon)$.*

Proof: Denote as *candidate* a node i such that $t_i \geq \log n - t$ for some parameter t that will be fixed later. Intuitively, $\log n - t$ is kind of a threshold that identifies nodes with high *id*'s. The leader will be the candidate with the maximum *id*.

We prove the lemma in two steps. We first show (claim 11) that (a) there are $\Theta(\log r)$ candidates, with probability $> (1 - \epsilon/2)$. This ensures that, with high enough probability, there is at least one candidate but not too many. We then show that (b) with probability $> (1 - \epsilon/2)$, $\max\{s_i\}$, where i indexes over the candidates, was chosen by only one candidate. This will suffice to prove that there is a unique node with $\max\{id_i\}$ with probability $\geq (1 - \epsilon)$.

To prove claim 11 we need the following:

Lemma 9 *([Che52], [AV79]):*

If X is binomial with parameters (n, p) then for all $0 < b < 1$

(1) $Probability(X \geq \lceil(1 + b)np\rceil) \leq \exp(-b^2 np/3)$

(2) $Probability(X \leq \lfloor(1 - b)np\rfloor) \leq \exp(-b^2 np/2)$.

Corollary 10 *If X is binomial with expectation c then*

(1) $Prob(X \geq 3c/2) \leq \exp(-c/12)$

(2) $Prob(X \leq c/2) \leq \exp(-c/8)$.

Proof: Let $b = 1/2$ and $np = c$ in lemma 9. ∎

Recall that a *candidate* is a node i whose $t_i \geq \log n - t$ for some parameter t. Let X be he number of candidates. The probability that a node is a candidate is $2^{t-\log n} = 2^t/n$ (= he probability to get $\log n - t$ *Tails* in $\log n - t$ coin tosses). As the number of nodes is n, we expect X to be 2^t. Let $c = 2^t$, then c is the expectation of X.

In the following claim we show that for a particular value of c the number of candidates s $\Theta(\log r)$ with probability $> 1 - \epsilon/2$.

Claim 11 *Let $c = 12\ln(4r)$, then $Prob(c/2 \leq X \leq 3c/2) > 1 - \epsilon/2$.*

Proof: By corollary 10 we have $Prob(c/2 \leq X \leq 3c/2) \geq 1 - [\exp(-c/12) + \exp(-c/8)] > 1 - 2/(4r) = 1 - \epsilon/2$. ∎

This concludes the proof of (a) in the proof of lemma 8.

Claim 12 *Let p be the probability that in k drawings from a domain of size d, the largest label (among those that were drawn) is drawn only once. Then, $p \geq 1 - (k/d)$.*

Proof: Let K be the number of possible results of a series of k drawings from a domain of size d, in which the largest label is drawn only once. We describe below a process Q of restricted drawings which ensures that the largest label is drawn only once. Let K' be the number of possible results of Q. Since K counts all possible drawings with unique max and K' counts only the size of a subset of these drawings, we have $K' \leq K$. Therefore, $p = K/d^k \geq K'/d^k$.

In Q we restrict the $(i+1)$'th drawing to be from all labels except for the maximum drawn label over the first i drawings. Clearly, $K' = d(d-1)^{k-1}$. Therefore we have $p \geq (d-1)^k/d^k = (1 - 1/d)^k > (1 - (k/d))$. ∎

Corollary 13 *If the number of candidates is $\leq g$ and s_i was chosen from the range $[1..2rg]$ then $\max_i\{id_i\}$ is unique with probability $> 1 - \epsilon/2$.*

Proof: Assume that all candidates have the same t_i. If this is not the case then we refine the *candidate* definition to be only those nodes that have the $\max_i\{t_i\}$. We have g drawings from a domain of size $2rg$. By claim 12 we have that $\max_i\{s_i\}$ (over P_i that are candidates) is unique with probability $\geq 1 - g/2rg = 1 - \epsilon/2$. ∎

This concludes the proof of (b) in the proof of lemma 8.

Let $g = 20 ln(4r)$ then by Claim 11 and corollary 13 we have that with probability $\geq 1 - \epsilon$ we have a unique node P_j with $id_j = \max\{id_i : i = 1, ..., n\}$; which concludes the proof of lemma 8. ∎

Corollary 14 *The domain d from which s_i is chosen needs to be $40r \ln(4r) = O(r \log r)$.*

Claim 15 *The time complexity of algorithm $ELECT$ is $O(D)$, where D is the diameter of the network.*

Remark: As a corollary we see that a leader can be chosen on a ring of unknown size with error probability ϵ with $O(nr \log n \log r)$ messages, each of size $O(\log \log n + \log r)$. Thus, the bit complexity is $O(n \log n \log \log n)$ (for fixed ϵ), an improvement on the $O(n \log^2 n)$ bound of [SS89] and of [IR81].

2.1 A different view of the algorithm

In Procedure $Choose(id_i)$ each node selects two random numbers t_i and s_i. The two can be combined into one number by tossing a biased coin to select t_i and eliminating s_i. More precisely, the probability of $Head$ in each coin toss is $p = O(\epsilon)$.

We can look at the process of choosing id's in a more general setting. We actually want each node to select a value j, according to some probability function p_j. We chose p_j to be $p_j = (1 - p)^{j-1}p$. A natural question is whether one can find another p_j that will result in better complexities. More precisely, we look for a probability function p_j that guarantees that the maximum value that was selected by a node is unique with high probability, and that the number of different values that were selected is minimal. In our case, the number of different values is $O(\log n)$.

The following claim [Alo89] indicates that our choice is optimal.

Claim 16 *Let p_j be a probability function for which the maximum value selected by any node is unique, i.e. was selected by only one node, with probability $\geq 1 - \epsilon$. Then, there are infinitely many n's, for which the number of different values that are selected by n nodes, is expected to be $\Omega(\log n)$.*

3 Networks with known bounds on size

In the sequel, we deal with the problem of electing a leader in an anonymous network, when some bounds on n - the size of the network - are known. We first show that if a lower bound L on the number of nodes is known, then our algorithm can be easily modified so that for $n = O(L)$, the message complexity is only $O(mr \log^2 r)$, and the messages size is only $O(\log r)$. If an upper bound of kL for constant $k \geq 1$ is also known, then we can also guarantee these worst case complexities.

Recall that a candidate is a node whose chosen value of t_i satisfies $t_i \geq \log n - t$. In the following we use t as a parameter to design and analyze the modifications of algorithm *ELECT* according to the additional knowledge about n.

Lemma 17 *Let $n > L$. The number of candidates is, for some setting of t, $\Theta((n/L) \log r)$ with probability $> 1 - \epsilon/2$.*

Proof: Set $t = \log c$, where $c = (n/L) 12 \ln(4r)$. Thus, the threshold for candidates is now $\log n - \log c = \log L - \log 12 \ln(4r)$. Similarly to claim 11, we have that the number of candidates is $\Theta(c) = \Theta((n/L) \log r)$ with probability $> 1 - \epsilon/2$. ∎

We use the knowledge of a lower bound L on n to improve complexities. The main idea is based on the observation that the threshold for the candidates, denoted as *thresh*, can be known in advance by all nodes. From the proof of lemma 17 it follows that *thresh* $= \log L - \log 12 \ln(2r)$. Since L and r are known in advance, after the *id* selection each node can check for itself if it is a candidate. Only candidates broadcast their *id*'s. Moreover, the *id*'s are reduced by *thresh* to yield smaller size messages.

In the full paper we prove:

Theorem 2 *If n is known to be lower bounded by L, $L \leq n$, then a leader can be elected, with probability $\geq 1 - \epsilon$, with $O(rm \log r \log(rn/L))$ expected message complexity, and each message is of size $O(\log r + \log \log(n/L))$ bits.*

Corollary 18 *If n is known to be lower bounded by L, and $n \leq kL$ (but the latter fact is unknown), then a leader can be elected with $O(rm \log(rk) \log r)$ expected message complexity, each message of size $O(\log r + \log \log k)$.*

We show now that if both bounds on n are known, $L < n \leq kL$, then we can use this to guarantee that all complexities are worst case. Let $t'_i := t_i - \log L + \log 12 \ln(4r)$. In the full paper it is proved that with probability $\geq 1 - \epsilon$, $max\{t_i'\} = O(\log(rn/L))$. (More precisely, $max\{t_i'\} < \log r + \log(n/L) + \log 12 \ln(4r)$.) Thus, for $k = n/L$, $max\{id_i\} < r \log r \log(12rk \ln(4r)) = id_{max}$. The value of id_{max} can be known in advance to all nodes, as r and k are both known. We modify algorithm $ELECT$ so that if a node's id is larger than id_{max} then it broadcasts an *abort* message. Upon receiving an *abort* message for the first time, P_i sends an *abort* message to all neighbors and aborts. In this case, which happens with probability $< \epsilon$, the algorithm fails.

Following the above discussion we have

Theorem 3 *If n is known to be in the range $L < n \leq kL$, then a leader can be elected, with probability $> 1 - \epsilon$, with a message complexity of $O(rm \log(rk) \log r)$, each message is of size $O(\log r + \log \log k)$ bits. Also, $O(\log r + \log \log k)$ bits of state information per node are required. The algorithm is without termination detection and all complexities are worst case.*

4 Leader election with termination detection

The algorithms presented in previous sections elect a leader without termination detection. In this section we address the question: "Under what conditions can a leader be elected with termination detection".

As was shown in [IR81] it is possible to elect a leader with termination detection in an anonymous network only if an upper bound on the network size is known. Schieber-Snir [SS89] give an algorithm for election with termination detection that succeeds with probability $1 - \epsilon$ using $O(n \log n + m)$ worst case message complexity, each message of size $O(\log(U/\epsilon))$, when $U > n$ is known. When the network size is known within a factor of two, i.e. $L < n \leq 2L$, they give an error-free algorithm with termination detection and with $O(n \log n + m)$ expected number of messages, each of size $O(\log n)$.

In this section we present two election algorithms with termination detection. Unlike [SS89] our algorithms have probability $\epsilon > 0$ of not succeeding. In the first algorithm it is assumed that n is known within a factor of two, i.e. an L is given for which $L < n \leq 2L$. The algorithm is a simple modification of algorithm $ELECT$. It succeeds with probability $1 - \epsilon$, and uses $O(mr \log^2 r)$ messages, each of size $O(\log n)$. For the case of a ring this algorithm reduces the known $O(n \log n)$ upper bound to an optimal algorithm with $\Theta(n)$ message complexity (for a fixed ϵ).

In the second algorithm it is assumed that n is known within any factor k, i.e., an L and k are given such that $L < n \leq kL$. The algorithm is similar to the first algorithm and has imilar complexities.

Upon termination of algorithm $ELECT$, max_i is the same at all the nodes, and the parent links of the nodes constitute a spanning forest of the network with one or more trees n it. The algorithm has been successful in electing a leader if the forest contains one tree. n the case that n is known to lie between L and $2L$ the tree of the elected node must be of ize greater than L. Moreover, if the size of a tree is greater than L than the root of that tree an safely assume the leadership since there can be only one such tree in a network with at most $2L$ nodes. Thus, to elect a leader with termination detection when n is known within a factor of two we provide the root of each tree in the algorithm with its size. If its size is greater than L then the root assumes leadership and broadcasts a $lead(id)$ message.

To provide the root of each tree with its size the broadcast mechanism of $ELECT$ is replaced by a broadcast and echo (algorithm pif from [Seg83]) and the size of each tree is collated on the echo phase.

Note that the modifications introduced above do not increase the message complexity by more than a constant factor. The messages sizes however increase to $O(\log n)$ due to the necessity of counting the number of nodes in the trees. Following Theorem 3 we get that:

Theorem 4 *If n is known to be in the range $L < n \le 2L$, then a leader can be elected with probability $> 1 - \epsilon$, by an algorithm with termination detection. The worst case message complexity is $O(mr \log^2 r)$, each message is of size $O(\log n)$ bits.*

By using similar techniques, a leader can be elected with termination detection and with the same complexities when it is known that $L < n \le kL$, for some constant k.

Theorem 5 *If n is known to be in the range $L < n \le kL$, then a leader can be elected with probability $> 1 - \epsilon$, with termination detection. The worst case message complexity is $O(kmr \log^2 r)$, each message is of size $O(\log n)$.*

Sketch of proof:

The problem with the case of $k > 2$ is that there might be several trees with the same id, all of size $> L$. However, there are at most k such trees. Thus, for each value of id_0 there are at most k nodes that initiate the message $lead(id_0)$. Let each one of these nodes randomly select a $label$ from the range $[1..2k/\epsilon]$. The $lead$ message will now consist of the pair $< lead(id_0), label >$. Since we are guaranteed with probability $> 1 - \epsilon/2$ that the largest label is unique, then a tree (with the new id) can be surrounded by similar trees only with probability $< \epsilon/2$. Thus, if there is a unique leader, then with probability $1 - \epsilon$, the algorithm will eventually distributively terminate.

The message complexity is the same as in the respective nondistributively terminating algorithm (theorem 3). The size of each message is, as in the case $k = 2$, $O(\log n)$. ∎

5 Election in complete networks

Consider the special case where the network is a complete graph. Using the previous results we obtain message complexities of more than $O(m) = O(n^2)$. In this section we show that election in a complete anonymous network is as easy as in networks with a linear number of links. Thus, we achieve, for example, message complexity of $O(n \log n \cdot r \log r)$.

The main idea is the following: given a network G we distributively select a sparse random subgraph G' that spans G and, with a very high probability, is connected. We apply the appropriate algorithm for leader election on G'. The elected leader may also be a leader of G. The complexities are now functions of n, m' and D' where m' is the number of links in G' and D' is the diameter of G'. Our main concern is, therefore, to distributively find G' with m' as small as possible.

A simple algorithm for finding such G' would be for each node in G to randomly select q out of its $n - 1$ incident link. Let $l = (v, u)$ be an edge of G' if and only if either v selected l or u selected l. Clearly, for each fixed q, $m' \leq qn = O(n)$. Fenner and Frieze showed in [FF82] the following theorem which guarantees that G' is connected with high probability.

Theorem 6 *Let G' be an undirected graph in which each vertex randomly chooses q neighbors, then for each fixed $q \geq 3$ the probability that G' is connected tends to 1 as n tends to infinity.*

Recall that the time complexity in all our algorithms is $O(D)$. For a complete graph this means $O(1)$ time. When using G' instead of G in order to reduce the message complexity, we result with an increase in time. However, the penalty is not too high: it can be shown [Alo89] that for fixed q and ϵ, the diameter of G' is $O(\log n)$ with probability $\geq 1 - \epsilon$.

Acknowledgement: We thank Noga Alon, Baruch Schieber and Michael Merritt for helpful discussions. In particular, Noga pointed out to us the results of subsection 2.1 and the reference [FF82].

References

[AAHK86] Abrahamson, Adler, Higham, and Kirkpatrick. Probabilistic solitude verification on a ring. In *Proceedings of the Fifth ACM Symposium on Principles of Distributed Computing*, August 11-13 1986.

[Alo89] N. Alon, 1989. Private Communication.

[Ang80] D. Angluin. Local and global properties in networks of processes. In *Proc. of the 12th Ann. ACM Symp. on Theory of Computing*, pages 82-93, May 1980.

[ASW85] Attiya, Snir, and Warmuth. Computing on an anonymous ring. In *Proc. of the Fourth ACM Symp. on Principles of Distributed Computing*, August 1985.

[AV79] D. Angluin and L.G. Valiant. Fast probabilistic algorithms for hamiltonian paths and matchings. *J. Comp. Syst. Sci.*, 18:155-193, 1979.

[Che52] H. Chernoff. A measure of asymptotic efficiency for tests of a hypothesis based on the sum of observations. *Annals of Math. Statistics*, 23:493-507, 1952.

[CV86] R. Cole and U. Vishkin. Deterministic coin tossing and accelerating cascades: micro and macro techniques for designing parallel algorithms. In *Proc. of the 16th Ann. ACM Symp. on Theory of Computing*, pages 206-219, May 1986.

[FF82] T.I. Fenner and A.M. Frieze. On the connectivity of random m-orientable graphs and digraphs. *Combinatorica*, 2:347-359, 1982.

[FS86] G. Frederickson and N. Santoro. Breaking symmetry in synchronous networks. In *VLSI Algorithms and Architectures, AWOC*, pages 82-93, 1986. Lecture Notes in Computer Science, No 227, Spring Verlag.

[GL83] A. G. Greenberg and R. Ladner. Estimating the multiplicity of conflicts in multiple access channels. In *Proc. of the 24th IEEE Annual Symp. on Foundation of Computer Science*, pages 384-392, October 1983.

[IR81] A. Itai and M. Rodeh. The lord of the ring or probabilistic methods for breaking symmetry in distributed networks. In *Proc. of the 28th IEEE Annual Symp. on Foundation of Computer Science*, pages 150-158, October 1981.

[Seg83] A. Segall. Distributed network protocols. *IEEE Trans. on Information Theory*, IT-29(1), January 1983.

[SS89] B. Schieber and M. Snir. Calling names on nameless networks. In *Proc. of the ACM Symp. on Principles of Distributed Computing*, August 1989. To appear.

A Distributed Solution for Detecting Deadlock in Distributed Nested Transaction Systems

Marta Rukoz*

MASI. Université Pierre et Marie Curie, 4 Place Jussieu

75230 Paris Cedex 05, France

* On leave from Universidad Central de Venezuela, Venezuela

Abstract. In systems where Nested Transactions are used, when a transaction commits, its locks are not released, they are inherited by its parent. Thus, the deadlock detection system must take nested transaction relationships into account or else some deadlocks cannot be detected. Besides, in the distributed Nested Transaction, it is not efficient neither to maintain nor to follow the edges of a global wait-for graph for the whole system. We propose a correct algorithm for detecting deadlocks in a distributed Nested Transaction. This algorithm does not require that the global wait-for graph be built and maintained nor that the edges of a global wait-for graph be followed in order for deadlocks to be detected.

Keywords. distributed computation, distributed databases, distributed transactions, nested transactions, deadlocks.

1.Introduction

Deadlock detection allows transactions to conflict (attempt to acquire the same resources) and to wait freely. A deadlock is a circular waiting situation which can involve many transactions [Bern87, Ceri 84]. The basic characteristic of a deadlock is the existence of a set of transactions such that each transaction waits for another one. This situation can be conveniently represented with a wait-for graph. A wait-for graph is a directed graph having transactions as nodes; an edge from transaction T1 to transaction T2 represents the fact that T1 waits for T2. Whenever a deadlock situation exists, the wait-for graph will indicate a cycle. Therefore, a system can detect deadlocks by constructing a wait-for graph and analyzing whether there are cycles in it.

In Nested Transactions (NT) systems, based on lock for concurrency control [Moss85,

Muel83], when a transaction commits, its locks are not released, they are inherited by its parent. Thus a deadlock detection algorithm for such NT systems must take nested transaction relationships into account or else some deadlocks cannot be detected. In [Moss85] a deadlock detection algorithm for NT has been proposed. The Moss's algorithm works by following edges of the wait-for graph, trying to find cycles. Another solution consists of constructing and maintaining the wait-for graph global and analyzing whether there are cycles in it. This global wait-for graph can be maintained by one of sites the system.

We propose an algorithm for detecting deadlocks in a distributed NT, which does not require that the global wait-for graph be built and maintained nor that the edges of a global wait-for graph be followed in order for deadlocks to be detected. In our algorithm each transaction maintains a representative wait-for graph which represents the waiting conditions between transactions in the trees of the level immediately below. This algorithm is proven correct by using the behavior and the locking rules of nested transactions.

In section 2, the NT are briefly reviewed and the problem of deadlock detection in NT is established. In section 3 we establish the environment in which we are studying this problem. In section 4, our algorithm for detecting deadlocks is presented and analysed. Finally, we offer our conclusions in section 5.

2. Nested Transactions

A Nested Transaction is a tree of component transactions (called subtransactions). A subtransaction appears atomic to its caller, (i.e., it is completely executed or it is not executed at all) and fails independently of the invoking transaction.

Because transaction relationships follow the pattern of a tree, we will often use tree terminology, or terms for familiar relationships, to express transaction relations. Thus, transactions having no subtransactions may be called leaf transactions. Transactions having subtransactions may be called parents, and their subtransactions are their children. Similarly, we will speak of ancestors and descendants. It is convenient to say that a transaction is an ancestor and descendant of itself, i.e., ancestor and descendant relations are reflexive. We use the terms superior and inferior for the non-reflexive version of ancestor and descendant respectively.

If a transaction T2 is a descendant of another transaction T1, we say that $T1 \geq T2$. Similarly, we say that $T1 > T2$ if T1 is a superior of T2. If a transaction T_1 is neither an ancestor nor a superior nor a descendant nor an inferior of another transaction T_2, we say that T_1 and T_2 are not comparable.

The behavior of a NT can be summarized by the following rules:

R1.- A transaction may abort at any time.

R2.- A transaction does not commit until all its children have committed or aborted. Then, when a transaction commits or aborts its parent must be informed.

R3.-When a transaction aborts, all its children must abort.

R4.- Committed transaction's results become permanent if and only if any ancestor of the committed transaction had committed.

Notice that by rules R3 and R4 a commitment of a transaction is not really a commit until all ancestor really commit.

Concurrency control based on locking

Each resource has a lock associated with it. Before a transaction T_1 may access a resource, the controller first examines the associated lock of the resource. If no transaction holds the lock, then the controller obtains the lock on behalf of T_1. If another transaction T_2 does hold the lock, then T_1 has to wait until T_2 releases it. The controller thereby ensures that only one transaction can hold the lock at any time, so only one transaction can access the resource at any time.

In NT systems based on this lock system, when a transaction commits, all its locks are inherited by its parent; that is, its parent holds all its locks. Then it is necessary to distinguish between a transaction that holds a lock, because the transaction wants to access the corresponding resource, and a transaction that holds a lock, because the transaction has inherited it. We will say that a transaction obtains a lock when the transaction wants to access the corresponding resource and hold it, and that a transaction holds a lock when the transaction has inherited the lock. A transaction can access a resource if and only if the transaction obtains the corresponding lock. The controller has to ensure that only one transaction can obtain the lock at any time. However, a transaction can hold and obtain a lock.

Then the locking rules are:

L1.- A transaction may obtain a lock if no other transaction has obtained the lock and any other transaction holding the lock is an ancestor of the requesting transaction.

L2.- When a transaction aborts, all its locks are simply discarded. If any of its superiors hold the same lock, they continue to do so.

L3.- When a transaction commits, all its locks are inherited by its parent (if any); that is, its parent holds all its locks.

L4.- When a transaction cannot obtain a lock, it has to wait until it can obtain the lock it needs.

L5.- Once a transaction holds or obtains a lock, the transaction cannot release it before committing or aborting.

Problem Description

The following example shows that NT relationships must be taken into account for deadlock detection systems or else some deadlocks may not be detected.

Example 1: Suppose the following NT

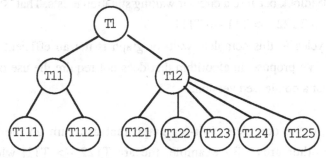

With the following wait relationships:

T111 awaits lock L1	T121 obtains lock L1
T122 awaits lock L2	T112 obtains lock L2
T124 awaits lock L3	T123 obtains lock L3
T125 awaits lock L3	

The classical wait-for graph is

T111 ---> T121; T122 ---> T112; T124 ---> T123; T125 ---> T123

Although this graph does not indicate deadlock, the graph is not complete because:

a.- T111 cannot necessarily obtain the lock when T121 commits. This is because the locking rule L1 implies that T111 cannot proceed until any other transaction holding the lock is an ancestor of T111. Furthermore, when a transaction commits, its locks are inherited by its parent (rule L3). Thus T111 cannot obtain the lock until T12 commits and T1 inherits all T12's locks. That is to say, T111 is indirectly waiting for T12, and this wait must be shown in the wait-for graph.

In the same way, T122 waits for T11.

b.- Furthermore, T11 cannot commit until all its children have committed (rule of behavior R2), and the wait-for graph must therefore show that T11 waits for T111 and T112. In the same way, T12 waits for T121, T122, T123, T124 and T125. Similarly T1 waits for T11 and T12.

The complete wait-for graph is:

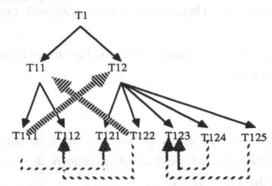

Thus there is a deadlock because a circular waiting situation exists. That is:

T111 --> T12 --> T122 --> T11 --> T111

To search the cycles in this complete wait-for graph is not an efficient solution in the distributed NT. We propose an algorithm that does not require the use of this complete wait-for graph but a condensed version.

Our solution

There are arcs in the complete wait-for graph that can sum up the wait situation represented by other arcs. By example, the arc T122 --> T11, which we call a representative arc, is added to the wait-for graph because T122 waits for T112. This arc can sum up the fact that T122 waits for all ancestors of T112 which are not an ancestor of T122. This arc, the hierarchical relation of NT and the transitivity of wait relationship allow the arc to obtain again the arc T122-->T112. Then the arc T122-->T112 is no longer necessary. In the same way the arc T111--> T121 is no longer necessary.

Besides, if the representative arc T122 --> T11 exists, then by transitivity of wait-for relationship and the fact that T12 waits for T122, we can construct an arc T12-->T11. This arc can sum up the fact that the oldest ancestor of T122 which is not an ancestor of T11 waits also for T11. The arc T12-->T11, which we call a condensed arc, can always be created when a transaction in the subtree rooted T12 waits for a transaction in the subtree rooted T11, then if there is a representative arc from a descendant of T12 to T11. Notice that T12 and T11 are brothers.

Furthermore, if the transactions are identified as in the example, that is, each identified subtransaction contains the identity of all its ancestors, the arcs that represent the tree relationship are no longer necessary.

Then it is sufficient to build and maintain a wait-for graph, WFG1, with the representative arcs, and to analyze the deadlock situation by means a condensed graph, WFG2, with the condensed arcs generated by the WFG1.

Notice that it is not necessary to maintain really WFG2.

Example 2: In the preceding example, the WFG1 graph contains only the arcs:

T111 --> T12; T122 --> T11; T124 --> T123 and T125 --> T123 to analyze a deadlock situation we use the WFG2 as follows:

T111 --> T12 means that an arc T11 --> T12 has to be added to WFG2, because T11 is the oldest ancestor of T111 which is not an ancestor of T12. In the same way T122-->T11 means that an arc T12 --> T11 also has to be added to WFG2. Then there is a deadlock situation.

Distribution of WFG1

We can see that when a representative arc, Ti --> Tj, is added to WFG1, this arc can close a cycle in the corresponding WFG2 only if there are arcs Tj -->..--> Tl --> Tp, where Tl.. Tp are brothers of Tj and Tp is an ancestor of Ti. So, the search of cycles can be simplified as follows: when a representative arc, say Ti --> Tj, is added to the WFG1 graph, the corresponding WFG2 to analyse is created only by considering the arcs of WFG1 which point to a node that is a brother of Tj. In the example, if T122 -->T111 is the last arc to be added to the WFG1 graph, the corresponding WFG2 to be analyzed should contain only the arcs: T11 --> T12; and T12 --> T13

Our algorithm is based on this solution: the WFG1 graph is distributed in hierarchical fashion, such that each WFG1 in the hierarchy contains the arcs that point to transactions in the same level of NT. Because when a transaction commits, its parent must be informed (the behavior rule R2), each WFG1 in the hierarchy is maintained by the appointed transactions parent. Thus when a transaction is informed that one of its children has committed, it can delete the corresponding arcs from its WFG1, if any exist. Therefore when a representative arc is added in the corresponding WFG1, the search of cycles is realized by analyzing the corresponding WFG2 to this WFG1.

3. Target Environment

We study the deadlock problem as it arises in Distributed Databases (DDB). A DDB consists of resources, controllers and processes. Associated with each controller is a set of resources which it manages and a set of constituent processes. A DDB is implemented by N computers S_1, .., S_n. A controller C_j at each computer S_j schedules processes, manages resources and carries out communication. The controllers communicate only by exchanging messages. Messages sent by controller C_i to another C_j arrive sequentially and in finite time. A process can request resources only from its own controller, but this controller may have to communicate with other controllers in order to reserve the particular resource. A process cannot execute unless it acquires all the resources for which it is waiting.

There is a NT running in the DDB. A transaction of a NT is implemented by a process which is executed on a computer. Each process is labeled with a tuple P_{ij} where T_i is the identity of the transaction to which the process belongs and S_j is the computer on which the process runs. We suppose that each identified transaction contains the identity of all its ancestors.

At some stages in a transaction's computation it may need a resource, at which time its associated process sends a request to its controller C_j. If the particular resource is available, the transaction may accede to the requested resource immediately; otherwise, the process has to wait to acquire the requested resource.

We assume that if a single transaction runs by itself in the DDB, it will terminate in finite time and eventually release all resources. When two or more transactions run in parallel, deadlock may arise.

In the discussion which follows, we assume that transactions are never aborted even in the presence of deadlock, because an aborting transaction merely breaks the cycle.

Notation

We use the following notation:

$l_i[x] =$ transaction T_i obtains lock on resource x.

$h_i[x] =$ transaction T_i holds lock on resource x.

$com(T_i) =$ transaction T_i has committed.

$rd(T_i,T_j) =$ process P_{im} has received a committed messages from process P_{jn} (via controllers C_m and C_n), where T_i is the parent of T_j.

$sd(T_i,T_j) =$ process P_{jm} has sent a committed messages to process P_{in} (via controllers C_m and C_n), where T_i is the parent of T_j.

'A' < 'B' = the action 'A' is executed before the action 'B'

Axioms

We have the followings axioms:

A1.- From behavior rule R2:

$com(T_j) < sd(T_i,T_j) < rd(T_i,T_j) < com(T_i) \ \forall j \ / \ T_j$ is a child of T_i

A2.- From locking rule L1:

$l_i[x]$ if $(\forall k \neq i \ \bar{l}_k[x])$ and $(\forall j \ / \ h_j[x] \Rightarrow T_j \geq T_i)$

A3.- From locking rule L3:

$com(T_i) \Rightarrow [(\bar{l}_i[x] \ \& \ h_j[x]) \ \forall x \ / \ l_i[x]$ where T_j is the parent of T_i]

$com(T_i) \Rightarrow [(\bar{h}_i[x] \ \& \ h_j[x]) \ \forall x \ / \ h_i[x]$ where T_j is the parent of T_i]

A4.- From locking rules L4 and L5:

$l_i[x] < com(T_i) < \bar{l}_i[x] \ \forall x \ / \ T_i$ wants to access the resource x

A5.- we assume also:

$com(T_j) < sd(T_i,T_j) < rd(T_i,T_j) < h_i[x] \ \forall x \ / \ l_j[x]$

4. Deadlock Detection

Our algorithm is based on the following propositions:

Proposition 1.

If a transaction T_i is waiting for a lock that is being used by transaction T_j ($l_j[x]$) such that $T_j > T_i$, then there is a deadlock.

Proof

If a transaction T_i is waiting for a lock that is being used by transaction T_j, this resource can be used by T_i if $(\forall k \neq i \ \bar{l}_k[x])$ and $(\forall p \ / \ h_p[x] \Rightarrow T_p \geq T_i)$ (Axiom A2). Then only after T_j releases it ($\bar{l}_j[x]$). By A4, we have that $l_j[x] < com(T_j) < \bar{l}_j[x]$. Consequently, T_i is waiting for $com(T_j)$ besides waiting for the lock.

Furthermore, by A1, T_j cannot commit until all its children have committed. Therefore, by recursivity and because $T_j > T_i$, we can conclude that $com(T_j) > com(T_i)$. T_j is then waiting for $com(T_i)$. Thus there is a deadlock.

Proposition 2.

If a transaction T_i is waiting for a lock that is being held or used by a transaction $T_j \ / \ T_i$ and T_j are not comparable, then T_i is waiting also for the oldest ancestor of T_j which is not also an ancestor of T_i.

Proof

If a resource x is being held or used by T_j, $com(T_j)$ is the only way that T_j releases resource x (because we suppose that transactions do not abort). $[com(T_j) \Rightarrow (\bar{l}_j[x]$ and $h_k[x]) \ \forall x \ / \ l_j[x]]$ and $[com(T_j) \Rightarrow [(\bar{h}_j[x]$ and $h_k[x]) \ \forall x \ / \ h_j[x]]$ where T_k is the father of T_j (A3). The same statement is true for T_k and its father transaction so, by extension,

T_j's locks will be held by any transaction $T / T \geq T_j$.

Let T_p be the youngest superior of T_j which is also a superior of T_i, that is: $T_p > T_j$ and $T_p > T_i$ and ($\forall k / T_k > T_i$ and $T_k > T_j \Rightarrow T_k \geq T_p$). From A2, $l_i[x]$ if ($\forall k / h_k[x] \Rightarrow T_k \geq T_i$). Thus T_i may obtain the lock only when $h_p[x]$. So by A3, T_i is waiting for the commitment of the oldest ancestor of T_j which is not also an ancestor of T_i.

Proposition 3.

When a transaction T_i starts to wait for a lock held by T_j, all T_i's ancestors start also to wait for T_j, that is ($\forall k / T_k \geq T_i \Rightarrow T_k$ waits for T_j). And, furthermore, they cannot commit until the lock is guaranteed.

Proof

By A1, we have that $\forall k / T_k > T_i \Rightarrow com(T_k) > com(T_i)$. Then $\forall k / T_k > T_i \Rightarrow T_k$ waits for $com(T_i)$

If T_i waits for a lock held by $T_j \Rightarrow com(T_i)$ waits for $com(T_j)$ (by A2 and A4). Thus, by transitivity of wait relationship T_k waits for $com(T_j)$.

We suppose that whenever a lock is released or inherited by another transaction, the corresponding controller is advised of this change.

When a transaction T_i starts to wait for a resource R, we will say that T_i awaits T_k, where T_k is the transaction that uses the resource R (if any exist), or else T_k is the youngest transaction that holds R. We will call this transaction T_k the awaited transaction.

Algorithm

1) When a transaction T_i starts to wait for a resource R, the corresponding controller C_j, realises:

1.a) If the awaited transaction T_k uses the resource R and $T_k > T_i$, then C_j detects a deadlock (proposition 1).

1.b) Else, if the awaited transaction T_k and T_i are not comparable, then C_j sends a message ('wait',i,k) to process P_{mn} via controller C_n, where T_m is the youngest superior of T_i which is also a superior of T_k ($T_m > T_k$ and $T_m > T_i$).

2) When a process P_{mn} receives a message ('wait',i,k) we have that:

$T_m > T_k \Rightarrow \exists r / T_r$ is a child of T_m and $T_r \geq T_k$

then P_{mn} adds an edge $T_i \dashrightarrow T_r$ to its WFG1, if one does not already exist.

3) When a process P_{mn} receives the commit message from its child P_{ro}, it deletes the edges $T_i \dashrightarrow T_r$ $\forall i$, from its WFG1.

We assume that these operations are atomic, that is:

$rd(T_m, T_r)$ = delete edges $T_i \dashrightarrow T_r$

4) When a transaction commits its locks are inherited by its parent. The controller associated with each resource inherited assigns the lock to some transaction which is waiting for it and can obtain it (if one exists), and sends corresponding waiting messages for all remaining transactions waiting on the new lock. That is, when a lock LR is inherited by a transaction, the controller C_j associated with the resource inherited R, assigns the lock to some transaction T_p which is awaiting R and can obtain it, then for each transaction T_i which is also waiting for L_R:

4.a) If $T_p > T_i$, then C_j detects a deadlock (proposition 1).

4.b) If T_p and T_i are not comparable, then C_j sends a message ('wait',i,p) to process P_{mn} via controller C_n, where T_m is the youngest superior of T_i which is also a superior of T_p.

The deadlock detection is initiated by any process P_{mn} which receives a message ('wait',i,k). P_{mn} analyses the condensed arcs of its WFG1, as follows:

If $\exists\ T_i \dashrightarrow T_r$ in WFG1 $\Rightarrow T_r$ is child of T_m and $\exists q\ /\ T_q$ is child of T_m and $T_q \geq T_i$
then P_{mn} adds an edge $T_q \dashrightarrow T_r$, if not already there, to WFG2.
If there is a cycle in its WFG2, P_{mn} can conclude that there is a deadlock.
Notice that WFG2 does not save.

<u>Analysis of the algorithm.</u>
We have to prove that the algorithm never claims there is a deadlock cycle when one does not in fact exist and that if there is a deadlock, it can be detected by our algorithm
Proposition 4.

If there is a cycle in a WFG2 $\in P_{mn}$, then there is a deadlock.

Proof
It is necessary to prove that there is an edge $T_q \dashrightarrow T_r$ in WFG2 if and only if T_q is waiting for T_r.
An edge $T_q \dashrightarrow T_r$ is added to WFG2 $\in P_{mn}$ if and only if $T_m > T_q$, $T_m > T_r$, $T_q \geq T_i$ and $T_i \dashrightarrow T_r \in$ WFG1. Then by proposition 3, if T_i is waiting for T_r, then T_q is also waiting for T_r . An edge $T_i \dashrightarrow T_r$ is added to WFG1 $\in P_{mn}$ if and only if P_{mn} receives a message ('wait',i,k) and T_r is a child of T_m and $T_r \geq T_k$ (part 2 of our algorithm). A message ('wait',i,k) is sent to P_{mn} (part 1b and 4b of our algorithm) if T_i

starts to wait for a transaction T_k where T_k and T_i are not comparable and $(\forall j / T_j > T_k$, and $T_j > T_i \Rightarrow T_j \geq T_m)$. Then by proposition 2, T_i is waiting for T_r.

An edge $T_i \dashrightarrow T_r$ is deleted from WFG1 $\in P_{mn}$ only when $com(T_r)$ and $h_m[x] \; \forall x / (l_r[x] \vee h_r[x])$ (part 3), therefore only when T_i is left to wait for T_r (transactions are never aborted). Furthermore, if T_i is left to wait for T_r because $com(T_r)$ and the lock is assigned to another transaction T_p so that T_i begins to wait for Tp, an arc representing this new waiting condition is added to the corresponding WFG1 (part 4b of our algorithm).

Proposition 5.

If a NT is in a deadlock situation then it can be detected by our algorithm.

Proof

Let T_A be the root of NT. A transaction $T_i \in$ NT starts to wait for another transaction $T_j \in$ NT if and only if T_i starts to wait for a lock that is being used by T_j or $\exists k \; \exists p / T_i \geq T_k$ and $T_j \geq T_p$ and T_k starts to wait for and lock that is being used or held by T_p (propositions 2 and 3). In both cases, the controller which manages the lock sends a 'wait' message to T_A because T_A is the youngest ancestor of T_i which is also ancestor of T_j. Then T_A adds an edge to its WFG1 which represents this wait. Thus, T_A has information about all wait situations between transactions in NT, and can detect the deadlock.The same proposition is true for any transaction T of NT which is also a NT so, by extension, if there is a deadlock situation it can be detected by our algorithm.

5. Conclusions

We have presented a deadlock detection algorithm for distributed NT which do not require that the global wait-for graph be built and maintained nor that the edges of a global wait-for grap be followed in order for deadlocks to be detected. However a distributed representative graph is built and maintained.

Our algorithm works in a hierarchical fashion, which is to say that any particular root process can detect deadlock occurring in the level of the trees immediately below that root. This hierarchical fashion is useful for NT, because NT have hierarchical relationships where the commitment of any particular root process depends on the commitment of transactions in the tree below that root. Furthermore if a root process fails, all transactions in the tree inmediately below that root must be aborted. Then if a root process fails, the detection of deadlocks in this tree is no longer necessary.

We have shown that the algorithm is correct. We have proven that our algorithm never claims there is a deadlock cycle when one does not in fact exist and that if there is a deadlock, it can be detected by our algorithm.

Our algorithm requires only $O(n)$ messages for detecting a cycle of length n (only one message for each waiting situation is needed). The edge-chasing algorithms requiere $O(n^2)$ messages for detecting a cycle of length n because each transaction has to diffuse the probe in the tree which it is root.

We are assuming that transactions are never aborted even when deadlock exists, because an aborting transaction merely breaks the cycle. In the case of abortion, the deadlock would already be resolved. When abortion does occur, it is necessary to update the corresponding WFG1. The controller of the aborted transaction must send a message (no-wait,i,j) to the controller of the youngest common ancestor of the transaction which had been awaiting the aborted one, in order to update its WFG1.

Our algorithm is meant to detect deadlocks for a single distributed nested transaction, not for multiple independent nested transactions. The algorithm can be easily extended to cover the deadlock detection for multiple independent nested transactions by adding to the system a root transaction that has all other nested transaction in the system as its children

ACKNOWLEDGEMENTS

I would like to express thanks to P. Blanc and C Girault for their helpful suggestions, as well as the referees who constructively criticized the previous version

REFERENCES

[Beer83] Beeri C, Bernstein P, Goodman N, Lai M and Shasha D (1983). A Concurrency Control Theory for Nested Transactions. Proc. 2nd ACM SIGACT SIGOPS Symposium on Principles of Distributed Computing.

[Bern87] Bernstein P, Hadzilacos V and Goodman N (1987). Concurrency Control and Recovery in Database Systems. Addison Wesley Publishing Company.

[Ceri84] Ceri S and Pelagatti G (1984). Distributed Database Principles and Systems. McGraw-Hill, New York.

[Chan83] Chandy M, Misra J and Haas L (1983). Distributed Deadlock Detection. ACM Transactions on Computer Systems, Vol. N°2, May 1983.

[Muel83] Mueller E., Moore I., and Popek G.. A Nested Transaction Mechanisme for LOCUS. Proc. of Operating Systems Principles. Bretton Woods NH. 1983

[Moss85] Moss E (1985). Nested Transactions: An Approach to Reliable Distributed Computing. Research Reports and Notes Information System Series MIT press 1985.

Distributed Deadlock Detection and Resolution with Probes

Beverly A. Sanders

Institut für Computersysteme
Swiss Federal Institute of Technology (ETH Zürich)
ETH Zentrum
CH–8092 Zürich, Switzerland

and

Philipp A. Heuberger

Sonnenweg 4
CH–8370 Sirnach, Switzerland

Abstract

We derive an algorithm for distributed deadlock detection and resolution which uses probes and allows an arbitrary priority scheme to choose a victim to abort after a deadlock has been detected. This algorithm is remarkable in that at least three incorrect versions of it have previously been published ([SiNa],[CKST87],[CKST89]). With careful attention to the properties of the wait–for–graph of the single resource model and definition of a simple and uniform framework for the underlying system, we are able to give an understandable and convincing derivation of the algorithm.

1. Introduction

Many distributed systems are vulnerable to deadlocks where a set of nodes wait indefinitely for the other members to take some action. A particularly important application, which motivated earlier work of the algorithm is in distributed databases where data objects must be locked by a transaction before they can be accessed. The single–resource model, which assumes that a node makes a single request and then blocks until the requested action is taken is appropriate for this application, and is consistent with commonly used 2–phase–locking concurrency control. A survey describing several other models is given in [Knapp].

Our goal is to develop an algorithm for distributed deadlock detection in the single resource model. We require that only actual deadlocks be detected and that all deadlocks eventually are detected and resolved by aborting some process. There are no spontaneous aborts of non–deadlocked processes. Deadlocks are detected with "probes", i.e. special messages that are sent along the edges of the wait–for–graph to detect a cycle. In addition to the correctness requirements already stated, an attempt is made to minimize the number of probe messages that must be sent. Further, we allow the victim to be chosen using an arbitrary priority scheme. In the first section, we describe a uniform and general operational model for the system, and indicate how the distributed database application is a special case. Then we state several useful properties and definitions relating to the system wait–for–graph. Next, we derive the deadlock detection algorithm. The final section compares our algorithm to previous approaches and points out an error in the algorithm in [CKST89].

2. Operational description and wait–for–graph

The aspects of a system relevant for deadlock detection are captured in the wait–for–graph. Formally, we consider the wait–for–graph, WFG, to be a pair (V,E), where V is a finite set of nodes (representing all possible transactions and data objects in the system), and E is a set of edges, ie ordered pairs of elements of V. An edge (u,v) in E represents the situation where u is waiting for v to do something. A node u is *blocked* if there is a node v such that (u,v) ∈ E. A node u is *active* if it is not blocked.

In the single resource model, there are several important restrictions on the way WFG can change. Only two actions are allowed in the normal case: 1) if u is active, then an edge (u,v) may be added, and 2) if u is active, then an edge (v,u) may be removed. The first action is called a request, the second a release. A special situation is an abort. In this case the victim node v, aborts by removing all edges to and from v. (Since releases and aborts are the only circumstances where an edge is removed from the WFG, only static deadlocks need be considered.) An important consequence of these restrictions is that each node has at most one outgoing edge. It is well known that in the single resource model a deadlock corresponds to a cycle in WFG.

It is not necessary to distinguish between transactions and resources in the development of the deadlock detection algorithm. The distributed data–base application is a special case where every edge has one member that is a transaction, and one member that is a data object (or data manager). A transaction t requesting a lock on r corresponds to adding edge (t,r) to WFG. Granting the lock corresponds to deleting edge (t,r) and immediately adding (r,t). The lock is held until it is released by deleting edge (r,t). At this point r would be active again and could grant a lock to another waiting transaction, t', introducing an edge (r,t'). Two–phase–locking is an additional constraint on the behavior of the transactions which disallows additional requests after any lock has been released by a transaction and does not impose any requirements on the deadlock detection algorithm.

The following definitions and properties of the wait–for–graph will be useful in the sequel. A *chain* is a set S of nodes where S ⊆ V which has the property that the elements of S can be arranged in a sequence $< s_0, s_1, ... s_{k-1} >$ where the sequence is part of the WFG, i.e. $\langle \forall i: 0 \le i < k-1 :: (s_i, s_{i+1}) \in E \rangle$. A chain together with the ordering relationship is called a *chain–sequence* where s_0 is the *startnode(S)*, and s_{k-1} is the *endnode(S)*. We will abbreviate chain–sequence with the term sequence when the meaning is clear. A chain or sequence S is *closed* if the successors of all nodes in S are in S: $\langle \forall s: s \in S :: (s,t) \in E \Rightarrow t \in S \rangle$. Since each node has at most one outgoing edge, and the elements in a sequence form a set, for any node u, there is a unique *closed sequence*, CS(u), with u as the first node. We use the notation (u < v) CS for u and v are the ith and jth, elements of CS, respectively, and i < j. Similarly for (u≤v)CS, (u ≤ v ≤ w)CS, etc. The fact that an element can appear at most once in a sequence is important in our derivation. A *cycle* in WFG is a closed chain S where for some u in S, successor(endnode(CS(u))) = u. In addition, if S is a cycle, then successor(endnode(CS(u))) = u holds for all u in S.

3. Derivation of the deadlock detection algorithm

3.0 Simple edge chasing

The predicate u.probe[v] is intended to capture the notion "node u holds a probe initiated by node v". In order for probes to be used to detect a deadlock, we need to require the following invariant:

    I 1   *invariant* $\langle \forall u,v :: u.probe[v] \Rightarrow u \in CS(v) \rangle$

When this invariant holds, from the definition of a cycle we have

    R1   *invariant* (u.probe[v] ∧ v is a successor to u) ⇒ deadlock .

R1 can be used to detect deadlock. In order to guarantee that a deadlock is always detected using R1, eventually for some node u in the cycle, endnode(CS(u)).probe[u] must hold.

Ignoring for the time being the problem of maintaining the invariant after an abort, as well as problems due to message transmission delays, a very simple algorithm would require that every node periodically send a probe message with its id to its successor. Any probe arriving at an active node would be discarded immediately and otherwise held long enough to test for deadlock by comparing the successor with the origin of the probe. If deadlock is not detected, the probe is immediately forwarded to the successor node. The only way the invariant I1 could be violated would be for some edge in the sequence between the initiator and the probe to be deleted, which cannot happen since (recall we are neglecting aborts at the moment) only edges incident on an active node, which must be the end node, can be removed.

3.1 Unique node detects deadlock

There are two main disadvantages to this algorithm: probes must repeatedly be initiated, and any or all nodes in a cycle can detect a deadlock. Since it is desirable to only abort one node in a cycle, resolution is made easier if a deadlock is only detected by one node. In the next refinement, we assume that the id's of the nodes in the system are totally ordered, and strengthen the invariant so that only the probe from the node in the deadlock cycle with the largest id will result in deadlock detection.

First, we define the notion of an antagonistic sequence. A sequence S is *antagonistic* (terminology from earlier papers) if the startnode of the sequence has the largest id in the sequence, ie $\langle \forall u: u \in S :: startnode(S) \geq u \rangle$. We define $AS(u)$ to be the largest antagonistic sequence with startnode u and strengthen the invariant to require that v.probe[u] will only hold if $v \in AS(u)$. In any cycle, there will a unique node u where $AS(u) = CS(u)$. We want this u's probe to result in deadlock detection.

The invariant I1 is strengthened to

   I2   *invariant* $\langle \forall u,v :: u.probe[v] \Rightarrow u \in CS(v) \wedge u \in AS(v) \rangle$

R1 still holds because I2 ⇒ I1. Since there is a unique node u where $AS(u) = CS(u)$, only one node will detect deadlock. In order to guarantee that a deadlock is always detected, eventually endnode(CS(u)).probe[u] must hold for the node u with $AS(u) = CS(u)$ in the cycle. In the distributed data–base application, the ordering of node ids can be defined so that the antagonistic sequences belonging to data–objects always have cardinality 1 and will never detect deadlock and abort. An obvious implementation would simply modify the above algorithm so that node u will also discard any probe it receives when holding it would result in violating I2, i.e., where initiator < u.

3.2 Probes are stored as long as valid

At this point, we consider a different approach which reduces the number of probe messages that need to be sent. The idea is that instead of holding a probe briefly and then passing it on (and falsifying u.probe[v]), a node will store any probe it receives until it must be deleted to maintain the invariant. In particular, active nodes will now store rather than automatically discard probes. As a result, unless a new edge is added to the WFG, a probe need be forwarded only once. A natural requirement is that if u.probe[v] holds, then x.probe[v] must also hold for all nodes x between v and u in CS(v). For all u, u.probe[u] is identically true. We strengthen I2 to give I3a:

I3a *invariant* $\langle \forall u,v :: u.probe[v] \Rightarrow u \in CS(v) \wedge u \in AS(v)$
$\wedge \langle \forall x : (v \le x \le u)CS(v) :: x.probe[v] \rangle \rangle$

Deletion of probes in order to maintain the invariant may be required in two situations: when deleting an edge in the WFG due to a release; and when some node aborts, deleting all incident edges. First consider the situation with releases. In particular, if u is the endnode of CS(v), and u.probe[v] holds, then clearly u.probe[v] must be falsified before the edge (w,u), where w $\in$ CS(v), can be deleted from WFG. (Since u is the endnode, and only this node is active in CS(v), u is the only node that we have to worry about). In general, there may be several probes that need to be deleted, and also several nodes x where x is a predecessor of u, and there is some v where x $\in$ CS(v) and u.probe[v] holds. Therefore, it is useful to keep track of the predecessor node x for each probe. We define a new predicate u.probe[v].x to represent u.probe[v] holds and and x is the node that forwarded v's probe to u. Since no probe was needed to establish u.probe[u], which is identically true, we introduce a new symbol Π for no predecessor. Thus, for all u, u.probe[u].Π is identically true. A new invariant I3b is introduced.

I3b *invariant* $\langle \forall u,v :: u.probe[v].w \Rightarrow u.probe[v] \wedge$
(w = predecessor of u in CS(v) $\vee$ w = Π) $\rangle$

R1 is still valid. Note that because w = predecessor of u in CS(v) $\vee$ w = Π, u.probe[v].w can hold for at most one value of w. (Recall that a node can appear at most once in CS(v)). In an implementation of the algorithm satisfying these invariants, each node would store any probe received, together with the identity of the node that forwarded it, in a variable u.probes unless doing so would violate I3, i.e., if initiator < u or the probe is already stored at the node with a different predecessor. For example, when a probe with initiator v arrives from w, then the pair (v,w) is added to u.probes, unless v < u or (v,x) $\in$ u.probes for x $\neq$ w. When an edge (w,u) is deleted, $\langle \forall x :: \neg u.probe[x].w \rangle$ must be established. Falsifying u.probe[x].w corresponds to deleting (x,w) from u.probes. In order to guarantee that a deadlock will eventually be detected, probes must be forwarded. Clearly, when a probe is received by node u, then either the probe must be forwarded or u must become active in a finite amount of time. Also, whenever a node u makes a request (i.e. adds an edge) then either the entire contents of u.probes must be forwarded or u must become active within a finite amount of time. These two conditions suffice to ensure that probe[v] will eventually be stored at every member of AS[v] . Note that we require for all nodes u.probe[u].Π, and thus u.probe[u] always holds. Forwarding the entire contents of u.probes after u makes a request incorporates the "probe initiation" for that request.

Now consider the problem of handling aborts. Let CS(v) = <v, ... w, y, ... ▷ be a closed sequence in the WFG which contains a cycle and y the node in the cycle that will be aborted. Some node between v and y is successor(t). After aborting y, CS(v) will be <v, ... w>. Therefore, u.probe[v] must be false for all u such that (y ≤ u)CS(v) before y is aborted. On the other hand, in order to keep the property that a probe need only be forwarded once, u.probe[v] should not be falsified for any u where (v ≤ u ≤ w)CS(v) To specify this requirement, we introduce a new predicate, y.abort which indicates that y has been selected as a victim in a deadlock cycle, and weaken invariant I3a in the situation where a member of a closed sequence has been chosen to be aborted.

I4   *invariant* $\langle \forall$ u,v :: u.probe[v] $\Rightarrow$ u $\in$ CS(v) $\wedge$ u $\in$ AS(v)

$\wedge$ (($\langle \forall$ x : (v $\leq$ x $\leq$ u)CS(v) :: x.probe[v] $\rangle$

$\vee \langle \exists$ y,z : v$\leq$ y $\leq$ z < u :: y.abort

$\wedge \langle \forall$ x : (v $\leq$ x < y)CS(v) :: x.probe[v] $\rangle$

$\wedge \langle \forall$ x : (y $\leq$ x $\leq$ z)CS(v) :: ¬ x.probe[v] $\rangle$

$\wedge \langle \forall$ x : (z < x $\leq$ u)CS(v) :: x.probe[v] $\rangle$))

$\rangle$

Thus y can safely be aborted when y.probe[v] is false for all v such that y $\in$ CS(v), and there is no u that satisfies the second conjunct in I4. The invariant suggests an implementation. A victim y that is preparing to abort sends a special clean message containing the id's of all probes in y.probes along CS(y) and sets y.probes = {(y,Π)}. When a node u recieves a clean message from its predecessor x, it falsifies u.probe[w].x for all w such that w $\in$ clean[y], then forwards the clean message to the next node. The only problem is that if x = endnode(CS(w)), then the next node, say u, is actually *before* the victim in the closed sequence CS(w), and deleting w's probe would violate I4. This situation is indicated by u.probe[w].t for some t $\neq$ x . Therefore, this possibility must be checked before accepting a clean message. If u.probe[w].t for some t $\neq$ x, then w is removed from the set of probes in the clean message before it is accepted. Once the clean message has traveled around the cycle, y can abort by deleting all its in and out edges in the WFG. Since accepting and forwarding any probe after sending the clean message would result in violating the invariant, probes are not accepted by y while y.abort holds.

3.3 Choosing the lowest priority node as victim

The next refinement introduces the possibility of priorities generated by an arbitrary mechanism to choose the victim node to be the node in the cycle with the lowest priority. This does not need to be the same as the one that detects deadlock. To do this, we will include an additional field in the probe which contains the id and priority of the node with the lowest priority between the start node v and the node u where u.probe[v]. For a node x, x.pri is the priority assigned to node x and we define a new predicate u.probe[v].w.(y,y.pri) which satisfies I5

l5   *invariant* $\langle \forall$ u,v :: u.probe[v].w.(y,y.pri) $\Rightarrow$ u.probe[v].w $\wedge$
               (v $\leq$ y $\leq$ u)CS(v) $\wedge$ $\langle \forall$ x : (v $\leq$ x $\leq$ u)CS(v) :: x.pri $\geq$ y.pri $\rangle$ $\rangle$

This could be implemented by including the pair (y,y.pri) with the probe messages. Before a probe is stored or forwarded, this field is checked. If the priority of the node u receiving the probe is lower than that which came with the probe, then (u,u.pri) is stored with the probe and this is also the value that is passed on. Then, when a deadlock is detected, the node in the priority field on the detecting probe will be the lowest priority node in the cycle. An abort message is sent to this node, which then aborts using the same procedure as before. Note that in particular, priorities can be assigned so that in the distributed data-base example, only transactions are ever selected as victim, and can also be coordinated with the scheduling policy to avoid cyclic restarts. This is discussed in [SiNa]. Because no node will hold a probe belonging to an active node, new priorities can be assigned each time a node makes a request. This is a useful generalization of the priority scheme in [SiNa],[CKST87],[CKST89].

4.0 Implementation in a distributed system

The invariant to be satisfied by the algorithm has been derived, and the basic ideas of an implementable algorithm based on probe messages described. In this section, we will discuss the algorithm in more detail, with particular attention to the problems introduced by message passing in a distributed system. We assume that message passing is reliable, and messages between two nodes are delivered in the order they are sent. An implicit assumption made in the previous discussion is that operations on the WFG as a result of requests and releases, as well as sending probes are atomic actions. In a distributed system, this assumption must be relaxed. For example, when sending a request to another node, the request is sent, and at some time later actually recieved by the destination. We will introduce program variables u.in and u.out which have type set of node and node $\cup$ ϕ, respectively. In principle, if (u,v) is an edge, then v $\in$ u.out and u $\in$ v.in. However, since releases are received some arbitrary time after they have been sent, the correspondence between the program variables and the edges of the WFG are not exact. We introduce the following mapping between actions that change the program variables u.in and u.out and changes to the abstract WFG.

u sends a request to v:
    when u sends the request, v inserted in u.out
    when v receives the request, u inserted in v.in and (u,v) inserted in WFG

u sends a release to v:
    when u sends the release, v removed from u.in and (u,v) removed from WFG
    when v receives release, u is removed from v.out

Notice that so far with this scheme:

l6   *invariant* $\langle \forall$ u,v :: v $\in$ u.in $\Rightarrow$ (v,u) $\in$ E$\rangle$

The other action which changes the WFG is an abort. Suppose that v is a victim. Aborting v requires sending releases to all nodes in v.in. The mapping to the changes in the WFG can be performed as above. Now, suppose that u ∈ v.out and (v,u) ∈ E. In order for the above invariant to hold, (v,u) cannot be removed from E and the abort action finished until v is removed from u.in. Therefore, in the abort procedure, v would send a withdraw message to u, u receives the withdraw message, removes v from u.in (and (v,u) from WFG), and sends an ack to v. The ack must be received before the abort procedure can be considered terminated.

Another action that must be considered is sending a probe. A probe should be sent from u to v only if, among other criteria, (u,v) ∈ E. However, node u can only read u.out, which may not accurately reflect the actual state of the WFG. There are two situations which may occur. A request has been to v, but not yet received, thus (u,v) ∉ E when a probe is forwarded. Since we want it to be sufficient to forward a probe once, it should be processed by v. Fortunately, because messages are delivered in order, the request will be delivered before the probe and (u,v) ∈ E will hold when the probe arrives. The other possibility is that v has sent a release which has not arrived at u when a probe is forwarded. This probe should be rejected by v. If v only accepts probes from u when u ∈ v.in, then the desired result is obtained.

Finally, we have clean and abort messages. Noninstantanous messages passing has no effect on clean or abort messages since the part of the WFG traveresed by these message is a deadlock cycle and does not change while these messages exist. Since messages are delivered in order, there will be no problems due to inappropriate interleaving of these messages and probes.

5.0 The algorithm

A precise statement of an the algorithm, which satisfies I1, I2, I3b, I4, I5, and I6, is given in this section. The flow of control to guarantee the invariants is simply that each action (which takes place at only one node) is executed atomically and that messages between two nodes are delivered and processed in the order they are sent. Additional rules, which have not been specified in the algorithms below, are needed to ensure liveness properties, i.e., that a deadlock will always be detected. It is sufficient to require that all probes in u.probes be forwarded at least once after a request is made or a new probe received (unless the edge in u.out is deleted first), and that all sent messages sent are eventually received. Because actions taken on probe receipt are idempotent, unless a change in the WFG which has occured in the meantime will result in the probe being discarded, no harm is done if a probe if forwarded more than once.

type

        probe = (id, predecessor, minpri-id: node, minpri: priority);
        clean = (victim: node, probes: set of probe)

variables at node u

    u.probes: set of probe, initially {(u, Π, u, u.pri)};
    u.abort: boolean, initially false;
    u.in: set of node, initially φ;
    u.out: node ∪ φ, initially φ;
    u.pri: priority

atomic actions at node u

    Send request to v

        If u.out = φ ∧ ¬u.abort then
            u.probes := u.probes − {(u, Π, u, u.pri)}; u.pri := new value;
            u.probes := u.probes ∪ {(u, Π, u, u.pri)};
            send(v,"request");
            u.out := v;
        end

    Receive request from v

        u.in := u.in ∪ v

    Send release to v

        If v ∈ u.in then
            while (∃ p:
                    p ∈ u.probes ∧ p.predecessor = v :: do u.probes := u.probes − p) end;
            u.in := u.in − v;
            send (v, "release");
        end

    Receive release from v

        u.out = φ

    Send probe p to v

        If ¬u.abort ∧ v ∈ u.out ∧ p ∈ u.probes then send(v, "probe", p) end

Receive probe p from v
    If v ∈ u.in then
        If p.id > u ∧ ¬⟨∃ q : q ∈ u.probes :: q.id = p.id ⟩ ∧ p.id ≠ u.out then
        (∗store probe∗)
        if p.minpri < u.pir then
            u.probes := u.probes ∪ (p.id, v, p.minpri–id, p.minpri)
        else u.probes := u.probes ∪ (p.id, v, u, u.pri)
        end
        elsif p.id = u.out then (∗conclude deadlock∗)
            send(p.minpri, "abort")
        end
    end

Receive abort message
    u.abort = true;
    clean := (u, u.probes);
    u.probes := {(u, Π, u, u.pri)};
    send(u.out, "clean", clean)

Receive clean message clean from v
    if clean.victim ≠ u
        while ⟨∃ p,q:
            p ∈ clean.probes ∧ q ∈ u.probes ∧ p.id = q.id ∧ q.predecessor = v ::
            u.probes := u.probes – q ⟩
        end;
        while ⟨∃ p,q:
            p ∈ clean.probes ∧ q ∈ u.probes ∧ p.id = q.id ∧ q.predecessor ≠ v ::
            clean.probes := clean.probes – q ⟩
        end;
        send(u.out, "clean", clean)
    else (∗clean.victim = u∗)
        send(u.out, "withdraw"); u.out := 0;
        while ⟨∃ v : v ∈ u.in :: send(v, "release"); u.in := u.in–v ⟩ end;
    end

Receive withdraw from v
    u.in := u.in – v;
    send(v, "ack");

Receive ack from v
    u.probes := {(u, Π, u, u.pri};
    u.abort := false

6. Comparison with previous work

6.0 Earlier attempts to derive a similar algorithm

Previous work priority based probe algorithms for deadlock detection and resolution which send probes along the edges of the WFG has been reported in ([SiNa],[CKST87] ,[CKST89]). The major difference in approach between the algorithm derived here and the earlier work is that we make no distinction is made between transactions and data managers. In the previous algorithms, data managers do not store probes, and only transactions are considered as nodes in the WFG. This introduces another level of "non–atomicity" and the algorithm requires complicated and difficult to understand rules for deleting and forwarding probes whenever the WFG changes. Further, the clean messages contains less information (only the detector of deadlock and victim). In order to avoid false deadlock in the algorithms in [CKST87] and [CKST89], the entire contents of u.probe must be deleted and re–established by retransmission of probes, incurring a considerable amount of unnecessary overhead. A more efficient scheme in [SiNa] was shown to be incorrect. Requiring data managers as well as transactions to store probes, recording the node which sent a probe, and the more informative clean messages of our version which indicate exactly which messages must be deleted from the probe queues, results in a much simpler and considerably more efficient algorithm. In addition, the lack of a sound foundation forced the authors to rely completely on error–prone operational reasoning in developing their algorithm. Because [CKST89] points out several errors in [SiNa], and corrects an error in [CKST87], we will only point out an error in the algorithm presented in [CKST89] which is due to improper definition of the abort phase. On page 14, the following actions are taken by a victim after receiving an abort message are described:

> a) It initiates a message clean(victim, initiator), sends it to the data manager where it is waiting.
> b) The victim enters abort phase only when its clean message returns to itself. Once it enters the abort phase, the victim releases all the locks it held, withdraws its pending request, and aborts. During this phase, it discards any probe or clean messsage that it receives. The victim enters abort phase only after receiving its clean message.

Until the victim receives the clean message, it will forward probes received from other nodes, which will not be deleted properly, thus allowing I1 to be violated after the victim aborts. Since the victim may receive and forward probes after sending the clean message but before aborting, the invariant I1 will be violated after the victim aborts by any such probe. This issue was discussed in section 3.2

6.1 An alternative approach to a priority probe algorithm

An interesting alternative priority based probe algorithm is given in [MiMe]. In this algorithm, probes are sent in the opposite direction of the edges of the WFG, and only the probe belonging to the node with the largest label need be stored. Each time a request is made by a node u, u receives a new label that is larger than the probes stored at any node for which there is an edge, and larger than the probe stored at the node it is waiting on. The algorithm has the interesting feature that nothing special needs to be done for deadlock resolution (ie no clean messages) before aborting the unique victim, and there is a simple extension which allows arbitrarily chosen priorities to select the node which has the lowest priority in the cycle to abort. The disadvantage is that every time a request is made by w, probes need to be propagated, potentially to *all* other nodes v for which w ∈ CS(v).

7.0 Conclusion

Distributed deadlock detection is a notoriously difficult problem, as indicated by the large number of published algorithms that have later been shown to be incorrect. Several are mentioned in [Knapp]. Many of these algorithms were "proved" correct, but with operational arguments. Others, for example [CKST87] and [CKST89], claim to have been extensively tested, but are still incorrect. Clearly formal methods are needed, but often result in tedious derivations that are not really illuminating to the reader. In this paper an attempt has been made, not to present a completely formal correctness proof in all its details, but to formalize those aspects of the problem that are most difficult. (It is straightforward to verify the invariants developed for each atomic action.) It is hoped that this approach has resulted in a presentation of the algorithm that is both convincing and interesting.

References

[CKST87] A.N. Choudhary, W.H. Kohler, J.A. Stankovic, D. Towsley. "A Priority Based Probe Algorithm for Distributed Deadlock Detection and Resolution" *Proceeding of the 7th International Conference on Distributed Systems* 1987. pp 162–168.

[CKST89] A.N. Choudhary, W.H. Kohler, J.A. Stankovic, D. Towsley. "A Modified Priority Based Probe Algorithm for Distributed Deadlock Detection and Resolution" *IEEE Trans on Soft Eng.* 15:1, January 1989. pp 10–17.

[Knapp] Edgar Knapp. "Deadlock Detection in Distributed Databases" *ACM Computing Surveys*, 19:4. December 1987.

[MiMe] Don Mitchell and Michael Merritt. "A Distributed Algorithm for Deadlock Detection and Resolution" *Proceedings of the AMC Symposium on Principles of Distributed Computing.* pp 282 – 284. 1984

[SiNa] M. K. Sinha and N. Natarajan, "A Priority Based Distributed Deadlock Detection Algorithm" *IEEE Trans on Soft Eng.* SE–11:1. January 1985. pp 67–80.

A NEW ALGORITHM TO IMPLEMENT CAUSAL ORDERING

André SCHIPER, Jorge EGGLI, Alain SANDOZ

Ecole Polytechnique Fédérale de Lausanne
Département d'Informatique
CH-1015 Lausanne, Switzerland
schiper@elma.epfl.ch.bitnet

Abstract

This paper presents a new algorithm to implement causal ordering. Causal ordering was first proposed in the ISIS system developed at Cornell University. The interest of causal ordering in a distributed system is that it is cheaper to realize than total ordering. The implementation of causal ordering proposed in this paper uses logical clocks of Mattern-Fidge (which define a partial order between events in a distributed system) and presents two advantages over the implementation in ISIS: (1) the information added to messages to ensure causal ordering is bounded by the number of sites in the system, and (2) no special protocol is needed to dispose of this added information when it has become useless. The implementation of ISIS presents however advantages in the case of site failures.

Keywords: distributed algorithms, ordering.

1. Introduction

The notion of global time does not exist in a distributed system. Each site has its own clock, and it is impossible to order two events E_1 and E_2 occurring on different sites of the system unless they communicate. It is however often necessary to order events in a distributed system.

One possible construction of a total ordering of events in a distributed system is described in [Lamport 78]. It is built using logical clocks defined in the same paper. To progress however, the algorithm requires each site to have received at least one message from every other site in the system, which means systematic acknowledgements of messages.

There does however exist a weaker ordering than total ordering: causal ordering. The implementation of such an ordering needs less message exchanging (no acknowledgements like the ones above are needed), and can prove to be sufficient in some applications.

This causal ordering should not be confused with the causality in the definition of logical clocks, which we call here "causal timestamping". Let us give an example enabling us to distinguish causal ordering from causal timestamping. Suppose an event SEND(M_1), corresponding to the site S_1 sending message M_1, and timestamped with logical time T_1. Suppose then a second event SEND(M_2), with timestamp T_2, occurring on site S_2 after S_2 has received message M_1. Lamport's logical clocks ensure that $T_1 < T_2$. Thanks to this "causal timestamping", event SEND(M_1) precedes event SEND(M_2) for every site in the system which will ever know of these events. This does not say anything about the order in which the messages M_1 and M_2 arrive at any given site in the system. Causal ordering of the events SEND(M_1) and SEND(M_2) means that every recipient of both M_1 and M_2 receives message M_1 before message M_2. This is not automatically the case in a distributed system, as shown in figure 1, where site S_3 gets message M_2 before message M_1, even though event SEND(M_1) occurs before event SEND(M_2).

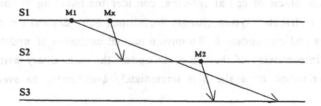

Figure 1. An example of the violation of causal ordering.

Causal ordering is described in [Birman 87] and has been implemented in the ISIS system developed at Cornell University [Birman 88a]. The implementation of causal ordering which we present here differs however from that of ISIS. It presents two advantages: (1) the information added to messages to ensure causal ordering of events is bounded (in the sense defined in section 4.2) by the number of sites in the system, and (2) the implementation does not require any complicated algorithm to clean up this additional information. The implementation of ISIS presents however advantages in the case of site failures. Causal ordering is also achieved through the *conversation abstraction* [Peterson 87]; this implementation however, uses explicit "send before" relations between messages, which is not the case in ours. The rest of the paper is organized in the following way: in section 2, we formally define causal ordering and show the usefulness of this notion. In section 3, we briefly present the idea of the implementation of causal ordering in ISIS. Finally in section 4, we develop a new algorithm to implement causal ordering.

2. Causal ordering of events

Causal ordering is linked to the relation "happened before" between events, noted "→", which we classically define as the transitive closure of the relation R described below (to simplify, we shall speak of sites rather than processes). Two events E_1 and E_2 are related according to R, iff any of the following two conditions is true:

1. E_1 and E_2 are two events occurring on the same site, E_1 before E_2;

2. E_1 corresponds to the sending of a message M from one site, and E_2 corresponds to the reception of the same message M on any other site.

With the relation →, we can formally define the causal ordering of two events E_1=SEND(M_1) and E_2=SEND(M_2), noted E_1^c→E_2, as follows:

E_1^c→E_2 iff (if E_1→E_2, then any recipient of both M_1 and M_2 receives message M_1 before message M_2)

To illustrate the usefulness of causal ordering, consider the handling of some replicated data on every site of a distributed system [Joseph 86, Birman 88b]. Each site controls one copy of the replicated data and can update it. To ensure mutual exclusion of updates, let's introduce a token. The site in possession of the token can update the data. Every write operation W_i on the local copy performed by a site S is immediately broadcasted to every other site (see figure 2).

In the example of figure 2, we have SEND(W_1)→SEND(W_2)→SEND(W_3)→SEND(W_4). Precedence of SEND(W_2) over SEND(W_3) is ensured by the sending of the token, since (1) SEND(W_2)→SEND(token), and (2) reception of the token happens before SEND(W_3). The causal ordering ensures that every site receives the updates in the same order (i.e. the order in which they happened initially). So every site updates its local copy in that order, which ensures global consistency of the set of copies.

It is important to realize that this ordering between events in the distributed system is not a total, but only a partial ordering. To see this, just consider a second replicated data, modified independently from the first one, and controlled by another token. Let's note X_j the updates of this data. Causal ordering of the events SEND(X_j), ensures again that every site sees these updates in the same order. However, one site S may well receive first some operation W_i and then X_j, whereas a second site S' might receive X_j before W_i. This shows that causal ordering of events is weaker than total ordering. Construction of a total ordering is however more expensive to achieve in terms of number of messages exchanged. The low cost of the implementation of causal ordering makes it an interesting tool for the development of distributed applications. Note that in the example above, if W and X are independent, there is no need for causal ordering of SEND(Wi) and SEND(Xj).

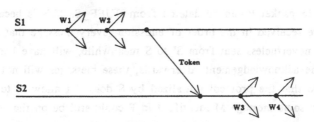

Figure 2. Handling of replicated data using causal ordering.

3. Implementation of causal ordering in ISIS

The implementation of causal ordering in ISIS is described in [Birman 87]. However, ISIS implements causal ordering together with atomic broadcasts (atomic broadcasts ensure that a broadcasted message is received by all sites that do not fail, or by none). For clarity, we shall only be interested here in the realization of causal ordering. The idea is the following: every message M carries along with itself every other message sent before M it might know of. To achieve this, every site S handles a buffer (noted BUFF_S) which contains, in their order of emission, every message received or sent by S (that is, every message preceding any future message emitted by S). Sending a message M from S to any site S' will require the following actions: message M is first inserted into buffer BUFF_S, a packet P is then built containing all the messages in BUFF_S, and finally this packet is sent to the destination site S' of M. When it arrives at S', the following actions are executed for every message in P: (1) if the message is already in buffer BUFF_S' (every message is given a unique id), it has already arrived at S' and is ignored. Else the message is inserted in BUFF_S'; (2) every message in the packet, of which S' is the destination site, is delivered to S' in the correct order.

As an example, consider figure 1. The packet sent from site S1 to S2 (resulting from the emission of message Mx) contains, in order, messages M1 and Mx. The packet sent from S2 to S3 (resulting from the emission of message M2) contains messages M1, Mx, and M2 (transmission of Mx is not necessary, but does take place if the algorithm described in [Birman 87] is respected). So message M1 is carried from site S1 to S3 over two different paths: <S1,S3> and <S1,S2,S3>. In this way, site S3 will always receive message M1 before message M2.

The algorithm, as described here, still has one major drawback: the information contained in BUFF_S increases indefinitely. Some protocol must be added to retrieve obsolete messages from the buffers. The simplified idea is the following: periodically each site S independently builds a request packet P containing the ids of messages in its buffer BUFF_S. Packet P is broadcasted to every other site. When some site S' receives the packet, it notes the source site S along with the identifiers (the corresponding messages must not be sent to S any more!) and acknowledges back to S. When S has received an acknowledgement from every site, the messages identified in packet P can be deleted from BUFF_S. This is because, if messages sent from S' to S are received in the order of emission, every message that could have been identified in P and nevertheless sent from S' to S meanwhile, will have been received by S before it receives the acknowledgement; afterwards, these messages will not be sent from S' to S any more. Note that the protocol initialized by S does not allow S' to delete messages from its own buffer: some message M identified in P could still be on the way to S', sent by another site S". After deleting message M from BUFF_S', S' would not be able to recognize the replicated message M.

4. Another algorithm to implement causal ordering

4.1. Some reflexions on the violation of causal ordering

The basic idea of our algorithm is the following. Rather than carrying around with a message every message which precedes it, let's try to answer the following question when a message M arrives at a site S: will any message preceding M arrive at S in the future? If the answer is yes, message M must not be delivered immediately. It will only be delivered to S when every message causally preceding M has arrived. For the moment, let's try to answer an easier question: is it possible to know that the causal ordering has been transgressed when a message arrives at a site?

If we consider Lamport's logical clocks, we can state the following proposition:

Proposition 1: if the causal order has been violated, then there exists a message M, timestamped $T(M)$, which arrives at destination S when the local time $T(S)$ is greater than $T(M)$.

Proof: consider two messages M_1 and M_2 sent to S, such that $SEND(M_1) \rightarrow SEND(M_2)$. It follows from the definitions that $T(M_1) < T(M_2)$. Suppose the causal ordering has been violated, i.e. M_2 arrives at S before M_1. After delivery of M_2, the logical time at S becomes greater than $T(M_2)$: $T(M_2) < T(S)$. Therefore, when M_1 arrives at S, $T(S)$ is greater than $T(M_1)$, which completes the proof.

However, the converse of Proposition 1 is not true, as shown in figure 3 where a message M, timestamped $T(M)$, arrives at site S which has logical time $T(S)$ such that $T(M) < T(S)$. This does not mean that the causal order has been violated, which shows that $T(M) < T(S)$ is a necessary, but not sufficient, condition for causal ordering violation.

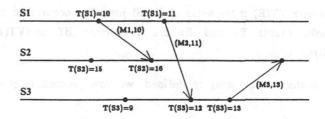

Figure 3. Transgression of causality cannot be detected with Lamport's logical clocks.

So there is no way of answering our second question about causality violation knowing only T(S) and T(M). The problem with Lamport's logical clocks is that they define a total order, whereas there exists only a partial ordering of the events in a distributed system.

A logical clock defining a weaker, partial order is the tool which will be sufficient to infer that the causal ordering was transgressed. This logical clock was recently proposed in [Mattern 89] and [Fidge 88]. For the sake of clarity, lets rapidly recall the principle. The logical time is defined by a vector of length N, where N is the number of sites in the system. We will note this logical time VT (vector time), VT(S) for the logical time on site S, and VT(M) for the timestamp of message M. The logical time of a site evolves in the following way (see figure 4):

- when a local event occurs at site S_i, the ith entry to the vector $VT(S_i)$ is incremented by one: $VT(S_i)[i]:=VT(S_i)[i]+1$.
- when S_i receives a message M, timestamped VT(M), the rule states:
  - for $j=i$, $VT(S_i)[j]:=VT(S_i)[j]+1$;
  - for $j \neq i$, $VT(S_i)[j]:=max(VT(S_i)[j],VT(M)[j])$.

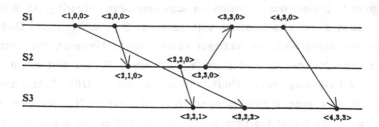

Figure 4. Mattern-Fidge logical clocks.

We also define the ordering relation "<" between logical vector times as follows: $VT_1<VT_2$ iff $VT_1[i] \leq VT_2[i]$, for all i. This relation is trivially reflexive, antisymmetric and transitive. Having defined relation <, it is possible to show that, given two events E_1 and E_2, then $E_1 \rightarrow E_2$ iff

$VT(E_1)<VT(E_2)$, where VT(E) is the value of VT(S) just after occurrence of event E on site S. In other words, events E_1 and E_2 are concurrent iff not($VT(E_1)<VT(E_2)$) and not($VT(E_2)<VT(E_1)$).

The logical time in the system being so defined, we now proceed to prove the following proposition:

> *Proposition 2: the causal ordering of events in the system is violated iff there exists a message M, timestamped VT(M), which arrives at destination S when local time VT(S) is such that VT(M)<VT(S).*

Proving the implication "causal ordering violation $\Rightarrow$ there exists M, VT(M)<VT(S)" is similar to the proof given above concerning Lamport's logical clocks. To prove the converse, we need the following lemma (the proof is given in [Schiper 89]):

> *Lemma 1: consider an event E_1, timestamped $VT(E_1)$, occurring at site S_i. For every event E_2 such that $VT(E_1)[i] \leq VT(E_2)[i]$, $E_1 \rightarrow E_2$ is true.*

Using lemma 1, we can now prove "there exists M, VT(M)<VT(S) $\Rightarrow$ causal ordering violation".

Proof: Suppose a message M was sent to site S by site S_i. If $VT(M)<VT(S)$, then in particular, $VT(M)[i] \leq VT(S)[i]$. Consider M' the message which made $VT(S)[i]$ take its current value (recall $S \neq S_i$!). Then $VT(M')[i] = VT(S)[i]$. By lemma 1, it follows from $VT(M)[i] \leq VT(M')[i]$ that SEND(M) $\rightarrow$ SEND(M'). Since M' arrived at S before M, the causal ordering has been violated.

4.2. The causal ordering algorithm

We are now going to present our algorithm for achieving causal ordering. As in the algorithm described in section 3, we also associate with each site S a buffer, noted ORD_BUFF_S, which will be sent along with the messages emitted by S. However, the contents of this buffer are not messages, but ordered pairs (S',VT), where S' is a destination site of some message and VT a timestamp vector. Unlike the earlier buffer BUFF_S, this one is bounded in size in the following sense: it holds at most (N-1) pairs, where N is the number of sites in the system. Note however that the time vectors in this buffer are not bounded, since their entries depend on the number of events having occurred on each site. The existence of an algorithm enabling to bound the time vectors in the system is an open problem. The causal ordering algorithm is composed of three parts:

- the insertion of a new pair in ORD_BUFF_S when site S sends a new message;
- the delivery of a message and the merge of the accompanying buffer with the destination site's own buffer;

- the deletion of obsolete pairs in the site's buffer (this part needs no exchange of messages).

4.2.1. Emission of a message

Consider a message M, timestamped VT(M) the logical time of emission, and sent from site S_1 to site S_2. The contents of ORD_BUFF_S_1 are sent along with the message. After the message is sent, the pair $(S_2,VT(M))$ is inserted in ORD_BUFF_S_1 (note that this pair was not sent with M). This information will be sent along with every message M' emitted from S_1 after message M. The meaning of this pair in the buffer is that *no message carrying the pair can be delivered to S_2 as long as the local time of S_2 is not such that $VT(M)<VT(S_2)$*. This ensures that any message M', emitted after M with destination S_2, will not be delivered before M, because the *only* way for S_2 to have a logical time greater than VT(M), is to receive message M or a message M' which depends causally on M, i.e. SEND(M)→SEND(M'). However, no message emitted after M will be delivered to S_2 before its logical time is greater than VT(M).

What happens if ORD_BUFF_S_1 already contains a pair (S_2,VT) when $(S_2,VT(M))$ is to be inserted in the buffer? The older pair can simply be discarded. To see this, we need the following lemma (see also point 4.2.2 and [Schiper 89] for a proof):

Lemma 2: for any site S, and any pair (S',VT) in buffer ORD_BUFF_S, the logical time VT(S) at S is such that: VT<VT(S).

Since, by lemma 2, VT is a time vector such that VT<VT(M), the pair (S_2,VT) becomes obsolete after the insertion of the pair $(S_2,VT(M))$. It follows that an ordering buffer contains at most (N-1) pairs, that is at most one for every site different from the site it is associated with.

Note that for the protocol to be correct there is no need to suppose that messages sent between two given sites arrive in the order in which they are emitted. If a message M_2 was to overtake message M_1, then M_2 would carry knowledge of M_1 in its accompanying buffer, and so the protocol ensures proper delivery independently of the order of arrival of messages.

Let's complete this point by noting that the algorithm adjusts well to the case of broadcasting a message M to a set DEST of destination sites. The solution consists of sending to every site S in DEST, *in the buffer accompanying M*, all the pairs $(S',VT(M))$, where S' is in DEST and S'≠S.

4.2.2. Arrival of a message

Suppose a message M arrives at its destination site S_2. If the buffer accompanying M contains no ordered pair (S_2, VT), then the message can be delivered. If such a pair does however figure in that buffer (there is at most one), message M cannot be delivered to S_2 as long as $VT < VT(S_2)$ is not true.

When a message can be delivered to site S_2, two actions must be undertaken: (1) merge the accompanying buffer with the destination site's own buffer, and (2) update the site's logical time. Consider the first point. Suppose the existence of a pair (S, VT), $S \neq S_2$, in the buffer accompanying message M. If ORD_BUFF_S_2 does not contain any pair $(S,...)$, then (S, VT) is introduced in the buffer (if $S = S_2$, the pair need not be introduced in ORD_BUFF_S_2). Now, if a pair (S, VT_1) already figures in the site's buffer, the meaning of these two pairs is the following:

- (S, VT_1): no message can be delivered to S as long as $VT_1 < VT(S)$ is not true;
- (S, VT): no message can be delivered to S as long as $VT < VT(S)$ is not true.

Conjunction of these two conditions can be translated into a single pair (S, VT_{SUP}) where $VT_{SUP} = \sup(VT_1, VT)$[1]. Indeed, VT_{SUP} is the smallest time vector such that $VT_1 < VT_{SUP}$ and $VT < VT_{SUP}$.

Note finally that delivery of a message forces the local time to progress, so that delivering of another message may be possible.

4.2.3. Example

Figure 5 shows an example illustrating a few typical situations solved by the causal ordering algorithm. In this figure, the end of an arrow points to the moment at which a message arrives at a destination site, whereas the corresponding circled number indicates the order in which the messages are delivered. Consider messages M_3 and M_5 sent to site S_4. The events SEND(M_3) and SEND(M_5) are concurrent, so messages M_3 and M_5 are delivered in the order of arrival. Now consider messages M_1, M_4 and M_6, sent to site S_3. The order of emission is SEND(M_1)→SEND(M_4)→SEND(M_6). The messages are delivered in this order.

4.2.4. Deletion of an obsolete pair in the ordering buffer

As has already been indicated, the number of pairs in the ordering buffer of a site is bounded. It can however be interesting to delete obsolete pairs from a buffer. The simplest solution consists of comparing message timestamps with buffer timestamps when messages are delivered. Namely, if message M, timestamped $VT(M)$ and sent by site S_1, is delivered to site S_2, then compare $VT(M)$ with the time vector of the pair (S_1, VT) in ORD_BUFF_S_2. If $VT < VT(M)$, then the pair has become obsolete and can be deleted from the local buffer, since the local time on S_1 is already greater than VT.

---

[1] $\sup(VT_1, VT_2)[i] = \max(VT_1[i], VT_2[i])$

4.2.5. Proof of the algorithm

Up to this point, we have tried to justify each step of the causal ordering algorithm. This however cannot be considered as a valid proof of its correctness. We are going to show in two steps that the causal ordering is indeed respected. The first step is the proof of the safety of the algorithm, the second its liveness.

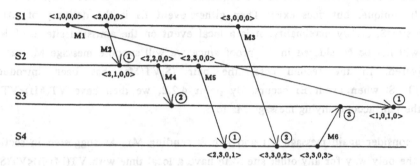

The circled numbers indicate on each site the delivery order of messages

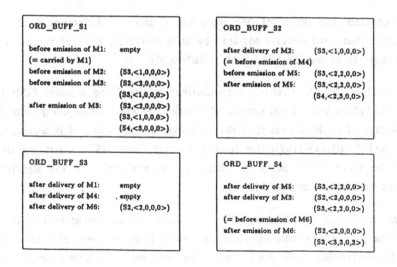

Figure 5. Example of the causal ordering algorithm.

Proof of the algorithm.

1. Safety: We must show that the handling of messages by the algorithm respects the causal ordering, i.e. if two messages M1 and M2 are sent to some site S and SEND(M1)→SEND(M2), then message M1 is delivered to site S before message M2. An equivalent statement is: if message M1 is sent to site S, then no message M2 such that SEND(M1)→SEND(M2) is delivered to S until M_1 itself has been delivered to S. This is what we are going to show. But first let's infer a couple of remarks from the algorithm.

Remark 1: by definition of the relation "happened before", it follows from $SEND(M_1) \rightarrow SEND(M_2)$ that there exists some maximal sequence $E_0,..,E_m$ of events such that $SEND(M_1)=E_0 \rightarrow E_1 \rightarrow .. \rightarrow E_{m-1} \rightarrow E_m = SEND(M_2)$ (we define maximality as follows: for all $0 \leq k < m$, and for every event E not in the sequence, $E_k \rightarrow E \rightarrow E_{k+1}$ is not true). This sequence need not be unique, but does exist. Then either event E_1 is the delivery of M_1 on its destination site S, or, by maximality, it is a local event on the emission site S_i of M_1. The first case will not be considered in the proof since we will suppose message M_1 has not yet been delivered. In the second case, the pair $(S,VT(M_1))$ has been introduced in ORD_BUFF_S_i when event E_1 occurs. By point 4.2.2, we then have $VT(M_1) < VT$ where (S,VT) is the pair accompanying message M_2 to S.

Remark 2: consider again message M_1 and site S_i sending M_1. As suggested in sections 4.1 and 4.2.1, the only way for any other site S' to have a local time with $VT(M_1)[i] \leq VT(S')[i]$ (or more generally such that $VT(M_1) < VT(S')$) is to have received a message M such that $SEND(M_1) \rightarrow SEND(M)$.

We can now proceed with the proof. We are going to show by induction on the events of destination site S that until message M_1 sent by S_i is delivered, none of these events is the delivery of a message M such that $SEND(M_1) \rightarrow SEND(M)$.

Base step: consider $E(S)_1$ the first event on destination site S and suppose $E(S)_1$ is not the delivery of M_1. Before event $E(S)_1$ occurs, $VT(S)[i]=0$, as every other component of $VT(S)$. For every message M in the system such that $SEND(M_1) \rightarrow SEND(M)$, M is accompanied by a pair (S,VT), and $VT[i] \geq 1 > VT(S)[i]$ (by remark 1, and since $E(S)_1$ is not the delivery of message M_1). So $VT < VT(S)$ is not true. Therefore, in application of the algorithm, event $E(S)_1$ is not the delivery of message M.

Induction step: now consider $E(S)_n$ the nth event on S and assume as induction hypothesis that none of the preceding events $E(S)_1,..,E(S)_{n-1}$ on S is the delivery of a message M such that $SEND(M_1) \rightarrow SEND(M)$. If M_1 has not yet been delivered, it follows from this hypothesis and remark 2 that $VT(E(S)_{n-1})[i] < VT(M_1)[i]$. Now remark 1 says that, if VT is the time vector of the pair (S,VT) accompanying a message M with $SEND(M_1) \rightarrow SEND(M)$, then $VT(M_1)[i] \leq VT[i]$, so VT is not such that $VT < VT(E(S)_{n-1}) = VT(S)$. The algorithm then ensures that $E(S)_n$ is not the delivery of a message M such that $SEND(M_1) \rightarrow SEND(M)$.

We can thus infer that, as long as message M_1 has not been delivered to S, no message happening after M_1 can be delivered to that site.

2. Liveness: To complete the proof, we must still show the liveness of our algorithm, i.e. that in the absence of failures every message in the system is indeed delivered.

Proof: ad absurdo. Suppose some message M has arrived at site S, and is never delivered. At the time of arrival, M was accompanied by a pair (S,VT) such that, for some i, $VT(S)[i]<VT[i]$. The number of messages that must be delivered to S before M is finite (it is smaller than the sum of $(VT[i]-VT(S)[i])$ over all such i). In the absence of failures and after some finite time, all these messages will have arrived at S. If every such message had been delivered, then we would have $VT(S)>VT$ and M could be delivered: contradiction. (This is because if $VT(S)>VT$ is not true, again $VT(S)[i]<VT[i]$, for some i. Let's call $n=VT[i]$. Then the nth event on site i was the emission of a message M' for S. If M' has been delivered to site S, then $VT(S)[i]>VT(M')[i]>VT[i]$: contradiction.)

So there exists at least another message M' which will not be delivered to S and should be before M. If (S,VT') is the pair corresponding to S in the accompanying buffer of M', then $VT'<VT$ and $VT'[i]<VT[i]$ for some i. We can thus apply the same reasoning to M' as to M, which completes the proof by finite decreasing induction.

4.3. Failures

Up to this point, we have not considered failures (this is because our implementation preserves the causal ordering even in the case of failures). Some failures however can have surprising effects. Consider figure 6, where message M1 is sent from site S1 to site S2 before message M2 is sent to site S3. A communication failure might prevent message M1 from arriving at its destination, but not message M2 from arriving at S3, though sent afterwards. To see this, consider the following sequence: message M1 is sent to S2, but arrives with a parity error; then M2 is sent but site S1 breaks down before retransmission of M1 is done.

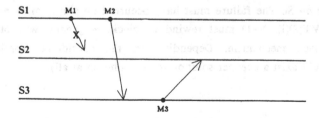

Figure 6. Possible effect of the failure of site S1.

What effect does this have on the causal ordering algorithm? Referring to figure 6, we see that message M3 will arrive at site S2 together with a pair (S2,VT(M1)). If M1 is not delivered, M3 will never be! As a matter of fact, site S3 will never be able to communicate with site S2 again (meaning messages from S3 will never be delivered to S2), since every other message from S3 to S2 will pile up behind message M3, waiting for message M1. For the same reason, any site having received a message from site S3 will be prevented by the algorithm of communicating with site S2. This of course is not a satisfying way to implement causal ordering in the case of failures.

Solutions to this problem can be conceived, but, as we will see, they need some sort of rollback mechanism to be introduced (i.e. in figure 6, for site S3 to recover a state preceding delivery of message M2). Let's note that the ISIS implementation resists to this kind of failure, since message M1 (which is at the heart of the problem) is sent to site S2 along two different paths: <S1,S2> and <S1,S3,S2>, so that message M3 cannot arrive at S2 before M1. This example clearly suggests that the only way to completely solve the problem of failures without rollback is an implementation like the one of ISIS.

Let's show how failures could be treated in our context. Once a failure has been discovered (in the example of figure 6, most likely by site S2) the remaining working sites must first agree to the time of failure, and then take appropriate actions to rewind their own logical time. Consider a failure of site S_i (site number i). To reach a global agreement on the time of failure, each site S must proceed as follows:

- consider the set $P=\{(S,VT_j)\}$ of all pairs accompanying a message M_j waiting to be delivered to S;
- consider then the subset $P_k=\{(S,VT_{jk})\}$ of P of pairs such that $VT_{jk}[i]>VT(S)[i]$. These pairs carry evidence of some message, emitted by the broken down site S_i, and not yet delivered to S;
- consider finally the number $MIN(S)=\min_k\{VT_{jk}[i]\}$. $MIN(S)$ indicates the number on S_i of the oldest event $SEND(M)$ such that message M was never delivered to site S.

When considering the minima of $MIN(S)$ over all the remaining working sites S, we get globally the oldest event $SEND(M)$ on S_i such that message M was never delivered. Call N this event number on S_i. The failure must have occurred on site S_i after event (N-1). Every site S such that $VT(S)[i]>(N-1)$ must rewind its clock. A general way of doing this is to introduce a rollback mechanism. Depending on the considered application's semantic however, there could exist a cheaper solution (or no solution at all).

5. Conclusion

We have shown in this paper how pairs (S,VT), composed of the destination site of some message, and of a Mattern-Fidge logical time vector, make it possible to ensure causal ordering. Such a pair (S,VT) carried by a message M says that the message cannot be delivered to site S before the local time VT(S) has become greater than VT. Actually, the pair (S,VT) indicates that at least one message preceding M must still be delivered to S. Compared to this, the implementation of ISIS forces any given message to carry along every causally preceding message in the system, whereas in our scheme, the message carries only some bounded information concerning their existence. On the other hand, we have seen that the implementation of ISIS does not need any special mechanism to treat failures, which can also be of advantage depending on the considered application. Actually a precise quantitative evaluation of the costs of these algorithms should be done. Depending on the characteristics of the application (semantics, real time aspects, etc...) the better suited algorithm could be chosen. We do not rule out the possibility of an algorithm combining advantages of both the ISIS system and our own implementation. Moreover, and independently from these considerations, we think that the proposed causal ordering algorithm will contribute to a better understanding of ordering problems in a distributed system, and, in particular, of the relation of causality.

Acknowledgments

We would like to thank the referees for their useful comments.

References

[Birman 87] K.Birman, T.Joseph, "Reliable Communications in Presence of Failures", ACM Trans. on Computer Systems, Vol 5, No 1 (Feb 1987), pp 47- 76.

[Birman 88a] K.Birman et al., "ISIS - A Distributed Programming Environment", Cornell University, June 1988.

[Birman 88b] K.Birman, "Exploiting Replication", in Lectures Notes Arctic'88, Tromso, July 1988.

[Fidge 88] C.Fidge, "Timestamps in Message-Passing Systems That Preserve the Partial Ordering", Proc. of the 11th Australian Computer Science Conference, Univ of Queensland, Feb 1988.

[Joseph 86] T.Joseph, K.Birman, "Low Cost Management of Replicated Data in Fault-Tolerant Distributed Systems", ACM Trans. on Computer Systems, Vol 4, No 1 (Feb 1986), pp54-70.

[Lamport 78] L.Lamport, "Time, Clocks, and the Ordering of Events in a Distributed System", Communications of the ACM, Vol 21, No 7 (July 1978), pp 558-565.

[Mattern 89] F.Mattern, "Time and Global States of Distributed Systems", Proc. of the International Workshop on Parallel and Distributed Algorithms, Bonas, France, October 1988, North-Holland 1989.

[Peterson 87] L.Peterson, "Preserving Context Information in an IPC Abstraction", IEEE Proc. of the 6th Symp. on Reliability in Distributed Software and Database Systems, March 1987.

[Schiper 89] A.Schiper, J.Eggli, A.Sandoz, "A New Algorithm to Implement Causal Ordering", Rapport Interne 89/02, EPFL-Laboratoire de Systèmes d'Exploitation, April 1989.

SYMMETRY BREAKING IN ASYNCHRONOUS RINGS WITH O(n) MESSAGES

by

Paul Spirakis[+,*], Basil Tampakas[+] and Athanasios Tsiolis[+]

+ Computer Technology Institute, Greece
* Courant Inst. Math. Sciences, U.S.A.

Abstract

The symmetry breaking problem is the problem of electing a leader in a network of indistinguishable processes. There is no deterministic solution for this problem. We provide here efficient probabilistic protocols for breaking symmetry in a unidirectional ring. For rings of unrestricted asynchrony, we provide a protocol needing only O(n) messages in the average. Yet, the average bit complexity of the protocol is still O(nlogn). We manage to get a message complexity below the Ω(nlogn) lower bound of [Burns, 80], by allowing our protocol to deadlock, with arbitrarily small probability, controllable by the implementer. The possibility of more than one leaders being elected is not allowed by our protocol.

1. Introduction

We address here the distributed election problem in ring networks under the assumption that the processes are indistinguishable (have no distinct identities). [Angluin, 80] has shown that no deterministic solution exists for the election problem (called also the symmetry breaking problem) in this case. Thus, if any solution exists, it must be a randomized algorithm. Assuming that the number n of nodes is known to the processors, [Itai, Rodeh, 81] provided randomized techniques which terminate with probability 1. For (completely) asynchronous processes, their algorithm reqquires O(nlogn) messages. For synchronous processes and simultaneous initiation, their protocol exchanges O(n) bits in time O(n) on the average. [Rodeh, Santoro, 85] presented a synchronous randomized algorithm for symmetry breaking in a ring without assumptions on initiation time. This algorithm terminates with probability 1 exchanging O(n) bits on the average but it requires $O(n^2)$ time units on the average. [Frederickson, Santoro, 86] provided a synchronous protocol which breaks symmetry without simultaneous initiation, with O(n) bits and time units on the average.

We provide here a symmetry breaking protocol for rings with unrestricted asynchronism. Its average bit complexity is O(nlogn). The message complexity of our protocol has to be contrasted with the Ω(nlogn) lower bound for the number of message passes for distributed elections, shown by [Burns, 80] and [Pachl, Korach, Rotem, 82]. We manage to get below the Ω(nlogn) lower bound not only because our processes choose names from the set {1,2,...,n} (and not from any arbitrary domain) but also because we trade a small possibility of deadlock with message efficiency. In fact, our protocol

This work was supported in part by the ESPRIT Basic Research Actions Project ALCOM and by the Ministry of Education of Greece.

is allowed to deadlock with arbitrary small probability, controllable by the implementer. The ring size (or at least a linear upper bound) is assumed to be known in advance by our protocol.

In the work of [Abrahamson et al, 86] efficient protocols are provided for the problem of <u>solitude verification</u> on an asynchronous unidirectional ring. Solitude verification combined with <u>attrition</u> (the method of reducing a set of contenders to just a few candidates) is usually used to solve the symmetry breaking problem. The [Abrahamson et al, 86] techniques can thus solve the symmetry breaking problem by using $O(n\log n + n\log(1/\varepsilon))$ bits on the average, with probability at most ε of electing <u>more than one</u> leaders. Our techniques is not based on solitude verification and, given that deadlock does not happen, it always elects a <u>unique</u> leader.

In the simultaneously appearing work of [Matias, Afek, 89] similar results are shown, for general networks, through different algorithms. [Matias, Afek, 89] allow for more than one leader to be chosen, with small probability.

In the sequel, the rings are assumed to be undirectional.

2. Efficient protocols for asynchronous rings

As [Burns, 80] and [Pachl, Korach, Rotem, 82] have shown, distributed elections in asynchronous rings require $\Omega(n\log n)$ message passes. However, this lower bound is mostly due to the fact that processes have distinct names chosen from an <u>arbitrary</u> domain. [Frederickson, Lynch, 84] indicated that if the identities are chosen from some <u>countable</u> set, then only $O(n)$ message are needed for <u>synchronous</u> rings. We show here that only $O(n)$ messages are needed for <u>symmetry breaking</u> in completely asynchronous rings, if we trade the possibility for deadlock with message complexity. A very small, controllable by the implementer, deadlock probability is enough to achieve $O(n)$ expected number of messages. We of course assume that communication links do not change the relative order of the sending of messages through them.

2.1 The general approach

2.1.1 The Challenges of the asynchronous setup

In an asynchronous setup, the following difficulties arise:

(a) No process may decide on its own to become inactive (or to stop propagation of activation messages) without being sure that some other processes remain active (else, the entire ring may stop without choosing a leader, in which case we have a <u>deadlock</u>).

(b) A process is unable to count time steps in order to deduce that a message it initiated has returned (contrast this with Archimedean networks (see e.g. [Vitanyi, 84], also [Spirakis, Tampakas, 88]), where some way of approximate time-out is possible).

(c) In case of spontaneous, non-simultaneous, awakening of processes, a process which has just been spontaneously awake must (possibly) undertake the task of starting other processes. It might choose to originate a wake-up message. If, later on, this process receives a wake-up message and decides to eliminate it, then the possibility of deadlock appears. On the other hand, a decision not to cut the wake-up messages may lead to high message complexity (e.g. $O(n^2)$).

Our approach is to allow a (small) probability of deadlock in the protocol in order to achieve a message complexity below nlogn. This is combined with the use of the [Itai-Rodeh, 81] protocol with the essential difference that we start it only when the vast majority of the ring processes are <u>repeaters</u> (i.e. they just pass on messages originated by other processes). Only a few processes (the <u>candidates</u>) originate messages to be sent around the ring. If the candidates running the Itai-Rodeh protocol are evenly distributed around the ring then we can prove that the average message complexity of the modified Itai-Rodeh protocol is $O(nx)$ where x is the number of candidates at the start of this modified protocol. Thus, our algorithms consist of two major stages.

(a) The <u>candidate creation stage</u> where, finally, only a few candidates are present. This stage allows for deadlock to happen, with a controllable small probability.

(b) The <u>election stage</u> where the symmetry breaking protocol of Itai & Rodeh is run, by candidates only.

We analyse here a way of implementing the candidate creation stage, which creates only $x=O(1)$ candidates, uses the technique of wake-up message elimination, and allows for deadlock with a probability of at most e^{-k} where k can be chosen in advance. The average message complexity of the protocol is then $O(nk+nx)$, leading to a linear message complexity asynchronous symmetry breaking algorithm when k is a constant.

2.1.2 <u>The election stage: (The modified Itai-Rodeh protocol and its complexity)</u>

Only candidate processes can become the leader. Initially most processes are repeaters and only x processes are <u>candidates</u>.

Each process v has the following variables, especially for this subprotocol:

(i)   candidate$_v$: a boolean variable indicating whether v is a candidate

(ii) ph$_v$:   the phase number (initially zero)

(iii) id$_v$:   an integer identification number between 1 and n. At the beginning of each phase, each candidate chooses id$_v$ at random. There might be more than one candidates with the same id.

(iv) buf$_v$:   a buffer containing at most one message.

Candidates originate messages to be sent around the ring. Both candidates and repeaters pass messages originated by other processes. A message here is of <u>type-b</u>, namely a quadruple

$$m = (ph_m, id_m, count_m, unique_m)$$

where ph_m and id_m are the phase number and the identification of the originator of the message; $count_m$ is the distance the message travelled (an integer between 1 and n). Each time a message is passed (to the left) $count_m$ is increased by one. Thus, each candidate can identify its own messages. Finally, $unique_m$ is a boolean variable, indicating whether any candidate, other than the originator, has been encountered during the traversal of the ring.

Let $nextphase_v$ be a procedure which increase the phase number ph_v, chooses at random a new value for id_v and sets buf_v to $(ph_v, id_v, 1, true)$. At any time a process can do any one of the following two activities.

A1. If a message of type-b is pending ($buf_v \neq$ "empty") then the message can be sent leftwards and "empty" is assigned to buf_v.

A2. At any time a process v can receive the message $(ph_m, id_m, count_m, unique_m)$ and then the following subprotocol E is executed:

subprotocol E

```
begin
 if           candidate_v = false & count_m=n then skip
 if           candidate_v = false & count_m<n then buf_v ← (ph_m, id_m, count_m+1,
                          unique_m)
 if           candidate_v = true then
              if  count_m=n then
                          begin
                             if unique_m then v is the leader
                             else nextphase_v
                          end
                          else /* count_m<n & candidate_v */
              if (ph_m,id_m) > (ph_v,id_v) then
                          begin
                          (ph_v,id_v) ← (ph_m,id_m);
                          candidate_v ← false;
                          buf_v ← (ph_m,id_m,count_m+1,unique_m)
                          end
              else if (ph_m,id_m) = (ph_v,id_v) then
                          buf_v ← (ph_m,id_m,count_m+1,false)
              else skip
end
```

We envision a message of type-b originating at a candidate (its originator) and moving leftwards until returning or until it is purged (not transmitted any further). The first two components of messages are compared lexicographically.

The following two properties of the above subprotocol can be proved as in [Itai, Rodeh, 81]:

Property 1: After the first message of type-b has been created by a candidate and until a leader is chosen, there exist messages and the originators of all messages with lexicographically maximal (ph_m, id_m) are candidates.

Property 2: On termination a unique leader is chosen.

Obviously the modified Itai-Rodeh subprotocol may diverge. Thus we consider average message complexity. If we assume an adversary scheduler at the election stage, then this scheduler will try to minimize message purges. Hence the ring will act almost synchronously. (We, of course, assume that a process can send and receive messages simultaneously, there by eliminating message purges). These considerations lead to an upper bound on the message complexity of the election stage.

Let the x candidates at the start of the election stage be the processes $v_1, v_2, \ldots, v_x$ at consecutive distances $y_1, y_2, \ldots, y_x$. Clearly $y_1 + y_2 + \ldots + y_x = n$.

We will condition the next lemma on the following hypothesis (to be shown in the analysis of the candidate creation stage).

Equidistribution Hypothesis

$\forall j \leq x$, the expected value of $v_1 + \ldots + v_j$ is $\theta(j\frac{n}{x})$.

Lemma 4.1 Given the equidistribution hypothesis, the average complexity of a single phase is $O(nx)$.

Proof sketch Consider the first phase. Let $p_1(i,d)$ be the probability that a message sent from process v_1 which chose the integer i travels distance d until it is purged.

$$p_1(i,d) = \begin{cases} (\frac{i}{n})^x & \text{when } d=n \\[2mm] (\frac{i}{n})^{j-1}(1-\frac{i}{n}) & \text{when } d=y_1+\ldots+y_j \end{cases}$$

The expected distance D travelled by the message originated at v_1, is (assuming $id_{v1}=i$)

$$D(i) = \sum_{j=1}^{x} d_j \, p_1(i,d_j) \text{ where } d_j = y_1 + \ldots + y_j$$

By the equidistribution hypothesis then,

$$D(i) = \sum_{j=1}^{x} \theta(j\frac{n}{x}) \, (\frac{i}{n})^{j-1}(1-\frac{i}{n}) = \frac{n}{x}(1-\frac{i}{n}) \, \theta(\sum_{j=1}^{x} j(i/n)^j)$$

i.e.
$$D(i) \leq \frac{n}{x} \theta(\frac{1-(i/n)^{x+1}}{1-(i/n)}) \leq \theta((\frac{n}{x})(1+\frac{i}{n}))$$

For all x candidates the number N of communications during the first phase becomes

$$N \leq x \sum_{i=1}^{n} \text{prob}(id=i) \, D(i)$$

i.e.
$$N \leq x \frac{1}{n} \sum_{i=1}^{n} D(i)$$

i.e.
$$N \leq \theta(x \, n)$$

In subsequent phases the number of candidates can only decreases, in which case N is even lower. $\square$

The analysis is complete by a Lemma of [Itai, Rodeh, 81].

Lemma 4.2 [Itai, Rodeh, 81] The expected number of phases to choose a leader in a ring of length n with m candidates (any $m \leq n$) is bounded by $e \frac{n}{n-1}$.
Hence

Corollary 4.1 The expected message complexity of the election phase is bounded by $O(nx)$. $\square$

2.2 The proposed protocol with O(n) messages

a. The protocol

Initially all nodes are in a <u>sleeping</u> state. Each node v has a counter $wcount_v$ (initially zero) that counts the number of wake-up messages that pass through it. The wake-up messages are considered to be of <u>type-a</u> and do not contain any other information than their type. In the sequel, k is a parameter, set by the algorithm implementor. The protocol consider of the following rules:

Protocol C_k

Rule 1 A <u>sleeping</u> node v

   1.1 If can become spontaneously <u>awake</u> and execute the Wake-up routine.

   1.2 If it receives a "wake-up" message it becomes awake, sets $wcount_v \leftarrow wcount_v + 1$ and execute the wake-up routine.

   1.3 If it receives a type-B message it becomes a repeater.

(<u>Note</u>: The Wake-up routine is the following:

     a. choose a number at random in $\{1, \ldots, n\}$

     b. If the number selected is 1 then the node becomes a candidate and sends a "type-B" message, else it stays an awake node and sends a "wake-up" message.

Rule 2 An <u>awake</u> node v

   2.1 If $wcount_v < k$ (k is a parameter) then on receipt of a "wake-up" message the $wcount_v$ increases by 1 and the node executes the Wake-up routine.

   2.2 If $wcount_v \geq k$ then the node becomes a <u>repeater</u>.

   2.3 If it receives a "type-B" message, it becomes a repeater.

Rule 3 A <u>candidate</u> node v

   3.1 It runs the election stage subprotocol, with $ph_v = 0$.

   3.2 If purges any received wake-up node.

Rule 4 A <u>repeater</u> node v

   4.1 It runs the election stage subprotocol, with $ph_v = 0$

   4.2 It purges any received "wake-up" messages.

b. The properties of Protocol C_k

Lemma 4.3 Protocol C_k may deadlock (in the candidate generation stage) with probability at most $\exp(-k)$.

Proof A deadlock will happen only if all nodes become repeaters. This is only possible if each node draws k times and fails to become a candidate. The probability of this is at most

$$(1-\frac{1}{n})^{nk} \le \exp(-k).$$

Lemma 4.4 Contitioned on the Equidistribution hypothesis, the average message complexity of Protocol C_k is $O(nk+xn)$ where x is the number of candidates at the beginning of the election stage.

Proof By Lemma 4.3 and Corollary 4.1. ▢

Lemma 4.5 The expected value of the maximum number, x, of candidates (at any time) in the Protocol C_k is $O(1)$.

Proof sketch This expected value is bounded above by the expected number of successes in the Bernoulli trials of nk trials and success probability $\frac{1}{n}$, which is k. ▢

Lemma 4.6 (Equidistribution hypothesis)

Let $v_1, v_2, \ldots, v_x$ be the candidate processes at the beginning of the election stage. Let their consequtive distance be $y_1, y_2, \ldots, y_x$. Then, $\forall_{j}<x$, the expected value of y_j is $\frac{n}{x}$.

Proof sketch By the symmetry in the candidate creation process. ▢

Corollary 4.2 For constant k, the expected message complexity of C_k is $O(n)$.

Proof By Lemma 4.4, 4.5 and 4.6. ▢

Remark The average _bit complexity_ of C_k remains $O(nlogn)$. (It is actually $O(kn+xnlogn)$) ▢

2.3 A modification of the election stage

If we allow a very small probability of multiple elections, we are able to use a more simple election algorithm with a linear number of messages too. In this case the type-B messages consist of two fields

$$m = (ph_m, id_m)$$

When an awake node becomes a candidate, chooses at random a value for the phase number, and a new value for the id_v, and sends the message. We give the modified subprotocol G.

```
if candidate = false then buf_v ← (ph_m, id_m)
if candidate = true then
    if (ph_m, id_m) = (ph_v, id_v) then
            v is the leader

    else
    if (ph_m, id_m) > (ph_v, id_v) then
      begin
        candidate = false;
```

$$buf_v \leftarrow (ph_m, id_m)$$
else skip

end

Two or more nodes may choose the same phase number and the same id with probability equal to $\frac{1}{n^4}$. So in the worst case the election stage may result in more than one winners with probability at most $\frac{1}{n^4}$.

Further research

Another possible implementation of the candidate creation stage could start by creating $\theta(n)$ candidates and then by quickly reducing their number through a randomized distributed sampling process. This protocol also allows a possibility for deadlock, since it is possible for all the candidates to be eliminated by the distributed sampling. The tradeoff between message efficiency and probability of deadlock is a subject of further work. Also, it seems that our protocol can be modified to run correctly even when processor know only an upper bound N on the size of the ring, such that $n \leq N \leq \beta n$ for some constant $\beta > 1$. The message and bit complexities are preserved in such a case.

References

[Abrahamson et al, 86] K. Abrahamson, A. Adler, L. Higham and D. Kirkpatrick, "Probability Solitude Verification on a Ring", Proc. of the 5th ACM Symp. on Principles of Distributed Computing, Aug. 1986, 161-173.

[Angluin, 80] D. Angluin, "Local and global properties in networks of processes", Proc. 12th ACM Symp. on Theory of Computing, April 1980, 82-93.

[Attiya et al, 85] C. Attiya, M. Snir, M. Warminth, "Computing on an anonymous ring", Proc. 4th ACM Symp. on Principles of Distributed Computing, Aug. 1985, 196-204.

[Burns, 80] Burns J.E., "A formal model for message passing systems", TR No. 91, CS Dept., Indiana Univ., May 1980.

[Frederickson, Lynch, 84] G. Frederickson, N. Lynch, "The impact of synchronous communication on the problem of electing a leader in a ring", Proc. 16th ACM Symp. on Theory of Computing, April 1984, 493-503.

[Frederickson, Santoro, 86] G. Frederickson, N. Santoro, "Breaking Symmetry in Synchronous Networks", VLSI Algorithms and Architectures, AWOK 1986, Lecture Notes in Computer Science, No. 227, Springer Verlag, pp. 26-33.

[Gafni, 85] E. Gafni, "Improvements in the time complexity of two message-optimal election algorithms", Proc. 4th ACM Symp. on principles of Distributed Computing, Aug. 1985, pp. 175-185.

[Itai, Rodeh, 81] A. Itai, M. Rodeh, "Symmetry breaking in distributive networks", Proc. 22nd IEEE Symp. on Foundations Computer Science, Oct. 1981, 150-158.

[Lamport, 78] Lamport, L., "Time clocks and the ordering of events in a distributed system", CACM Vol. 21, No. 7, 558-565.

[van Leeuwen, Santoro, Urrutia, Zaks, 87] J. van Leeuwen, N. Santoro, J. Urrutia and S. Zaks, "Guessing Games and Distributed Computations in Synchronous Networks", 14th ICALP, INCS No. 267, pp. 347-356, Springer-Verlag, 1987.

[Matias, Afek, 89] Y. Matias, Y. Afek "Simple and Efficient Election Algorithms for Anonymous Networks", 3rd International Workshop on Distributed Algorithms, Proceedings, September 1989.

[Overmars, Santoro, 86] M. Overmars, N. Santoro, "An improved election algorithm for synchronous rings", preliminary draft, Carleton University, March 1986.

[Pachl, Korach, Rotem, 82] Pachl J., E. Korach and D. Rotem, "A technique for proving lower bounds for distributed maximum-finding algorithms", Proc. 14th ACM STOC, 1982, pp. 378-382.

[Reif, Spirakis, 84] J. Reif, P. Spirakis, "Real Time Synchronization of Interprocess Communication", ACM Transactions of Programming Languages and Systems, April 1984.

[Reif, Spirakis, 85] J. Reif, P. Spirakis, "Unbounded Speed Variability in Distributed Systems", SIAM Journal of Computing, February 1985.

[Ricart, Agrawala, 81] G. Ricart, A. Agrawala, "An Optimal Algorithm for Mutual Exclusion in Computer Networks", CACM: Vol. 24, No. 1, Jan. 1981.

[Santoro, Rotem, 85] N. Santoro, D. Rotem, "On the Complexity of distributed elections is synchronous graphs", Proc. 11th Int. Workshop on Graphtheoretic Concepts in Computer Science, June 1985, 337-346.

[Spirakis, Tampakas, 88] Spirakis P. and B. Tampakas, "Efficient Distributed Algorithms by Using the Archimedean Time Assumption", 5th STACS (1988), Lecture Notes in Computer Science No. 294, pp. 248-264, also in Theoretical Informatics and Applications, Gauthier-Villars, Vol. 23, No. 1, 1989, pp. 113-128.

[Vitanyi, 84] P. Vitanyi, "Distributed elections in an Archimedean ring of processors", Proc. 16th ACM Symp. on Theory of Computing, April 1984, 542-547.

Designing distributed algorithms
by means of
formal sequentially phased reasoning
(extended abstract)

F.A. Stomp

University of Nijmegen

Department of Computer Science

Toernooiveld, 6525 ED Nijmegen, The Netherlands

E-mail address: frank@cs.kun.nl

W.P. de Roever

Eindhoven University of Technology

Department of Mathematics and Computing Science

POB 513, 5600 MB Eindhoven, The Netherlands

E-mail address: mcvax!eutrc3!wsinwpr

Abstract: Designers of network algorithms give elegant informal descriptions of the intuition behind their algorithms (see [GHS83, Hu83, MS79, Se82, Se83, ZS80]). Usually, these descriptions are structured as if tasks or subtasks are performed *sequentially*. From an operational point of view, however, they are performed *concurrently*. Here, we present a design principle that formally describes how to develop algorithms according to such sequentially phased explanations. The design principle is formulated using Manna and Pnueli's linear time temporal logic [MP83]. This principle, together with Chandy and Misra's technique [CM88] or Back and Sere's technique [BS89] for designing parallel algorithms, is applicable to large classes of algorithms, such as those for minimum-path, connectivity, network flow, and minimum-weight spanning trees. In particular, the distributed minimum-weight spanning tree algorithm of Gallager, Humblet, and Spira [GHS83] is structured according to our principle.

1 Introduction

Designers of complex network algorithms, see, e.g., [GHS83, Hu83, MS79, Se82, Se83, ZS80], usually describe their algorithms on the basis of *tasks* or *subtasks* – sometimes referred to as *phases* and *subphases*. Their (informal) descriptions are structured as if groups of nodes in the network perform these (sub)tasks *sequentially*, although in reality (i.e., operationally speaking) they are performed *concurrently*. Current design methodologies (see, e.g., [CM88, BS89]) lack an appropriate principle for *formally* developing such sequentially phased algorithms. *In this paper we formulate a formal design principle that captures this sequential structure in network algorithms.* It closely resembles the designers' intuitions as given by the informal descriptions and thus preserves the natural flavor of their original explanation. Furthermore, this principle can also be used to design formally new algorithms.

The sequential decomposition of a concurrently performed task into subtasks can already be discerned in a simple broadcast protocol, viz., Segall's PIF-protocol [Se83] (cf. also [DS80] and [F80]). Here, the whole protocol performed by the nodes in some network can be decomposed into two subtasks: the *first one* broadcasting some information and unwinding a directed tree, and the *second one* reporting that the nodes have indeed received the information. Following this pattern of sequential reasoning the distributed minimum-weight spanning tree algorithm of Gallager, Humblet, and Spira [GHS83], hereafter referred to as Gallager's algorithm, can be described in essentially four subtasks, which from a logical point of view are performed sequentially (see [SR87a, SR87b]). *That algorithm displays, however, an additional feature: that of "interference".* Expanding groups of nodes perform a certain task repeatedly, with different groups performing their tasks concurrently w.r.t. another. Now a task performed by one group can be disturbed temporarily due to interference with the task of another group. *Our design principle is geared to cope naturally with this kind of interference.*

In order to design a distributed program that solves a certain task which can be split up logically into subtasks as if they are performed sequentially, we propose the following strategy:
First develop distributed programs which solve the subtasks. Methodologies for doing so are described in [CM88] and [BS89]. Next, combine these programs to construct one which solves the whole task. Our design principle describes how to accomplish this combination. (In [CM88] there has not been given any methodological advice how to accomplish this kind of combination. Our technique generalizes one transformation principle described in [BS89], because it is able to cope with repeatedly performed tasks and with temporary disturbances of the kind discussed above.)
In essence, it is required to prove the *verification conditions* (A) and (B) below.

(A) Prove that for each distributed program S, solving a subtask, a specification consisting of, for each node j,

    (1) a precondition p_j and a postcondition q_j, and

    (2) a pair of state-assertions (I_j, T_j)

holds. I_j is an invariant for the program executed by node j. Furthermore, I_j is an invariant for program S; It has been incorporated in the specification in order to deal with the above-mentioned kind of interference, which occurs in, e.g., Gallager's algorithm (cf. [SR87a, SR87b]). T_j expresses that node j has completed its contribution to the subtask associated with program S.

(B) Prove that each node can participate in at most one subtask at a time and that all nodes which participate in more subtasks, participate in these subtasks in the same order.

One is then entitled to conclude that the program consisting of all (atomic) actions occurring in those programs associated with the subtasks solves the whole task as if the nodes perform the subtasks sequentially. Astonishingly, this simple design principle underlies the development of such complicated algorithms as Gallager's and those described in [Hu83, MS79, Se82, Se83, ZS80].

How can one understand the inherently sequential intuition present in this design principle for concurrent computations?

Its semantic foundation lies in considering computation sequences in a specific form in which all operations associated with one subtask are performed consecutively. Although it might not be the case at all that each computation sequence of the program solving the whole task is in this specific form, *reasoning about this program by means of computation sequences in this specific form is correct*, since any computation sequence of the program turns out to be *equivalent* to one in that form. In order to define this notion of equivalence (see [L85]) the notion of an event is needed: an event is an occurrence of the execution of some atomic action. Now each computation sequence defines a partial ordering of its events. This partial order is a causal relation in which all events generated at a single node are ordered according to their temporal occurrence in this sequence. Additionally, in an asynchronous model of computation the event of sending a message precedes the event of receiving it; in a synchronous model these events are identical. Two computation sequences are *equivalent* if their first states are identical and if they define the same partial order of events. In essence, equivalent computation sequences differ only in the way events generated at different nodes are interleaved (w.r.t. the partial order defined by these sequences). Moreover, if two *finite* computation sequences are equivalent, then their last states coincide. This argument justifies, e.g., Elrad and Francez's *safe decomposition principle* [EF82] (cf. also [Pa88]) as demonstrated by Gerth and Shrira [GS86]. This principle states the following: if $S_{1,m} \parallel \cdots \parallel S_{n,m}$ is partially correct w.r.t. precondition p_{m-1} and postcondition p_m ($n \geq 1$, $m = 1, \cdots, d$ for some natural number $d \geq 2$) and if no communication occurs between $S_{i,m}$ and $S_{j,m'}$ for $1 \le i, j \le n$, $i \ne j$, $1 \le m, m' \le d$, and $m \ne m'$, then $(S_{1,1}; S_{1,2}; \cdots; S_{1,d}) \parallel \cdots \parallel (S_{n,1}; S_{n,2}; \cdots; S_{n,d})$ is partially correct w.r.t. p_0 and p_d.

To reason formally about such arguments, Katz and Peled have proposed to use interleaving set temporal logic [KP87, KP88] as a formalism. Their logic allows one to reason about a program's behavior by considering only particular representatives of the program's computation sequences, such as the very sequences in the specific form introduced above.

From the discussion above it follows that if in some program, solving a certain task which can be split up logically into two subtasks as if they are performed sequentially, each node always performs operations associated with one subtask before operations associated with the other, then the following holds: each computation sequence of the program is equivalent to a computation sequence, in which all operations associated with the first subtask are performed before all operations associated with the second one. This is, e.g., the case for the program in figure 1 below, which describes the PIF-protocol [Se83] (cf. [DS80, F80]), where in order to illustrate our decomposition of a task into two subtasks in a few words, it is assumed that the network constitutes a tree.[1] The nodes perform the following task: some message $info(v)$, for a certain argument v, initially in the message queue of node k (viewed as the root of the tree), has to be sent to all nodes in the network. Node k has to be informed that all nodes in the network have received this message indeed and that the value v has been recorded by them. The two subtasks constituting this task have been described above and consist of a broadcasting phase followed by a reporting phase. In the program below (see figure 1), boxes labeled A_i^n indicate which operations of node i are associated with the nth subtask ($n=1,2$). Note that the boxes do not necessarily correspond with the body of a "response" (since they are the outcome of a *semantical* analysis). *Now our principle justifies that one can reason formally about this protocol as if first A^1 programs are executed by the nodes, and thereafter only A^2 programs.* In the full paper [SR89] the specific assertions I_j, T_j, p_j, and q_j for all nodes j have been defined in case of the PIF-protocol.

Our principle is a broad *semantic* generalization of Elrad and Francez's *safe decomposition principle* [EF82] (cf. also [GS86, Pa88]). Their decompositions, however, i.e., the programs (called *layers* in [EF82]) describing the subtasks, are restricted by the syntax of the whole program; This is not true for our decompositions as has already been observed above. In contrast with their principle, and the one described in [FF89], our principle also applies to reasoning about *repeatedly* performed tasks by expanded groups of nodes, such as in, e.g., Gallager's algorithm. Methods for verifying Gallager's algorithm appear in [SR87a, SR87b, CG88, WLL88]. We [SR87a, SR87b] have reasoned

---

[1] A decomposition is also possible in the case of an arbitrary connected network.

about its correctness on the basis of (sub)tasks. In those papers, however, the underlying proof principles have not been formulated. Neither has a formalism for them been given. Welch, Lamport, and Lynch [WLL88] give a correctness proof in the context of I/O-automata, using a (partially-ordered) hierarchy of algorithms. Chou and Gafni [CG88] consider a simplified version of Gallager's algorithm, a distributed version of Boruvka's algorithm [B26]. The problem of finding a simple proof principle for the sequentially phased reasoning of the full version of Gallager's algorithm clearly emerges in [CG88], since in the full version of that algorithm one has to cope with temporary disturbances of the kind discussed above. In order to reason about such disturbances along the lines of [CG88], another principle would be required. In our case, due to the collection of assertions (I_j, T_j) for nodes j, merely an *interference-freedom* argument for I_j and T_j must be given.

---

loop executed by node k (the root)

```
response to receipt of info(v)
begin
  valₖ:=v;
  for all edges e ∈ Eₖ
    do send info(valₖ) on edge e od
end
```
A_k^1

```
response to receipt of ack(v) on edge C
begin
  Nₖ(C):= true;
  if ∀C ∈ Eₖ.Nₖ(C)
  then doneₖ:=true
  fi
end
```
A_k^2

loop executed by node $i \neq k$ (a non-root)

```
response to receipt of info(v) on edge
C
begin
  valᵢ:=v; inbranchᵢ:=C; Nᵢ(C):=true;
  for all edges e ∈ Eᵢ ∧ e ≠ inbranchᵢ
    do send info(valᵢ) on edge e od;
```
A_i^1

```
  if ∀C ∈ Eᵢ.Nᵢ(C)
  then send ack(valᵢ) on inbranchᵢ
  fi
end
```

```
response to receipt of ack(v) on edge C
begin
  Nᵢ(C):= true;
  if ∀C ∈ Eᵢ.Nᵢ(C)
  then send ack(valᵢ) on inbranchᵢ
  fi
end
```
A_i^2

Notation used: E_i denotes the set of edges adjacent to node i. Variable val_i is used to record the argument of the info-message received by node i; $N_i(C)$ records whether any message has been received along edge C, $C \in E_i$. For node i different from k, variable $inbranch_i$ records the identification of the edge along which the info-message has been received. (These variables are used for unwinding the directed tree.) Variable $done_k$ records whether the whole task has been completed.
Initially, node k's message queue contains one info-message and the message queues of all other nodes are empty. Furthermore initially $\neg done_k$ holds for node k, and $\neg N_i(C)$ for all nodes i and edges $C \in E_i$. The initial values of the other variables are irrelevant.

Figure 1 : Segall's PIF-protocol

The rest of this paper is organized as follows: in section 2, we introduce some notation and conventions. Our design principle is formulated in section 3. For ease of exposition we have restricted ourselves to synchronous communication. Section 4 contains some conclusions. In appendix I of the full paper [SR89] we have discussed how to formulate our principle for the asynchronous case. Appendix II of that paper shows how to transform programs represented by lists of responses (cf. the program above) into our own notation for representing distributed algorithms. In Appendix III of [SR89] a fully worked out illustration of the principle, applied to the PIF-protocol, can be found.

2 Conventions and notations

A distributed algorithm is performed by nodes in a fixed, finite, and undirected network (V, E), and consists of at least two nodes. The network is viewed as a graph. Two adjacent nodes communicate by means of messages. Since edges are undirected, each node can both send and receive messages along any of its adjacent edges. Except for delivering messages properly any edge can damage, lose, duplicate, and reorder messages in transit.

For ease of exposition it is assumed that communication is *synchronous*. (In the full paper [SR89] we have shown how our results can be extended to an *asynchronous* model of communication.) In order to avoid bothering about the actual syntax of programs, distributed algorithms are represented by a quintuple $< V', S, \{p_i \mid i \in V'\}, \{q_i \mid i \in V'\}, A >$. (In [SR89] we have shown how a program represented by lists of responses, as in e.g., section 1, can be represented by such a quintuple.) The interpretation of the five components is the following: V' is a subset of V containing all nodes that actually execute the algorithm. S is a set of states that can occur when the algorithm is executed (cf. the definition below). $\{p_i \mid i \in V'\}$ and $\{q_i \mid i \in V'\}$ are collections of state-assertions. For all $i \in V$, assertion p_i describes the initial values of node i's variables; assertion q_i describes the final values of node i's variables, provided that the algorithm terminates. Finally, A is a collection of atomic actions which can occur when the nodes in V' execute the algorithm (see the definition below). Each action a has an enabling condition $en(a)$ associated with it.

Given an algorithm represented by a quintuple as above, it is assumed that the set A of actions can be partitioned into sets A_j of node j's internal actions and sets $A_{j,i}, i \neq j$, of actions involving a transmission of a message from node j to node i $(i, j \in V')$. The set of all actions that can be performed by node j (possibly simultaneously with other nodes), i.e., the set $A_j \cup \bigcup_{i \in V'} A_{j,i} \cup \bigcup_{i \in V'} A_{i,j}$, will be denoted by $act(A, j)$.

Definition

A computation sequence of an algorithm as above is a maximal sequence $s_0 \overset{a_0}{\to} s_1 \overset{a_1}{\to} s_2 \cdots$ such that for all $n \geq 0$ the following is satisfied: s_n is a state occurring in the set S, a_n is an action occurring in the set A, action a_n is enabled in state s_n, i.e., $en(a_n)$ holds in s_n, and s_{n+1} is the state resulting when a_n is executed in state s_n. Each computation sequence is assumed to be fair, i.e., if it is infinite, then every action infinitely often enabled in the sequence is taken infinitely often.

3 Our design principle

In this section we present a design principle that formalizes sequentially phased design of distributed algorithms. The principle itself is formulated in subsection 3.3. In subsection 3.2 the *verification conditions* of the principle, i.e., conditions to be verified in order to apply the principle, are presented. Subsection 3.1 describes some basic observations for solving tasks from the class considered here.

3.1 General observations

Assume that a collection V' of nodes performs a certain task specified by means of a pair of sets of state-assertions $\{p_i \mid i \in V'\}$ (the preconditions) and $\{q_i \mid i \in V'\}$ (the postconditions). Consequently, in order to solve this task by some distributed algorithm $\mathcal{A}$ we must find a collection of actions A and a collection of states S such that $\mathcal{A}$ is described by the quintuple $< V', S, \{p_i \mid i \in V'\}, \{q_i \mid i \in V'\}, A >$.

We shall assume that this task can be split up logically into two subtasks as if they are performed sequentially. (The general case is a straightforward extension as shown at the end of this section.) It is attractive to design $\mathcal{A}$ in two stages: In the first stage algorithms $\mathcal{B}$ and $\mathcal{C}$ are designed that solve the two subtasks. Such a decomposition enables us to concentrate on one subject at a time. Methodologies for developing these algorithms are described in [CM88] and [BS89]. In the second stage $\mathcal{A}$ itself is designed by combining algorithms $\mathcal{B}$ and $\mathcal{C}$. Our design principle describes how to accomplish this combination.

Obviously, since the whole task can be split up *logically* into two subtasks, there exist intermediate assertions r_i, $i \in V'$, such that the two subtasks are solved by distributed algorithms $\mathcal{B}=< V', S, \{p_i \mid i \in V'\}, \{r_i \mid i \in V'\}, B >$ and $\mathcal{C}=< V', S, \{r_i \mid i \in V'\}, \{q_i \mid i \in V'\}, C >$ (for certain sets B and C of actions) (cf. [CM88, BS89]).

The remainder of this section describes how to combine these algorithms in order to obtain $\mathcal{A}$.

3.2 Verification conditions

We now present conditions of two kinds which are required for a sound application of our principle. Some conditions that algorithms $\mathcal{B}$ and $\mathcal{C}$ should satisfy in order to design $\mathcal{A}$ with this principle are described in subsection 3.2.1. Each of them can be verified by concentrating on one algorithm at a time. Conditions referring to both $\mathcal{B}$ and $\mathcal{C}$ are formulated in subsection 3.2.2.

3.2.1 Conditions on algorithms describing subtasks

Let $\mathcal{D}=< V', S, \{pre_i \mid i \in V'\}, \{post_i \mid i \in V'\}, D >$ be an algorithm. Node j's computation can be characterized by means of an invariant $I_j^{\mathcal{D}}$ ($j \in V'$). Introducing such invariants is the standard technique to ensure that our design principle (see subsection 3.3) can also be used for designing algorithms in which a (sub)task performed by some group of nodes can be disturbed temporarily (due to interference of the kind discussed in section 1).

Except for the invariant $I_j^{\mathcal{D}}$, we can be more precise about node j's behavior. If node j has completed its participation at a certain point in some computation sequence of $\mathcal{D}$, then j cannot perform any action from that point onwards. The states in which node j cannot perform any action anymore are characterized by an assertion $T_j^{\mathcal{D}}$ ($j \in V'$).

These assertions can be characterized in linear time temporal logic [MP83] as follows:
($\Box$ denotes the *always*-operator)

(a) $\forall j \in V'.\Box(pre_j \Rightarrow I_j^{\mathcal{D}})$ holds for all computation sequences of $\mathcal{D}$.

   Therefore, initially $I_j^{\mathcal{D}}$ holds for all nodes j in V'.

(b) $\forall j \in V'.\Box((I_j^{\mathcal{D}} \wedge \neg T_j^{\mathcal{D}})U(I_j^{\mathcal{D}} \wedge T_j^{\mathcal{D}}))$ holds for all computation sequences of $\mathcal{D}$, where U denotes the weak until-operator,
   i.e., for all nodes j in V', $I_j^{\mathcal{D}}$ is an invariant and for all computation sequences the following holds: "node j participates in the algorithm until it has completed its participation".

(c) $\forall j \in V'.\forall d \in act(D, j).\Box ((I_j^{\mathcal{D}} \wedge T_j^{\mathcal{D}}) \Rightarrow \neg en(d))$ holds for all computation sequences of $\mathcal{D}$,
   i.e., if a certain node has completed its participation in the algorithm, then it cannot perform any action. (Cf. section 2 for the definitions of $act(D, j)$ and of $en(d)$.)

(d) $\forall j \in V'.\Box((I_j^{\mathcal{D}} \wedge T_j^{\mathcal{D}}) \Rightarrow \Box(I_j^{\mathcal{D}} \wedge T_j^{\mathcal{D}}))$ holds for all computation sequences of $\mathcal{D}$,
   i.e., once a node has completed its participation in the algorithm, then it will never participate in the algorithm anymore.

Furthermore, we require that if in a certain state some node has not (yet) completed its participation in algorithm $\mathcal{D}$, then the whole algorithm cannot be completed.

(e) $\forall j \in V'.\Box((I_j^{\mathcal{D}} \wedge \neg T_j^{\mathcal{D}}) \Rightarrow \exists d \in D.(en(d)))$ holds for all computation sequences of $\mathcal{D}$.

Finally, node's j postcondition is established when it has completed its participation in the algorithm.

(f) $\forall j \in V'.\Box((I_j^{\mathcal{D}} \wedge T_j^{\mathcal{D}}) \Rightarrow post_j)$ holds for all computation sequences of $\mathcal{D}$.

3.2.2 Conditions for combining subtasks

Let $\mathcal{B}=< V', S, \{p_i \mid i \in V'\}, \{r_i \mid i \in V'\}, B >$ and $\mathcal{C}=< V', S, \{r_i \mid i \in V'\}, \{q_i \mid i \in V'\}, C >$ be algorithms which solve the two subtasks. Assume that $\mathcal{B}$ and $\mathcal{C}$ satisfy the collection of pairs of assertions (I_j^B, T_j^B), resp., (I_j^C, T_j^C), where the assertions have the above interpretation $(j \in V')$. In order to solve the whole task, we shall design an algorithm $\mathcal{A}$ with actions from B and C in which each node j in V' first participates in $\mathcal{B}$ and then participates in $\mathcal{C}$, provided that j actually participates in both subtasks. As a consequence of this strategy, no node in V' will participate in both subtasks at the same time. Therefore, we require that if a certain node has not completed its participation in one subtask, then it cannot execute any action associated with the other subtask.

Define for some assertion P and for some set of actions AC the predicate $disabled(P, AC)$ expressing that if assertion P holds, then all actions in AC are disabled: Formally, $disabled(P, AC)$ holds iff $\Box(P \Rightarrow \forall a \in AC. \neg en(a))$ is satisfied. It is required that the following conditions are satisfied:

(g) $\forall j \in V'. disabled(I_j^B \wedge \neg T_j^B, act(C, j))$ holds for all computation sequences of $\mathcal{B}$,
    i.e., if a certain node has not completed its participation in algorithm $\mathcal{B}$, then it cannot participate in algorithm $\mathcal{C}$, and similarly

(h) $\forall j \in V'. disabled(I_j^C \wedge \neg T_j^C, act(B, j))$ holds for all computation sequences of $\mathcal{C}$.

Also, we require that if some node has completed its participation in the second subtask, i.e., the one solved by algorithm $\mathcal{C}$, then no action associated with the first subtask which can be executed by that node is enabled. This condition ensures that every node in V' that actually participates in both subtasks will participate in the first subtask before it participates in the second one.

(i) $\forall j \in V'. disabled((I_j^C \wedge T_j^C, act(B, j))$ holds for all computation sequences of $\mathcal{C}$,
    i.e., after completing its contribution to algorithm $\mathcal{C}$, no node can ever participate in algorithm $\mathcal{B}$. (The assertion $disabled$ has been defined above.)

Also, it must be shown that the reasoning about each one of the algorithms is not invalidated by actions of the other algorithm, i.e., *interference freedom* of specifications must be shown.

Let, for assertions P_1 and P_2 and for a set of actions AC, the assertion $Int\text{-}free(P_1, P_2, AC)$ denote the following: for any action a in AC, if a is executed in a state satisfying $P_1 \wedge P_2$, then P_1 is not invalidated by a.

(j) $Int\text{-}free(I_j^B \wedge \neg T_j^B, I_k^C \wedge \neg T_k^C, act(C, k))$,
    $Int\text{-}free(I_j^B \wedge T_j^B, I_k^C \wedge \neg T_k^C, act(C, k))$,
    $Int\text{-}free(I_j^C \wedge \neg T_j^C, I_k^B \wedge \neg T_k^B, act(B, k))$,
    $Int\text{-}free(I_j^C \wedge T_j^C, I_k^B \wedge \neg T_k^B, act(B, k))$, holds for nodes $j, k \in V'$, $j \neq k$.

3.3 The design principle

After solving the two subtasks by means of the algorithms $\mathcal{B} =< V', S, \{p_i \mid i \in V'\}, \{r_i \mid i \in V'\}, B >$ and $\mathcal{C} =< V', S, \{r_i \mid i \in V'\}, \{q_i \mid i \in V'\}, C >$ as above, formulating the design principle in order to obtain an algorithm $\mathcal{A} =< V', S, \{p_i \mid i \in V'\}, \{q_i \mid i \in V'\}, A >$ solving the whole task is straightforward. Observe that a node is participating in the whole task iff it is participating in one of the subtasks. Therefore, we define the set of actions A as the union of the sets B and C.

Given algorithms $\mathcal{B}$ and $\mathcal{C}$. Prove that the verification conditions (a) through (j) above are satisfied for $\mathcal{B}$ and $\mathcal{C}$. Conclude that the algorithm $< V', S, \{p_i \mid i \in V'\}, \{q_i \mid i \in V'\}, B \cup C >$ indeed solves the whole task.

Observe that as a consequence of the requirement that for any node participating in a certain subtask all the node's actions associated with the other subtask are disabled (cf. the conditions (g) and (h) above), it follows that the set of actions B and C can be chosen disjoint.

Note that we have dealt above with partial correctness only. If it is required to design an always terminating algorithm $\mathcal{A}$, then one must additionally prove a verification condition that both B and C always terminate (notation as above). This holds because the whole task terminates iff both its subtasks terminate. Formally formulating the condition that a certain algorithm terminates is straightforward and therefore omitted.

In order to establish the validity of the principle above we have shown that every finite computation sequence of $\mathcal{A}$ is equivalent (in the sense of section 1) to a finite one in which every action associated with the first subtask is performed before other actions associated with the second subtask. The proof is similar to the soundness proof in [SR88] and is therefore omitted.

From the discussions above it follows that our principle can also be used for the designing algorithms hierarchically. That is, if the task solved by $\mathcal{A}$ is a subtask of yet another task, the the same principle can be applied for solving the other task. (The pairs of assertions $(I_j^B \vee I_j^C, T_j^C)$, where I_j^B, I_j^C, and T_j^C have been used in order to construct $\mathcal{A}$, satisfy conditions (a) through (f) above.)

In case the whole task can be split up into more than two subtasks we proceed as follows: First design algorithms $\mathcal{D}$ solving the subtasks. Prove that for each such $\mathcal{D}$ there exist pairs of assertions $(I_j^{\mathcal{D}}, T_j^{\mathcal{D}})$ for each node j in V' satisfying the conditions (a) through (f) above. Then prove that each node can participate in one subtask at a time (cf. conditions (g) and (h) above). Thereafter prove that the nodes participate in the subtasks in some fixed order (cf. condition (i) above). Finally, prove interference freedom of specifications (cf. condition (j) above). Then conclude that the whole task is solved by an algorithm consisting of actions of all those algorithms that solve the subtasks.

4 Conclusion

We have presented a design principle which allows formal derivation of complex network algorithms by means of sequentially phased reasoning. This principle is applicable to a large class of algorithms (as e.g., as in [GHS83, Hu83, MS79, Se82, Se83, ZS80]) and allows structuring of their design according to logical (sub)tasks. We have decided to keep the formulation of the principle as simple as possibly. As a consequence, it is not immediately applicable for derivation of the PIF-protocol

[Se83] when the network does not constitute a tree. The reason is that a message associated with the first subtask can be received by a node, when that node is participating in the second subtask (cf. section 1). In this case an adjustment of the design principle would be required. (Verification conditions (h) and (i) must be adjusted.) In essence, it has to be required that if a node is participating in the second subtask or has completed its participation in that subtask, then the arrival of a message associated with the first subtask does not affect the respective assertions attached to that node.

As structured verification and design of complex algorithms yields more insight in their correctness, we envisage that new language constructs will be designed in order to obtain better structured programs. In particular, we believe that a better structuring of programs can be achieved by means of a construct for describing subtasks and another one for building programs solving some task from programs which solve the subtasks.

In the future we will investigate how our principle can be extended for applications to network algorithms when edges and nodes can fail.

Acknowledgement: We thank R. Koymans and R. Gerth for valuable discussions. We also thank N. van Diepen and H. Partsch for their remarks concerning the presentation of our results.

References

[AFR80] Apt K.R., Francez N., and de Roever W.P., A proof system for communicating sequential processes, ACM TOPLAS, 2-3 (1980).

[B26] Boruvka O., O jistém problému minimálním, Práca Moravské Přírodovědecké Společnosti (1926) (in Czech.).

[BS89] Back R.J.R. and Sere K., Stepwise refinement of action systems, Proc. of the international conference of mathematics and program construction (1989).

[CG88] Chou C.T. and Gafni E., Understanding and verifying distributed algorithms using stratified decomposition, Proc. of the ACM Symp. on Principles of Distr. Comp. (1988).

[CL85] Chandy K.M and Lamport L., Distributed snapshots: determining global states of distributed systems, ACM Trans. on Comp. Syst. 3-1 (1985).

[CM88] Chandy K.M. and Misra J., Parallel program design: a foundation, Addison-Wesley Publishing Company, Inc. (1988).

[DS80] Dijkstra E.W. and Scholten C.S., Termination detecting for diffusing computations, Letters 1-4 (1980).

[Ev79] Even S., Graph algorithms, Computer Science Press, Inc.(USA), (1979).

[EF82] Elrad T. and Francez N., Decomposition of distributed programs into communication closed layers, Science of Computer programming, 2 (1982).

[F80]   Francez N., Distributed termination, ACM-TOPLAS, 2-1 (1980).

[FF89]   Fix L. and Francez N., Semantics-driven decompositions for the verification of distributed pro-
           grams, manuscript (1989).

[GHS83]   Gallager R.T., Humblet P.A., and Spira P.M., A distributed algorithm for minimum-weight
           spanning trees, ACM TOPLAS, 5-1 (1983).

[GS86]   Gerth R.T. and Shrira L., On proving closedness of distributed layers, LNCS-241 (1986).

[Hu83]   Humblet P.A., A distributed algorithm for minimum-weight directed spanning trees, IEEE
           Trans. on Comm., 31-6 (1983).

[KP87]   Katz S. and Peled D., Interleaving set temporal logic, Proc. of the ACM Symp. on Principles of
           Distr. Comp. (1987).

[KP88]   Katz S. and Peled D., An efficient verification method for parallel and distributed programs,
           Proc. of the REX-workshop (1988).

[L85]   Lamport L., Paradigms for distributed programs: computing global states. LNCS-190 (1985).

[MP83]   Manna Z. and Pnueli A., Verification of concurrent programs: A temporal proof system, Foun-
           dations of computer science IV, part 2, MC-tracts 159 (1983).

[MS79]   Merlin P.M. and Segall A., A failsafe distributed routing protocol, IEEE Trans. on Comm., 27-9
           (1979).

[Pa88]   Pandya P.K., Compositional verification of distributed programs, Ph.D. thesis, Tata institute of
           fundamental research, Bombay, India (1988).

[Se82]   Segall A., Decentralized maximum-flow algorithms, Networks 12 (1982).

[Se83]   Segall A., Distributed network protocols, IEEE Trans. on Inf. Theory. IT29-1 (1983).

[SR87a]   Stomp F.A. and de Roever W.P., A correctness proof of a distributed minimum-weight spanning
           tree algorithm (extended abstract), Proc. of the 7th ICDCS (1987).

[SR87b]   Stomp F.A. and de Roever W.P., A fully worked out correctness proof of Gallager, Humblet, and
           Spira's minimum-weight spanning tree algorithm, Internal Report 87-4, University of Nijmegen
           (1987).

[SR88]   Stomp F.A. and de Roever W.P., A formalization of sequentially phased intuition in network
           protocols, Internal Report 88-15, University of Nijmegen (1988).

[SR89]   Stomp F.A. and de Roever W.P., Designing distributed algorithms by means of sequentially
           phased reasoning (full paper), Internal Report 89-8, University of Nijmegen (1989).

[SS84]   Schlichting R.D. and Schneider F.B., Using message passing for distributed programming, Proof
           rules and disciplines, ACM TOPLAS 6-3 (1984).

[WLL88]   Welch J.L., Lamport L., and Lynch N.A., A lattice-structured proof of a minimum spanning
           tree algorithm, Proc. of the ACM Symp. on Principles of Distr. Comp. (1988).

[ZS80]   Zerbib F.B.M. and Segall A., A distributed shortest path protocol, Internal Report EE-395,
           Technion-Israel Institute of Technology, Haifa, Israel (1980).

Possibility and Impossibility Results in a Shared Memory Environment

Gadi Taubenfeld*
Computer Science Department
Yale University
New Haven, CT 06520

Shlomo Moran†
Computer Science Department
Technion, Haifa 32000
Israel

Abstract. We focus on unreliable asynchronous shared memory model which support only atomic read and write operations. For such a model we provide a necessary condition for the solvability of problems in the precence of multiple undetectable crash failures. Also, by using game-theoretical notions, a necessary and sufficient condition is provided, for the solvability of problems in the precence of multiple undetectable initial failures

Our results imply that many problems such as consensus, choosing a leader, ranking, matching and sorting are unsolvable in the presence of a single crash failure, and that variants of these problems are solvable in the presence of $t - 1$ crash failures but not in the presence of t crash failures.

We show that a shared memory model simulate various message passing models, and hence our impossibility results hold also for those message passing models. Our results extend and generalize known impossibility results for various asynchronous models.

1   Introduction

This paper investigates the possibility and impossibility of solving certain problems in an unreliable asynchronous shared memory system which supports only atomic read and write operations. The faulty behaviours we consider are undetectable initial failures and undetectable crash failures. Initial failures are a very weak type of failures where it is assumed that processes may fail only prior to the execution and that no event can happen on a process after it fails. Initial failures are a special case of crash (fail stop) failures in which a process may become faulty at any time during an execution.

There has been extensive investigation about the nature of asynchronous message passing systems where undetectable crash failures may occur. The work in [FLP] proves the nonexistence of a (nontrivial) consensus protocols that can tolerate a single crash failure, for a completely asynchronous message passing system. Various extensions of this fundamental result, also for a single crash failure, prove the impossibility of other problems in the same model [MW, Ta1, BMZ]. Other works study the possibility of

---

*Supported in part by the National Science Foundation under grant CCR-8405478, by the Hebrew Technical Institute scholarship, and by the Guttwirth Fellowship.

†Supported in part by Technion V.P.R. Funds - Wellner Research Fund, and by the Foundation for Research in Electronics, Computers and Communications, administrated by the Israel Academy of Sciences and Humanities.

solving variety of problems in asynchronous systems with numerous crash failures, and in several message passing models [ABDKPR,BW,DDS,DLS,TKM].

In [DDS], Dolev, Dwork and Stockmeyer studied the consensus problem in partially synchronous message passing models. They showed that by changing the broadcast primitives it is possible to solve the consensus problem in the presence of $t-1$ crash failures but not in the presence of t crash failures. They also identify five critical parameters that may effect the possibility of achieving consensus. By varying these parameters they defined 32 models and found the maximum resiliency for each one of them.

In [LA] an impossibility result for the binary consensus problem is shown for an asynchronous shared memory system, such as we consider here, where a single processes may (crash) fail. In [Abr,CIL,Her] a weaker result than that of [LA] proves the impossibility of the consensus problem in the presence of $n-1$ crash failures. This last impossibility result is used in [Her] to derive a hierarchy of atomic operations (objects) such that no operation at one level has a wait-free (i.e., (n-1)-resilient) implementation using only operation from lower levels. Systems that support only atomic read and write operations are shown to be at the bottom of that hierarchy. In particular, it is impossible to implement using atomic read and write operations a common data types such as sets, queues, stacks, priority queues, lists and most synchronization primitives.

Initial failures may occur in situations such as recovery from a breakdown of a network. Necessary and sufficient conditions are provided in [TKM2], for solving problems in asynchronous message passing systems where up to half of the processes may fail prior to the execution, with and without a termination requirement. Protocols that solve the consensus, the leader election and the spanning tree problems in a message passing model, which can tolerate initial failures of up to half of the processes were designed in [FLP,BKWZ]. As for shared memory model, a leader election protocol that can tolerate up to $n-1$ initial failure is presented in [Ta2]. Recently, a complete combinatorial characterizations, for the solvability of problems in asynchronous shared memory and message passing models where crash failures may occur using *random protocols* was given in [ChM].

We concentrate, in this paper, on an asynchronous shared memory model and proved possibility and impossibility results within that model. For every $t < n$, where n is the number of processes, we define a class of problems that are unsolvable in such a system in the presence of t crash failures. This implies a (necessary) condition for solving a problem in such an unreliable system. Also, we provide a necessary and sufficient conditions for solving problems in an asynchronous shared memory model where only undetectable initial failures may occur. Similar condition for initial failures in a message passing model appears in [TKM2]. However, unlike in [TKM2] we do not need to assume that only up to half of the processes may fail. Our results extend and generalize previously known impossibility results for asynchronous systems.

It appears that the necessary and sufficient condition which we give here for initial failures assuming only deterministic protocols, is the same as the complete characterization which is given in [ChM] for crash failures assuming randomize protocols. An interesting result that follows from the similarities between these characterizations is that in a shared memory model which support only atomic read and write operations, a problem can be solved by a *deterministic* protocol that can tolerate up to t *initial* failures (without assuming termination) if and only if the problem can be solved by a *randomize* protocol that can tolerate up to t *crash* failures. Similar result holds also for message passing models.

We show that many problems such as consensus, choosing a leader, ranking, matching and sorting are unsolvable (in a nontrivial way) in the presence of a single crash failure, and that, for any t, there are variants of these problems that are solvable in the presence of $t - 1$ crash failures but not in the presence of t crash failures. An example is the consensus problem with the assumption that for each input vector, $| \#1 - \#0 | \geq t$. (i.e., the absolute difference between the number of ones and the number of zeros is at least t.) Following is a simple protocol that solves this problem assuming up to $t - 1$ crash failures. Each process sends its input value to everybody, waits until it gets $n - t + 1$ inputs, and decide 1 (0) iff their sum is more (less) then $(n - t + 1)/2$. The fact that $| \#1 - \#0 | \geq t$ guarantees that all the processes will decide the same.

We show that a shared memory model can simulate several of the message passing models which are considered in [DDS], and hence all our impossibility results hold also for those message passing models. In particular, the impossibility results for crash failures presented in this paper implies similar results, for an asynchronous message passing model, which appear in [TKM1].

To prove our result, for the crash failures case, we first identify a class of *protocols* that cannot tolerate the (crash) failure of t processes, when operating in an asynchronous shared memory system. Then, we identify those *problems* which force every protocol which solves them to belong to the above class of protocols. Hence, these problems can not be solved in an asynchronous system where t processes may fail.

The class of protocols for which we prove the impossibility result (for crash failures) is characterized by two requirements on the possible input and decision (output) values. For the input, it is required that (for each protocol) there exists a group of at least $n - t$ processes and there exist input values such that after all the $n - t$ processes in the group read these input values, the eventual decision value of at least one of them is still not uniquely determined. The requirement for the decision values is that the decision value of any (single) process, say p_i, is uniquely determined by the input values of all the processes together with the decision values of all the processes except p_i.

In order to prove the above result for protocols, we use an axiomatic approach for proving properties of protocols (and problems) which is due to Chandy and Misra [CM1,CM2]. The idea is to capture the main features of the model and the features of the class of protocols for which one wants to prove the result by a set of axioms, and to show that the result follows from the axioms. We will present five axioms capturing the nature of asynchronous shared memory systems which support only atomic read and write operations, a single axiom expressing the fact that at most t processes may crash fail, and two axioms defining the class of protocols for which we want to prove the impossibility result (for crash failures). We then show that no protocol in the class can tolerate t faulty processes, by showing that the set of the eight axioms is inconsistent.

The rest of the paper is organized as follows. In Section 2 the notions of a problem and a protocol are defined. In Section 3 the properties of asynchronous shared memory systems are stated. In Section 4 the notions of dependency and robustness are introduced. In Section 5, a special class of protocols is identified and it is proved that all its members cannot tolerate t crash failures. We also show that any non-trivial fault-tolerant protocol has to have some special property. In Section 6, we identify the class of problems that can not be solved in the presence of t crash failures. In Section 7, we give a complete characterization for the solvability of problems in the presence of initial failures. In section 8, we show that a shared memory model can simulate various message passing models. A full version of this paper (which includes all the proofs) appeared as [TM].

2 Definitions and Basic Notations

Let I and D be sets of input values and decision (output) values, respectively. Let n be the number of processes, and let $\bar{I}$ and $\bar{D}$ be subsets of I^n and D^n, respectively. A problem T is a mapping $T : \bar{I} \rightarrow 2^{\bar{D}} - \{\emptyset\}$ which maps each n-tuple in $\bar{I}$ to subsets of n-tuples in $\bar{D}$. We call the vectors $\vec{a} = (a_1, ..., a_n)$ where $\vec{a} \in \bar{I}$, and $\vec{d} = (d_1, ..., d_n)$ where $\vec{d} \in \bar{D}$, the input vector and decision vector respectively, and say that a_i (resp. d_i) is the input (resp. decision) value of process p_i.

Following are some examples of problems, which we will also refer to later in the paper (the input vectors for all problems are from I^n for an arbitrary set I): (1) The *permutation* problem, where each process $p_i (i = 1..n)$ decides on a value v_i from D, $D \equiv 1, ..., n$, and $i \neq j$ implies $v_i \neq v_j$; (2) The transaction commitment problem, where $I = D = \{0, 1\}$, and all processes are to decide on "1" if the input of each process is "1", otherwise all processes are to decide on "0"; (3) The *consensus* problem, where all processes are to decide on the same value from an arbitrary set D; (4) The (leader) *election* problem, where exactly one process is to decide on a distinguished value from an arbitrary set D; and (5) The *sorting* problem, where all processes have input values and each process p_i decides on a value identical to the ith smallest input value.

A *protocol* $P \equiv (C, N, R)$ consists of a nonempty set C of *computations*, a set of process id's (abbv. processes) $N \equiv \{p_1, ..., p_n\}$, and a (possibly infinite) set R of registers. A computation is a *finite* sequence of events. There are four types of events. A *read* event, denoted $([read, r, v], p_i)$, represents reading a value v from register r by process p_i. A *write* event, denoted $([write, r, v], p_i)$, represents writing a value v into register r by process p_i. An *input* event, denoted $([input, a], p_i)$, represents reading an input value a by process p_i. A *decide* event, denoted $([decide, d], p_i)$, represents deciding on a value d by process p_i. We use the notation (e, p_i) to denote an arbitrary event, which may be an instance of any of the above types of events. For an event (e, p_i) we say that it occurred *on* process p_i. An event is *in* a computation iff it is one of the events in the sequence which comprises the computation.

The value of a register r at a computation x is the last value that was written into that register. We use $\perp$ to denote the undefined value. A value of a register is undefined as long as no value was written into that register. We define, using pascal-like notations, the function *value* which receives as parameters a computation and a register and returns the value of that register in the computation. Let $\langle x; y \rangle$ be the sequence obtained by concatenating x and y, and let *null* denotes the empty computation.

function *value* $(r:\text{register}, x: \text{computation})$: value;
begin
    if $x = null$ **then** $value := \perp$
    else if $x = \langle x'; (e, p_i) \rangle$ /* for some computation x' and event (e, p_i)
        then if $(e, p_i) = ([write, r, v], p_i)$ **then** $value := v$ /* for some write event
           else $value := value(r, x')$
end.

In the rest of this paper Q denotes a set of processes where $Q \subseteq N$. The symbols x, y, z denote computations. An *extension* of a computation x is a computation of which x is a prefix. For an extension y of x, $(y - x)$ denotes the suffix of y obtained by removing x from y. For any x and p_i, let x_i be the subsequence of x containing all events in x which are on p_i. Computation y *includes* computation x iff x_i is a prefix of y_i for all p_i.

Definition: Computations x and y are *equivalent w.r.t.* p_i, denoted by $x \overset{i}{\sim} y$, iff $x_i = y_i$.

Note that the relation $\overset{i}{\sim}$ is an equivalence relation. For a computation x and process p_i, we define the extensions of x which only have events on p_i.

Definition: $Extensions(x, i) \equiv \{ y \mid y$ is an extension of x and $x \overset{j}{\sim} y$ for all $j \neq i \}$.

Process p_i *reads* input a in a computation x iff the input event $([input, a], p_i)$ is in x. Process p_i *decides* on d in a computation x iff the decision event $([decide, d], p_i)$ is in x. A computation x is *i-input* iff for some value a, p_i reads input a in x. We assume that a process may read and decide only once.

A *protocol* $P \equiv (C, N, R)$ *solves* a problem $T : \bar{I} \rightarrow 2^{\bar{D}} - \{\emptyset\}$ iff (1) For every input vector $\vec{a} \in \bar{I}$, and for every decision vector $\vec{d} \in T(\vec{d})$, there exists a computation $z \in C$ such that in z processes $p_1, ..., p_n$ read input values $a_1, ..., a_n$ and decide on $d_1, ..., d_n$; (2) For every computation $z \in C$ and $\vec{a} \in \bar{I}$ if in z processes $p_1, ..., p_n$ read input values $a_1, ..., a_n$ and decide on $d_1, ..., d_n$, then $\vec{d} \in T(\vec{a})$; and (3) In any "sufficiently long" computation on input in $\bar{I}$ all processes decide (this last requirement is to be defined precisely later). It is also possible to define solvability so that (1) is replaced by the requirement that for each input vector $\vec{a} \in \bar{I}$, there exists a computation with $\vec{a}$ as input. In such a case we will say that a protocol P *minimally solves* a problem T. It will be shown in section 6 that it is possible to prove the impossibility result for the former definition of solvability, and then to derive from it a result for the latter one.

We define when a set of input events is *consistent*. Intuitively, this is the case when all the input events in the set can occur in the same computation. Let P be a protocol that solves $T : \bar{I} \rightarrow 2^{\bar{D}} - \{\emptyset\}$. For any input vector $\vec{a} \in \bar{I}$, the set $\{([input, a_1], p_1) , ..., ([input, a_n], p_n)\}$ is a consistent set of input events (w.r.t T); and any subset of a consistent set of input events is also consistent. For simplicity we consider here only computations whose set of input events is consistent. Fix a protocol, $P \equiv (C, N, R)$, that solves a problem $T : \bar{I} \rightarrow 2^{\bar{D}} - \{\emptyset\}$.

3 Shared Memory Model

In this section we characterize an asynchronous shared memory model which supports atomic read and write operations.

Definition: An *asynchronous read-write protocol* (abbv. asynchronous protocol) is a protocol that satisfies the following properties,

P1: Every prefix of a computation is a computation.

P2: Let $\langle x; (e, p_i) \rangle$ be a computation where (e, p_i) is either a write event or a decision event, and let y be a computation such that $x \overset{i}{\sim} y$, then $\langle y; (e, p_i) \rangle$ is a computation.

P3: For any computation x, process p_i and input value a, if the set of all input events in x together with $([input, a], p_i)$ is consistent then exists y in $Extensions(x, i)$, such that $([input, a], p_i)$ appears in y.

P4: For computations x and y and process p_i, if $\langle x; ([read, r, v], p_i) \rangle$ is a computation, and $x \stackrel{i}{\sim} y$ then $\langle y; ([read, r, value(r, y)], p_i) \rangle$ is a computation.

P5: For a computation x and an event $([read, r, v], p_i)$, the sequence $\langle x; ([read, r, v], p_i) \rangle$ is a computation only if $v = value(r, x)$.

Property $P2$ means that if some write event or decision event can happen at a process p_i at some point in a computation, then this event can happen at a later point, provided that p_i has taken no steps between the two points. Property $P3$ means that a process which has not yet read an input value may read any of the input values not conflicting with those already read by other processes. Property $P4$ means that if a process is "ready to read" a value from some register then an event on some other process cannot prevent this process from reading some value from that register (although it may prevent this process from reading a specific value which it could read previously). Property $P5$ means that it is possible to read only the last value that is written into a register.

We will consider in this paper only deterministic protocols which mean that at any point in a computation a process may perform at most one non-input action; in case the current action of a process is reading an input then the process may read one of several possible input values. I.e., if $\langle x; (e, p_i) \rangle$ and $\langle x; (e', p_i) \rangle$ are computations and both (e, p_i) and (e', p_i) are not input events then $(e, p_i) \equiv (e', p_i)$. This assumption does not restrict the generality of the results which will hold also for non-deterministic protocols.

We say that process p_i is *enable* at computation x iff there exists an event (e, p_i) such that $\langle x; (e, p_i) \rangle$ is a computation. It follows from the above five properties that an enable process cannot become not enable as a result of an event on some other process.

4 Classes of Protocols

In this section we identify two classes of protocols, called *dependent(t)* protocols, and *robust(t)* protocols. In a dependent(t) protocol every process tries to decide on a certain value, and additional conditions hold, to be defined below. A decision is irreversible, that is, once a process decides on a value, the decision value cannot be changed. The important features of dependent(t) protocols are the requirements on the possible input and decision (output) values. For the input, it is required that there exists a group of at least $n - t$ processes and there exist input values such that after all the $n - t$ processes read these input values, the eventual decision value of at least one of them is still not uniquely determined. The requirement for the decision values is that the decision value of any (single) process p_i is uniquely determined by the input values of all the processes together with the decision values of all the processes except p_i.

Typical examples of dependent(t) protocols are the protocols that solve any of the problems described in the Introduction, and Section 2, where various assumptions, depending on the value of t, are made about the set of input vectors for each of these problems. We prove in the next section that for every $1 \leq t \leq n$, no protocol in the class of dependent(t) protocols can tolerate t process failures. The following definition generalizes the notion of *valency* of a computation from [FLP]. Let d be a possible decision value and let U, W be sets of values.

Definition: A computation x is (i, W)-*valent* iff (1) for every $d \in W$, there is an extension of x in which p_i decides on d, and (2) for every $d \notin W$, there is no extension of x in which p_i decides on d.

A computation is i-*univalent* iff it is $(i, \{d\})$-*valent* for some (single) value d. It is i-*multivalent* otherwise. Note that an $(i, \emptyset)$-*valent* computation is i-*multivalent*, however it will follow from the sequel that no computation in a protocol studied here is $(i, \emptyset)$-*valent*.

Definition: Let y and y' be (i, W)-*valent* and (i, W')-*valent*, respectively. Then y and y' are i-*compatible* iff $W \cap W' \neq \emptyset$. They are *compatible* iff they are i-*compatible* for all $i = 1..n$.

Using the above notions we can now characterize dependent(t) protocols formally.

Definition: A *dependent(t) protocol* is a protocol that satisfies the requirements:

D1(t): There exists a computation x, set of processes Q and process $p_i \in Q$, such that $|Q| \geq n - t$, for every $p_j \in Q$ x is j-input, and x is i-multivalent. (non-triviality.)

D2: For any two computations x and y which are both i-*univalent*, if each process read the same input value in both x and y, and if each processes $p_j \neq p_i$ decide on the same value in both x and y then x and y are i-*compatible*. (dependency.)

Notice that $D1(t)$ implies $D1(t + 1)$. It is not difficult to see why any protocol that solves the variant of the consensus problem, with the assumption that for each input vector $|\#1 - \#0| \geq t$, must satisfy $D1(t)$. The proof of that fact is similar to the proof of Lemma 2 in [FLP]. Requirement $D2$ means that an external observer who knows all the input values and all decision values except one can always determine the missing decision value. All protocols which solve the problems mentioned in the Introduction and in Section 2 satisfy $D2$.

Next we identify the class of protocols which can tolerate t crash failures ($0 \leq t \leq n$). A crash failure of a process means that no subsequent event can happen on this process. Informally, a protocol is robust(t) if, in spite of a failure of any group of up to t processes at any point in the computation, each of the remaining processes eventually decides on some value.

In order to define robust(t) protocols formally, we need the concept of a *Q-fair sequence*. Let Q be a set of processes, a *Q-fair sequence* w.r.t. a given protocol is a (possibly infinite) sequence of events, where: (1) Each finite prefix of the sequence is a computation; (2) For an *enable* process $p_i \in Q$ at some prefix x, there exists another prefix y that extends x such that there is an event (e, p_i) in $(y - x)$.

It follows from $P5$ and requirement (1) that the sequence $\langle x; ([read, r, v], p_k) \rangle$ is a prefix of a Q-fair sequence only if $v = value(r, x)$. A Q-fair sequence captures the intuition of an execution where all enable processes which belong to Q can proceed. Notice that a Q-fair sequence may be infinite and in such a case it is not a computation. It follows from $P1 - P5$ that, in asynchronous protocols, for every set of processes Q, any computation is a prefix of a Q-fair sequence.

Definition: A *robust(t) protocol* $(0 \leq t \leq n)$ is a protocol that satisfies:

R(t): For every set Q of processes where $|Q| \geq n - t$, every *Q-fair sequence* has a finite prefix in which any $p_i \in Q$ decides on some value.

Requirement $R(0)$ means that in any "long enough" execution of a protocol, if no process fails then each process (eventually) decides on a value. In fact, $R(0)$ formally expresses requirement (3) from the definition of *solves* given in Section 2. From $R(0)$ and from the fact that every computation is a prefix of some N-fair sequence it follows that (in asynchronous robust(0) protocols) no computation is $(i, \emptyset)$-*valent*.

Lemma 1: In any asynchronous robust(1) protocol, for any two computations x and y and for any process p_i, if $x \overset{j}{\sim} y$ for any $j \neq i$, and $value(r, x) = value(r, y)$ for any $r \in R$, then x and y are *j-compatible* for any $j \neq i$.

Proof: It follows from $P1 - P5$ that the computation x is a prefix of some $(N - \{p_i\})$-fair sequence, and there are no events on p_i in that sequence after x. Apply requirement $R(1)$ to the above sequence to conclude that there exists an extension z of x such that $x \overset{i}{\sim} z$ and any $p_i \neq p_j$ has decided in z. From $P1 - P4$, it follows that $w \equiv \langle y; (z - x) \rangle$ is also a computation. Clearly, for any $i \neq j$, z and w are *j-compatible*. Hence also, for any $i \neq j$, x and y are *j-compatible*. $\quad\square$

We postpone the formal definition of initial failures to Section 7. In the next two sections we consider only crash failures.

5 Impossibility Results for Protocols

In this section we investigate a class which is the intersection of all the previous classes. This class is defined by the entire eight axioms and is called the class of RObust(t) Asynchronous Dependent(t) Protocols (abbv. ROAD(t) P's), where $1 \leq t \leq n$. We prove in this section that the class of ROAD(t) P's is empty.

Lemma 2: In any ROAD(t) P, for any two computations x and y and any process p_i, if, (1) p_i did not read different input values in x and y, (2) $x \overset{j}{\sim} y$ for any $j \neq i$, and (3) $value(r, x) = value(r, y)$ for any $r \in R$, then x and y are *compatible*.

Proof: It follows from $P1 - P5$ that the computation x is a prefix of some $(N - \{p_i\})$-fair sequence, and there are no events on p_i in that sequence after x. Apply requirement $R(1)$ to the above sequence to conclude that there exists an extension z' of x such that $x \overset{i}{\sim} z'$ and for any $p_i \neq p_j$, p_j has decided in z'. By $P3$ there is an extension z of z' in which all processes except maybe p_i read their input and $z \overset{i}{\sim} z'$. From $P1 - P4$, it follows that $w \equiv< y; (z - x) >$ is also a computation. By $P1 - P5$ and $R(0)$, there are two *i-univalent* extensions $\hat{z}$ and $\hat{w}$ of z and w respectively, in which p_i read the same input value. From $D2$, $\hat{z}$ and $\hat{w}$ are *compatible*, hence also x and y are *compatible*. $\quad\square$

THEOREM 1: In any ROAD(t) P, for any process p_i and any *j-multivalent* computation x, if x is *i-input* and p_i is enable at x then there exists a *j-multivalent* extension $\hat{x}$ of x such that $\neg(x \overset{i}{\sim} \hat{x})$.

Proof: To prove the theorem we first assume to the contrary: for some process p_i and some *j-multivalent* computation x where x is *i-input* and p_i is enable at x, there is no *j-multivalent* extension $\hat{x}$ of x such that $\neg(x \overset{i}{\sim} \hat{x})$. Then we show that this leads to a contradiction. It follows from the assumption that for any extension m of x such that p_i is enable at m, the unique extension of m by a single event on p_i is *j-univalent*. Let us denote that *j-univalent* extension of m by $\Phi(m)$.

Since x is *j-multivalent*, there exists an extension z of x ($z \neq x$) such that z and $\Phi(x)$ are not *j-compatible*. Let z' be the longest prefix of z such that $x \overset{i}{\sim} z'$. From the assumption it follows that $\Phi(x)$ and $\Phi(z')$ are not *j-compatible*. Consider the extensions of x which are also prefixes of z'. Since $\Phi(x)$ and $\Phi(z')$ are not *j-compatible*, there must exist extensions y and y' (of x) such that $\Phi(y')$ and $\Phi(y)$ are not *j-compatible*, and y is a one event extension of y'. Therefore, $y = < y'; (e, p_h) >$ for some event (e, p_h) where $p_i \neq p_h$. For later reference we denote $w \equiv < \Phi(y'); (e, p_h) >$. We do not claim at this point that w is a computation. There are four possible cases.

Case 1: (e, p_h) is not a write event. By $P2$ and $P4$, $(\Phi(y') - y') = (\Phi(y) - y)$ and hence for any $p_k \neq p_h$, $\Phi(y') \overset{k}{\sim} \Phi(y)$. Also, the values of all registers are the same in both $\Phi(y)$ and $\Phi(y')$, and obviously p_h does not read different input values in $\Phi(y')$ and $\Phi(y)$. By Lemma 2, $\Phi(y')$ and $\Phi(y)$ should be *compatible*. Hence, we reach a contradiction. At this point we know that (e, p_h) is a write event and (from $P2$) that w is a computation.

Case 2: $(\Phi(y') - y')$ is not a write event. For every $p_k \neq p_i$, $w \overset{k}{\sim} \Phi(y)$. Also, the values of all registers are the same in both w and $\Phi(y)$. Since y is *i-input* obviously p_i reads the same input values in w and $\Phi(y)$. By Lemma 2, w and $\Phi(y)$ are *compatible*. Since, w is an extension of $\Phi(y')$ then $\Phi(y')$ and $\Phi(y)$ should be *compatible*. Hence again we reach a contradiction.

Now we know that for some registers r_1 and r_2, and values v_1 and v_2, $(\Phi(y') - y') = ([write, r_1, v_1], p_i)$, and $(y - y') = ([write, r_2, v_2], p_h)$.

Case 3: $r_1 \neq r_2$. Since the two write events on p_i and p_h are independent, the values of all registers are the same in w and $\Phi(y)$. Also, for every process p_k, $w \overset{k}{\sim} \Phi(y)$. This leads to a contradiction as in the second case.

Case 4: $r_1 = r_2$. Clearly, $value(\Phi(y'), r_1) = value(\Phi(y'), r_2) = value(\Phi(y), r_1) = value(\Phi(y), r_2) = v_1$. Hence, the values of all registers are the same in $\Phi(y')$ and $\Phi(y)$. Also, for any $p_k \neq p_h$, $\Phi(y') \overset{k}{\sim} \Phi(y)$. By Lemma 2, $\Phi(y')$ and $\Phi(y)$ are *compatible*. Hence, again we reach a contradiction. □

THEOREM 2: There is no ROAD(t) P.

Proof: By $D1(t)$, there exists a computation x, process p_i and set of processes Q, such that $|Q| \geq n - t$, for every $p_j \in Q$ x is *j-input*, $p_i \in Q$, and x is *i-multivalent*. Using Theorem 1, we can construct inductively starting from the computation x a Q-fair sequence such that all the finite prefixes of that sequence are *i-multivalent*. This contradicts requirement $R(t)$. □

Consider the eight requirements mentioned so far. Apart from requirement $D2$, all the requirements capture very natural concepts: $P1 - P5$ and $R(t)$ express the well known notions of asynchronous and robust protocols respectively, while $D1(t)$ requires that a given solution is not trivial. This motivates the question of what can be said about protocols that satisfy all the above requirements expect $D2$. For later reference we call these protocols Decision(t) Asynchronous Robust(t) Protocols (abbv. DEAR(t)

P's). A simple example for a DEAR($n-1$) protocol, is a protocol where there is only one shared register, each processes first writes its input value into the shared register, then it reads the value of the shared register and decide on that value. It follows from the impossibility result of Theorem 2 that DEAR(t) P's cannot satisfy requirement $D2$. Also, since $D2$ is only used in the proof of Lemma 2, DEAR(t) P's have to satisfy the negation of Lemma 2. These observations leads to the following theorem.

THEOREM 3: In any DEAR(t) P, there exist two computations x and y, and there exists process p_i, such that: (1) p_i did not read different input values in x and y, (2) $x \overset{j}{\sim} y$ for any $j \neq i$, (3) $value(r, x) = value(r, y)$ for any $r \in R$, and yet x and y are not i-compatible.

Proof: Immediate from Lemma 1 and the negation of Lemma 2. $\quad\square$

Theorem 3 gives the intuition for the nonexistence result for ROAD(t) P's as stated in Theorem 2. This result follows from a conflict between two requirements. One is requirement $D2$ which means that at any time a process may be forced by the group of all other processes to a situation where it has only one possible decision left. As opposed to that requirement there is the necessary condition given in Theorem 3 which means that there exist two computations such that the sets of values some process may still decide on in each one of this computations are disjoint and those computation are indistinguishable from the point of view of the group of all other processes.

6 Impossibility Results for Problems

In this section we identify the problems that cannot be solved in an unreliable asynchronous shared memory environment which support only atomic read and write operations. We do this by identifying those problems which are solved only by ROAD(t) protocols. Hence, the impossibility of solving these problems will follow from Theorem 2. Results for completely asynchronous message passing systems which are similar to those presented in the sequel appear also in [TKM1].

We say that a problem can be solved in an environment where t processes may fail, if there exists a robust(t) protocol that solves it. Since we assume an asynchronous shared variable environment where t processes may fail, any protocol that solves a problem should satisfy properties $P1 - P5$, and the requirement $R(t)$. Thus, we are now left with the obligation of identifying those problems which force any protocol that solves them also to satisfy requirements $D1(t)$ and $D2$. Let Q denote a set of processes, and $\vec{v}$ and $\vec{v'}$ be vectors. We say that $\vec{v}$ and $\vec{v'}$ are Q-equivalent, if they agree on all the values which correspond to the indices (of the processes) in Q. A set of vectors H is Q-equivalent if any two vectors which belong to H are Q-equivalent. Also, we define: $T(H) \equiv \bigcup_{\vec{a} \in H} T(\vec{a})$.

Definition: A problem $T : \bar{I} \to 2^D - \{\emptyset\}$ is a *dependent(t) problem* iff it satisfies:

T1(t): There exists a set of processes Q where $|Q| \geq n-t$, and there exists a Q-equivalent set $H \subseteq \bar{I}$ such that $T(H)$ is not a Q-equivalent set.

T2: For every $\vec{a} \in \bar{I}$, every set of processes Q where $|Q| = n - 1$, and every two different decision vectors $\vec{d}$ and $\vec{d'}$, if both $\vec{d}$ and $\vec{d'}$ belong to $T(\vec{a})$ then they are not Q-equivalent.

Requirement $T1(t)$ means that $n - t$ input values (in an input vector) do not determine the corresponding $n - t$ decision values (in the decision vectors). Any problem that does not satisfy requirement $T1(t)$ can easily be solved in a completely asynchronous environment where t processes may fail. (Each process sends its input value to all other processes, then it waits until it receives $n-t$ values; assuming it does not satisfies $T1(t)$, it has now enough information to decide.) Note that $T1(t)$ implies $T1(t+1)$. Requirement $T2$ means that a single input vector cannot be mapped into two decision vectors that differ only by a single value.

THEOREM 4: A dependent(t) problem cannot be solved in an asynchronous shared memory system which support only atomic read and write operations and where t failures may occur.

A problem $T : \bar{I} \to 2^{\bar{D}} - \{\emptyset\}$ *includes* a problem $T : \bar{I}' \to 2^{\bar{D}'} - \{\emptyset\}$ iff $\bar{I}' = \bar{I}$, and for every $\vec{a'} \in \bar{I}'$: $T'(\vec{a'}) \subseteq T(\vec{a'})$. It is easy to see that a protocol P *minimally solves* a problem T iff there exists a problem T' which is included in T such that P *solves* T'. A problem $T' : \bar{I} \to 2^{\bar{D}'} - \{\emptyset\}$ is a *sub-problem* of a problem $T : \bar{I} \to 2^{\bar{D}} - \{\emptyset\}$ iff $\bar{I}' \subseteq \bar{I}$, and for every $\vec{a'} \in \bar{I}'$: $T(\vec{a'}) = T'(\vec{a'})$. It is easy to see that if a protocol P *solves* (*minimally solves*) a problem T then P *solves* (*minimally solves*) any sub-problem T' of T.

Nowhere up to now, have we assumed anything about the process ids, hence the results we proved hold even if all processes have distinct id's which are mutually known.

7 Initial Failures

In this section we give complete characterization of the problems that can be solved in an asynchronous shared memory environment where t processes may initially fail. We use the intuitive appeal of a game-theoretical characterization by reducing the question of solvability in the model under consideration to whether there is a winning strategy to a certain game which we describe below. Similar results for message passing model appears in [TKM2, Section 4]. However, unlike in [TKM2] we do not need to assume here that only up to half of the processes may fail.

Informally, a protocol can tolerate up to t initial failures if in spite of a failure of any group of up to t processes at the beginning of the computation, each of the remaining processes eventually decides on some value. We now characterize such protocols formally.

Definition: A protocol *can tolerate up to t initial failures* iff for every set Q of processes where $|Q| \geq n - t$, every Q-fair sequence which consists only of events on processes which belong to Q, has a finite prefix in which any $p_i \in Q$ has decided.

The class of protocols that can tolerate up to t initial failures strictly includes the class of protocols that can tolerate only up to $t - 1$ initial failures. To see that the inclusion is strict consider the *rotating(t)* problem, where each process p_i has to decide on a value from the set of input values of processes $p_{i(mod\ n)+1}, ..., p_{i+t-1(mod\ n)+1}$. We say that a problem can be solved in an environment where t initial failures may occur, if there exists a protocol which can tolerate up to t initial failures that solves the problem.

The game $G_1(T, t)$, corresponding to a problem $T : \bar{I} \to 2^{\bar{D}} - \{\emptyset\}$ and a number t ($0 < t \leq n-1$), is played by two players A (Adversary) and B, according to the following rules. Each play of the game begins with a move of player A and in the subsequent moves both players move alternately. The game is played on a board which has n empty circles drawn in a straight line. The circles are numbered from 1 to n. At the first move player A chooses $n - t$ input values from (the set of input values) I and "places" them on arbitrary $n - t$ empty circles. Then player B chooses $n - t$ decision values from (the set of decision values) D and uses them to *cover* all the $n - t$ input values placed by player A in the previous move. The other subsequent moves consist of player A choosing a *single* value from I, in each move, and placing it on an empty circle, and then player B choosing a single value from D and covering the previous value placed by player A. The play is completed when all the n circles are covered with decision values from D. We emphasize that at any time each player knows all the previous moves.

We denote by $a_i \in I$ and $d_i \in D$ the values players A and B placed on the i'th circle in the course of the play, respectively. For simplicity we assume that the final vector $(a_1,...,a_n)$ belongs to $\bar{I}$. Player B has *won* the play iff $\vec{d} \in T(\vec{a})$. Player B has a *winning strategy* in the game $G_1(T,t)$, denoted B *wins* $G_1(T,t)$, if it can always win each play. For simplicity we assume that the processes have distinct identities.

THEOREM 5: A problem T can be minimally solved in an asynchronous shared memory environment where t processes may initially fail $(0 < t \leq n - 1)$, iff player B wins $G_1(T,t)$.

Examples of problems that can be shown to be unsolvable using the above theorem (in the model under consideration), are transaction commitment, sorting and rotating(t). To show the impossibility for transaction commitment we demonstrate that B has no winning strategy. The adversary can choose at its first move $n - t$ "1" values; B then must also use $n - t$ "1" values since player A may later choose only "1" values. Then A can add the value "0" and B loses.

8   Simulations of Various Message Passing Models by a Shared Memory Model

In this section we examine all the 32 message passing models considered by Dolev, Dwork and Stockmeyer [DDS]. For each of 30 out of those models we will either prove that it can be simulated by an asynchronous shared memory model which support only atomic read and write operations (abbv. shared memory model), or will prove that it cannot. By saying that model A can *simulate* model A' we mean that whenever there is a protocol that solves some problem in the presence of t failures in model A', this protocol can be translated to a protocol which solves the same problem in the presence of t failures in model A. Evidently, all the impossibility results that we proved so far hold for any model that can be simulated by a shared memory model.

We informally review some of the results presented in [DDS]. The authors identify five critical parameters in message passing systems that may effect the possibility of achieving consensus. The digits 0 and 1 below refer to situations that are unfavorable or favorable for solving a problem, respectively. The notion of atomic step is used for an undivided sequence of events on some process. A process which executes an atomic step cannot fail before completing that step. The five parameters are:

Processes: (0) *Asynchronous* - Any finite numbers of events can take place between

mb \ pc	00	01	11	10	00	01	11	10
00	0 Yes	0 Yes	n No	0 ?	0 No	0 No	n No	0 No
01	0 Yes	0 Yes	n No	0 ?	1 No	n No	n No	1 No
01	n No	n No	n No	n No	N No	N No	N No	N No
01	0 No	0 No	n No	n No	0 No	0 No	n No	n No
			s=0				s=1	

Figure 1: Each entry in the table is defined by different setting of the five system parameters, processes (p), communication (c), messages (m), transmission mechanism (b), and receive/send (s).

any two consecutive events on a process. **(1)** *Synchronous* - There is a constant $\Psi \geq 1$ such that for any computation $\langle x; y \rangle$, if there are $\Psi + 1$ events on some process in y then there is an event on any nonfaulty process in y.

Communication: (0) *Asynchronous* - Any finite numbers of events can take place between the sending and receiving of a certain message. **(1)** *Synchronous* - There is a constant $\Delta \geq 1$ such that, every message that is sent is delivered within Δ attempt which are made to accept it.

Messages: (0) *Unordered* - Messages can be delivered out of order. **(1)** *Ordered* - If the sending m_1 is sent before the message m_2 (w.r.t. real time), and both message are sent to the same process, then m_1 must be received before m_2.

Transmission Mechanism: (0) *Point to point* - In an atomic step a process can send to at most one process. **(1)** *Broadcast* - In an atomic step a process can send to all processes.

Receive/Send: (0) *Separate* - In an atomic step a processes cannot both receive and send. **(1)** *Atomic* - In an atomic step a processes can received and send.

By varying the above five parameters the authors defined 32 models and found the maximum resiliency for each one of them. These results are summerized together with our results, in the table in Figure 1. In an entry of the table the letters $0, 1, n$ describe the maximum resilience for the relevant model as proved in [DDS]. (Recall that n is the number of processes, thus when n appears in an entry it means that it is possible to tolerate any number of faulty processes.) The words **"Yes"** and **"No"** state whether the particular model can be simulated by a shared variable model, while **"?"** declares that we do not know the answer.

Acknowledgements: We are grateful to Michael J. Fischer, Shmuel Katz and Lenore D. Zuck for helpful discussions concerning this work.

References

[Abr]   Abrahamson, K. On achieving consensus using shared memory, *ACM-PODC* 1988, 291-302.

[ABDKPR] Attiya, H., Bar-Noy, A., Dolev, D., Koller, D., Peleg, D., and Reischuk, R. Achievable cases in an asynchronous environment, *ACM-FOCS* 1987, 337-346.

[BMZ]   Biran, O., Moran S., and Zaks, S. A Combinatorial characterization of the distributed tasks which are solvable in the presence of one faulty processor, *ACM-PODC* 1988, 263-275.

[BW]   Bridgland, M., and Watro, R. Fault-tolerant decision making in totally asynchronous distributed systems, *ACM-PODC* 1987, 52-63.

[ChM]   Chor, B., and Moscovici, L. Solvability in asynchronous environments, manuscript, 1989.

[CIL]   Chor, B., Israeli, A., and Li, M. On processor coordination using asynchronous hardware, *ACM-PODC* 1987, 86-97.

[CM1]   Chandy, M., and Misra, J. On the nonexistence of robust commit protocols, Unpublished manuscript, November 1985.

[CM2]   Chandy, M., and Misra, J. How processes learn, *Distributed Computing* 1986, 40-52.

[DDS]   Dolev, D., Dwork, C., Stockmeyer, L. On the minimal synchronism needed for distributed consensus, *JACM 34*, 1, 1987, 77-97.

[DLS]   Dwork, C., Lynch, N., Stockmeyer, L. Consensus in the presence of partial synchrony, *JACM 35*, 2, 1988, 288-323.

[FLP]   Fischer, M., Lynch, N., Paterson, M. Impossibility of distributed consensus with one faulty process, *JACM 32*, 2, 1985, 374-382.

[Her]   Herlihy, P.M. Impossibility and universality results for wait-free synchronization, *ACM-PODC* 1988, 276-290.

[LA]   Loui, C.M., and Abu-Amara, H. Memory requirements for agreement among unreliable asynchronous processes, *Advances in Computing Research 4*, 1988.

[MW]   Moran, S., and Wolfstahl, Y. An extended impossibility result for asynchronous complete networks, *IPL 26*, November 1987, 145-151.

[Ta1]   Taubenfeld, G. Impossibility Results for Decision Protocols, Technion Technical Report #445, January 1987. Revised version, Technion TR #506, April 1988.

[Ta2]   Taubenfeld, G. Leader election in the presence of $n - 1$ initial failures, *Yale technical report YALEU/DCS/TR-709* (May 1989).

[TKM1] Taubenfeld, G., Katz, S., and Moran, S. Impossibility results in the presence of multiple faulty processes, Technion Technical Report #492, January 1988.

[TKM2] Taubenfeld, G., Katz, S., and Moran, S. Initial failures in distributed computations, Technion Technical Report #517, August 1988.

[TM]   Taubenfeld, G., and Moran, S. Possibility and impossibility results in a shared memory environment, *Yale technical report YALEU/DCS/TR-708* (May 1989).

COMMUNICATION HEURISTICS IN DISTRIBUTED COMBINATORIAL SEARCH ALGORITHMS

Alfred Taudes
Department of Applied Computer Science
Institute of Information Processing and Information Economics
Vienna University of Economics and Business Administration
Austria, A-1090 Vienna, Augasse 2-6

Abstract

Algorithms for combinatorial search problems such as the travelling salesman problem, the polynomial problem or game-tree searching have been prime candidates for a distributed implementation as these problems offer substantial parallelism on the programm level. However, a number of experimental studies show that naive approaches to distributed combinatorial search tend to yield only a moderate speedup. The problem is to find a communication strategy that is able to limit stand-stills and superfluous searching of individual processors by distributing the work-load and intermediate results among the processors effectively and that causes only moderate communication overhead. To tackle the problem of the diffusion of commonly useful intermediate results between processors linked by "slow" communication lines without shared memory, we propose a formal method to derive optimal and adaptive communication strategies based on *Dynamic Programming in Markov Chains*. The key idea of our approach is to compare the running time to be expected under the current contents of the local copy of the shared state with the search and communication effort when acquiring the intermediate result of another processor via an exchange of messages. Using this method we study communication strategies for various distributed combinatorial search problems: for the distributed determination of the maximum of a vector, for a distibuted version of a simple variant of alpha-beta pruning, and for distributed branch and bound methods, where we examine the set partitioning problem.

1 Introduction

We are concerned with the distributed solution of combinatorial search problems. Our motivation for studying this area is the new hardware situation created by the advent of low-cost high-speed interconnected workstations, such as described in [5]. Finkel and Manber ([5]) motivate their development effort for "DIB", a programming environment for distributed backtracking, as follows: "In the next few years, professionals from many areas will have access to multicomputers and advanced workstations connected by networks. A *multicomputer* is a collection of machines, each with its own local store, that cooperate by exchange of messages. A network of workstations is similar in that each machine can act independently, but can cooperate with others through messages. Algorithms that take advantage of these architectures are of great importance. Such algorithms can employ workstations that are frequently idle (e.g. workstations that are used as personal computers) to help solve computationally intensive problems."

One class of computationally intensive problems offering substantial parallelism on the program level and thus a considerable potential for speedup on this kind of computational device are combinatorial search problems. Algorithms solving these problems search a space of combinatorial objects such as permutations, board-positions or assignments for an optimum. Many important algorithms in Operations Research and Artificial Intelligence are combinatorial search algorithms. At first glance a distributed implementation of such an algorithm looks trivial: "Just let each processor search a part of the space and only take care that no double work is done."

However, practical experience shows the deficiencies of this simple approach. Kumar et al. ([12]), for instance, report: "For many problems, heuristic domain knowledge is available, which can be used to avoid searching some (unpromising) parts of the search space. This means that parallel processors following a simple strategy (such as divide the search space statically into disjoint parts and let each one be searched by a different processor) may end up doing a lot more work than a sequential processor. This would tend to reduce the speedup that can be obtained by parallel processing." Similarly [9] state at the beginning of their theoretical work on distributed randomized branch and bound algorithms that "The fundamental problem is to allocate the node-expansion steps to the processors so that they can all be performing useful work. A successful solution must ensure that processors will not spend much time performing useless node expansions, and that the overhead for interprocessor communication is not excessive." Kumar et al. study various distributed implementation alternatives for the travelling salesman and the vertex cover problem on the BBN-Butterfly Multiprocessor. Generally, it turns out that the main problem is to find a compromise between redundancy of search and communication effort: "If the frequency of transfer is high, then the redundancy factor can be small; otherwise it can be very large. The choice of frequency of transfer is effectively determined by the cost of communication. If comunication cost is low (e.g. on shared-memory multiprocessors) then it would be best to perform communication after every node expansion." For their configuration they find that the best communication strategy is a "cautious" shared-memory policy, where the global shared memory is only accessed if the local solution is not within a "tolerable limit" of the global one: this policy both avoids the contention caused by an unrestricted access to shared memory and the redundancy of search arising in the case of too little coordination between the processors.

Other works relevant to this problem are those by Vonberger ([17]) and Vornberger et al. ([18]). Vornberger ([17]) performs experiments with a distributed version of a branch and bound algorithm for the travelling salesman problem on a ring of 16 personal computers. His first approach to a distributed implementation is as follows: A "master" starts solving the original problem and the distribution of work-load is accomplished via "requests" of unsolved problem instances by idle processors. The experiences with this simple solution to the load-balancing and "knowledge coordination" problem *are not good*. The experiments show that at the beginning the search space is extremely unevenly distributed and that therefore a bulk of requests of idle processors strains the network. It also turns out that usually the problem sent in the course of a request is quickly solved, so that immediately after a communication the requesting processor is idle again and "disturbs" the sender once more. For these two reasons the distribution of the work-load is extremely uneven. Furthermore, the only reason to communicate is that a processor has finished searching his local search space. Therefore, the situation often arises in which there are considerable differences between the local bounds of the different processors causing a waste of resources for the solution of problem instances that cannot possibly lead to an improvement of the optimum. Vornberger takes these problems as the starting point for the improvement of the implementation via three experimentally determined heuristics:

- All processor start solving the initial problem and dynamically create their local search space. Then a certain portion of it is disregarded to avoid double work. Thus a satisfactory initial work-load is created.

- In the case of a request more than one unsolved problem is sent. The number of communicated problems "depends on some heuristic arguments such as the toal number of subproblems in the heap and the difference between the lowest bound in the heap and the cost of the temporary solution.".

- Request are not only submitted at the end of a local search but also "at certain intervals (depending on the increase of the smallest lower bound in the heap by a certain constant)".

With this implementation Vornberger obtains a *nearly linear speedup*. In [18] Vornberger and Monien compare various distributed versions of the alpha-beta and the SSS-algorithm for game-tree searching on the ring architecture. Here they find, among other things, that "the main reason for the low speedup is the fact that all three versions (of the implementation) visit too many nodes. The trade-off between "avoiding idle times" and "waiting for a sharper bound" allows an 8-fold increase in performance while running Alpha-Beta on 16 processors."

Similar problems arose in the development of V, a distributed version of the operating system UNIX. Cheriton ([2]) reports that "... the *handling of shared state* was recognized as the primary challenge of distributed systems. Shared memory is the most natural model for handling shared state. Shared memory can be implemented across multiple machines i.e. by caching referenced data as virtual memory pages and implementing a consistency protocol between the page frame caches on different machines. The major disadvantage is the cost of consistency operations when contention arises. Thus, we have been investigating efficient mechanisms for implementing consistency between network nodes, software structuring techniques that reduce contention and non-standard forms of consistency that are less expensive than conventional consistency, so-called *problem oriented shared memory*." Cheriton ([2]) also describes experiments done with V: "We have programmed several example problems using this model, including the travelling salesman problem, alpha-beta search, zero-finding and matrix multiplication." He reports that "Although the speedup for some programs, such as matrix multiplication, did suffer from the communication overhead, the major significant problem was the superflous processing that often arises as a result of parallelizing the computation."

As can be seen from these examples, at the present state-of-the-art communication problems in distributed combinatorial search problems are solved in an experimental and thus problem- and configuration-dependent way. No general method for programming such algorithms exhibiting "optimal" communication patterns is currently known to the author. In this paper we deal with the problem of distributing the intermediate results used as cut-off criteria in combinatorial search problems and develop a formal method to find heuristics for a resource allocation strategy that is balanced between the communication effort and the size of the search space explicitly inspected. This method is demonstrated for the distributed determination of the maximum of a vector, for a distributed variant of alpha-beta pruning and for distributed set partitioning. Furthermore, a version allowing for the adaptive construction of an efficent policy is presented.

2 A Method for Determining Communication Heuristics

2.1 Basic Definitions

The theoretical computer underlying our investigations is the MRAM-machine. A Multi-Random Access Machine (MRAM) is a finite collection of RAMs (or the definition of a RAM see e.g. [1] p.5), each with a read-only identification register and additionally the communication instruction SEND(i), which sends the content of the local accumulator to the accumulator of the RAM with identification i. We assume that the communication functions according to a NO-WAIT SEND protocol (see e.g. [6] p.119), i.e. that the SEND-command is non-blocking and that an interrupt handler checks whether a message has been received. We study combinatorial search algorithms on this machine. A MRAM combinatorial search program is a finite set of RAM-programs $R = \{r_1, \cdots, r_k\}$, each one proofing for all elements e_{ik} of a countable set E_k that either $e_{ik} = \max_{j=1,\ldots,i} e_{jk}$ or $e_{ik} < \max_{j=1,\ldots,i} e_{jk}$ (maximum search) or $e_{ik} = \min_{j=1,\ldots,i} e_{jk}$ or $e_{ik} > \min_{j=1,\ldots,i} e_{jk}$ (minimum search), respectively. [1] We define the *width of a MRAM combinatorial search program* as the number of elements of the search space exlicitely inspected by all RAMs of the configuration, and we shall look for algorithms minimizing this quantity. The execution of the communication command shall take $d, d \in N$, times the number of cycles it takes to inspect one element of the search space. [2]

This notion of the "quality of a non-serial algorithm" conflicts with the usual definition of the time-complexity of a PRAM-program as the maximum of the number of cycles taken by each RAM of the theoretical parallel computer (see e.g. [15] p.25). We choose this measure to limit the complexity of the problem: as we only deal with the problem of optimal diffusion of intermediate results of search processes in the absence of global memory and with "slow" communication lines, we want to separate the effects of a communication for work-load allocation from the effects of a communication to distributed results.

In our case, the number of cycles it takes to exchange a message can be interpreted as the "opportunity cost" for searching the local search space, and in order to obtain an efficient distribution of intermediate results an individual RAM has to solve the following decision problem at each search step: "Can I save a portion of the search space large enough to offset the effort for communication when using the result(s) obtained currently by another RAM?" However, this model is also supported by a number of applications where our definition of complexity is the relevant one: in many practical combinatorial search problems the search space is enormous and only a limited amount of time is available for producing a "good" solution. Thus a single RAM never "runs out of work" and a solution where a larger portion of the search space has been scrutinized is better than a result relying on less inspections. A well-known example for this class of problems is computer-chess, others are decision support systems involving search problems, for instance an on-line train routing advisory system proposing "favourable" travelling routes to passengers, or search problems in robotics or real-time systems.

2.2 Optimal Communication Policies

To make the decision-rule given above precise, we need a measure for the "quality" of an intermediate result (bound) $\min_{j=1,\ldots,i} e_{jk}$. A suitable choice is the expected number of inspections when continuing the search of the local set E_k with the current bound, whereby we have to consider that this value changes in the course of the execution. Such a measure can be obtained by modelling the development of the bound in the

---

[1] For ease of presentation we restrict our attention to minimization problems in the sequel. The results hold in an analogous way for maximization problems, too.

[2] This model can be viewed as a modification of Leiserson and Magg's DRAM model ([13]), which consists of an unlimited number of RAMs whereby the communication speed depends on the load of the network.

couse of an execution as the realisation of a Markov Chain, i.e. of a stochastic process with discrete parameter space, discrete state space and finite memory: the contents of RAM-registers are integers, they are changed in discrete steps (execution cycles) and if the algorithm is well-defined, the current state of a RAM can only depend on the input, i.e. the starting state, and a finite number of previous states. A Markov Chain is well-defined if a vector of state-probabilities $q = \{q_1, \cdots, q_I\}$, where $1, \cdots, I$ denotes the states, and the transition matrix $P = \{p_{ij}\}$ $i, j = 1, \cdots, I$, where p_{ij} denotes the probability to move from state i to state j in one step, are given. In our case P is a lower triangular matrix: $\min_{j=1,\cdots,l} e_{jk} \le e_{jk}$ $\forall l < m$ and thus $p_{ij} = 0$ $\forall i < j$. If we define c_{ij} as the expected effort for the inspection of one element of E_k when starting in state i, i.e. with bound i, and moving to state j, the total expected search effort when starting in search step t in state i $(E(C)_{it})$ can be obtained by $E(C)_{it} = \sum_{j=1}^{i} p_{ij} \cdot (c_{ij} + E(C)_{jt+1})$ $i = 1, \cdots, I, t = 1, \cdots, T$ ([8]).

In order to decide on a possible communication, each RAM has to compare this value with the search effort to be expected when starting with the bound of another RAM plus the cost of the communication and possible improvements for the other RAM. But our MRAM-machine does not have shared memory. Therefore the current state of another RAM is not known. However, as previous states are known, either because of former communications or due to the fact that the starting state $\sup(\sup E_1, \cdots, \sup E_k)$ is common to all RAMs. Furthermore, all RAMs operate under the same probability law. Neglecting possible effects on the search effort of the RAM contacted and using the well-known result that the vector of state-probabilities after k transitions is given by $q \cdot P^k$ ([7] p.13), we obtain the following functional euqation for the optimal decision function, which for each state and search step provides the optimal decision between the alternatives "proceed with local search without communication" or "communicate":

$$E(C)_{it_m} = \min \left\{ \begin{array}{l} \sum_{j=1}^{i} p_{ij}(c_{ij} + E(C)_{jt+1_m}) \\ \sum_{j=1}^{i-1} p_{pj_k}(c_{ij} + E(C)_{jt+1_m}) + (\sum_{j=i}^{I} p_{pj_k})(c_{ii} + E(C)_{it+1_m}) + 2d \end{array} \right. \qquad \forall i, t$$

(1)

where

p - state of the RAM contacted k steps ago,

k - number of search steps passed since last communication,

p_{ij_k} - element of the k-step transition matrix P^k.

If more than one RAM can be asked for a bound, one has more than one alternative to local search and chooses the processor with the smallest resulting effort. If a "central coordinator" is used to collect the local bound (e.g. as in the "star architecture" ([2])), k is the sum of the numbers of inspections of all processors.

Using the the fact that $E(C)_{iTm} = 0$ $\forall i$ the decision function can be determined in principle via backward induction However, as stated, this task can be intractable or even impossible: T is usually enormous and for more complicated algorithms it is very hard to determine P from the input distribution, which is also often not known or not known precisely. We deal with the first problem by developing asymptotic and myopic policies for the case when $T \to \infty$. These strategies can be easily implemented and produce an upper bound on the communication frequency. The second problem is tackled by the construction of Bayesian policies, whereby P is "learned" during the execution of the search algorithm.

2.3 Communication-Conservative Heuristics

We start out for the first goal by noting that the only result for a communication is a state-change. As the best state we can expect to reach is $\min(\min E_1, \cdots, \min E_k)$, we can set $v_{1t} = 0 \; \forall t$ and consider "relative values" $v_{it} = E(C)_{it} - E(C)_{1t} \; i = 2, \cdots, I$ only. For this situation it follows easily, e.g from the fact that $v_{it} \geq 0 \; \forall i, t$ and that $\lim_{t \to \infty} v_{it} \leq \sum_{t=1}^{\infty} \max_{ij} c_{ij} \cdot (1 - p_{i1})^i$, that $\lim_{t \to \infty} v_{it} = v_i$ exists $\forall i$. Thus we can obtain an upper bound for the expected search effort when starting in state i until "absorption", i.e. until reaching state 1, by solving the following set of equations:

$$v_i = \begin{cases} \sum_{j=1}^i p_{ij}(c_{ij} + v_j) & \text{if } i = 2, \cdots, I \\ 0 & \text{else.} \end{cases} \tag{2}$$

This enables us to formulate the follwing theorem as a simplification of the exact case:

Theorem 1 *If we assume that we can communicate just once (myopic policy), an optimal policy is to communicate if another RAM was in state p k inspections ago and the intermediate result $\min_{j=1,\cdots,I} e_{jk} = i$ is such that*

$$\sum_{j=1}^{i-1} p_{pj_k} v_j + (\sum_{j=i}^{I} p_{pj_k}) v_i + 2d < v_i. \tag{3}$$

The first term represents the expected results of a successful communciation, the second one the case when no better bound can be obtained. Due to the fact that we consider asymptotic values and that only one communication is allowed, this decision rule provides an upper-bound on the communication time.

Obviously, the following corollary can be derived from it:

Corollary 1 *It is optimal not to communicate in a combinatorial minimum search algorithm on a MRAM-Machine if $v_I < 2d$.*

In other words, if the expected search effort for the whole problem is smaller than the cost of a communication, i.e. two message sends, it is optimal not to communicate. Then the additional programming effort introduced by message passing is not compensated by an improvement of the search speed. Thus $v_I/2$ gives a lower bound on the speed of communication devices needed to justify coordination.

While being considerably simpler than the exact version, this formula is still too complicated. In order to decrease the cost of evaluating the decision rule, one can derive upper bounds. Obviously, $\sum_{j=1}^{i-1} p_{pj_k} v_j + (\sum_{j=i}^{I} p_{pj_k}) v_i < p_i^* \cdot w_i$ with $p_i^* = (p_{I1_k}, p_{I2_k}, \cdots, p_{Ii-1_k}, p_{Ii_k}, p_{Ii+11_k}, \cdots, p_{II_k})$ and $w_i = (v_1, v_2, \cdots, v_{i-1}, v_i, v_i, \cdots, v_i)^t$. From the properties of the R_∞-Norm it follows that $|p_i^* \cdot w_i|_\infty \leq (I-1) \cdot \max p_i^* \cdot \max w_i \leq (I-1) \cdot \max P^k \cdot \max w_i \leq (I-1) \cdot (\max P)^k \cdot \max w_i$.

2.4 Adaptive Communication Policies

If P is not known or not known precisely in advance, it can be learned during the execution of the search algorithm starting from a prior distribution on P. A natural candidate for this distribution is the Matrix Beta distribution, which is the conjugate distribution to the transition count $F = \{f_{ij}\}$, where f_{ij} denotes the number of transitions from state i to state j during sampling, i.e. in our case during an execution (see [14] p.141):

$$f(P|A) = \prod_{i,j=1}^{I} \frac{\Gamma(a_{i1} + a_{i2} + \cdots + a_{im-1})}{\prod_{j=1}^{I} \Gamma(a_{ij})} p_{ij}^{a_{ij}-1}, \tag{4}$$

with

$A = \{a_{ij}\}$ - matrix of parameters, $a_{ij} > 0$, $i, j = 1, \cdots, I$.

Then all previously derived results hold with p_{ij} replaced by $(a_{ij} + f_{ij})/(\sum_{j=1}^{m} a_{ij} + \sum_{j=1}^{m} f_{ij})$, the mean of the a posteriori distribution $f(P|A, F)$ (see [14] p. 150). However, the continuous revision of the decision function based on the current estimate of P is very costly. Thus less adaptive but also less costly policies such as revising the policy only after an execution of the search algorithm are worth studying.

3 Examples

3.1 Determining the Maximum of a Vector

To demonstrate the method, let us start with a well-known problem: one has to find the maximum of an unsorted vector of integers equally distributed in the interval $[1, \cdots, I]$. In this case a search step resembles to the inspection of one element of the vector and the cost of an inspection consists of the cost for a compare-operation (c_v) and the cost of an inversion-operation (c_c) if a new maximum is found. This problem is characterized by the following transition matrix:

$$P = \begin{pmatrix} \frac{1}{I} & \frac{1}{I} & \cdots & \frac{1}{I} & \frac{1}{I} \\ 0 & \frac{2}{I} & \cdots & \frac{1}{I} & \frac{1}{I} \\ \cdots & \cdots & \cdots & \cdots & \cdots \\ 0 & 0 & \cdots & \frac{I-1}{I} & \frac{1}{I} \\ 0 & 0 & \cdots & 0 & 1 \end{pmatrix}.$$

The expected search costs per step in each state are

$$C = \begin{pmatrix} c_v & c_v + c_c & \cdots & c_v + c_c & c_v + c_c \\ c_v + c_c & c_v & \cdots & c_v + c_c & c_v + c_c \\ \cdots & \cdots & \cdots & \cdots & \cdots \\ c_v + c_c & c_v + c_c & \cdots & c_v & c_v + c_c \\ c_v + c_c & c_v + c_c & \cdots & c_v + c_c & c_v \end{pmatrix}.$$

One can use P and C to determine an exact policy according to formula (1). To obtain asymptotic myopic policies, one has to solve (2). In this case, $v_i = \frac{c_c}{I-i} \sum_{j=i+1}^{I} v_j$ and it can be easily shown by induction that $v_i = c_c \cdot H_{I-i}$ with $H_i = \sum_{j=1}^{i} \frac{1}{j}$ - i-th harmonic number, a well-known result (see e.g. [10] p. 94) which is usually obtained by inspecting the generating function. Now one is able to apply (3) or to find an upper bound to (3) as indicated in section 2.3: for this problem we find that a RAM should only communicate if it is in a state i for which $G_{ik} > 0$, $G_{ik} = c_c \cdot H_{I-i} \cdot (1 - ((I-1) \cdot (\frac{I-1}{I})^k)) + 2d$. Corollary 1 yields that one only should think about communicating intermediate results if $d < (\log I)/2$ - a big difference to the "naive" upper-bound $I/2$. Note that in this case the function $(i, k) \to G_{ik}$ is monotone, i.e. for each state i there either exists a k^* such it pays to communicate $\forall k > k^*$ or it does not pay to communicate at all. This is a very important property from the implementation point of view, as only these cut-off points have to be stored and checked for in an execution.

3.2 Alpha-Beta Pruning

We study a simplified version of alpha-beta pruning ([11]): one has to determine $\min_{i=1,\cdots,n} \max_{j=1,\cdots,m} a_{ij}$, whereby we assume that the a_{ij} are equally distributed in the interval $[1, a]$, i.e. we only evalutate the game-tree one move ahead. In this case a search step resembles to the inspection of the moves successive to one of the moves possible currently. Let the cost of this operation be c.

This problem is characterized by the following transition matrix:

$$P = \begin{pmatrix} 1 & 0 & \cdots & 0 & 0 \\ (\frac{1}{a})^m & 1 - \frac{1}{a^m} & \cdots & 0 & 0 \\ (\frac{1}{a})^m & (\frac{2}{a})^m & \cdots & 0 & 0 \\ \cdots & \cdots & \cdots & \cdots & \cdots \\ (\frac{1}{a})^m & (\frac{2}{a})^m & \cdots & 1 - \frac{\sum_{j=1}^{a-2} j^m}{a^m} & 0 \\ (\frac{1}{a})^m & (\frac{2}{a})^m & \cdots & (\frac{a-1}{a})^m & 1 - \frac{\sum_{j=1}^{a-1} j^m}{a^m} \end{pmatrix}.$$

and $c_{ij} = \frac{c}{a^{m-1}} \cdot \sum_{k=1}^{m} a^{m-k}(i-1)^{k-1} \ \forall i, j$. Thus $v_i = \frac{c \cdot (\sum_{j=1}^{m} a^{m-j+1}(i-1)^{j-1} + \sum_{j=1}^{i-1} j^m v_j)}{\sum_{j=1}^{i-1} j^m}$

and one should communicate in states where $v_i > (a-1) \cdot (\frac{a^m-1}{a^m})^k v_i + 2d$. Once again the decision function is monotone.

3.3 Set Partitioning

For more complex discrete optimization problems exact formulas for the average case behaviour of algorithms are not available. However, for our purpose simplified models of these algorithms yielding upper bounds on the expected behaviour often suffice and, as shown for instance by [16], such an approximation often yields a satsifactory precise image of the actual ressource consumption. We demonstrate this possibility for the set partitioning problem, one of the classical problems in combinatorial optimization. This problem is as follows: try to find a setting of n binary variables $x = (x_1, \cdots, x_n)$ such that

$$c \cdot x \ \to \ \text{Min.}$$
$$s.t. \ A \cdot x \ = \ e$$

where A is an $m \times n$ matrix of zeroes and ones, c is an arbitratiy n vector and e is a vector of m ones (for a more detailed description of the problems and a list of applications see e.g. [3] p.151 ff.). One method to solve this problem is partial enumeration ([3] p. 185 f.): after grouping the columns of A into blocks B_j, $j = 1, \cdots, k$, where $a_{il} = 1$ $\forall l \in B_j$ and $a_{il} = 0$ $\forall l \in \cup_{m=j+1}^{k} B_m$ and ordering the columns within a block by increasing c_i, one step-wise assigns 1 to variables (=columns) which satisfy constraints (=rows) additional to those satisfied by the current assignment without violating any of these contraints. As soon as the sum of the c_i's of the current assignment is not less than the current minimum or a block is exhausted the algorithm backtracks.

Thus the enumeration process can be modelled as a tree, where the nodes represent assignments. Therefore, the memory of the Markov Chain of the search algorithm resembles to the stack of previous assignments, which in our case implies that the state space of the chain is very large. However, an upper bound on the expected behaviour can be found as follows: we interpret the enumeration of a path from the root to a leaf as a search-step. The expected cost per step is the length of such a path, whereby an enumeration halts as soon as the sum of the c_i's exceeds the current bound or a new solution has been found, i.e. all constraints are satisfied. In such a case a state change occurs, provided that the newly found feasible assignment improves the current solution. Suppose, for instance, that the c_i and a_{ij} take the values $\{0, 1\}$ with equal probability. Then the transition matrix is

$$
P = \begin{pmatrix}
1 & 0 & \cdots & 0 & 0 \\
\frac{1}{2^n}\begin{pmatrix} n \\ 0 \end{pmatrix} & 1 - \frac{1}{2^n}\begin{pmatrix} n \\ 0 \end{pmatrix} & \cdots & 0 & 0 \\
\cdots & \cdots & \cdots & \cdots & \cdots \\
\frac{1}{2^n}\begin{pmatrix} n \\ 0 \end{pmatrix} & \frac{1}{2^n}\begin{pmatrix} n \\ 1 \end{pmatrix} & \cdots & 1 - \frac{1}{2^n}\sum_{j=0}^{n-2}\begin{pmatrix} n \\ j \end{pmatrix} & \\
\frac{1}{2^n}\begin{pmatrix} n \\ 0 \end{pmatrix} & \frac{1}{2^n}\begin{pmatrix} n \\ 1 \end{pmatrix} & \cdots & \frac{1}{2^n}\begin{pmatrix} n \\ n-1 \end{pmatrix} & 1 - \frac{1}{2^n}\sum_{j=0}^{n-1}\begin{pmatrix} n \\ j \end{pmatrix}
\end{pmatrix}.
$$

and $c_{ij} = \sum_{k=1}^{m} k \cdot \{[\frac{1}{2^k} \cdot \sum_{l=i}^{n}\begin{pmatrix} k \\ l \end{pmatrix}] + [(\frac{1}{2^k} \cdot \sum_{l=1}^{i-1}\begin{pmatrix} k \\ l \end{pmatrix}) \cdot \frac{(m \cdot k)!}{m^m}]\}$. Thus $v_i = \frac{\sum_{j=1}^{i-1} p_{ij}(c_{ij}+v_j)}{1-p_{ii}}$ and message passing should take place if the bound is such that $v_i > (n-1) \cdot (\frac{2^n-1}{2^n})^k v_i + 2d$. Again the decision function is monotone.

4 Conclusion

We have developed a general methodology for obtaining communication heuristics for distributed combinatorial search problems. Both an exact and an approximate method for the determination of a coordination policy are derived. These results are applied to the problems of the distributed determination of the maximum of a vector, to a simple distributed variant of alpha-beta pruning and to distributed set partitioning. Furthermore, the adaptive determination of optimal communication rules is explored. However, a lot remains to be done in this field: Can we find closed-form expressions for problems other than those studied here? Is it possible to analyze whole classes of algorithms? Currently the RAMs are "selfish", in that they do not consider benefits for the partner of the communication. Can this aspect be introduced? The cost of communication, d, is assumed to be a constant. In reality, d varies according to the work-load of the network. How robust to these variations are the strategies derived here? One, of course, can always choose an upper or lower bound of d and use the method developed here, but is it possible to extent the approach to allow for an adaptability of the parameter d? When should a new policy be determined in the case of adaption? These and other questions related to the practical application of the method are currently under investigation: a simulator of a MRAM and real-life implementations are in development.

References

[1] Aho, A.V., J.E. Hopcroft und J.D. Ullman, *Data Structures and Algorithms*, Reading, Mass. u.a., Addison-Wesley, 1985

[2] Cheriton D.R., The V Distributed System, *Communications of the ACM*, Vol. 31 (March), No. 3, 314-334, 1989

[3] Christofides N., A: Mingozzi, P. Thot, C. Sandi (eds.), *Combinatorial Optimization*, New York a.o., John Wiley & Sons, 1979

[4] Ferguson C. und R.E. Korf, Distributed Tree Search and its Applications to Alpha-Beta Pruning, *Proceedings of the AAAI Conference 1987*, 128 - 132

[5] Finkel R., und U. Manber, DIB - A Distributed Implementation of Backtracking, *ACM Transactions on Programming Languages and Systems*, Vol. 9, No. 2 April 1987, 235-256

[6] Giloi W.K., *Rechnerarchitektur*, Heidelberg, Springer, 1981

[7] Howard R.A., *Dynamic Probabilistic Systems, Vol I: Markov Models*, Wiley, New York, 1971

[8] Howard R.A., *Dynamic Probabilistic Systems, Vol II: Semi-Markov and Decision Processes*, New York, 1971

[9] Karp, R.M., und Y. Zhang, A Randomized Parallel Branch-and-Bound Procedure, Working Paper, University of California, Berkeley, 1988

[10] Knuth, D.E. *Fundamental Algorithms*, Reading, Mass. u.a., Addison-Wesley, 1. The Art of Computer Programming, 1973

[11] Knuth D.E. und R.W. Moore, An Analysis of Alpha-Beta Pruning, *Artificial Intelligence*, Vol. 6, 293-326, 1975

[12] Kumar V., K. Ramesh und V.N. Rao, Parallel Best-First Search of State-Space Graphs: A Summary of Results, *Proceedings of the AAAI Conference 1987*, 122 - 127

[13] Leiserson C.E. und B.M. Maggs, Communication-Efficient Parallel Algorithms for Distributed Random-Access Machines, *Algorithmica*, Vol. 3 (1988), 53 - 77

[14] Martin J.J., *Bayesian Decision Problems and Markov Chains*, R.E. Krieger, New York, 1975

[15] Parberry I., *Parallel Complexity Theory*, New York u.a., John Wiley & Sons, 1987

[16] Smith D.R., Random Trees and the Analysis of Branch and Bound Procedures, *Journal of the Association for Computing Machinery*, Vol. 31, No. 1, January 1984, 163-188

[17] Vornberger O. und B. Monien, Parallel Alpha-Beta versus Parallel SSS, in: Barton, Dagless, Reijns (eds): *IFIP Conference on Distributed Processing*, North-Holland 1987

[18] Vornberger O., Implementing Branch-and-Bound in a Ring of Processors, in: Goos, Hartmanis (eds): *Lecture Notes in Computer Science, CONPAR 86 - Conference on Algorithms and Hardware for Parallel Processing*, 158 - 164, Springer, 1986

The Role of Inhibition in Asynchronous Consistent-Cut Protocols

Kim Taylor *

Cornell University Department of Computer Science
4130 Upson Hall, Ithaca, NY 14850

Abstract

We present results regarding *consistent-cut* protocols. Consistent-cut protocols are based on finding a *consistent global state* in an underlying distributed computation; they are used for a variety of applications such as checkpointing and deadlock detection. We formally define what it means for a protocol to be *non-inhibitory*, which intuitively means that it does not prevent any actions from occurring in an underlying computation. We prove that there is no non-inhibitory consistent-cut protocol for non-FIFO asynchronous systems. We also give a lower bound on communication for non-inhibitory consistent-cut protocols for FIFO systems of one message per bidirectional channel (up to $\frac{1}{2}(n^2 - n)$). We present two protocols, one non-inhibitory requiring up to two messages between each pair of neighboring nodes in a network and the other inhibitory and requiring only $3(n - 1)$ messages total. In most networks these results illustrate a tradeoff between the amount of necessary communication and the willingness to inhibit actions of the underlying system. Additionally, our inhibitory protocol also works for non-FIFO systems, thus illustrating that the inhibitory condition is exactly what is required to develop consistent-cut protocols for non-FIFO systems which satisfy our model.

1 Introduction

In this paper we investigate the problem of developing *consistent-cut* protocols in asynchronous systems. Consistent-cut protocols are based on finding a *consistent global state* [4] in a underlying computation, a set of local states that do not directly depend on one another and may occur simultaneously. Consistent-cut protocols have applications in checkpointing and rollback recovery [9], deadlock detection [3], and distributed databases [2].

We consider whether or not consistent-cut protocols are *non-inhibitory*, i.e. do not prevent operations which would otherwise take place in the underlying system. For example, non-inhibitory protocols cannot delay the sending and reception of messages which would take place if the protocol were not being run. We have observed that a variation on the "echo" algorithm of Chang [6] and on the checkpointing algorithm of

---

*Supported by an AT&T Ph.D. Scholarship

Chandy and Lamport [4] - without delaying actions of the underlying system - finds a consistent cut in systems with FIFO channels but sends up to two messages between each pair of connected nodes. On the other hand, a two-phase commit variant suspends system send events for an interval but requires only $3(n-1)$ messages total. Whether or not the less expensive algorithm is indeed better depends upon the degree of degradation caused by the suspension of events in the underlying application.

This paper presents the following results regarding consistent-cut protocols in asynchronous systems. (1) There is no non-inhibitory protocol for non-FIFO systems. (2) Any non-inhibitory protocol for FIFO systems requires one message between each pair of neighboring nodes. (3) There is a non-inhibitory protocol for FIFO systems using up to two messages between neighboring nodes. (4) There is an *inhibitory* protocol for both FIFO and non-FIFO systems using exactly $3(n-1)$ messages, where n is the number of nodes in the network. Results (2) through (4) illustrate a tradeoff between the amount of communication necessary in consistent-cut protocols and whether or not they inhibit actions of the underlying system. Results (1) and (4) indicate that the property of inhibition is exactly what is required for a non-FIFO network to achieve a consistent cut in the systems that satisfy our model.

2 Model and Definitions

2.1 System Model

Our goal is to model reliable asynchronous distributed systems. By asynchronous, we mean: (1) there is no global clock, (2) there are no bounds on message transmission time, and (3) there are no assumptions made concerning the relative speed of processors. By reliable we mean that processes do not fail and that the communication medium eventually delivers all messages sent, message contents are not permuted, and no messages are delivered that were not sent. We also assume that communication channels are bidirectional and that the network is connected.

The model is similar to that of Chandy and Misra [5] and to that used in our related work [13]. A system is characterized by a set of possible executions, or *runs*, which are composed of sequences of *events*. Unlike the models mentioned, we explicitly include the *enabling* of events by past event sequences [15] and we explicitly separate protocol events from underlying system events. These two features allow us to define *non-inhibitory* protocols as those whose events never disable those of the underlying system. We also include mechanisms for sending multiple messages atomically (in one indivisible process operation) and for receiving a message and sending responses in one atomic operation. Our impossibility and lower bound results immediately generalize to weaker models without one or both of these primitives, and they are not necessary in algorithm 2.

The basic entity in our system model is the *event*. Let $\mathcal{I} = 1, 2, ..., N$ be process identifiers. Then $\mathcal{E} = (E_1, E_2, ..., E_N)$ is a vector of sets of possible events, where events in the (possibly infinite) set E_i correspond to operations performed by process i. There are four types of events: (1) *sends*, (2) *receives*, (3) *receive-sends*, and (4) *internal events*. A send event is parameterized by a set of up to N *messages* (maximum of one per process). A message consists a string of bits, a unique identifier, and two process identifiers indicating the sender and receiver of the message. A receive event is parameterized by a single message. A receive-send is parameterized by one to $N + 1$ messages, the first corresponding to a received message and the remainder corresponding to a (possibly empty) set of messages sent in the same atomic step. A *local history of i* is any sequence of events, denoted $e_1^i, e_2^i, ...$, such that each element of the sequence is a member of the set E_i. A *local state* is any finite prefix of a local history. *Local_states$_i$* is the set of all possible local states of E_i. The null *initial state* is an element of *Local_states$_i$* for all i. Concatenation of events to local states is denoted by "." as in $l = l' \cdot e$. If local state s is a prefix of local history h, then predicate *Prefix*(s, h) is true.

Our model also includes $\mathcal{M} = (M_1, ..., M_N)$, a vector of *enabling relations*. An enabling relation M_i specifies that events may take place based on prerequisite events. Specifically, M_i is an *enabling relation on E_i* iff it satisfies $M_i \subseteq$ *Local_states$_i$* $\times E_i$. If $(l_i, e_i) \in M_i$ then we say l_i enables e_i. An enabling relation is *finite-branching* iff it contains a finite number of events enabled by each local state. We will require that our enabling relations be finite-branching.

Finally, a *channel* set $\mathcal{C}$ is a set of unordered pairs of elements from $\mathcal{I}$. Pair (i, j) is in the set iff process i can send a message directly to process j and vice-versa.

We can now define our system model. A *system* $\mathcal{S}$ is a quadruple $(\mathcal{I}, \mathcal{C}, \mathcal{E}, \mathcal{M})$ consisting of a process identifier set $\mathcal{I} = 1, ..., N$, a channel set $\mathcal{C}$, an N-vector of event sets $\mathcal{E}$, and an N-vector of enabling relations $\mathcal{M}$ such that (1) for each process i, M_i is a finite-branching enabling relation on E_i, (2) for each message from i to j in $\mathcal{E}$, (i, j) is in $\mathcal{C}$, and (3) for any two processes i and j, there is a path $(i, i_1), (i_1, i_2,), ..., (i_k, j)$ in $\mathcal{C}$.

In order to guarantee that runs of a system correspond to executions of a potentially-real distributed system, we impose a temporal ordering on the events in them based on *causality* as introduced by Lamport [11]. We define two relations on vectors of N local histories, one per process. First, e_1^i *happens-immediately-before* e_2^j, denoted $e_1^i \mapsto e_2^j$, iff (1) i equals j and e_2^j is the next event after e_1^i in the local history of i (j), or (2) e_1^i includes the sending of a message and e_2^j includes its reception. Next, *happens-before*, denoted $\rightarrow$, is the transitive closure of happens-immediately-before. Therefore, if $e_1^i \rightarrow e_2^j$ then either (1) $e_1^i \mapsto e_2^j$, or (2) there exists an event e_3^k such that $e_1^i \rightarrow e_3^k$ and $e_3^k \rightarrow e_2^j$.

We can now define the runs of a system. First of all, a *partial run* of a system $\mathcal{S} = (\mathcal{I}, \mathcal{C}, \mathcal{E}, \mathcal{M})$ is a vector of N local states $(l_1, ..., l_N)$, one per process, such that (1) for every receive there is a corresponding send (of a message having the same unique identifier), (2) → is a partial order on the set of events, (3) for any event e in local state l_i, there is an enabling local state l (possibly the null initial state) immediately before e in l_i, i.e. $(l, e) \in \mathcal{M}$. An *initial partial run* is composed solely of null initial states.

We say that event e is *forever-enabled* in a local history if it is enabled by some local state l in the history (i.e. $(l, e) \in \mathcal{M}$), it is not in the history, and it is enabled by all local states for which l is a prefix. A *total run* of system S is a vector of local histories that satisfies conditions (1)-(3) on partial runs above and, in addition, satisfies: (4) there are no forever-enabled send or internal events, and (5) there are no forever-enabled receive or receive-send events for which there is a corresponding send event. We often refer to a total run as simply a "run." We let $r[i]$ denote the local history of i in run r. We say that run r *extends* partial run r' iff $\forall i \,.\, Prefix(r'[i], r[i])$. A total run is maximal in the sense that it cannot be extended. For the special case of *first-in-first-out (FIFO)* systems, in which messages are guaranteed to arrive in the order in which they are sent, we add an additional constraint on total runs: for any two messages m_1 and m_2, both from process i to process j, if $send(m_1) \to send(m_2)$ then $receive(m_1) \to receive(m_2)$.

2.2 Protocols

In this section we formally define protocols, non-inhibitory protocols, and consistent-cut protocols. We define protocols in an additive fashion, so as to separate the activities of the protocol from those of the underlying system. We desire that any protocol (inhibitory or non-inhibitory) allow the system to accomplish its original tasks as well as the protocol task. For example, we would not want to consider a consistent-cut protocol in which each process simply halts after sending its first message. We will require that the projection of the system events in the run of a protocol be some valid run of the original system.

Protocols will map a system $S = (\mathcal{I}, \mathcal{C}, \mathcal{E}, \mathcal{M})$ to a new system $\mathcal{P}(S) = (\mathcal{I}, \mathcal{C}, \mathcal{E}', \mathcal{M}')$ under certain constraints. The events in $\mathcal{E}$ are called the *system events* and the events in $\mathcal{E}' - \mathcal{E}$ are called the *protocol events*. Given a sequence composed of both system and protocol events, the function *SysEvents* maps it to a sequence containing only the system events in their original order. Formally, a *protocol* $\mathcal{P}$ is a function which maps a system $S = (\mathcal{I}, \mathcal{C}, \mathcal{E}, \mathcal{M})$ to a system $\mathcal{P}(S) = (\mathcal{I}, \mathcal{C}, \mathcal{E}', \mathcal{M}')$ such that (1) $\mathcal{E} \subseteq \mathcal{E}'$ (2) $\mathcal{M}' = (M_1', ..., M_N')$, where M_i' is an enabling relation on E_i', and (3) for all total runs $r' = (h_1', ..., h_N')$ of $\mathcal{P}(S)$, where h_i' is the local history of process i, run $r = (SysEvents(h_1'), ..., SysEvents(h_N'))$ is a total run of the original system S. Note that the possible projected runs of the underlying system may only be a subset of the original possible runs. For example, at points where the original system had a choice between performing internal events and send events, it may be forced to perform only internal events or to forego all system activity for some number of protocol steps.

A protocol is *non-inhibitory* iff for all local states l and events e, if $(SysEvents(l), e) \in \mathcal{M}$ then $(l, e) \in \mathcal{M}'$. In other words, if a sequence of system events enables some system

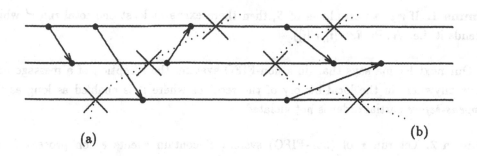

Figure 1: Inconsistent (a) vs. consistent (b) cuts.

event in the original system, then the same sequence with protocol events interspersed will enable that system event in the protocol. This implies that the protocol cannot prevent system events from occurring which would otherwise, including delaying them for an interval.

Given a run r, a prefix of the run is typically called a *consistent cut* if it is also a partial run. Thus, a *consistent cut* of run r is a vector of local states of r, denoted $cut(r) = (l_1, ..., l_N)$, such that for any message m from i to j if $receive(m)$ is in l_j then $send(m)$ is in l_i. (See figure 1. The states of (b) form a consistent cut whereas those of (a) do not.) For simplicity we assume that consistent-cut protocols create only one cut in the system; our results can be easily extended to the multiple-cut case. Formally, protocol $\mathcal{P}$ is a *consistent-cut protocol* iff, for every system $\mathcal{S}$, every run r in $\mathcal{P}(\mathcal{S})$ contains a unique N-vector of local states $cut(r)$ such that the set $\{cut(r)|r \in \mathcal{P}(\mathcal{S})\}$ satisfies: (1) every $cut(r)$ is a consistent cut, not equal to the initial partial run, and (2) if $l_i = cut(r)[i]$ and run r' also contains l_i, then $l_i = cut(r')[i]$. The second condition implies that the occurrence of the cut is deterministic with respect to the sequence of local events leading up to it, i.e. if process i's cut state immediately follows sequence of events l_i in one run and the exact same sequence l_i occurs in a different run, then i's cut state in the later run will immediately follow the same sequence. This is necessary if some local action is to be performed immediately and exactly once as a result of the occurrence of the cut; for example, taking a checkpoint. (One can devise algorithms which determine the existence of a cut "after the fact" which do not satisfy condition (2)[7], for example by sending histories to a central processor which determines a suitable prefix and distributes the result. Our results do not address protocols of this type.)

3   Lemmas

Our first lemma says that any partial run can be extended to a total run. A constructive proof is contained in [14].

Lemma 1. If r is a partial run of S, then there exists at least one total run r' which extends it, i.e. $\forall i \, . \, Prefix(r[i], r'[i])$.

Our next lemma says that, in a non-FIFO system, the reception of a message may occur anywhere in the local history of the receiver where it is enabled as long as the *happens-before* partial order is not violated.

Lemma 2. Let run r of (non-FIFO) system S contain events e_j on process j and $send(m)$ on process i, where m is from i to j, i.e. there are local states l_i and l_j such that $Prefix(l_i \cdot send(m), r[i])$ and $Prefix(l_j \cdot e_j, r[j])$. Also, let $l_j \cdot e_j$ not contain $receive(m)$ and let l_j enable $receive(m)$. If $e_j \not\to send(m)$ then there exists a run r' also in S such that $Prefix(l_i \cdot send(m), r'[i])$ and $Prefix(l_j \cdot receive(m), r'[j])$. (See figure 2. The crossed solid line indicates "not happens-before" and the dashed lines connect the sending and reception of m.)

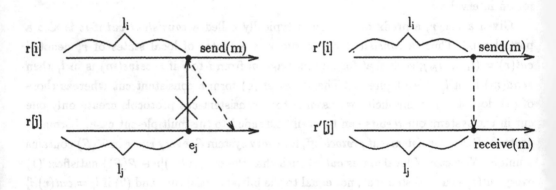

Figure 2: Lemma 2.

Proof: The proof proceeds by first showing that there is a partial run r'' of S where $Prefix(l_i \cdot send(m), r''[i])$ and $r''[j] = l_j$ (without e_j). Then $receive(m)$ is added to r'' still resulting in a partial run which can be extended to a total run r' by lemma 1.

We find a partial run of r, which satisfies the conditions on r'' above, iteratively. Let $MinSends(l_x, y)$ be the minimum local state of process y in run r which includes the sending of all messages received by x from y in local history l_x. Let $max(l_1, l_2)$, where l_1 and l_2 are local states of a single process in a single run, be the largest sequence of the two. Initialize a vector of local states s as follows: $s[j] = l_j$, $s[i] = max(l_i \cdot send(m), MinSends(l_j, i))$, and $s[x] = MinSends(l_j, x)$ for x not equal to i or j. This is not necessarily a partial run. On each step of the iteration, find a message m' from any process a to any other process b whose reception is in s but whose sending is not. Add events from $r[a]$ to $s[a]$ until the necessary send is included.

We next make an observation to be used extensively in the remainder of the proof. Consider any message m' causing inconsistency above. Either $receive(m')$ is in the original cut, or is included as the result of adding states until the sending of some m'' is included, so $receive(m') \rightarrow send(m'')$. This argument can be continued resulting in a chain of messages $send(m') \rightarrow receive(m') \rightarrow send(m'') \rightarrow receive(m'') \ldots \rightarrow receive(m^0)$ where $receive(m^0)$ is in the original set of local states s. (See figure 3. The solid circles represent the original set of states.)

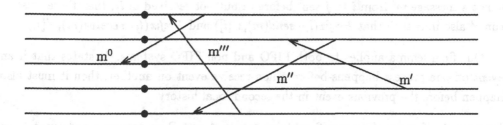

Figure 3: Proof of Lemma 2: Message chains during iterative construction.

We now show that (1) the iteration terminates, and (2) the local state of j is not changed, i.e. upon termination $s[j] = l_j$. Suppose that the iteration above never terminates. Then there must be message chains where two messages m_1 and m_2 are sent by the same process. If $m_1 \rightarrow m_2$ in the chain then $m_2 \rightarrow m_1$ also because there is a local state which includes m_2 but not m_1. This cannot occur, hence the iteration terminates. Now suppose that during the iteration state $s[j]$ is changed due to message m'. There must be a chain of messages ending with $receive(m^0)$ in the original states and $send(m') \rightarrow receive(m^0)$. There are three cases depending on what process has $receive(m^0)$. (1)If it is a process x, x not i or j, then by the definition of the original set of states s and $MinSends$ there must be a message m_x sent after $receive(m^0)$ from x to j such that $receive(m_x) \rightarrow e_j$; but $e_j \rightarrow send(m')$, $send(m') \rightarrow receive(m^0)$, and $receive(m^0) \rightarrow send(m_x) \rightarrow receive(m_x)$, resulting in circularity. (2) If it is process j then there is a circularity as in the proof of termination above. (3) If it is process i then either (a) m^0 arrives before $send(m)$ or (b) m^0 arrives after $send(m)$ but before the sending of a message m_x to j as in the definition of $MinSends$. In case (a), $e_j \rightarrow send(m')$, $send(m') \rightarrow receive(m^0)$, and $receive(m^0) \rightarrow send(m)$. This violates the assumption that $e_j \not\rightarrow send(m)$. Case(b) is analogous to case (1). Hence $s[j] = l_j$.

Let r'' be the final s. Then r'' is a partial run of S such that $r''[j] = l_j$ and $Prefix(l_i \cdot send(m), r''[i])$. Since $receive(m)$ is enabled by l_j, adding event $receive(m)$ to $r''[j]$ still results in a partial run of S. By lemma 1 this can be extended to a full run r'. ∎

Lemma 2 does not quite hold for a FIFO system because adding the reception of m could violate the FIFO condition. If, however, there is no message m' that is sent to j prior to m but has not been received in l_j, then adding $receive(m)$ to l_j cannot violate FIFO. This fact along with the proof of lemma 2 is sufficient to state its FIFO counterpart without proof.

Lemma 3. Let run r of FIFO system S contain events e_j on process j and $send(m)$ on process i, where m is from i to j, i.e. there are local states l_i and l_j such that $Prefix(l_i \cdot send(m), r[i])$ and $Prefix(l_j \cdot e_j, r[j])$. Also, let $l_j \cdot e_j$ not contain $receive(m)$ and let l_j enable $receive(m)$. If (1) $e_j \not\mapsto$ (does not happen before) $send(m)$ and (2) there is not a message m' from i to j sent before m but not received in l_j, then there exists a run r' also in S such that $Prefix(l_i \cdot send(m), r'[i])$ and $Prefix(l_j \cdot receive(m), r'[j])$.

Our final lemma applies to both FIFO and non-FIFO systems. It states that if an event on one process happens-before a non-receive event on another, then it must also happen before the previous event in the second local history.

Lemma 4. If run r of system S contains events A and B on process i and event C on process j such that (1) $A \mapsto B$, (2) $C \to B$, and (3) B is not a receive event, then $C \to A$.

Proof: Since C and B are on different processes and B is not a receive, C cannot happen immediately before B. Therefore, by the definition of happens-before, there exists events $X_1, ... X_m$ such that $C \mapsto X_1 \mapsto ... X_m \mapsto B$. Since B is not a receive, only A can happen immediately before it. Therefore $X_m = A$ and $C \mapsto X_1 ... \mapsto A$, so $C \to A$. ∎

4 Impossibility and Lower-Bound Theorems

In this section we prove two results regarding non-inhibitory consistent-cut protocols: that one does not exist for non-FIFO systems, and that any for FIFO systems requires one message between each pair of directly connected nodes.

Theorem 1. There is no non-inhibitory consistent-cut protocol for non-FIFO systems.

Proof: Suppose that there is such a protocol $\mathcal{P}$, and let S be any non-FIFO system. For any run r in $\mathcal{P}(S)$, there must be a set of local states $cut(r) = (l_1, ... l_N)$ as in the definition of a consistent-cut protocol. Let run r be a run in $\mathcal{P}(S)$ in which there is a system send event of a message m_i from i to j immediately after l_i and similarly a send of m_j from j to i immediately after l_j. By the definition of a non-inhibitory protocol, such system events cannot be disabled, i.e. if $(SysEvents(l_i), send(m_i)) \in \mathcal{M}$ then $(l_i, send(m_i)) \in \mathcal{M}'$. Let $l_i = l'_i \cdot e_i$ and $l_j = l'_j \cdot e_j$. (See figure 4(a). The '×' indicates the local states of the cut.) Also let the receptions of messages m_i and m_j be enabled by local states l'_j and l'_i, respectively. Again, a non-inhibitory protocol cannot prevent such enablings.

Suppose $e_j \not\mapsto send(m_i)$. Then by Lemma 2 there exists a run r' in $\mathcal{P}(S)$ such that $Prefix(l_i \cdot send(m_i), r'[i])$ and $Prefix(l'_j \cdot receive(m_i), r'[j])$. By the definition of a

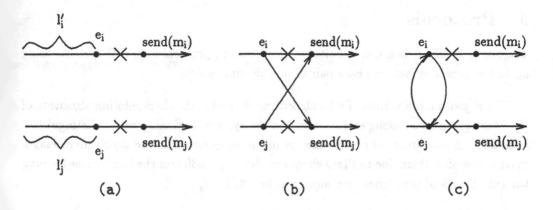

Figure 4: Proof of Theorem 1. (a) Run r. (b) From lemma 2. (c) From lemma 4.

consistent-cut protocol, there must be a cut $cut(r') = (k_1, ...k_N)$. However, k_j cannot be l'_j or a prefix of it. If it were then, by condition (2) of the definition, k_j would be an element of $cut(r)$ also. Then by the uniqueness of cut states $k_j = l_j$. This is impossible, given that k_j is equal to l'_j or a prefix of it, since $l_j = l'_j \cdot e_j$. It follows that the reception of m_i is in $cut(r')$ but the sending is not. This contradicts the assumption that $\mathcal{P}$ is a consistent-cut protocol. Hence the assumption that $e_j \not\rightarrow send(m_i)$ must be false.

A symmetric argument holds for e_i and $send(m_j)$. Hence $e_j \rightarrow send(m_i)$ and $e_i \rightarrow send(m_j)$. (Figure 4(b).) Since $e_j \mapsto send(m_j)$ and $e_i \mapsto send(m_i)$, it follows from Lemma 4 that $e_i \rightarrow e_j$ and $e_j \rightarrow e_i$. (Figure 4(c).) Thus r is not a possible run. ∎

Theorem 2. Any non-inhibitory consistent-cut protocol for FIFO systems requires one message between each pair of neighboring nodes.

Proof: Suppose that P is such a protocol but sends no messages between nodes i and j. We arrive at a contradiction similar to that of theorem 1; we refer to it for brevity. Let run r of $P(S)$ with $cut(r) = (l_1, ...l_N)$ send messages m_i, m_j immediately after l_i, l_j as before, with the receptions of m_i and m_j enabled in l'_j and l'_i, respectively. Additionally assume that run r contains no system messages sent by i to j before l_i or by j to i before l_j.

In run r there is no message m'_i satisfying $send(m'_i) \rightarrow send(m_i)$ but $receive(m'_i)$ is not in l_j, as in condition (2) of lemma 3. It then follows from arguments identical to those of theorem 1 (using lemma 3 rather than lemma 2) that $e_j \rightarrow send(m_i)$ and symmetrically $e_i \rightarrow send(m_j)$. The remainder of the proof follows theorem 1 exactly. ∎

5 Protocols

Theorem 3. There is a non-inhibitory consistent-cut protocol for FIFO systems using up to two messages between each pair of neighboring nodes.

The algorithm is a variant of echo algorithms [6] and of the checkpointing algorithm of [4]. Messages are sent along every channel in the system, beginning with a distinguished initiator I. A consistent cut occurs because any message sent after the algorithm messages must arrive after them due to FIFO channels. "{Cut}" indicates the local states forming the cut. Proofs of correctness are contained in [14, 13, 4].

Algorithm 1. Non-inhibitory Consistent-Cut Protocol

- Initiator I: Send(cut,I,j) to all neighbors j. {Cut}

- Other processes i, immediately (atomic receive-send) upon first receiving a message of the form (cut, k, i): Send(cut, i, j) to all neighbors $j \neq k$. {Cut}

Theorem 4. There is an inhibitory consistent-cut protocol for both FIFO and non-FIFO systems using $3(n-1)$ messages, where n is the number of nodes in the network.

Our inhibitory protocol is a variant of the classic two-phase commit [8], where a spanning tree of the network is used to minimize communication. It is inhibitory because it disables send events between the two phases of messages. Again there is a distinguished initiator I. Three messages, $PrepareCut, Cut$, and $Resume$ are sent respectively up, down, and back up the tree. System send events are disabled as Cut moves down the tree and re-enabled as $Resume$ moves up the tree.

Algorithm 2. Inhibitory Consistent-Cut Protocol

1. Let T be a spanning tree of the network rooted at I. At each process i, let variable $parent(i)$ and list $children(i)$ contain the parent and children of i in T.

2. Initiator I: Send $PrepareCut$ to $children(I)$.

3. Each internal node i, after receiving $PrepareCut$: Send $PrepareCut$ to $children(i)$.

4. Leaf nodes i, after receiving $PrepareCut$: Disable system send events; Send Cut to $parent(i)$. {Cut}

5. Each internal node i, after receiving Cut from all $children(i)$: Disable system send events; Send Cut to $parent(i)$. {Cut}

6. Initiator I, after receiving Cut from all $children(i)$: {Cut} Send $Resume$ to all $children(I)$.

7. Internal nodes i, after receiving $Resume$ from $parent(i)$: Send $Resume$ to all $children(i)$; Enable previously disabled system send events.

8. Leaf nodes i, after receiving *Resume* from *parent(i)*: Enable previously disabled system send events.

The proof that this algorithm attains a consistent cut for FIFO and non-FIFO systems is contained in [14]. Since a spanning tree of the network contains exactly $n-1$ links and three messages are sent along each of them, the algorithm uses exactly $3(n-1)$ messages.

Theorems 2, 3, and 4 illustrate a tradeoff in many FIFO systems between inhibiting actions of an underlying system and requiring more communication. In particular, for completely connected networks the inhibitory algorithm 2 requires only $3(n-1)$ messages whereas the non-inhibitory algorithm 1 requires up to $n^2 - n$ messages. Indeed, by Theorem 2, no non-inhibitory protocol can do better than $\frac{1}{2}(n^2 - n)$ messages. Also, theorems 1 and 4 illustrate that inhibition is exactly what is required for consistent-cut protocols in non-FIFO systems corresponding to our model.

6   Conclusions and Related Work

In this paper we have given formal definitions for *non-inhibitory* protocols and *consistent-cut* protocols. We have shown that there is no non-inhibitory consistent-cut protocol for non-FIFO systems, and given a lower bound on the communication necessary for such a protocol in a FIFO system. In the future we would like to also give a lower bound for inhibitory consistent-cut protocols. We have presented two consistent-cut protocols, one non-inhibitory and one inhibitory, which illustrate a tradeoff between communication complexity and inhibition of underlying system activity for most FIFO networks. In addition, the inhibitory protocol works for non-FIFO systems, illustrating that inhibition is exactly the property required to achieve a consistent-cut in non-FIFO systems corresponding to our model.

It should be noted that there are non-inhibitory consistent-cut protocols for non-FIFO systems which do not satisfy our model [12, 10]. These protocols rely upon piggybacking information onto messages. This is not possible in our model, due to the distinction between protocol and system messages which is necessary to formalize the notion of inhibition. The impossibility results are circumvented in that case because piggybacking results in the reception of messages in the exact order that they are packaged together. Hence an implicit ordering mechanism is present which is not available in the "pure" non-FIFO systems that we consider. This distinction illustrates that it is precisely the loss of ordering in pure non-FIFO systems which prevents the attainment of consistent-cut protocols in a non-inhibitory manner.

In related work, Awerbuch [1] observes tradeoffs between communication complexity and execution time in "synchronizers" similar to our algorithms. Awerbuch does not consider the issue of inhibition whereas we do not consider execution time.

Our model includes both indivisible multiple-send events and indivisible receive-send events. Our impossibility and lower-bounds results still hold in weaker models which do not include these primitives, as does the proof of correctness of our inhibitory protocol. However, it has yet to be proven whether or not these primitives are indeed necessary to develop a non-inhibitory protocol for the FIFO systems we are modeling.

Acknowledgments: I would like to thank Prakash Panangaden for many helpful discussions throughout the development of this work and Willy Zwaenepoel for critical observations leading to the definition of non-inhibitory and to algorithm 2, as well as Ken Birman, Ajei Gopal, and Amitabh Shah for commenting on versions of this paper.

References

[1] B. Awerbuch. Complexity of network synchronization. *J.A.C.M.*, 32(4), Oct. 1985.

[2] K. Birman and T. Joseph. Reliable communication in the presence of failures. *A.C.M. Transactions on Computer Systems*, 5(1), February 1987.

[3] G. Bracha and S. Toueg. Distributed deadlock detection. *Distributed Computing*, 2(3):127–138, 1987.

[4] M. Chandy and L. Lamport. Finding global states of a distributed system. *A.C.M. Transactions on Computer Systems*, 3(1):63–75, 1985.

[5] M. Chandy and J. Misra. How processes learn. In *Proceedings of the Fifth A.C.M. Symposium on Principles of Distributed Computing*, pages 204–214, 1985.

[6] E. Chang. Echo algorithms: depth parallel operations on graphs. *I.E.E.E. Transactions on Software Engineering*, SE-8(4):391–400, 1982.

[7] A. Gopal and S. Toueg, January 1989. Personal communication.

[8] J. Gray. Notes on database operating systems. In *Lecture Notes in Computer Science 60*. Springer-Verlag, Berlin, 1978.

[9] R. Koo and S. Toueg. Checkpointing and rollback-recovery for distributed systems. *IEEE Transactions On Software Engineering*, SE-13(1):23–31, January 1987.

[10] T. Lai and T. Yang. On distributed snapshots. *Information Processing Letters*, 25:153–158, 1987.

[11] L. Lamport. Time, clocks, and the ordering of events in a distributed system. *Communications of the A.C.M.*, 21(7):558–565, 1977.

[12] F. Mattern. Virtual time and global states of distributed systems. Technical Report SFB124-38/88, University of Kaiserslautern, Dept. of Computer Science, Oct. 1988. Submitted for publication in *Proceedings of Parallel and Distributed Algorithms*.

[13] P. Panangaden and K. Taylor. Concurrent common knowledge: A new definition of agreement for asynchronous systems. In *Proceedings of the Seveth A.C.M. Symposium on Principles of Distributed Computing*, pages 197–209, Aug. 1988.

[14] K. Taylor. The role of inhibition in asynchronous consistent-cut protocols. Technical Report 89-995, Cornell University, Dept. of Computer Science, April 1989.

[15] G. Winskel. Event structures. Technical Report 95, University of Cambridge, Computer Laboratory, 1986.

How to Construct an Atomic Variable
(Extended Abstract)

John Tromp

Centrum voor Wiskunde en Informatica

Kruislaan 413, 1098 SJ Amsterdam, The Netherlands

Email: tromp@cwi.nl

Abstract

We present solutions to the problem of simulating an atomic single-reader, single-writer variable with non-atomic bits. The first construction, for the case of a 2-valued atomic variable (bit), achieves the minimal number of non-atomic bits needed. The main construction of a multi-bit variable avoids repeated writing (resp. reading) of the value in a single write (resp. read) action on the simulated atomic variable. It improves on existing solutions of that type in simplicity and in the number of non-atomic bits used, both in presence and in accesses per read/write action.

1 Introduction.

Communication plays a vital role in any distributed system, allowing multiple processors to share and exchange information. Conventionally this communication is based on mutually exclusive access to a shared *variable*. This is the case not only in a shared memory system, but also at the two endpoints of a link in a message based system. Unfortunately, this exclusive nature of access may force a user of such a variable to wait for another one and therefore impedes the parrallellism inherent in distributed systems. In the last years a growing interest has evolved around *wait-free* variables, which can be accessed concurrently without any form of waiting. The main focus of interest is on the question of how to construct such variables in terms of lower-level hardware, like flip-flops.

Peterson was one of the first to investigate this question in [7], giving a construction for a single-writer, multi-reader, multi-bit atomic variable from single-writer, multi-reader atomic bits. Later, Lamport, in his fundamental work [2], developes formalisms and theories besides giving solutions to some of the problems. It is worth noting that most papers use the word "register" instead of variable—we often use the latter to avoid associations with physical, limited size (seldom more than 64 bits) registers.

The ultimate goal is to build a variable accessible to any fixed number of users—each having write and read capabilities—which can hold any fixed number of values, and whose accesses behave atomically. The latter means that for any sequence of operations on the variable, the partial precedence order among those operations must have a total extension (for external consistency) such that each read operation returns the value from the write operation which is the last to precede it in the total order (for internal consistentency).

The construction of this "ultimate" variable is not done directly from the most primitive kind of variable. Rather, this task is more conveniently split into two subtasks: the construction of atomic, multi-bit, single-writer, single-reader variables and next the construction of atomic, multi-bit, multi-user variables from the former type.

This partition can be justified by the nature of the problems involved. In the first construction, the multi-bit value is to be *distributed* over a multiple number of bits. In the second construction, the

Paper	used	write	read
[7]	$3b + 10$	$3b + 13$	$3b + 23$
[3]	$4b + 39$	$b + 5$	$b + 26$
this	$4b + 8$	$b + 2$	$b + 4$

Table 1: worst case number of bits

value of the multi-user variable is *replicated* among all users[1] along with control information which allows each user to identify the most recently written value. This is the more complex problem, as witnessed by the fact that many proposed (and often proven) solutions were later found to be erroneous. The interested reader is referred to [1, 4, 6, 9, 10].

In this paper we attack the first problem, and also give special attention to the case of constructing a single-bit atomic variable.

2 Results of the paper

There are basically two approaches that can be taken in order to construct a multi-bit variable from a linear number of single bits. The first was taken by G.L. Peterson in [7] and involves keeping 3 copies of the multi-bit value, called the *tracks* (in the original paper, they are called *buffers*). Apart from the 3 tracks, there are some *control* bits which we collectively call the *switch*. In this approach the writer writes the new value to all three tracks. The reader reads from all tracks, but in a different order. The switch allows the reader to determine which track was read without interference from the writer.

In Kirousis et. al. [3], the second approach was taken. The idea is that the writer and the reader access only a single track, and that the switch ensures that they never access the same track simultaneously. The price to be paid for the reduced number of track-accesses is the necessity of 4 tracks.

In this paper a simplification of the latter construction is presented. Table 2 gives a comparison of these constructions for a b-bit atomic variable. The "used" column displays the total number of safe bits used in the construction ("space complexity"). The "write" ("read") column gives the worst case number of safe bits that must be accessed in a write (read) action on the atomic variable. A trade-off between time and space is clearly visible.

We also present a solution to the special case of constructing an atomic bit with a minimal number of non-atomic bits. This problem was solved independently and earlier by J. Burns and G. Peterson [8].

3 Preliminaries and Problem Statement

in the single-writer case

In this paper we consider variables which can be written by one user, called the *writer*, and read by another, the *reader*. Both users may be accessing the variable concurrently without ever having to wait for one another. This means that no assumptions are made about the relative speed of the users, and that the correct operation of the variable is not impaired by halting either one. As stated in the introduction, we aim to construct an atomic, multi-bit, single-writer, single-reader variable. The objects we use in this construction are *safe*, single-bit, single-writer, single-reader variables, or simply *safe bits*. These are the mathematical counterparts of flip-flops, in the sense that real-life flip-flops can be argued to satisfy the *safety* property. Before giving rigorous definitions for the notions of safe and atomic, we first state some preliminary definitions.

---

[1] to have a communication path between any pair of users, we need to maintain $\Omega(n^2)$ copies.

In order to distinguish the accesses to the constructed atomic variable (the *higher level*) from the accesses to the safe bits (the *lower level*), we call the former *actions*, and the latter *subactions*. As we will see, each higher-level action is composed of a number of subactions—where the *wait-free* condition requires this number to be bounded.

Let V be a variable and $\mathcal{A}$ (the set of accesses) the union of a set of writes $\mathcal{W}$ to V and a set of reads $\mathcal{R}$ from V. The result of a read is a value which is said to be *returned* by that read. Each access $a \in \mathcal{A}$ occupies a *time interval* $(s(a), f(a))$, where $s(a)$ is the start time and $f(a)$ the finish time of access a. All start and finish times are assumed to be pairwise disjoint. We define a precedence relation $\rightarrow$ on the accesses in $\mathcal{A}$ as follows: $a \rightarrow b$ iff $f(a) < s(b)$. We assume that the set $\{w | w \rightarrow r\}$ is finite for any read r. We call the pair $(\mathcal{A}, \rightarrow)$ a *run*, The writes in $\mathcal{W}$ are totally ordered by $\rightarrow$, and so are the reads in $\mathcal{R}$, in accordance with the requirement that a user can only perform one access at a time.

We relate the reads to the writes in terms of a reading function: A partial function $\pi : \mathcal{R} \rightarrow \mathcal{W}$ is a reading function if for every read $r \in \mathcal{R}$ on which π is defined, $\pi(r)$ writes to V the value returned by r. Unless explicitly stated, the reading function will in fact be total (non-total reading functions will be needed in the definition of safety). We call the triple $(\mathcal{A}, \rightarrow, \pi)$ a *system execution*, We can now define atomicity:

Definition 1 *A system execution* $\sigma = (\mathcal{A}, \rightarrow, \pi)$ *of the variable V is atomic iff there is a total extension* $\rightarrow'$ *of* $\rightarrow$ *consistent with* π, *i.e. for every read* $r \in \mathcal{R}$, *$\pi(r)$ is the last write preceding r in the total order* $\rightarrow'$.

In the case of a single writer, a simplification of the general definition above can be given which avoids the use of a total ordering:

Definition 2 *A system execution* $\sigma = (\mathcal{A}, \rightarrow, \pi)$ *of the single-writer variable V is atomic iff the following three properties hold for all* $r, r_1, r_2 \in \mathcal{R}$ *and* $w \in \mathcal{W}$:

A0 *not* $(r \rightarrow \pi(r))$

A1 *if* $r_1 \rightarrow r_2$, *then not* $(\pi(r_2) \rightarrow \pi(r_1))$

A2 *not* $(\pi(r) \rightarrow w \rightarrow r)$

Equivalence of definitions 1 and 2 in the single-writer case is shown in [5, 11]. Thus, in atomic runs, the partially ordered set of accesses can be linearized while respecting the logical read/write order. In addition to definition 2, we have:

Definition 3 σ *is regular iff A0 and A2 hold.* σ *is safe iff* $(\mathcal{A} - \mathcal{R}', \rightarrow, \pi)$ *is atomic, where* $\mathcal{R}' = \{r \in \mathcal{R} | \exists w \in \mathcal{W}(w \not\rightarrow r \wedge r \not\rightarrow w)\}$ *is the set of reads which overlap a write (in which case π is left undefined).*

Thus, in a safe run, a read overlapping a write may return any value in the domain of the variable. The other actions will then be totally ordered, such that each non-overlapping read returns the value written by the last preceding write.

Definition 4 *Variable V is atomic (regular,safe) iff for each of its runs* $(\mathcal{A}, \rightarrow)$, *there exists a reading function π, such that the system execution $(\mathcal{A}, \rightarrow, \pi)$ is atomic (regular,safe).*

It is clear from these definitions that an atomic variable is regular, and that a regular variable is safe. We call a reading function *normal* if it satisfies A0, i.e. it doesn't map a read to a write which starts after the read finishes. In practice, only normal reading functions are considered.

See [2] on some characteristic properties of safe and regular bits. The following result is of particular interest to us. To make a safe bit regular, it suffices never to write to the safe bit its current value, i.e. to only *change* the bit. Since this is the approach taken in this paper, we will use safe from now on as a synonim for regular.

It remains to define what it means to construct an atomic variable from safe bits. Such a construction is defined by an *architecture* and a pair of *protocols*, one for each user. The architecture specifies the number of safe bits, their names and how they are connected among the users. Each safe bit can be connected to the reader and the writer in one of only two ways: changed by the writer and read by the reader, or changed by the reader and read by the writer. The user that can change a bit is said to be the *owner*. Bits which are both changed and read by the same user are *local variables* and therefore not considered part of the architecture (which specifies only *shared* bits).

A protocol specifies how the writer (reader) can change (read) the atomic variable in terms of changes to and reads from the safe bits. We consider only *wait-free* protocols, i.e., the number of safe bit accesses in a single protocol execution must be bounded by a fixed constant. This requirement forbids solutions in which a user might have to wait for a safe bit to change value.

A read or write action on the atomic variable consists of an execution of the corresponding protocol. We use the terms "action" and "protocol execution" interchangeably. A construction is initialised by an initial write that sets the atomic variable to the value 0. This allows the definition of a reading function on every read action. All other shared bits and local variables are also initialised to 0. Finally, each run of the construction must satisfy the atomicity criterion.

In the next section we consider the special case of a 2-valued atomic variable. The general case of a b-bit (2^b-valued) atomic variable is dealt with in section 5 and further.

4 Optimal Construction of Atomic Bits

4.1 Lower Bound on the Number of Safe Bits Needed to Construct an Atomic Bit

In [2], Lamport proves the following lower bound:

Lemma 1 *A construction of an atomic bit from non-atomic, safe bits requires at least 2 bits owned by the writer, and at least 1 bit owned by the reader.*

4.2 Upper Bound on the Number of Safe Bits Needed to Construct an Atomic Bit

We show how to attain the optimal number of shared safe bits, which is 3. As shown above, the reader will be the owner of one of these, so we simply call that bit "R." One of the two bits owned by the writer will be used to hold the value of the simulated atomic bit, we therefore call it "V." For the other bit owned by the writer, we consider "W" to be an appropriate name. To sum up, we have the following 3 safe bits:

Writer $\rightarrow \boxed{V} \rightarrow$ Reader .... value of simulated atomic bit

Writer $\rightarrow \boxed{W} \rightarrow$ Reader .... flag for writer

Writer $\leftarrow \boxed{R} \leftarrow$ Reader .... flag for reader

In the protocols, we make use of the following statements. The owner of a safe bit B can execute the statement "change B" to change its value. Remember that during this change, the value flickers between 0 and 1. Local variables have lower case names to distinguish them from the shared bits. In all the protocols presented here, the local variables are 2-valued (bits), and are used to hold a copy of V. For this purpose there is a statement "read loc := V," whose effect is to read V and store the result in the local variable *loc*. Given the safety of a shared bit, we know that the changes to and reads from it obey the conditions A0 and A2 (see definition 4), for some reading function. The next statement we consider is the conditional "if test then statement." There is no else part, because it just so happens that we don't need it in any of our protocols. The semantics are obvious—if the test succeeds, then the statement is executed, otherwise it is skipped. The test is either "W==R"[2] or "W<>R." Performing such a test is done by first reading the flag owned by the other user (e.g. the writer reads R in its test). This read is implicit in the test, and is not stated explicitly in the protocol as a separate read statement. In order to be able to compare this value against the value of one's own flag, we assume that the owner of a flag keeps track of its value. This abbreviated notation for tests will prove to make the protocols more concise and readable. The final statement in our repertoire is "return loc," with loc again a local bit. It is used by the reader to exit the execution of its protocol and to specify the return value.

WRITER PROTOCOL	READER PROTOCOL
change V	1. if W==R then return v
if W==R then change W	2. read x := V
	3. if W<>R then change R
	4. read v := V
	5. if W==R then return v
	6. read v := V
	7. return x

The writer can be seen to follow a change of V with a so-called *handshake*, in which it effectively tries to make W different from R. Conversely, the reader, in line 3, tries to make R equal to W. This handshake mechanism helps the reader to decide when a new value has been written to the atomic bit. In line 1, the reader may decide to return a value which was read in an earlier read action and which it considers to be recent enough. Otherwise it does a handshake sandwiched between two reads of V. The value of the later read is returned in line 5 if the handshake is seen to have taken effect. If not, then the reader concludes that W has been changed by the writer and it returns the value of the earlier read in line 7. Line 6 then assures an appropriate value for v if the next read action would return in line 1. In the next section we present a rigorous proof based on this intuitive explanation.

4.3 Correctness

Let $(\mathcal{A}, \rightarrow)$ be a run of the atomic bit. Then we can find a lower level run for each of the three safe bits, consisting of all the accesses to that safe bit and the precedence relation defined from their start and finish times. Let π' be the reading function that makes the run on V safe. Let $\mathcal{W}$ be the set of write actions in $\mathcal{A}$, and $\mathcal{R}$ the set of read actions in $\mathcal{A}$. We must prove the atomicity of $\sigma = (\mathcal{A}, \rightarrow, \pi)$ for some reading function π. We define π in the natural way as follows. Let $r \in \mathcal{R}$ be any read action and let loc be the local variable returned by r. We can define ρ, the subread of r's return value, as the last subread from V into loc before r returns. E.g. if r returns in line 7 then ρ is the read in line 2 of r, and if r returns in line 1, then ρ is the read in line 4 of some earlier read action. Let w be the write action which executed $\pi'(\rho)$ in the first line of its protocol. Then we define $\pi(r) = w$.

Proof of A0 Intuitively, since the underlying bits are safe, a read action can only return the value of a past or concurrent (overlapping) write action. We formally prove A0 by contradiction: Assume that for some $r \in \mathcal{R}$, $r \rightarrow \pi(r)$. Let ρ be the subread of r's return value as above. Then $f(\rho) < f(r)$ and by definition of π, $s(\pi(r)) < \pi'(\rho)$. Together these imply that $\rho \rightarrow \pi'(\rho)$, which contradicts the safety of π'.

Proof of A1 The proof is again by contradiction. Let $r_1, r_2 \in \mathcal{R}$ be such that $r_1 \rightarrow r_2$ and $\pi(r_2) \rightarrow \pi(r_1)$. We assume without loss of generality that r_1 is the first such read action. Let

---

[2]This notation for equality comes from the language C and helps to line up the statements.

$\rho_i, i \in \{1, 2\}$ be the subread from V of r_i's return value. For notational convenience, we use the element-of-set symbol $\in$ to denote that a safe bit access is part of a read or write action. Then $\rho_1 \in r_1$ if r_1 returned in line 5 or line 7. Otherwise, if r_1 returned in line 1, then by the assumption above, ρ_1 is in the previous read action. Defining ω_i as $\pi'(\rho_i)$, we also have $\omega_i \in \pi(r_i)$. This clearly implies that $\omega_2 \to \omega_1$. According to the reader protocol and because $\pi(r_1) \neq \pi(r_2)$ implies $\rho_1 \neq \rho_2$, we have that $\rho_1 \to \rho_2$. For this new-old inversion to occur on safe bit V, it is necessary that $s(\omega_1) < f(\rho_1)$ (to satisfy A0) and that $s(\rho_2) < f(\omega_1)$ (to satisfy A2). This means that

$$\text{the value of } W \text{ doesn't change between } f(\rho_1) \text{ and } s(\rho_2). \tag{1}$$

We now consider all three possible cases of the position of ρ_1.

read x := V in line 2 Then r_1 returned in line 7 of its protocol execution, so in line 5, it sees W different from R. But in line 3 R is made equal to W. Because ρ_2 is either the read in line 6 of this protocol execution, or a later read, we have found a contradiction with 1 above.

read v := V in line 4 Then r_1 returned in line 5 of its protocol execution, after seeing W equal to R. Since $\rho_1 \to \rho_2$, ρ_2 must be part of some later read action which sees W different from R in line 1 of its protocol execution. This contradicts 1 again.

read v := V in line 6 Then r_1 returned in line 1 of its protocol execution (which immediately succeeds that of ρ_1) after seeing W equal to R. This case therefore reduces to the previous one.

We have shown that the assumed violation of A1 leads to a contradiction.

Proof of A2 The proof is once again by contradiction. Let $r \in \mathcal{R}, w \in \mathcal{W}$ be such that $\pi(r) \to w \to r$. Let ρ be the read from V of r's return value as usual, and ω the write to V in w. From $\pi'(\rho) \in \pi(r)$ and $\omega \in w$ follows $\pi'(\rho) \to \omega$. By the safety of V, $\neg(\omega \to \rho)$, in other words, $s(\rho) < f(\omega)$. Hence $\rho \notin r$, and r must have returned in line 1 of its protocol execution after seeing W equal to R. After ω however, write action w makes sure that W is different from R. So R must have been changed between ρ and r. According to the reader protocol, this is done in line 4, and is followed by a **read v := V** statement. This read between ρ and r contradicts the definition of ρ. This completes the proof. $\square$

Lemma 1 and the given construction prove the following

Theorem 1 3 *safe bits are necessary and sufficient to construct a single-reader, single-writer, atomic bit.*

5 The 4-track Protocol

We return to the general problem of constructing a b-bit atomic variable with a linear number of safe bits. Among these bits several will be on b-bit tracks, whose purpose is to hold the values of the atomic variable. The remaining bits, that are not part of a track, are called control bits, or collectively, the switch. The full paper [11] contains an explanation of why 4 tracks might be necessary (no *proof* is known to me). It remains to show that 4 tracks suffice.

We conveniently split the 4 tracks into 2 groups T_0, T_1 of 2 tracks $T_{i,0}, T_{i,1}$ each. In order to avoid collisions, the writer always tries to go to the group other than where it sees the reader. The reader in turn wants recent values, hence it tries to go to the group where it sees the writer. Both the reader and the writer use part of the switch to signal the other user about the group they are in. For the moment this involves an atomic bit W for the writer, and an atomic bit R for the reader. In addition, the switch has two *trackdisplays* D_0, D_1, one for each group, displaying the most recently completed track. For the moment, these too are atomic bits. Later we will show how to use safe bits instead. Now when the writer completes a write action, the new value will be on track T_{W,D_W}.

In summary, the architecture consists of 4 tracks of b safe bits each and the following 4 atomic bits, which comprise the switch:

Writer → $\boxed{D_0}$ → Reader   group 0 trackdisplay

Writer → $\boxed{D_1}$ → Reader   group 1 trackdisplay

Writer → $\boxed{\text{W}}$ → Reader   writer's group

Writer ← $\boxed{\text{R}}$ ← Reader   reader's group

We can now informally state the writer protocol. The writer starts by reading R, the group that the reader is in, and compares it to W, the writer's group. If they are equal, then the reader must have left the other group, so the writer simply writes to a track in that other group, and changes W afterwards. It chooses the displayed track so that it doesn't have to change the trackdisplay. If R is different from W, then the writer writes to the other track in its group and changes the trackdisplay D_W afterwards.

The reader protocol is then as follows: The reader starts by reading W to see if the writer has vacated the reader's group. In that case the reader changes R and follows the writer to the other group.

Next, the reader reads the trackdisplay D_R of its group. It then reads the track T_{R,D_R} and returns the obtained value.

In a programming language, closely related to that introduced in section 4.2, the above protocols look like:

```
WRITER PROTOCOL              READER PROTOCOL

1.   if R==w then            if W<>r then
2.      w := 1-w                r := 1-r
3.      write track T[w,d[w]]    change R
4.      change W             endif
5.   else                    read d := D[r]
6.      d[w] := 1-d[w]       read track T[r,d]
7.      write track T[w,d[w]]
8.      change D[w]
9.   endif
```

The lower-case local variables hold copies of the similarly named shared bits. An array notation is used for the tracks and displays instead of the index notation that we reserve for the text. The access to a track has been compressed to a single statement since we can ignore how many bits must be changed and in what order. For notational convenience, we do not mention the value to be written in the writer protocol or the value to be read in the reader protocol. Since each protocol execution involves exactly one track access, the meaning should be obvious.

Consider a run of the above construction. Each action contains lower-level accesses to the atomic bits of the switch and to the safe bits of a track. By definition 1, the partial order on the accesses to each atomic bit can be extended to a total one. Intuitively, the accesses to different atomic bits can then also be totally ordered. In [5], it was shown that this is indeed the case, if the precedence relation is defined in terms of a global time[3]. Using this total ordering on all atomic bit accesses, we can model a run by a sequence of *state transitions*, each transition corresponding to an atomic bit access. In this model, the states of the writer are:

0 idle, i.e., before the atomic read of R in line 1,

1 between the atomic read of R and the atomic change of W in line 4, when it is writing track $T_{1-W, D_{1-W}}$,

---

[3]This *global time assumption* is equivalent to the *interval axiom*: if $a \to b \wedge b \not\to c \wedge c \to d$, then $a \to d$.

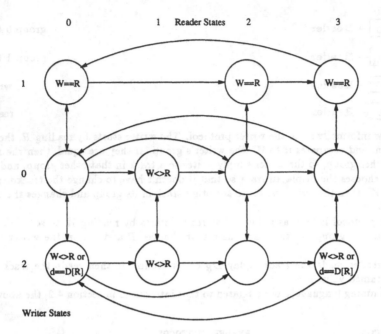

Figure 1: state diagram of 4-track construction

2 between the atomic read of R and the atomic change of D_w in line 8, when it is writing track $T_{W,1-D_W}$.

Thus, the writer is always moving from state 0 to either state 1 or state 2 (depending on the outcome of the test), and then back to state 0. The states of the reader are:

0 idle, i.e., before the atomic read of W in line 1,

1 between the atomic read of W and the atomic change of R in line 3,

2 just before the atomic read of D_R in line 5,

3 after the atomic read of D_r, when it is reading track $T_{R,d}$.

Thus the reader is always moving from state 0 to either state 1 and then to state 2 or directly to state 2, then on to state 3, and finally back to state 0.

Now figure 1 shows all possible transitions in a run of the 4-track construction. It can be easily checked that the invariants in the nodes hold. Note that it is impossible for both the writer and the reader to be in state 1.

Lemma 2 *The 4-track construction is collision-free.*

Proof. We denote the combined writer and reader state in a pair (ws, rs). Collisions can only occur in states $(1, 3)$ and $(2, 3)$, when both the writer and the reader are accessing a track.

In the former case, the writer is in group $w = 1 - W$, while the reader is in group $r = R$. From the diagram we see that $W = R$ in state $(1, 3)$, so the users are accessing tracks in different groups.

In state $(2, 3)$, the writer writes on track $d_w = 1 - D_W$ in group $w = W$, while the reader reads from track d in group R. The diagram shows that either $W \neq R$ or $d = D_R$, so the users are again accessing different tracks. $\square$

5.1 Correctness

Given lemma 2, it remains to show that for every run $(\mathcal{A}, \rightarrow)$, there exists a reading function π such that $\sigma = (\mathcal{A}, \rightarrow, \pi)$ satisfies the three atomicity conditions. As before we may assume that the set of all atomic bit accesses is totally ordered by $\rightarrow$, hence we can use the state model. Naturally, we choose the reading function π to map a read action to the write action that last writes to the track before the read action reads from that track. As such, it is induced by the reading functions that make the track-bits safe. Lemma 2 makes this a valid definition. We now prove each of the three conditions in turn.

Proof of A0 The reading function is obviously normal by the safety of the track-bits.

Proof of A2 The proof is by contradiction. Let $r \in \mathcal{R}, w \in \mathcal{W}$ be such that $\pi(r) \rightarrow w \rightarrow r$.[4] Assume without loss of generality that w writes on track $T_{0,0}$ and that $D_1 = 0$ at time $f(w)$. Then at the same time, $W = 0$ and $D_0 = 0$.

Consider now the 4 possible tracks that r can read from:

$T_{0,0}$ This contradicts our choice of the reading function π, since $\pi(r)$ must either equal w or succeed it.

$T_{0,1}$ In this case, r reads $d = 1$ from D_0, which requires that the writer changes D_0 to 1 between $f(w)$ and the read of D_0. But according to the writer protocol, this change is preceded by the writing of track $T_{0,1}$, implying $w \rightarrow \pi(r)$ and hence leading to a contradiction. The last two cases are similar and we need only show that the track read by r must have been written after w.

$T_{1,0}$ In this case, r reads 1 from W, which requires that the writer changes W to 1. This is preceded by the writing of track $T_{1,0}$.

$T_{1,1}$ In this case, r reads $d = 1$ from D_1, which requires that the writer changes D_1 to 1. This is preceded by the writing of track $T_{1,1}$.

In all three cases, we see that r cannot read a value older than that of w, because the display (W, D_0, D_1) doesn't change until the new track has been written. In other words, once the display is set, every new read action must read either the track on display or a more recently written one.

Proof of A1 We claim that A1 follows from A2 and show this by deriving a violation of A2 from a violation of A1. Let $r_1, r_2 \in \mathcal{R}$ be such that $r_1 \rightarrow r_2$ and $\pi(r_2) \rightarrow \pi(r_1)$. By definition of π and lemma 2, r_1 accesses some track, say $T_{0,0}$, after $\pi(r_1)$ does so. But since $\pi(r_1)$ ends its track access by atomically changing a safe bit and thereby finishing its protocol, we have that $f(\pi(r_1)) < f(r_1) < s(r_2)$, hence with $w = \pi(r_1)$, $\pi(r_2) \rightarrow w \rightarrow r_2$, violating A2. $\square$

5.2 Space Complexity

Now that the 4-track construction has been proven correct, we consider its "space complexity." Using the 3 safe bit construction to implement each of the four atomic bits, we see that 12 bits suffice for the switch. But we can do better, because those atomic bits are used in a special way. In particular, since the W and R bits are used for handshaking, there is exactly one atomic read of W between an atomic change of W and an atomic change of R (and vice versa). Hence there is at most one atomic change of W between two consecutive atomic reads of W (and vice versa). With the trackdisplay bits D_0, D_1 the situation is more complicated. When the reader changes groups (say, to 0), and atomically reads D_0, there can be at most one atomic change of D_0 before the writer leaves group 0.

We will show that, because of these properties, we can implement any of the four atomic bits, call it B, with 2 safe bits B_0, B_1. The problem with safe bits is their flickering. If, for example, R was only a safe bit, then while being changed by the reader, the writer could first see the new value,

---

[4]It will be clear from context whether we mean the write action w or the similarly named writer's local copy of W.

change groups, then see the old value and write to the displayed track in the old group. With 2 safe bits, the following scheme can be applied to alleviate the flickering problem. We represent the value of atomic bit B as the exclusive-or (xor,$\oplus$) of 2 safe bit values: $B = B_0 \oplus B_1$. The change of atomic bit B is then replaced by a change of safe bit B_b, where b is the old value of B. Thus, B_0 and B_1 are changed alternatingly. For the purpose of reading B, two local copies b_0, b_1 of B_0 and B_1 are kept. Normally then, an atomic read of B is replaced by a safe read of B_b, where $b = b_0 \oplus b_1$ is the old value of B. In this case, new-old inversions are eliminated, since the flickering bit is no longer examined once the new value is obtained. This procedure suffices for reading W and R, since the handshaking ensures that each safe bit change is noticed by the other user. It also suffices if the reader sees the writer in the same group and wants to read the trackdisplay, because the writer will change the display at most once (before moving to the other group). If on the other hand the reader sees the writer in the other group, then any local copies it would have of the trackdisplay bits in that other group would probably be out of date. In this case it can simply read both safe bits of that display one after the other, because again the writer will change the display at most once before moving to the other group.

The new architecture of the switch is as follows:

Writer $\rightarrow \boxed{D_{0,0}} \rightarrow$ Reader

Writer $\rightarrow \boxed{D_{0,1}} \rightarrow$ Reader   group 0 trackdisplay

Writer $\rightarrow \boxed{D_{1,0}} \rightarrow$ Reader

Writer $\rightarrow \boxed{D_{1,1}} \rightarrow$ Reader   group 1 trackdisplay

Writer $\rightarrow \boxed{W_0} \rightarrow$ Reader

Writer $\rightarrow \boxed{W_1} \rightarrow$ Reader   writer's group

Writer $\leftarrow \boxed{R_0} \leftarrow$ Reader

Writer $\leftarrow \boxed{R_1} \leftarrow$ Reader   reader's group

The corresponding protocols are:

```
WRITER PROTOCOL                 READER PROTOCOL

1.   if R[1-w]==W[1-w] then      if W[r]<>R[r] then
2.     w := 1-w                    change R[r]
3.     write track T[w,x[w]]       r := 1-r
4.     change W[1-w]               read d[0] := D[r,0]
5.   else                         read d[1] := D[r,1]
6.     x[w] := 1-x[w]           else
7.     write track T[w,x[w]]       read d[d[0]⊕d[1]] := D[r,d[0]⊕d[1]]
8.     change D[w,1-x[w]]       endif
9.   endif                      read track T[r,d[0]⊕d[1]]
```

The writer's local variables d_0, d_1 have been renamed to x_0, x_1 to emphasize that x_i now represents the eXclusive-or of $D_{i,0}$ and $D_{i,1}$. The reader's local variable d has been replaced by d_0 and d_1, where d_i is meant to hold a copy of $D_{r,i}$. All shared and local variables are initialized to 0 as usual. Because the switch now consists of eight safe bits, we call it the "Safe Byte Switch."

We can now state the main theorem:

Theorem 2 *A single-reader, single-writer b-bits atomic variable can be constructed from $4b+8$ safe bits.*

The proof of correctness of the new construction will appear in the full paper [11], which also discusses the use of atomicity testing automata in automated verification methods and their application to the presented constructions.

6 Conclusions

We have presented and proven correct the following two constructions:

- an atomic bit from 3 safe bits

- an atomic b-bit variable from $4b + 8$ safe bits

The first achieves the optimal number of non-atomic bits needed (optimal space complexity). The second needs only 2 extra bit accesses in a write action, and at most 4 extra bit accesses in a read action on the atomic variable (in addition to the b accesses to the bits on a track), making its time complexity very near (if not equal) to optimal. The cost for this "speed" is in the space complexity, which is about a factor 4/3 from optimal, since Peterson showed the neccessity and sufficiency of 3 tracks. A main advantage of the 4-track construction as given here, is its simplicity and transparency—the purpose of the bits in the architecture and the workings of the protocols can be easily understood.

References

[1] B. Bloom, *Constructing Two-writer Atomic Registers*, IEEE Transactions on Computers, vol. 37, pp. 1506–1514, 1988.

[2] L. Lamport, *On Interprocess Communication Parts I and II*, Distributed Computing, vol.1, 1986, pp. 77–101

[3] L.M. Kirousis, E. Kranakis, P.M.B. Vitányi, *Atomic Multireader Register*, Proc. 2nd International Workshop on Distributed Computing, Amsterdam, July 1987.

[4] M. Li, J. Tromp, P.M.B. Vitányi, *How to Share Concurrent Wait-Free Variables*, (to appear)

[5] Baruch Awerbuch, Lefteris M. Kirousis, Evangelos Kranakis, Paul M.B. Vitányi, *On Proving Register Atomicity*, 1980.

[6] G.L. Peterson and J.E. Burns, *Concurrent reading while writing II: the multiwriter case*, Proc. 28th IEEE Symposium on Foundations of Computer Science, pp. 383–392, 1987.

[7] G.L. Peterson, *Concurrent reading while writing*, ACM Transactions on Programming Languages and Systems, vol.5, No.1, 1983, pp. 46–55

[8] J.E. Burns, G.L. Peterson, *Sharp Bounds for Concurrent Reading While Writing*, Technical Report, Georgia Institute of Technology GIT-ICS-87/31

[9] R. Schaffer, *On the correctness of atomic multi-writer registers*, Technical Report MIT/LCS/TM-364, MIT lab. for Computer Science, June 1988.

[10] P.M.B. Vitányi, B. Awerbuch, *Atomic Shared Register Access by Asynchronous Hardware*, Proc. 27th IEEE Symposium on Foundations of Computer Science, pp. 233–243, 1986. (Errata, Ibid.,1987)

[11] J. Tromp, *How to Construct an Atomic Variable*, (to appear).

Electing a Leader when Processor Identity Numbers are not Distinct*
(Extended Abstract)

M. Yamashita
Department of Electrical Engineering, Hiroshima University
Saijo, Higashi-Hiroshima, 724 Japan.
mak%csl.hiroshima-u.ac.jp@RELAY.CS.NET

T. Kameda
School of Computing Science, Simon Fraser University
Burnaby, B.C., V5A 1S6 Canada.
tiko%lccr.sfu.cdn@ubc.csnet

1. Introduction

The **leader election problem (LE)** is the problem of electing a unique leader (processor) in the sense that the elected leader knows that it has been elected and the other processors know that they have not been elected [5,6]. Suppose that each processor has a unique identity number. Then the LE can be regarded as the **maximum finding problem** in the obvious way. As the number of processors in a network increases, keeping the identity numbers of all processors different becomes difficult, and the probability that a network accidentally includes processors having the same identity number increases. Thus an LE algorithm, which works even if more than one processor happens to have the same identity number, is desired from the viewpoint of fault tolerance. The objective of this paper is to explore the possibility and limit of such LE algorithms, when processor identity numbers are not distinct. A possible application of such a "fault tolerant" LE algorithm would be to reduce the complexity of identity number administration as follows: We distribute the identity number administration for the whole network in such a way that each distributed administration is responsible for keeping its "local" processor identity numbers distinct. Usually, each administrator does not need to enforce global uniqueness of identity numbers. When globally unique processor identity numbers are required, by invoking an LE algorithm first, we will be able to give each processor a distinct name under the central control of the elected leader.

An **anonymous network** is a network such that no processor has an identity number, or equivalently, all of the processors have the same identity number. Therefore, an anonymous network is an extreme case of the problem under consideration. The systematic investigation of anonymous networks was begun by Angluin [2]. Johnson and Schneider [4] introduced the concept of "similarity relation". Intuitively, a pair of processors belong to the similarity relation if and only if it is possible that these two processors behave just the same way and produce the same output. Recently, we investigated four problems, including the LE [8,9]. We considered six cases, depending on what network attribute information (e.g., the number of processors) an algorithm can use. These

* This work was supported in part by the Natural Sciences and Engineering Resarch Council of Canada under Grant No. A5340 and a Scientific Research Grant-in-Aid from the Ministry of Education, Science and Culture of Japan.

problems were analyzed using the concept of "view" (see Section 3) For each combination of the four problems and six cases, we characterized the class of networks for which the LE is solvable.

The LE algorithms for anonymous networks proposed in the literature can be used for our purpose here, just by ignoring the identity numbers. It is, however, more desirable to extract useful information from the identity numbers (even if there are duplicates) for the following reasons; first, the set of anonymous networks on which the LE is solvable is quite small even if algorithms can use the network topology information [8,9], and second, in most "practical" networks almost all processors would have unique identity numbers, which should help algorithms a lot in finding a unique leader. This paper will investigate the following two basic questions:

(1) How to find the number of processors with the same identity number?

(2) How to characterize the class of networks on which the LE is solvable?

Related Work: Recently, Merritt [7], Bar-Yehuda and Kutten [3], and Afek and Saks [1] have investigated the LE under the assumption that processors have unique identity numbers, and processors and/or links are subject to failures. [1] and [3] investigate the LE on an asynchronous network in which certain links are down and certain links are up. Down links may come up at any time: however, once a link is up, then it remains so during the execution of the algorithm. They propose several leader election algorithms and analyze their message complexities. [7] investigates the "stopping-fault" and "Byzantine" elections on a synchronized network, assuming that the number of faulty processors is bounded by a constant. It proposes several "stopping-fault" election protocols and authenticated protocols for Byzantine election. The Byzantine election problem, in general, subsumes the LE we will investigate in this paper, since processors with duplicated identity numbers can be simulated by those suffering from Byzantine failures. However, the Byzantine election algorithms such as those in [7] cannot be used for our purpose here, since they cannot distinguish between two correct processors having the same identity number.

In the next section, we define basic terminology. In Section 3, we develop a general method before treating individual cases. In Section 4, we investigate networks under the assumption that each processor knows at least the number of processors. In Section 5, the case where each processor knows at most an upper bound on the number of processor is investigated.

2. The Model and Basic Definitions

A network N is modeled by a pair (G, id), where $G = (V, E)$ is an undirected, connected, simple graph (i.e., it has neither self-loops nor parallel edges) and id is a function from the vertex set V to the set of non-negative integers. The vertex set V represents the processors, the edge set E represents the bidirectional links among processors, and $id(v)$ is the identity number of processor v. For convenience, we name the processors with unique names $v_1, ..., v_n$; these names, however, are not known to the processors, so that no algorithm discussed in this paper will directly use them. Processor v only knows its identity number $id(v)$ and its degree $deg(v)$, the number of processors adjacent to v, and algorithms can make use of them.

A network is **asynchronous** in the sense that no assumption is made about the relative speeds of processors and the amount of communication delay. Neither is any assumption made about the order of message delivery, such as FIFO. Finally, no processor or communication link fails. Communication is carried out by sending and receiving messages through links. The **port-to-port (PP)** communication mode has been studied extensively in the past. In this mode, a processor has a distinct port to access each of its links; however, the processor does not know which processor is at the other end of the link corresponding to a port. The PP mode provides the following communication instructions:

(1) send a message M via port j,

(2) receive a message M from port j.

Each processor can accommodate an input queue of unbounded length for each link incident to it. Let port j be the port of processor u for the link connecting processors u and v. When processor u executes instruction (1), M is sent to the input queue of v for the link, in finite time, with no error. By instruction (2) executed by processor u, the first message in the input queue for the link is transferred to the local variable M. If the input queue is empty, a special symbol is assigned to M. Besides the PP mode, this paper will investigate the following three communication modes.

(1) **broadcast (BC)**: same as the PP mode except for the send instruction. It provides "send a message M" as the send instruction. By the instruction "send M" executed by processor u, M is sent via all ports j of u simultaneously.

(2) **port-to-mailbox (PM)**: same as the PP mode except for the receive instruction. It provides "receive a message M (from mailbox)" as the receive instruction. All messages arriving at a processor are stored in one mailbox queue. By the instruction "receive M" executed by processor u, the first message in u's mailbox is transferred to the local variable M. If the mailbox is empty, a special symbol is assigned to M.

(3) **mailbox-to-mailbox (MM)**: provides "send M" instruction of the BC mode and "receive M" of the PM mode.

We assume that each processor "knows" the network $N = (G, id)$ in some sense specified below. The following four cases will be discussed:

(1) *net*: each processor knows everything about N.

(2) *size*: each processor knows the order n of G.

(3) *upb*: each processor knows an upper bound on the order n of G.

(4) *none*: no network attribute information is available.

A (distributed) algorithm may include send, receive and compute instructions. From time to time processors (**initiators**) spontaneously "wake up" and start the same algorithm (e.g., an LE algorithm), and the execution of the algorithm starts on the network. Some processors may not wake up at the initiation time. The algorithm can initially use the information assumed to be available. The next action of the algorithm on a processor at any time must be determined uniquely by its initial information and its history of communications (i.e., the list of all the messages sent or received so far together with the times at which they were processed). The algorithm execution on the *network* will terminate when the algorithm terminates on every processor.

An algorithm A for the LE must work on any network N using the available network attribute information about N, decide whether it can solve the LE for N, and solve the LE correctly if it can. (If A determines that it cannot solve the LE for N, then it reports this fact.) For an LE algorithm A, let $Nets(A)$ denote the set of networks N on which A can solve the LE under any circumstance. (In general, the behavior of A depends both on the timing of communications among the processors and on the naming (labeling) of the ports to access them. $N \in Nets(A)$ if and only if A can solve the LE for N no matter what the communication timing and the port labeling are. Thus by accident, A may solve the LE for N even if $N \notin Nets(A)$.) For each communication mode $c \in \{PP, BC, PM, MM\}$ and network attribute information $I \in \{net, size, upb, none\}$, let $ALG_{c,I}$ be the set of all algorithms that correctly work on any network N with communication mode c using network attribute information I about N. Define $D_{c,I}$ as follows:

$$D_{c,I} = \{N \mid N \in Nets(A) \text{ for some } A \in ALG_{c,I}\}.$$

Property 2.1 *For any communication mode c,*

$$D_{c,none} \subseteq D_{c,upb} \subseteq D_{c,size} \subseteq D_{c,net}. \quad \square$$

Property 2.2 *For any network attribute information I,*

$$D_{MM,I} \subseteq D_{BC,I} \cap D_{PM,I} \subseteq D_{BC,I} \cup D_{PM,I} \subseteq D_{PP,I}. \quad \square$$

3. View and the Leader Election Problem

Several useful concepts for dealing with the LE were introduced in [8,9]. In this paper, we will use their generalizations. We can assume, without loss of generality, that the algorithm on processor v uses integers, 1, 2, $\cdots$, $deg(v)$, to specify ports. More formally, let $G = (V, E)$ be a graph. A **labeling** (or **port numbering**) of G is a set σ of functions $\{\sigma[v] \mid v \in V\}$ such that, for each v, $\sigma[v]$ is a bijection from the set of edges incident on v onto the set of positive integers $\{1, \cdots, deg(v)\}$.

Consider a network $N = (G, id)$ in communication mode $c \in \{PP, PM, BC, MM\}$. Fix a labeling σ and let $v_1, \cdots, v_d$ be the processors adjacent to v. The **view** $T_\sigma(v)$ for v is an infinite, labeled, rooted tree, defined recursively as follows. The label of the root of $T_\sigma(v)$ is the identity number $id(v)$ of v, and for each vertex v_i adjacent to v in G, $T_\sigma(v)$ has a vertex x_i and an edge from the root to x_i with label $l(v, v_i)$ given by

$$l(v, v_i) = \begin{cases} (\sigma[v](v, v_i), \sigma[v_i](v, v_i)) & \text{if } c = PP \\ (\sigma[v](v, v_i), *) & \text{if } c = BC \\ (*, \sigma[v_i](v, v_i)) & \text{if } c = PM \\ (*, *) & \text{if } c = MM, \end{cases}$$

where $*$ is a special label which is not a number. x_i is now the root of $T_\sigma(v_i)$ for v_i. Note that the vertices of $T_\sigma(v)$ come from V, but they are not labeled as such. For example, x_i in the above definition is a local name and it is labeled only by $id(v_i)$, and not by v_i.

Two views T and T' are said to be **similar**, written $T \equiv T'$, if they are isomorphic (including edge and vertex labels, but ignoring local names for the vertices). Note that there may be many vertices v in V having similar views. Let $\Gamma_\sigma(N)$ denote the set of all dissimilar views, i.e., $\Gamma_\sigma(N) = \{T_\sigma(v) \mid v \in V\}$ with one representative from each "similarity class". We may omit σ and/or N from T_σ and $\Gamma_\sigma(N)$, respectively, whenever they are obvious from the context. Intuitively, the view of a processor represents the maximum information that the processor can obtain, in the worst case, by exchanging messages with others. (Note that, in "practical" cases, the processor may be able to obtain much more information than view. For example, its history of communications would be invaluable information, since the history of communications for each processor would be distinct because of the asynchrony of network.) For any $d \geq 0$, let $T^d(v)$ denote $T(v)$ truncated to depth d, where depth is the distance (in the number of edges) from the root. An algorithm is said to be **pseudo-synchronous** if it has the following form (for processor v).

Let $p := 0$ and $k := deg(v)$;
do forever {
  $p := p + 1;$

Process information in v's local memory;
if the termination condition holds then
    send a $(done, p)$ message via each port j and terminate;
Send messages via some ports (a sequence of send instructions);
Send an $(end\text{-}phase, p)$ message via each port j;
Receive messages until a total of k $(done, p)$ or $(end\text{-}phase, p)$
messages have been received;
$k := k - k'$, where k' is the number of $(done, p)$ messages received;
} od

The pth iteration of the **do** loop is called phase p. We now show that any algorithm A can be converted into a pseudo-synchronous algorithm. The execution of A on a processor consists of a sequence of processing, message exchanges, processing, message exchanges, $\cdots$, and so forth. Informally, we modify A to send/receive an $(end\text{-}phase, p)$ message via each port j at the end of the pth message exchange, regardless of whether the pth message exchange sends any message via port j. The resulting algorithm will be pseudo-synchronous, and it will run correctly on any network on which A runs, since the added send/receive instructions are provided in any communication mode. We thus have the following property.

Property 3.1 *There exists an LE algorithm for a network N if and only if there is a pseudo-synchronous LE algorithm for N.* $\square$

A pseudo-synchronous algorithm A, by definition, may perform local information processing which depends on the times at which messages are sent or received. However, we can assume, without loss of generality, that A does not perform such time-dependent local information processing. We can show this informally as follows. Suppose that A performs such local information processing. Since A must work correctly under any communication timing, A must work correctly when the network works as if it were synchronous, i.e., in each processor, phase p starts at time p and the messages sent or received in phase p are processed at the end of this phase. Consider a pseudo-synchronous algorithm A' which is constructed from A by replacing, for each p, the time-dependent local information processing in phase p by the local processing in phase p when the network works as if it were synchronous. (Note that the replaced local information processing is independent of the communication timing.) Then A' also works correctly. We use the following lemma as a basis of subsequent discussions.

Lemma 3.1 *Let c be any communication mode in $\{PP, PM, BC, MM\}$ and I be any network attribute information in $\{net, size, upb, none\}$. There is an algorithm A for solving the LE on any network N in a class K of networks in communication mode c, using network attribute information I on N, if and only if there is a pseudo-synchronous algorithm B for solving the LE on any G in K such that, using I in each phase $p+1$ $(p \geq 0)$, each processor v sends $T_\sigma^p(v)$, and nothing else, to every one of its neighbors.*

Proof (outline). The significance of this lemma is that all information that the processors running A exchange is contained in $T_\sigma^p(v)$. The if part is trivial, so we concentrate on the only if part. By Property 3.1, we can assume without loss of generality that A is pseudo-synchronous. We need to show that B can simulate A using only the information contained in $T_\sigma^p(v)$. B at processor v can determine the state of execution of A in phase p at v, if v has at its disposal a copy of A, the given information I about attributes of N, and $T_\sigma^p(v)$, by simulating the execution of A through phases 1 to p at each processor w on $T_\sigma^p(v)$. A pseudo-synchronous algorithm B satisfying the conditions of this lemma may operate as follows: In each phase p, B constructs $T_\sigma^p(v)$ using the messages $T_\sigma^{(p-1)}(u)$ sent from each neighbor u and simulates A for the first p phases. If A does not terminate in the simulation, B sends $T_\sigma^p(v)$ to every neighbor. B terminates since A does. $\square$

Corollary 3.1 *For any network N, each processor v can construct $T^d(v)$ for any nonnegative integer d.* □

Theorem 3.1 *For each communication mode c in $\{PP, PM, BC, MM\}$ and each network attribute information I in $\{net, size, upb, none\}$, a network N is in $D_{c,I}$ only if for any labeling σ, there is a processor v having a unique view $T_\sigma(v)$.*

Proof. Suppose that there is an algorithm A for solving the LE for a network N that does not satisfy the necessary condition of the theorem. Namely, for some σ, there exists u ($\neq v$) such that $T_\sigma(u) \equiv T_\sigma(v)$ for some v in V. By Lemma 3.1, there exists a pseudo-synchronous algorithm B satisfying the condition of that lemma. Consider the computation of B on N with σ. B on u and v works under the same situation, since $T_\sigma(u) \equiv T_\sigma(v)$. Thus B on u decides that u is the leader if and only if B on v decides that v is the leader, a contradiction. □

Theorem 3.1 states that a necessary condition for a network to have an LE algorithm is that for each labeling σ, there is a unique processor in terms of its view. A view is by definition an infinite tree and, therefore, deciding whether two views $T(u)$ and $T(v)$ are similar appears to be difficult. The following lemma asserts that the decision can be made by comparing $T^d(u)$ and $T^d(v)$, where $d = n^2$. The proof of the lemma is analogous to that of Lemma 3.1 in [8,9] and, therefore, is omitted,

Lemma 3.2 *For each communication mode c in $\{PP, PM, BC, MM\}$, $T(u) \equiv T(v)$ if and only if $T^d(u) \equiv T^d(v)$, for any integer $d \geq n^2$.* □

Corollary 3.2 *For each communication mode c in $\{PP, PM, BC, MM\}$ and each network attribute information I in $\{net, size, upb, none\}$, a network N is in $D_{c,I}$ only if, for all σ, there is a processor v having a unique "partial" view $T_\sigma^d(v)$, for any integer $d \geq n^2$.* □

Let $\Gamma_\sigma^d(N)$ define the set of partial views $\{T_\sigma^d(v) \mid v \in V\}$.

Lemma 3.3 *Suppose that an upper bound b on the number of processors in N is available. Then there is an algorithm for computing $\Gamma_\sigma^d(N)$ for any integer d.*

Proof (outline). Let $j = \max\{b, d\}$ and $k = j^2 + j - 1$. By Corollary 3.1, we can construct $T_\sigma^k(v)$. Then we can construct $\Gamma_\sigma^d(N)$ from $T_\sigma^k(v)$ by Lemma 3.2, since every element in $\Gamma_\sigma^d(N)$ must appear in $T_\sigma^k(v)$ as a subtree whose root is within distance $b - 1$ from the root of $T_\sigma^k(v)$. □

4. Computing with Known Number of Processors

This section investigates networks under the assumption that each processor knows at least the number n of processors. The first aim is to show that for each combination of communication mode c in $\{PP, BC, PM, MM\}$ and network attribute information I in $\{net, size\}$, there is a **universal** LE algorithm A in the sense that $Net(A) = D_{c,I}$ holds. Next we will investigate the PP and PM in detail and show that, for any c in $\{PP, PM\}$, $D_{c,size} = D_{c,net}$ holds. This equality states that no LE algorithm can take advantage of knowing the network, besides n, on which it is being executed, as the initial network attribute information. The essential information that an LE algorithm can use is the number of processors. We then will characterize the class $D_{c,size}$ ($= D_{c,net}$), for each communication mode c in $\{PP, PM\}$. Whether or not $D_{c,size} = D_{c,net}$ holds in the BC and MM cases is also an interesting question but is left as future work.

We will also investigate the problem we posed in Section 1, i.e., the problem of finding $Dmax$, the maximum number of processors with the same identity number. In what follows, we call this problem the **maximum duplication number** problem (**MDN**, for short).

4.1 General Results

Theorem 4.1 *For each combination of communication mode c in $\{PP, BC, PM, MM\}$ and network attribute information I in $\{net, size\}$, there is a universal LE algorithm A (i.e., $Net(A) = D_{c,I}$).*

Proof (outline). We give a sketch of an LE algorithm A and then show that $Net(A) = D_{c,I}$. Since the set of views truncated to finite depths is enumerable, we can fix a total order $<$ among these finite views. On each processor v in network N, A computes $\Gamma_\sigma^d(N)$, where $d = n^2$ and n is the number of processors. By Lemma 3.3, it is possible. If $|\Gamma_\sigma^d(N)| = n$, then since each processor has a unique view, the processor v with the smallest view $T_\sigma^d(v)$ with respect to $<$ is elected.

Since the number of different networks with n processors is finite, so is the number of different networks which are consistent with the network attribute information that A has. One of them is the network on which A is being executed. Let CAN be the set of such the candidates. If $|\Gamma_\sigma^d(N)| < n$, let Δ be the set of views T^d such that for any network N' in CAN and labeling ρ for N', if $\Gamma_\rho^d(N') = \Gamma_\sigma^d(N)$ then the number of processors in N' having partial views similar to T^d is one. Clearly Δ is computable. If Δ is empty, then A reports that it cannot solve the LE. Otherwise, i.e., if Δ is not empty, then the processor v with the smallest view $T_\sigma^d(v)$ in Δ with respect to $<$ is elected.

Now we show $Net(A) = D_{c,I}$. Clearly, it is sufficient to show $D_{c,I} \subseteq Net(A)$. The key observation here is that by definition of view, if $\Gamma_\sigma^d(N) = \Gamma_\rho^d(N')$ then A on any processor cannot determine on which network it is being executed, in the worst case. Suppose that an LE algorithm A' can elect a leader w for N, even in the case Δ is empty. By Lemma 3.1, without loss of generality, we can assume that A' is pseudo synchronous. By definition of Δ, there is a network N' and a labeling ρ such that there are at least two processors u and v in N' satisfying $T_\sigma(w) \equiv T_\rho(u) \equiv T_\rho(v)$. Let A' run on N'. Since $T_\sigma(w) \equiv T_\rho(u) \equiv T_\rho(v)$, both u and v are elected, since A' on u and v works in the same situation, a contradiction. $\square$

Theorem 4.2 *For any communication mode c in $\{PP, BC, PM, MM\}$, there is an algorithm using n for deciding whether or not $Dmax = 1$ on any network N.*

Proof (outline). We give a sketch of an algorithm A for deciding whether or not $Dmax = 1$. A first constructs Γ_σ^d, where $d = n^2$. If $|\Gamma_\sigma^d| < n$, then $Dmax > 1$, since each view is unique if each processor has a unique identity number. Otherwise, i.e., if $|\Gamma_\sigma^d| = n$, $Dmax = 1$ if and only if each view $T_\sigma^d(v)$ in Γ_σ^d has a unique label $id(v)$ as its root label. $\square$

4.2 Networks in Port-to-port or Port-to-Mailbox Communication Mode

Lemma 4.1 *For any network $N = (G, id)$ in communication mode c in $\{PP, PM\}$, the cardinality of the set $\{v \mid T(v) \equiv T\}$ is the same for all $T \in \Gamma_\sigma(N)$.*

Proof (outline). Suppose that $T_\sigma(u) \equiv T_\sigma(v)$ and let $e = (x, y)$ and $e' = (x', y')$ be edges occurring in the same relative position in $T_\sigma(u)$ and $T_\sigma(v)$,
respectively. Since $T_\sigma(u) \equiv T_\sigma(v)$, we have $l(e) = l(e')$. Then by definitions of PP and PM, we can observe that $\overline{x} = \overline{x}'$ if $\overline{y} = \overline{y}'$, where $\overline{z}$ denotes the name of the vertex (processor) in G corresponding to the local name z in the view.

Suppose that $T(u) \not\equiv T(v)$ for some u and v, and that the number of vertices having views similar to $T(u)$ is greater than the number of those having views similar to $T(v)$.

Let $u_1, \cdots, u_k$, $k > 1$, where $u_1 = u$, be the vertices such that $T(u_i) \equiv T(u)$ $(1 \leq i \leq k)$. Since G is connected, there exists a path connecting the root and a vertex z in $T(u)$ such that $\overline{z} = v$. For each i $(1 \leq i \leq k)$, define z_i as a vertex satisfying both $T(\overline{z_i}) \equiv T(v)$ and $L(T(u_i), z_i) = L(T(u), z)$, where $L(T, w)$ denotes the label sequence attached to the shortest path connecting the root and w in T. Clearly there exists z_i since $T(u) \equiv T(u_i)$. To derive a contradiction to the assumption that the number of vertices having views similar to $T(u)$ is greater than the number of those having views similar to $T(v)$, it is sufficient to show that $\overline{z_i} \neq \overline{z_j}$ for any $i \neq j$. Suppose that $\overline{z_i} = \overline{z_j}$ for some $i \neq j$. Then using the observation above, we can show $u_i = u_j$, a contradiction. $\square$

Lemma 4.1 does not hold for communication mode BC or MM. Consider, for example, a star network with four processors. Intuitively, when PP or PM is adopted, since the processor located at the center can send a distinct message through each port, the three peripheral processors can distinguish each one from the other two, i.e., these three processors have unique views. Thus all the processors have unique views and Lemma 4.1 holds. However, when BC or MM is adopted, since each peripheral processor receives the same message from the center processor, the three peripheral processors cannot distinguish one from the others, i.e., all peripheral processors have similar views. Clearly, the views of the center and peripheral processors are different. Thus Lemma 4.1 does not hold.

For any labeling σ, let $c_\sigma(N)$ be the cardinality of the set $\{v \mid T_\sigma(v) \equiv T\}$ for some T in $\Gamma_\sigma(N)$.

Theorem 4.3 *For any communication mode c in $\{PP, PM\}$,*

$$D_{c,size} = D_{c,net}.$$

Proof (outline). We give a sketch of an algorithm B for solving the LE that uses the number of processors as the network attribute information, and that satisfies $Net(B) = D_{c,net}$.

B works in the same way as A in the proof of Theorem 4.1. Clearly B can elect a leader if $|\Gamma_\sigma^d(N)| = n$. If $|\Gamma_\sigma^d(N)| < n$, on the other hand, B reports that B cannot solve the LE.

Now we show $Net(A) = D_{c,net}$. Suppose that an algorithm B' can elect a leader even if $|\Gamma_\sigma^d(N)| < n$. By Lemmas 3.2 and 4.1, the number of processors having partial views similar to T^d is the same for all $T^d \in \Gamma_\sigma^d(N)$. Thus $c_\sigma(N) = |\{v \mid T_\sigma^d(v) \equiv T\}|$ for all $T \in \Gamma_\sigma^d(N)$. Since $c_\sigma(N) > 1$, for any processor u, there is a processor v ($\neq u$) such that $T_\sigma^d(u) \equiv T_\sigma^d(v)$, a contradiction to Corollary 3.2. $\square$

Corollary 4.1 *For any communication mode c in $\{PP, PM\}$,*

$$D_{c,size} = \{N \mid c_\sigma(N) = 1 \text{ for any labeling } \sigma\}. \quad \square$$

Let $Deg = \{deg(v) \mid v \in V\}$ and $Id = \{id(v) \mid v \in V\}$. Let $\#_d(j)$ and $\#_i(j)$ denote $|\{v \in V \mid deg(v) = j\}|$ and $|\{v \in V \mid id(v) = j\}|$, respectively. The greatest common divisor of a set $\{j_1, j_2, \cdots, j_k\}$ of integers is denoted by $GCD\{j_1, j_2, \cdots, j_k\}$.

Theorem 4.4

$$\{N \mid GCD\{n, \#_d(j), \#_i(k) \mid j \in Deg \text{ and } k \in Id\} = 1\} \subseteq D_{c,size},$$

where n is the number of processors.

Proof. That $c_\sigma(N)$ divides n directly follows from Lemma 4.1. On the other hand, that $c_\sigma(N)$ divides both $\#_d(j)$ and $\#_i(k)$ follows from the fact that $T_\sigma^d(u) \equiv T_\sigma^d(v)$ implies both $id(u) = id(v)$ and $deg(u) = deg(v)$. The rest follows from Corollary 4.1. $\square$

This theorem is quite powerful. For instance, if a network $N = (G, id)$ with a prime number of processors is *not* in $D_{c,size}$, then N is both anonymous and regular, i.e., G is a regular graph and id is a constant function, since $c_\sigma(N)$ must be n if $c_\sigma(N) \neq 1$, when n is prime. Any network N with relatively prime $\#_r(j)$ and $\#_{r'}(j')$ (where the subscripts $r, r' \in \{d, i\}$) is in $D_{c,size}$, and so is any network N with $|Id| > n/2$.

Another application of Lemma 4.1 is the following.

Theorem 4.5 *There is an algorithm for solving the MDN on any network N in communication mode PP or PM, if the network size n is known.*

Proof (outline). Let b_j denote the number of partial views in $\Gamma_\sigma^d(N)$ such that the label $id(v)$ attached to the root is j, where $d = n^2$. We give a sketch of an algorithm A for solving the MDN. On each processor v, A constructs $\Gamma_\sigma^d(N)$. A next computes $c_\sigma(N)$ and b_j. $c_\sigma(N)$ is computable because $c_\sigma(N) = n / |\Gamma_\sigma^d(N)|$ by Lemma 4.1. Again by Lemma 4.1, the number of processors with identity number j is then $b_j c_\sigma(N)$. A finally computes $Dmax = \text{Max}\{b_j c_\sigma(N)| j \in Id\}$. □

4.3 $D_{PP,size}$ and $D_{PM,size}$

Let $G_X = (X, E')$ be the subgraph of G induced by $X \subseteq V$, i.e., $E' = E \cap (X \times X)$.

Theorem 4.6 $N (= (G, id)) \in D_{PP,size}$ *if and only if for any k (> 1), V cannot be partitioned into $g = n/k$ subsets, $V_1, \cdots, V_g$, satisfying the following four conditions:*

(1) *for any i, $1 \leq i \leq g$, and any two vertices u and v in V_i, $id(u) = id(v)$,*

(2) *for any i, $1 \leq i \leq g$, $|V_i| = k$,*

(3) *for any i, $1 \leq i \leq g$, G_{V_i} is a regular graph such that it contains a perfect matching (1-factor) if its degree is odd, and*

(4) *for any i and j, $1 \leq i, j \leq g$ and $i \neq j$, $K_{V_i,V_j} = (V_i // V_j, E \cap (V_i \times V_j))$ is a regular bipartite graph.*

Proof (outline). Only if part: It suffices to show that if $c_\sigma(N) = k$, then there is a partition of V which satisfies conditions (1)-(4). Fix any labeling σ. We introduce a **quotient network** which is induced by the equivalence classes $V_1, \cdots, V_g$, defined by the equivalence relation $\equiv$ (i.e., u and v are in V_i if and only if $T_\sigma(u) \equiv T_\sigma(v)$). Intuitively, it is obtained from N by collapsing all vertices of V_i into one vertex for each i. Let $N/\sigma = (H, id')$ be the quotient network of N induced by σ. Note that $H = (W, A)$ is not necessarily simple. There are two natural correspondences π and τ between the two vertex sets W and V and the two edge sets A and E, respectively; for any $w \in W$, $\pi(w)$ is the set of vertices in V which are collapsed into w (i.e., $\pi(w)$ is V_i for some i), and for any $a \in A$, $\tau(a)$ is the set of edges in E which are represented by a in H. Then we can show the following:

(a) If $a \in A$ is a self-loop at w with label (j, j) for some j, then $\tau(a)$ forms a matching (i.e., 1-factor) on $G_{\pi(w)}$.

(b) If $a \in A$ is a self-loop at w with label (j, j') for some $j \neq j'$, then $\tau(a)$ forms a 2-factor on $G_{\pi(w)}$.

(c) If $a = (w, w') \in A$ is not a self-loop, then $\tau(a)$ forms a bipartite matching between $\pi(w)$ and $\pi(w')$.

We now show that the equivalence classes defined by $\equiv$ satisfy conditions (1)-(4). By definition of view and Lemma 4.1, conditions (1) and (2) hold. By (a) and (b), condition (3) holds. Condition (4) follows from (c).

If part: Given a partition, $V_1, ..., V_g$, satisfying conditions (1)-(4), we show how to construct a labeling σ with $c_\sigma \geq n/g$. Informally, we construct σ as follows: >From the given partition $\{V_i\}$, the quotient network N/σ is determined except for labeling. Consider any labeling for N/σ, and define a labeling for N by τ, i.e., if $e \in \tau(a)$ then define $l(e) = l(a)$, where a is an edge of N/σ. Then the quotient network of N induced by the labeling defined above coincides with N/σ and, therefore, this labeling is what we are looking for. $\square$

By definitions of PP and PM, clearly $D_{PM,size} \subseteq D_{PP,size}$. Now we make clear the difference between the two by characterizing $D_{PM,size}$ using the concept of "consistent labeling". An r-regular graph $G = (V, E)$ is said to have a **consistent labeling** if there is a labeling σ such that for each vertex $v \in V$ the set $\{\sigma[v_i](v_i, v) \mid v_i \text{ is adjacent to } v\}$ coincides with the set $\{1, \cdots, r\}$, i.e., the labels attached to the other end (port) of edges incident to v are distinct.

Theorem 4.7 $N (= (G, id)) \in D_{PM,size}$ *if and only if, for any k (> 1), V cannot be partitioned into $g = n/k$ subsets, $V_1, \cdots, V_g$, satisfying the following four conditions:*

(1) *for any i, $1 \leq i \leq g$, and any two vertices u and v in V_i, $id(u) = id(v)$,*

(2) *for any i, $1 \leq i \leq g$, $|V_i| = k$,*

(3) *for any i, $1 \leq i \leq g$, G_{V_i} (is regular and) has a consistent labeling, and*

(4) *for any i and j, $1 \leq i, j \leq g$ and $i \neq j$, $K_{V_i,V_j} = (V_i \mathbin{/\!/} V_j, E \cap (V_i \times V_j))$ is a regular bipartite graph.*

Proof (outline). The if part can be shown using an argument similar to that in the if part proof of Theorem 4.6. We concentrate on the only-if part. Let σ be a labeling satisfying $c_\sigma = k$. V can be partitioned into $g = n/k$ equivalence classes, $V_1, \cdots, V_g$, defined by $\equiv$. Using the same argument as in the proof of Theorem 4.6, this partition satisfies conditions (1), (2) and (4). We now show that it also satisfies condition (3). Since each vertex in V_i has a similar view, G_{V_i} is regular. We claim that for any i, $1 \leq i \leq g$, G_{V_i} has a consistent labeling. If G_{V_i} is empty then it satisfies (3), so it is not empty. Assume that $T_\sigma(u) \equiv T$ for all u in V_i. T contains infinite number of subtrees T' such that $T \equiv T'$. Let L be the set of labels $(*, j)$ attached to edges (x, y) in T such that the two subtrees rooted at x and y are similar to T. Since G_{V_i} is not empty, neither is L. Fix any label $(*, j)$ in L, and let $(\overline{x}, \overline{y})$ and $(\overline{x}', \overline{y}')$ in $V_i \times V_i$ be any two edges having a label (h, j) for some h. Recall that $\overline{z}$ denotes the name of the vertex in G corresponding to the local name z in the view. Then $\overline{x} = \overline{x}'$ because, if there were such vertices $\overline{x}$ and $\overline{x}'$ $(\overline{x} \neq \overline{x}')$, counting the number of edges (u, v) in $V_i \times V_i$ with label (h, j) for some h, each vertex u in V_i would have at least two vertices v and w adjacent to u in V_i such that the edges connecting u and each of v and w were labeled by (j, h) for some h. Therefore, $|L|$ is the degree of G_{V_i}. Although the set $\{j| (*, j) \in L\}$ may not coincide with $\{1, \cdots, |L|\}$, by renaming the labels we can easily construct a consistent labeling for G_{V_i}. $\square$

5. Computing without Network Size Information

We first should clarify what the *upb* information means. Suppose that an upper bound $\overline{n}$ on the number n of processors such that $\overline{n} - n \leq 1$ is available. Then knowing $\overline{n}$ is just as good as knowing n. Therefore, we assume that each processor does not know the accuracy of the given upper bound. Let $Net(A)$ denote the set of networks for which P is solved by A no matter how large an upper bound on n is given. Let $\mathbf{T}$ be the set of all networks $N = (G, id)$ such that G is a tree.

Lemma 5.1 *For any communication mode c in $\{PP, BC, PM, MM\}$, $N = (G, id) \in \mathbf{T}$ if and only if, for any labeling σ, there is no network $N' = (G', id')$ and labeling σ' for N' satisfying the following two conditions simultaneously:*

(1) *The numbers of processors in N and N' are different.*

(2) $\Gamma_\sigma(N) = \Gamma_{\sigma'}(N')$.

Proof (outline). The if part is easy, because we can show that this lemma holds for PP, arguing as in the proofs of Theorems 5.3 and 5.4 in [8,9]. We now turn to the only-if part. By definition of view, if $T_\sigma(u) \equiv T_\sigma(v)$ for some c, then $T_\sigma(u) \equiv T_\sigma(v)$ for MM. For MM, we show that for any $N \in \mathbf{T}$, if there is a network N' satisfying $\Gamma_\sigma(N) = \Gamma_{\sigma'}(N')$, then N and N' are isomorphic including identity numbers. To this end, we give a deterministic procedure B for constructing N from any $T \in \Gamma_\sigma(N)$, provided $N \in \mathbf{T}$. If such B exists, since N is determined uniquely from $\Gamma_\sigma(N)$, the equality $\Gamma_\sigma(N) = \Gamma_{\sigma'}(N')$ implies that N is isomorphic to N'.

For T, B repeats the following pruning, along each path starting from the root of T. Suppose that x is the vertex of T under consideration. Let y be any child vertex of x. By definition of view, y has at least one child vertex z such that the subtree rooted at z is similar to that rooted at x. Then z (and an edge connecting y and z) is removed from T. $\square$

Lemma 5.2 *For any communication mode c in $\{PP, BC, PM, MM\}$,*

$$D_{c,ubp} \subseteq D_{c,net} \cap \mathbf{T}.$$

Proof (outline). It is sufficient to show $D_{PP,upb} \subseteq \mathbf{T}$. Assume that $N = (G, id) \in D_{PP,upb}$ for some non-tree graph G. By Lemma 5.1, there is a network $N' = (G', id')$ and a labeling σ' for N' satisfying the two conditions in that lemma. Consider any LE algorithm A. Without loss of generality, by Lemma 3.1, we can assume that A is pseudo synchronous. Since $\Gamma_\sigma(N) = \Gamma_{\sigma'}(N')$, for any processor u of N, there is a processor v of N' with a view similar to $T_\sigma(u)$. Since A on u and v works under the same situation, A elects a leader for N, and also for N'. However, it is a contradiction, since $c_{\sigma'}(N') \geq 2$. $\square$

Lemma 5.3 *For any communication mode c in $\{PP, BC, PM, MM\}$,*

$$D_{c,net} \cap \mathbf{T} \subseteq D_{c,none}.$$

Proof (outline). For any fixed integer $d > 0$, by modifying algorithm B in the proof of Lemma 5.1, we can construct, for each c, an algorithm B_d that (i) without using any network attribute information, can decide whether or not the network $N = (G, id)$ on which it is being executed belongs to $\mathbf{T}$ and the network size n is no more than d, and (ii) if so, reports N. Therefore, for each c, the algorithm A_d that invokes B_d first and then, using the network information A_d can get from B_d, invokes the LE algorithm in the proof of theorem 4.1, satisfies $N(A_d) = D_{c,net} \cap \mathbf{T}_d$, where $\mathbf{T}_d$ is the set of all networks in $\mathbf{T}$ with size no more than d. By definition of $D_{c,I}$, it is clear that this lemma holds. $\square$

Theorem 5.1 *For any communication mode c in $\{PP, BC, PM, MM\}$,*

$$D_{c,upb} = D_{c,none} = D_{c,net} \cap \mathbf{T}. \quad \square$$

Theorem 5.2 *For any communication mode c in $\{PP, BC, PM, MM\}$, and network attribute information I in $\{upb, none\}$, $N \in \mathbf{T}$ if and only if the MDN is solvable.*

Proof. By Lemmas 4.1 and 5.1, for PP, if the MDN is solvable for N then $N \in \mathbf{T}$. On the other hand, using algorithm B_d in the proof of Lemma 5.3, if $N \in \mathbf{T}$ then N can be constructed. Thus the MDN is solvable. $\square$

6. Summary

The following table summarizes the results about characterizations of $D_{c,I}$ we have obtained in this paper.

	net	size	upb	none
PP	Th. 4.3 and 4.6	Th. 4.3 and 4.6	Th. 5.1	Th. 5.1
BC	?	?	Th. 5.1	Th. 5.1
PM	Th. 4.3 and 4.7	Th. 4.3 and 4.7	Th. 5.1	Th. 5.1
MM	?	?	Th. 5.1	Th. 5.1

References

[1] Y. Afek and M. Saks, "Detecting Global Termination Conditions in the Face of Uncertainty", *Proc. 6th ACM Symp. on Principles of Distributed Computing*, Vancouver, B.C., 109-124, 1987.

[2] D. Angluin, "Local and global properties in networks of processors", *Proc. 12th ACM Symposium on Theory of Computing*, Los Angeles, California, 82-93, 1980.

[3] R. Bar-Yehuda and S. Kutten, "Fault Tolerant Leader Election with Termination Deatection", *Tech. Rept., Duke University*, CS-1986-12, 1986, Durham.

[4] R. E. Johnson and F. B. Schneider, "Symmetry and similarity in distributed systems", *Proc. 4th ACM Symp. on Principles of Distributed Computing*, Minaki, Ontario, 13-22, 1985.

[5] A E. Korach, S. Moran, and S. Zaks, "Tight lower and upper bounds for some distributed algorithms for a complete network of processors", *Proc. 3rd ACM Symp. on Principles of Distributed Computing*, 199-207, 1984.

[6] G. LeLann, "Distributed systems - Towards a formal approach", *Information Processing '77*, 155-160, 1977.

[7] M. Merritt, "Elections in the presence of faults", *Proc. 3rd ACM Symp. on Principles of Distributed Computing*, New York, 134-142, 1984.

[8] M. Yamashita and T. Kameda, "Computing on anonymous networks", *Proc. 7th ACM Symp. on Principles of Distributed Computing*, Tronto, Ontario, 117-130, 1988.

[9] M. Yamashita and T. Kameda, "Computing functions on an anonymous network", *LCCR Tech. Rept., Simon Fraser University*, 87-16, 1987, Vancouver, B.C..

LIST OF THE REFEREES

M. Adam
B. Awerbuch
R. Bar-Yehuda
J-C. Bermond
O. Biran
H. Bodlaender
B. Braschi
N. Budhiraja
B. Caillaud
B. Charron-Bost
T. Chandra
R. Cohen
A. Couvert
R. Dechter
W. Fernandez de la Vega
N. Francez
R. Fujimoto
Y. Gold
A. Gopal
O. Grumberg
P. Hell
J-M. Helary
M. Hofri
A. Itai
C. Jard
S. Katz
J-C. Konig
E. Korach
G. Kissin
O. Kraemer
D. Krizanc
E. Lazard
Y. Lavallee
C. Lavault
U. Lemberg
D. Le Metayer

F. Mattern
H. Mehl
B. Monien
S. Moran
M. Naimi
J. Pachl
P. Panangaden
A. Petit
N. Plouzeau
S. Porat
M. Raynal
Y. Reshef
R. Rom
C. Roucairol
B. Rozoy
M. Santha
N. Santoro
A. Segall
R. Shani
O. Shmueli
M. Sidi
S. Skyum
P. Sole
K. Taylor
G. Tel
S. Toueg
M. Trehel
J. Tromp
D. Trystram
P. Vitanyi
O. Vornberger
D. Wagner
O. Wolfson
D. Wybranietz
M. Yoeli
S. Zaks

Vol. 352: J. Díaz, F. Orejas (Eds.), TAPSOFT '89. Volume 2. Proceedings, 1989. X, 389 pages. 1989.

Vol. 354: J.W. de Bakker, W.-P. de Roever, G. Rozenberg (Eds.), Linear Time, Branching Time and Partial Order in Logics and Models for Concurrency. VIII, 713 pages. 1989.

Vol. 355: N. Dershowitz (Ed.), Rewriting Techniques and Applications. Proceedings, 1989. VII, 579 pages. 1989.

Vol. 356: L. Huguet, A. Poli (Eds.), Applied Algebra, Algebraic Algorithms and Error-Correcting Codes. Proceedings, 1987. VI, 417 pages. 1989.

Vol. 357: T. Mora (Ed.), Applied Algebra, Algebraic Algorithms and Error-Correcting Codes. Proceedings, 1988. IX, 481 pages. 1989.

Vol. 358: P. Gianni (Ed.), Symbolic and Algebraic Computation. Proceedings, 1988. XI, 545 pages. 1989.

Vol. 359: D. Gawlick, M. Haynie, A. Reuter (Eds.), High Performance Transaction Systems. Proceedings, 1987. XII, 329 pages. 1989.

Vol. 360: H. Maurer (Ed.), Computer Assisted Learning – ICCAL '89. Proceedings, 1989. VII, 642 pages. 1989.

Vol. 361: S. Abiteboul, P.C. Fischer, H.-J. Schek (Eds.), Nested Relations and Complex Objects in Databases. VI, 323 pages. 1989.

Vol. 362: B. Lisper, Synthesizing Synchronous Systems by Static Scheduling in Space-Time. VI, 263 pages. 1989.

Vol. 363: A.R. Meyer, M.A. Taitslin (Eds.), Logic at Botik '89. Proceedings, 1989. X, 289 pages. 1989.

Vol. 364: J. Demetrovics, B. Thalheim (Eds.), MFDBS 89. Proceedings, 1989. VI, 428 pages. 1989.

Vol. 365: E. Odijk, M. Rem, J.-C. Syre (Eds.), PARLE '89. Parallel Architectures and Languages Europe. Volume I. Proceedings, 1989. XIII, 478 pages. 1989.

Vol. 366: E. Odijk, M. Rem, J.-C. Syre (Eds.), PARLE '89. Parallel Architectures and Languages Europe. Volume II. Proceedings, 1989. XIII, 442 pages. 1989.

Vol. 367: W. Litwin, H.-J. Schek (Eds.), Foundations of Data Organization and Algorithms. Proceedings, 1989. VIII, 531 pages. 1989.

Vol. 368: H. Boral, P. Faudemay (Eds.), IWDM '89, Database Machines. Proceedings, 1989. VI, 387 pages. 1989.

Vol. 369: D. Taubner, Finite Representations of CCS and TCSP Programs by Automata and Petri Nets. X. 168 pages. 1989.

Vol. 370: Ch. Meinel, Modified Branching Programs and Their Computational Power. VI, 132 pages. 1989.

Vol. 371: D. Hammer (Ed.), Compiler Compilers and High Speed Compilation. Proceedings, 1988. VI, 242 pages. 1989.

Vol. 372: G. Ausiello, M. Dezani-Ciancaglini, S. Ronchi Della Rocca (Eds.), Automata, Languages and Programming. Proceedings, 1989. XI, 788 pages. 1989.

Vol. 373: T. Theoharis, Algorithms for Parallel Polygon Rendering. VIII, 147 pages. 1989.

Vol. 374: K.A. Robbins, S. Robbins, The Cray X-MP/Model 24. VI, 165 pages. 1989.

Vol. 375: J.L.A. van de Snepscheut (Ed.), Mathematics of Program Construction. Proceedings, 1989. VI, 421 pages. 1989.

Vol. 376: N.E. Gibbs (Ed.), Software Engineering Education. Proceedings, 1989. VII, 312 pages. 1989.

Vol. 377: M. Gross, D. Perrin (Eds.), Electronic Dictionaries and Automata in Computational Linguistics. Proceedings, 1987. V, 110 pages. 1989.

Vol. 378: J.H. Davenport (Ed.), EUROCAL '87. Proceedings, 1987. VIII, 499 pages. 1989.

Vol. 379: A. Kreczmar, G. Mirkowska (Eds.), Mathematical Foundations of Computer Science 1989. Proceedings, 1989. VIII, 605 pages. 1989.

Vol. 380: J. Csirik, J. Demetrovics, F. Gécseg (Eds.), Fundamentals of Computation Theory. Proceedings, 1989. XI, 493 pages. 1989.

Vol. 381: J. Dassow, J. Kelemen (Eds.), Machines, Languages, a Complexity. Proceedings, 1988. VI, 244 pages. 1989.

Vol. 382: F. Dehne, J.-R. Sack, N. Santoro (Eds.), Algorithms and D Structures. WADS '89. Proceedings, 1989. IX, 592 pages. 1989.

Vol. 383: K. Furukawa, H. Tanaka, T. Fujisaki (Eds.), Logic Programm '88. Proceedings, 1988. VII, 251 pages. 1989. (Subseries LNAI)

Vol. 384: G.A. van Zee, J.G.G. van de Vorst (Eds.), Parallel Computir 1988. Proceedings, 1988. V, 135 pages. 1989.

Vol. 385: E. Börger, H. Kleine Büning, M.M. Richter (Eds.), CSL '8 Proceedings, 1988. VI, 399 pages. 1989.

Vol. 386: J.E. Pin (Ed.), Formal Properties of Finite Automata a Applications. Proceedings, 1988. VIII, 260 pages. 1989.

Vol. 387: C. Ghezzi, J.A. McDermid (Eds.), ESEC '89. 2nd European So ware Engineering Conference. Proceedings, 1989. VI, 496 pages. 1989

Vol. 388: G. Cohen, J. Wolfmann (Eds.), Coding Theory and Application Proceedings, 1988. IX, 329 pages. 1989.

Vol. 389: D.H. Pitt, D.E. Rydeheard, P. Dybjer, A.M. Pitts, A. Poign (Eds.), Category Theory and Computer Science. Proceedings, 1989. V 365 pages. 1989.

Vol. 390: J.P. Martins, E.M. Morgado (Eds.), EPIA 89. Proceedings, 198 XII, 400 pages. 1989 (Subseries LNAI).

Vol. 392: J.-C. Bermond, M. Raynal (Eds.), Distributed Algorithms Proceedings, 1989. VI, 315 pages. 1989.